Elinor Ostrom and the Bloomington School of Political Economy

Also of Interest

DANIEL H. COLE AND MICHAEL D. MCGINNIS, EDS.
Elinor Ostrom and the Bloomington School of Political Economy

Volume 1, Polycentricity in Public Administration and Political Science
Volume 2, Resource Governance
Volume 3, A Framework for Policy Analysis
Volume 4, Policy Applications and Extensions

VINCENT OSTROM
The Political Theory of a Compound Republic: Designing the American Experiment (3rd edition; 2008)

VINCENT OSTROM
The Quest to Understand Human Affairs: Natural Resources Policy and Essays on Community and Collective Choice, volume 1.
Edited by Barbara Allen (2011)

VINCENT OSTROM
The Quest to Understand Human Affairs: Essays on Collective, Constitutional, and Epistemic Choice, volume 2.
Edited by Barbara Allen (2012)

Interior design and typesetting by Patty Lezotte.

Elinor Ostrom and the Bloomington School of Political Economy

Volume 3, A Framework for Policy Analysis

Edited by Daniel H. Cole and Michael D. McGinnis

LEXINGTON BOOKS
A division of
ROWMAN & LITTLEFIELD PUBLISHERS, INC.
Lanham • Boulder • New York • Toronto • Plymouth, UK

Published by Lexington Books
An imprint of The Rowman & Littlefield Publishing Group, Inc.
4501 Forbes Boulevard, Suite 200, Lanham, Maryland 20706
www.rowman.com

Unit A, Whitacre Mews, 26-34 Stannary Street, London SE11 4AB

British Library Cataloguing in Publication Information Available

Library of Congress Cataloging-in-Publication Data Available

ISBN 978-0-7391-9111-8 (cloth : alk. paper)
ISBN 978-1-4985-5452-7 (pbk. : alk. paper)
ISBN 978-0-7391-9110-1 (electronic)

∞™ The paper used in this publication meets the minimum requirements of American National Standard for Information Sciences—Permanence of Paper for Printed Library Materials, ANSI/NISO Z39.48-1992.

Printed in the United States of America

Contents

Acknowledgments xi

Introduction to Volume 3 xiii

PART I: IMPLEMENTING INSTITUTIONAL ANALYSIS

1 Selections from Y673 Syllabus: Institutional Analysis and Development—Micro 3
Elinor Ostrom

2 An Institutional Framework for Policy Analysis and Design 13
Margaret M. Polski and Elinor Ostrom

3 Appendix A: The Institutional Analysis and Development Framework 49
Elinor Ostrom, Clark Gibson, Sujai Shivakumar, and Krister Andersson

4 The IAD Framework in Action: Understanding the Source of the Design Principles in Elinor Ostrom's *Governing the Commons* 87
Michael D. McGinnis

PART II: POLYCENTRICITY IN REGIONAL PUBLIC ECONOMIES

5 Public Economy Organization and Service Delivery 111
Elinor Ostrom and Vincent Ostrom

6 Metropolitan Governance and Institutional Collective Action 147
Richard C. Feiock

7 Structuring Institutional Analysis for Urban Ecosystems: A Key to Sustainable Urban Forest Management 171
Sarah K. Mincey, Miranda Hutten, Burnell C. Fischer, Tom P. Evans, Susan I. Stewart, and Jessica M. Vogt

PART III: DEVELOPMENT AND NESTED GOVERNANCE

8 Levels, Scales, Linkages, and Other "Multiples" Affecting Natural Resources 203
Amy R. Poteete

9 Selections from *Aid, Incentives, and Sustainability: An Institutional Analysis of Development Cooperation* 223
Elinor Ostrom, Clark Gibson, Sujai Shivakumar, and Krister Andersson

10 Nested Governance for Effective REDD+: Institutional and Political Arguments 275
Prakash Kashwan and Robert Holahan

PART IV: INTEGRATING MULTIPLE ACTORS, INTERESTS, AND PERSPECTIVES

11 Analysing Decentralised Natural Resource Governance: Proposition for a "Politicised" Institutional Analysis and Development Framework 303
Floriane Clement

12 Building Negotiated Agreement: The Emergence of Community-Based Tourism in Floreana (Galápagos Islands) 343
Esteban Ruiz-Ballesteros and Eduardo S. Brondizio

PART V: FOUNDATIONS FOR FUTURE EXTENSIONS

13 Institutional Analysis, Policy Analysis, and Performance Evaluation 371
Vincent Ostrom

14 Learning from the Field 389
Elinor Ostrom

Index 413

Contributors 421

Acknowledgments

As editors, we are deeply indebted to Joseph Parry of Lexington Books for responding so positively to our initial suggestion, now several years ago, to put together a four-volume compendium of readings in honor of our dear colleagues Elinor and Vincent Ostrom, and of the broader Bloomington School of Political Economy that they are responsible for initiating. Both Joseph Parry and Emily Roderick, also from Lexington, exhibited extraordinary levels of patience with us, as completion of this third volume was inordinately delayed, in part, by the movement of one of the editors to a full-time administrative position at Indiana University.

Our gratitude to Patty Lezotte for her invaluable assistance in all aspects of the publishing process, from helping us locate potential readings in the Ostrom Workshop archives, arranging for permission from copyright holders to allow us to reproduce previously published materials, polishing our rough drafts and putting all these diverse materials into a common format, overseeing the indexing process (completed by Joanna Broderick), and then typesetting the volume as a whole. Patty has spent her entire professional career at the Ostrom Workshop, and her skills at editing, proofreading, typesetting, and record keeping are legendary, as is her good-natured patience with overly distracted academics. She is truly a joy to work with, and these volumes could never have looked so good without her professional care.

We also thank the Ostrom Workshop, now under the direction of Lee Alston, for their generosity in allowing Patty the time to work on this legacy project, in addition to her work on the many exciting new initiatives being undertaken by a new generation of Workshoppers. The Indiana University Foundation, which holds the copyright for the published and unpublished papers of Vincent and Elinor Ostrom, generously allowed us permission to reprint their papers in this collection. We are also grateful to the editors of the publications in which these papers originally appeared in print, who granted us permission for republication, most for no compensation or at a steep discount. We are particularly grateful to the authors of the papers included here for permitting us to reproduce their work, even, in a few cases, works that still had a few rough edges, having never been completed for publication.

Our experience has been that anyone who ever worked closely with Elinor or Vincent Ostrom came away from that experience with a deep appreciation of their impressive intellectual power, and their basic humanity. Editing these volumes has been a work of love for us, and we again thank them both for letting us get to know them, and to learn so much from them.

Introduction to Volume 3

Before she was awarded a Nobel Memorial Prize in Economic Sciences in 2009, Elinor Ostrom was best known, within her home discipline of political science, as the driving force behind the *Institutional Analysis and Development (IAD)* framework, which has been applied to a wide range of policy settings (Ostrom 1999; McGinnis 2011b). The analysis of public policy can be approached along many alternative pathways, and this volume sheds new light on this well-trodden path.

This volume collects fourteen papers that explore the historical development of this framework, illustrate its application to specific policy problems, and highlight recent extensions that ensure it will remain a vibrant focus of research for years to come. Three chapters were previously unpublished; only one (chapter 13) had been included in earlier collections of papers from the Bloomington School (Cole and McGinnis 2015a, 2015b; McGinnis 1999a, 1999b, 2000; V. Ostrom 1991, 2011, 2012; Sabetti and Aligica 2014; Sabetti, Allen, and Sproule-Jones 2009; Sproule-Jones, Allen, and Sabetti 2008).

Understanding Institutional Diversity (Ostrom 2005) remains the most comprehensive and authoritative explication of the entire analytical apparatus of the IAD framework, and the role it plays in the broader context of the Bloomington School of Political Economy. Whereas that book focused on the IAD as a tool for rigorous scientific research, in this book we collect examples of *policy-relevant applications* of IAD to a wide range of policy sectors. Although adherents of the Bloomington School strive to balance scientific rigor and policy relevance (McGinnis 2011b), most published works lean toward the analytical side. Consider, for example, the special issue of *Policy Studies Journal* dedicated to the IAD framework, which consists entirely of research articles, not policy analyses per se (Blomquist and deLeon 2011).

The best published examples of the use of IAD for policy analysis date back to the 1990s: Ostrom (1992) and Ostrom, Schroeder, and Wynne (1993). As long-time Workshoppers, we knew the Ostrom archives included several examples of direct policy applications, and we decided to publish a few of the best in this volume. More recently, the IAD (and the related Social-Ecological Systems [SES] framework) has been applied to a wider range of environmental policy issues, especially related to global warming. We have included a few recent examples, and this strand of literature will be covered in more depth in the fourth and final volume of this compendium on *Elinor Ostrom and the Bloomington School of Political Economy*.

The first half of this introduction highlights how the mode of analysis based on the IAD framework clarifies the range of intellectual challenges and social dilemmas that must be overcome to realize effective policy reform. The second half highlights what we consider to be the most important contributions made in each chapter.

Understanding Action Situations and Policy Processes

Over the years, the IAD framework has undergone subtle changes (as illustrated in Kiser and Ostrom 1982; Ostrom 1986a, 1989, 1999, 2007, 2010, 2011; Oakerson 1992; Ostrom, Gardner, and Walker 1994; Ostrom and Ostrom 2004; Ostrom, Cox, and Schlager 2014; Cole, Epstein, and McGinnis 2014a, 2014b). The authors of papers included here highlight different aspects of this framework, or interpret some components in different ways, but all share common presuppositions. As will become apparent in later chapters, this framework is especially useful as a device to organize the questions policy analysts ask as they learn more about some particular real-world policy process.

At the core of this approach to understanding policy lies an *action situation*, an abstraction of decisional settings in which individuals and corporate actors interact with each other by making choices that jointly determine the outcomes of some particular aspect of a policy question. Decisions and outcomes are influenced by the beliefs and incentives of individual actors, as shaped by the responsibilities and social expectations attached to any official position they may hold, and by the information available to them. These action situations are also shaped by preexisting conditions, grouped for analytical purposes into three categories: (1) the "nature of the good" under consideration, including all relevant biophysical conditions; (2) the social ties and cultural attributes that characterize the individuals interacting on that policy problem; and (3) the existing configuration of laws, regulations, rules, norms, and shared understandings held by the participants to be relevant to deliberations on that policy area.

Biophysical, sociocultural, and legal-institutional factors interact in complex ways to shape patterns of interactions among relevant actors as well as policy outcomes. These interaction patterns and outcomes are then evaluated by the same actors, and perhaps others as well, and these evaluations (and the outcomes that triggered them) feed back into all three of the categories of preexisting conditions, thereby setting the stage for the next round of action situations to take place.

Unfortunately, the dynamism embedded in this framework is not very effectively represented in its canonical depiction (see figure 2.1 in chapter 2, and figure 1.2 in Ostrom 2005, 15). The representation conveys an inappropriate sense that any one policy situation can be understood in isolation from the many other policy situations with which it is, in the real world, complexly interrelated.

Instead, we presume that there is no such thing as an institution-free context (Cole, Epstein, and McGinnis 2014). Every existing situation is shaped, in complex ways, by the preexisting configurations of rules, norms, and shared understandings. No policy reform can be applied to a completely blank slate. Instead, all policy advocates necessarily are engaged in efforts to introduce purposeful interventions into an already complex ecosystem of institutional arrangements.

Action situations are created by groups seeking to cope with newly emerging challenges as well as those that recur on a regular basis, albeit in changing detail. And they link these action situations together in chains of decisions, some of which are repeated so frequently that they become important institutional arrangements within which policy participants operate. Some sequences of action situations take the form of legally required processes or the standard operating procedures found in any formal organization.

Organization provides structure to the actions of individuals seeking at least some shared goals, by assigning particular tasks to different individuals or subunits of that organization, and by setting in place sequences of decisions that become institutionalized procedures in their own right. Within the IAD framework, a formal organization is a complex configuration of institutional arrangements and action situations.

> An organization is composed of one or more (usually more) action situations linked together by prescriptions specifying how outcomes from

> one situation become inputs into others. Organizations may be thought of as a tree or a lattice with situations at each node. A particular set of rules structures the situation at each node. A general set of rules partially structures all internal situations and specifies the paths that may be chosen from one situation to the next. (Ostrom 2005, 57)

Although some action situations occur in regular sequences, many action situations will generally be active concurrently (Ostrom 2005, 56). Policy participants weave their ways through complex ecologies of action situations along multiple paths, which may proceed in a logical sequence, or become trapped in endless repetition, or double back upon themselves.

If we identify each significant decision mode as an action situation, then we need to identify the sources of the conditions that define this action situation. There has to have been some path of decisions that led us to our current plight. Some relevant decisions may be lost to the mist of deep time, but most will be identifiable, and can be imagined to have come out differently, or even to be changed to a different outcome by concerted action.

For analytical purposes, it is especially useful to conceptualize a policy process as a path through a complex network of linked action situations, with the outcome from any one node affecting the likely outcomes that will emerge from subsequent decision nodes. Some action situations will have only trivial consequences on others, but for many decisions of interest, the associated action situation may have very significant implications for later decisions, including ones to be made by other sets of actors. In effect, each *consequential* action situation constitutes a mini-critical juncture that shapes the opportunities and probabilities of subsequent steps, thereby imposing a form of path dependence at the micro level. Although the term "path dependence" is usually associated with more macro-level phenomena (North 1990), this same effect occurs in micro-level paths traced through the policy landscape.

In terms of the IAD framework, any collective decision to intervene in an ongoing policy process constitutes either a new action situation to be added to the existing system, or is a particular realization of a form of intervention that had already been incorporated into that system. Interventions frequently seek to influence the outcome of a focal action situation in an indirect manner, by effecting changes in other action situations that determine one or more of the factors that determine which outcomes are generated by that focal action situation (see chapter 4 for an extended illustration of this logic). Most interventions are intended to change the beliefs, identities, incentives, or behavior of the actors making decisions in the focal action situation or in ones that are closely adjacent to it.

Each action situation denotes a nexus where a group of decision makers jointly confront important decisions related to some particular policy concern. To use the IAD framework, each of these critical decision nodes needs to be given separate consideration, and analysts face the difficult challenge of understanding how multiple action situations interact to jointly produce policy outcomes.

Two forms of connections between action situations have been examined in the IAD-based literature. The first is based on a long-standing distinction among different levels, or kinds, of decision situations. The IAD framework differentiates among three kinds of choice settings: (1) operational-choice settings in which the choices of the relevant actors directly impact tangible outcomes, (2) policymaking or collective-choice settings in which the actors shape the rules that constrain actors in operational-choice arenas, and (3) settings for constitutional choice in which decisions are made concerning which actors have standing in different choice situations as well as which kinds of alternative institutional mechanisms are available to them as they make their collective deliberations and operational-level choices (Ostrom 2005, 58–62). Although the IAD framework asks researchers to consider processes at all three of these levels, in most cases analysts focus on action situations occurring at only one or two of these levels.

A second form of linkage is manifested through an action situation's "working components," which define how the relevant actors interact in the context of that situation. In her presidential address to the Public Choice Society, Ostrom (1986a) acknowledges that this approach was inspired by the "rules of the game" that game theorists use to define game models, but she insists that a more general approach is needed to extend analysis to more informal settings in which real-life policy actors interact, especially since these boundedly rational actors are themselves influenced in subtle ways by social norms, shared understandings, and myriad other contextual factors.

Ostrom (2005) justifies this complexification of game models in detail. Briefly, each action situation is configured by interlocking components, which are related in the following manner:

> *Participants*, who can either be individuals or any of a wide diversity of organized entities, are assigned to *positions*. In these positions, they choose among *actions* in light of their *information*, the *control* they have

> over *action-outcome linkages*, and the *benefits and costs* assigned to actions and outcomes. (Ostrom 2005, 188; emphasis added)

The seven working components are italicized in their first occurrence in this quotation. Each of these component elements may be modified by concerted action, but for the purposes of studying any one "focal" action situation, each component is fixed for that period of time. Furthermore, any effort to change any of these components would itself have to take place within the context of some other action situation. For example, congressional elections determine which individuals can vote on bills that will be considered by the next Congress.

McGinnis (2011c) defines as "adjacent" any action situation whose outcome directly impacts any of the "working components" of the focal action situation that lies at the heart of that particular analysis. This type of connection between action situations was implicit in the distinction among operational, collective, and constitutional levels of analysis. Examples of specific linkages between action situations were posited in a few earlier works (e.g., Ostrom 1986b), then addressed more explicitly in general (McGinnis 2011c, and chapter 4 of this volume, previously unpublished) and in particular policy settings (Mincey et al. 2013, reproduced as chapter 7 of this volume). This line of investigation remains to be fully developed.

In sum, the "rules of the game" or "working components" of any single action situation are presumed to have been determined by the operation of other action situations, either at the same or different levels of choice. The following sequence of sentences from Ostrom (2005) demonstrates just how profound the implications of this conceptualization for policy analysis are:

- Rarely do action situations exist entirely independently of other situations (p. 55).
- Where one draws the boundaries on the analysis of linked situations depends on the questions of interest to the analyst (p. 58).
- An institutional theorist must self-consciously posit the kind of information participants possess, the relevant preference structure of the participants, and the process they use for choosing among actions. Assumptions about information, preferences, and choice mechanisms are thus the essential components [that] need to be specified in order to generate hypotheses about interactions and outcomes that can be tested in a particular type of action situation or linked set of action situations (p. 99).

- To dig under that situation, however, to think about changing it, one needs to know a lot about the underlying structure leading to the social dilemma (p. 189).

Unfortunately, the resulting networks of adjacent action situations can be very complex. If each action situation is envisioned as a nexus of strategic competition, then actors dissatisfied with the outcome of any particular action situation could engage in "level-shifting strategies" (Ostrom 2005, 62–64) to seek to influence the outcomes of the collective- or constitutional-choice processes where the basic contours of the focal action situation was established. Since there may be no logical limit to deployment of this strategy, and since each of the working components in any one action situation have been determined by outcomes from adjacent action situations, anyone seeking to use the IAD framework to understand the implications or improve the outcomes of a fully articulated network of action situations may be overwhelmed by the immensity of the analytical task.

However, it is not necessary to know everything about everything before one can make a decision regarding a specific thing. So, if policy advocates perceive that an unacceptable policy outcome is driven primarily by the decisions made by rule-makers, and that these rule-makers are susceptible to be persuaded otherwise, then the logical choice would be to focus on lobbying efforts. Alternatively, if certain pieces of information were not made available to some actors in a timely fashion, reformers could revise the procedures in place in whatever organization was responsible for distributing that information to selected actors. It is not necessary to know the entire network of adjacent action situations, so long as the analyst can identify critical deficiencies in the current understanding of the situation, and follow the trail of connections to locate the appropriate and most effective point of intervention.

The rationale that lies behind development of such a complex analytical framework is worth further justification, and for that we draw, once again, from the words of Elinor Ostrom.

> The language developed in this book to identify the working components of action arenas that exist everywhere . . . ; to analyze the similarities and differences in rules, norms, and strategies . . . ; and then to group similar rules together by the component of the action situation they directly affect . . . , is undoubtedly more complex than many contemporary scholars would prefer. This complexity of language has not been introduced lightly. A scholar should also keep analysis as simple as possible—given the prob-

> lem to be analyzed. Just as important, however, is developing a mode of analysis that enables scholars, policymakers, and participants in ongoing processes to grapple with the problems they face by digging through the layers of nested systems in which these processes exist. . . . Thus, we need a consistent, nested set of concepts that can be used in our analysis, research, and policy advice in a cumulative manner. (Ostrom 2005, 256–57)

Building this capacity for analytical complexity is required if institutional analysts and direct participants are to properly understand "the complex, polycentric systems of governance that are created by individuals who have considerable autonomy to engage in self-governance" (Ostrom 2005, 258).

Overview of This Volume

This volume is organized in five parts. Part I provides detailed explanations of the components of the IAD framework as well as guidelines for its practical implementation in research projects or policy analyses. Parts II and III cover empirical applications of the IAD and related frameworks to, respectively, the study of metropolitan governance in the United States and to questions of international development and environmental policy. Part IV illustrates ways in which the complicating factors of power inequities, patterns of policy discourse, and the diverse interests of multiple actors operating at different levels of aggregation can be integrated into policy analyses based on the core IAD framework. Finally, in the two chapters in Part V, Vincent and Elinor Ostrom raise critical concerns that should be kept in mind by future researchers as they continue to build upon the analytical frameworks bequeathed to us by these pioneers of the Bloomington School of Political Economy.

Part I: Implementing Institutional Analysis

Chapter 1 consists of introductory material from the course syllabus for Elinor Ostrom's last graduate seminar. For more than two decades, she yearly taught this general introduction to institutional analysis and development, with particular attention to its application to processes operating at the micro level. Although the list of assigned readings changed from year to year, something very similar to this material was included every time.

In these introductory remarks, she succinctly summarizes the core foundations of the Ostrom Workshop approach to research and policy analysis. She begins by introducing four central pillars of this approach: (1) a focus on individuals as fallible, yet capable, decision makers (2) who use institutions to organize their collective problem-solving endeavors; (3) the need to develop better frameworks and theory to understand behavior; and (4) the active application of these concepts to diverse areas of policy concern. She warns students that they will be exposed to a wide range of theoretical conceptualizations and methodological tools, and highlights the role that the IAD (and in recent years the SES) frameworks will play in helping students integrate these diverse viewpoints.

Ostrom advises novice institutional analysts to remain open to learning from what they observe in real-world settings, and to avoid becoming too fond of any one theoretical perspective or mode of policy solution. For example, she cautions against thoughtless invocation of the phrase "the State" to designate some disembodied policymaker, and to focus instead on the individuals and organizations that are specifically responsible for framing, making, and implementing any particular policy decision.

Another point that comes through clearly concerns the balance between the promise and the limitations of policy analysis and design. After assuring the beginning student that the tools to be covered in this course will help them understand how groups have been able to craft effective institutions to cope with specific policy concerns, she cautions them against any presumption that this knowledge will enable any of them to put forward a comprehensive design for the ideal society (V. Ostrom 1991, 1997).

In our experience, students taking this course of study sometimes came away too harshly skeptical of any attempt to recommend policy intervention, even of a limited kind, in hopes that the people most directly involved would be able, if simply left alone by outsiders, to design their own institutions. This volume is intended to counter that overgeneralization of the Ostroms' warnings about the hubris of social planning, and to bring this line of work back into the mainstream of policy analysis and scholarly research. Later chapters demonstrate that it is indeed possible to use the IAD framework, and related analytical tools, to offer constructive policy advice, provided those making recommendations retain a healthy dose of humility.

In chapter 2, Margaret Polski (a student whose professional career focused on active participation in the policymaking community) and Elinor Ostrom provide a comprehensive overview of how the IAD framework can be used for purposes of policy analysis. Although previously unpublished, this paper has been cited on many occasions, and we are pleased to be able to include it in this volume.

The authors use an especially appealing list of questions to organize their presentation of the IAD framework and its application to policy analysis. These questions help structure an analyst's initial consideration of the policy situation being studied, as each draws attention to particularly important dimensions of consideration. In effect, the authors lead the reader through the components of the IAD framework step by step, and at the completion of this exercise the analyst should have a sound foundation for completing a comprehensive institutional analysis.

At this point, it may be useful to remind ourselves of the utility of an analytical framework, as compared to a causal theory or a formal model. Unlike more detailed analytical tools, there is no way to reduce application of the IAD framework to a recipe or simple set of instructions. Textbooks in statistical analysis, in contrast, lay out straightforward sequences of steps and specific criteria for comparison of alternative models, and anyone following those same steps should end up with exactly the same conclusions. That is not the case here.

Institutional analysis, when done in the Ostrom manner, does not follow an unambiguous path, nor does it offer any all-purpose standard for evaluation. Instead, the IAD framework helps guide a researcher through the long process of fully understanding all relevant aspects of a real-world policy situation, which is, by its very nature, highly complex and thus subject to multiple interpretations and evaluations. But application of this framework is, ultimately, only an initial step in any full analysis. The remaining steps are up to the researcher, and they remain an exercise in creative artisanship and not the routine implementation of specific rules of analysis.

Chapter 3 gives the reader a more in-depth overview of the critical distinctions that analysts should be aware of when they examine each component of the IAD framework in their particular policy situation. This chapter was originally published as a technical appendix to a report to Sida, the Swedish International Development Cooperation Agency, by a team of Workshop researchers, led by Elinor Ostrom. An extended selection of excerpts from the substantive portions of this report is included as chapter 9 in this volume, but this appendix was written with a broader audience in mind. (A related version is included in Gibson et al. 2005.) This appendix locates each component of the IAD framework within relevant literatures in policy analyses and the social sciences more generally.

The IAD framework incorporates a rich set of concepts and distinctions that may seem to some observers as a tangle of nearly impenetrable jargon. McGinnis (2011a) provides a glossary meant to make it easier for newcomers to this tradition to understand the terminology used by scholars deeply influenced by the Ostroms; since this terminology continues to be expanded and revised, an updated version is being maintained online (http://mypage.iu.edu/~mcginnis/iad_guide.pdf).

Since both of us have been fortunate to teach the course referred to in chapter 1, we can personally attest that this problem was especially noticeable with the arrival of each year's new cohort of graduate students eager to learn from the Ostroms and their colleagues. Chapter 4 was prepared by one of us (McGinnis) for distribution to members of the Y673 class several years ago, and we have included it here in hopes that it can help clarify the process involved in implementing the mode of institutional analysis exemplified in the many publications of Vincent and Elinor Ostrom.

The specific piece of research selected to illustrate application of this research framework is *Governing the Commons* (1990). Ironically, Elinor Ostrom makes only a passing reference to the IAD framework in this, her best-known and her most highly influential book. She avoided such side discussions in hopes that her presentation would be understandable to a wide audience, and she definitely accomplished that goal. For the purposes of this volume, however, we need to delve more deeply into the conceptual underpinnings of the conclusions for which she is so widely known.

This chapter directs attention to the separable action situations that lie at the heart of Ostrom's analysis of the many cases of community management of common-pool resources covered in that widely read volume. Each of the core action situations of appropriation, maintenance, rule-making, and monitoring is identified, and their interactions examined. By going through this exercise, it becomes easier to understand how Ostrom was able to discern the operation of the eight "design principles" that have proven to be the single most important take-away point from *Governing the Commons.* In effect, these design principles, when present, facilitate the smooth adjustment among, or the coevolution of, these core action situations. Each design principle points to ways in which changes in biophysical conditions, social and cultural attributes, and institutional arrangements adjust to each other, and thus effectively coevolve toward a sustainable balance. This chapter concludes with a series of questions inspired by each of these design principles (from Ostrom 2005, 270–71).

The presentation in chapter 4 draws upon the concept of linked action situations developed elsewhere (McGinnis 2011c). As discussed above, the concept of networks of adjacent action situations introduced there was intended to inspire later efforts to understand specific policy settings. One example along those lines is included as chapter 7 of this volume.

Part II: Polycentricity in Regional Public Economies

Part II includes three chapters focused on different aspects of policy and governance in US metropolitan areas. The first substantive example, chapter 5, dates back to a time (1977) before the IAD framework had been explicitly formulated. However, the Ostroms' contribution to a conference where policy analysts provided contrasting evaluations of the prospects for metropolitan reform in Detroit draws from exactly the same vein of thought that led, in time, to the IAD framework, *Governing the Commons*, and a Nobel Prize. In terminology, it draws more explicitly on the initial articulation of polycentric governance (V. Ostrom, Tiebout, and Warren 1961; see Cole and McGinnis 2015a). The Ostroms conclude their analysis by reviewing a series of questions concerning the range of options that were then available to Detroit city officials, including ones that they might not have considered otherwise. Given the ever-expanding inventory of policy instruments, contemporary officials have a broader menu of options available to them, but still face the same challenges as expressed here.

In chapter 6, Richard Feiock updates this line of research on metropolitan governance by introducing an Institutional Collective Action (ICA) perspective focused explicitly on the behavior of the formal units of governance in metropolitan areas. It is not exactly the same as the IAD framework, especially since it focuses its attention on the actions of local public administrators. Feiock and his colleagues work very much in the mainstream of public administration scholarship, and this ICA framework is every bit as interdisciplinary in spirit as is the IAD framework. Here the focus lies on understanding the range of institutional arrangements that are available to metropolitan officials confronting long-term problems, ranging from informal policy networks to individual contracts, collaborative councils, and more fully consolidated regional authorities. Each option is best suited for a different set of conditions, and this line of research continues to be very productive (see Feiock and Scholz 2009).

In chapter 7, a team of Workshop affiliated faculty, students, and postdocs demonstrates how the IAD framework, initially developed for application to natural resource governance in primarily underdeveloped regions, can also be used to understand important policy concerns within metropolitan areas. They explicitly expand the core action situation in their analysis to more fully explore the nature of the working components within that action situation, and draw specific connections to adjacent action situations in which the available range of choice open to actors is set, and what positions each actor holds, what information they have access to, and how their choices are aggregated into overall policy outcomes. In doing so, they illustrate the usefulness of the network concept first introduced, in an abstract way, by McGinnis (2011c), and yet also demonstrate the limitations of that line of research. Although the complexity revealed by this analytical exercise makes it difficult for them to offer specific policy recommendations, their analysis provides a promising basis for further elaborations. From our perspective as long-term Workshoppers, we find it especially gratifying to see that this team nicely connects the current state of the IAD framework to the core concept of polycentric governance of metropolitan areas that lies at the heart of the Bloomington School of Political Economy.

Part III: Development and Nested Governance

Part III shifts attention to particular aspects of development policy. In chapter 8, Amy Poteete, also a long-time Workshopper, sets the context for considering questions of natural resources management from the perspectives of different levels, scales, and forms of linkages. Her discussion effectively encourages institutional analysts to open their minds to complex interplay of processes (or action situations) that determine changes in biophysical conditions, institutional arrangements, economic transactions, and social-cultural forces, with these processes operating at divergent speeds in widely disparate geographic scales. This same openness is equally valid for policy analysts working in any policy sector, and for citizens in any society.

Chapter 9 consists of extended excerpts from chapters 1, 4, 5, and 11 of the Ostrom Workshop report to Sida discussed above. This analysis was inspired by the question of why so few tangible results have thus far been obtained from a long history of economic assistance to many countries throughout the developing world. This report was commissioned by a development agency with a strong reputation for professionalism in the delivery of economic assistance to particular countries with which they developed long-term relationships. Sida's executives were genuinely puzzled as to why the results of their efforts were so disappointing.

Our selections highlight the theme of ownership and their construct of a development assistance octangle, a multiconnected network of public, private, and community organizations from both the donor and recipient countries. (Much of this material was published, in different form, in Gibson et al. 2005.) We also sought to reinforce our point that many IAD-inspired scholars tend to operate by asking a disciplined series of questions structured by the elements of the IAD framework.

Critics of development policy have long drawn attention to the relatively small amounts of money devoted to development aid, or to the general absence of competitive markets or secure property rights in the recipient countries, or to other missing institutions needed to support prosperous economies and democratic political systems. To this list the Ostrom-led team added the missing ingredient of making sure that the recipients of this aid saw themselves as full partners in these endeavors. In the end, this team of policy analysts drew upon the multifaceted IAD framework to identify the many ways in which the actual practice of development assistance fell short of getting local recipients fully involved in all of the most critical steps of the process, or in IAD-based language, in all of the core action situations ranging from basic operationalization to the details of policy design and to overall constitutional design of the overall process.

Selections from chapters 4 and 5 of the Sida report demonstrate how these analysts used a series of questions to structure their understanding of the basic relationship between government officials in the donor and recipient countries. These questions cover pretty much the same material as those in chapters 2, 4, and 5 of this volume, focused this time on the nature of the action situation defined by ongoing negotiations between these two governments, and the lessons that might be drawn from their analysis.

This selection concludes with one of the general lessons they draw in the final chapter on this report. Although Sida officials had long emphasized the importance of nurturing a sense of local ownership among recipients of their aid, the results remained disappointing. The authors demonstrate that this notion of ownership needs to be extended to cover the full range of core action situations, ranging over the entire spectrum from first identifying user demands to the final dissolution of a project that has run its course.

Chapter 10 examines a relatively new initiative in international environmental policy that has also fallen short of fully engaging local recipients in all program stages. Here the primary actors are United Nations agencies and community-based forestry management organizations, but a remarkably similar range of problems emerge in this area as well. It remains to be seen how this particular policy initiative will work out in practice, and this preliminary analysis highlights a wide range of potential problems that future analysts should keep in mind.

Part IV: Integrating Multiple Actors, Interests, and Perspectives

The two chapters in Part IV introduce additional complications that must, in some way, be better incorporated into policy analyses based on the IAD template. In chapter 11, Floriane Clement, a scholar with only a marginal connection to the Ostrom Workshop, demonstrates why it is important to integrate questions of power into these analyses. Other scholars closely tied to the Ostroms, notably Agrawal (2003) and Epstein et al. (2014) have pointed to the unfortunate tendency of analysts working within this tradition to focus on the problem-solving aspect of policy problems and overlook, or at least downplay, the extent to which policy outcomes are driven by who has the most power to shape policy.

Clement does an excellent job of adding considerations of power and discourse analysis into the IAD framework in a natural manner. Since power is often exerted through subtle means of conceptualizations of policy alternatives, the incorporation of discourse analysis is especially welcome. In most works using the IAD framework, the attributes of the community are taken as given, although they may be changed, over long periods of time, by the experiences of that community as they govern themselves (see V. Ostrom, 1997). Clement puts this factor front and center, and thus makes an important contribution to this line of analysis.

In chapter 12, a long-term leader among Ostrom Workshop scholars, Eduardo Brondizio, and his colleague Esteban Ruiz-Ballesteros demonstrate how regional conditions and cross-level connections involving both the ecological and governmental aspects of resource management can be more explicitly integrated into detailed policy analyses based on the IAD framework. The resulting framework is quite complex, but this only goes to show how much the IAD framework remains a work in progress, one that is continually being refined and updated by those researchers and policy analysts who find it a useful tool to organize their own analyses, and to more clearly convey their findings to others. The process of refining and updating is closely associated with the Ostroms' commitment to empirically informed and policy-relevant political theory.

Part V: Foundations for Future Extensions

This volume demonstrates the continuing elaboration of the IAD-based mode of policy analysis or points toward continuing weaknesses that remain to be addressed in subsequent elaborations. In Part V, we include two papers in which Vincent and Elinor Ostrom separately offered words of encouragement and guidance for those seeking to further improve upon the analytical foundations they provided for us.

Chapter 13 remained unpublished until its inclusion in part one of Barbara Allen's two-volume collection of Vincent Ostrom's work (Ostrom 2011), and we thought it was well worth reproducing here. Originally written in 1982, when the IAD framework was first being formulated, this paper highlights the critical importance of evaluating the performance of public officials in the implementation of public policy. That theme was then emerging in public administration in a big way because of the new public management and decentralization and devolution movements, but in this paper Vincent demonstrates a broader concern with the evaluation of all of the many efforts that go into the implementation of policies, including those by community members and private organizations. Implementation is the process through which abstract policies have tangible impacts on the real world. It is often seen as primarily a technical exercise in the application of policy directives, but in practice this remains a very interactive, and an intrinsically political, process. Remarkably, the word "implementation" has rarely been used by Ostrom Workshop scholars, and we hope this chapter inspires future IAD-inspired researchers to remedy this unfortunate oversight.

In chapter 14, we give Elinor Ostrom the final word, from her contribution to a collection of autobiographical reflections by eminent economists. She devotes most of her attention to the early years of her career, before the IAD framework began to take shape in the 1980s. She acknowledges the formational influences of two scholars, Vincent Ostrom and Herbert Simon. From her husband and career-long collaborator, she drew the foundational concept of polycentricity (V. Ostrom, Tiebout, and Warren 1961), and from Herbert Simon (thus far the only other PhD in political science to have been awarded the Nobel Memorial Prize in Economic Sciences), Elinor Ostrom came to appreciate the ubiquity of bounded rationality in human behavior. Amazingly, individuals with significantly constrained cognitive abilities can nonetheless bind themselves together to devise and operate organizations and institutional configurations that enable them to effectively cope with situations of seemingly overwhelming complexity (see Simon 1972, 1981).

Elinor Ostrom concludes this essay by pointing to the fundamental similarity of the challenges facing public officials, policy analysts, and ordinary citizens—all of whom must decide the best they can in the presence of bewildering complexity, incomplete information, limited cognitive capabilities, and conflicting normative and strategic considerations. She leaves us with a powerful expression of her remarkably resilient yet realistic and restrained sense of optimism, secure in her knowledge that communities of fallible yet capable individuals can find innovative ways to jointly accomplish both "the long-term sustainability of common-pool resources and the efficient provision of public goods," despite the daunting complexity of those tasks.

The IAD framework was built to serve as a foundation for the kinds of institutional analyses needed to understand and nurture the diverse forms of creative public entrepreneurship that are so critical to the long-term sustainability of democratic self-governance (V. Ostrom 1997). This connection was nicely summarized by Elinor Ostrom in *Understanding Institutional Diversity* (2005, 132–33):

> As scholars and policy analysts, we need to learn the artisanship of working with rules so as to improve how situations operate over time. Human beings are neither all-knowing saints nor devilish knaves. The institutions they grow up in—families, schools, playgrounds, neighborhoods—differentially reward or punish them over time so that intrinsic and extrinsic motivations are learned and developed over time. The situations they find themselves facing as adults in the workplace and their community also affect which norms they use and the outcomes they reach. When individuals learn the artisanship of crafting rules, they can experiment and learn to create more productive outcomes (as well as participants) over time. Learning to craft rules that attract and encourage individuals who share norms of reciprocity and trustworthiness, or who learn them over time, is a fundamental skill needed in all democratic societies.

References

Agrawal, Arun. 2003. "Sustainable Governance of Common-Pool Resources: Context, Methods, and Politics." *Annual Review of Anthropology* 32: 243–62.

Blomquist, William, and Peter deLeon, eds. 2011. "The Design and Promise of the Institutional Analysis and Development Framework." Special issue, *Policy Studies Journal* 39(1) (February): 1–183.

Cole, Daniel H., Graham Epstein, and Michael D. McGinnis. 2014a. "Digging Deeper into Hardin's Pasture: The Complex Institutional Structure of 'The Tragedy of the Commons.'" *Journal of Institutional Economics* 10: 353–69.

———. 2014b. "Toward a New Institutional Analysis of Social-Ecological Systems (NIASES): Combining Elinor Ostrom's IAD and SES Frameworks." Indiana Legal Studies Research Paper No. 299; Indiana University, Bloomington, School of Public & Environmental Affairs Research Paper No. 2490999. Available at SSRN: http://ssrn.com/abstract=2490999.

Cole, Daniel, and Michael D. McGinnis, eds. 2015a. *Elinor Ostrom and the Bloomington School of Political Economy: Volume 1, Polycentricity in Public Administration and Political Science*. Lanham, MD: Lexington Books.

———, eds. 2015b. *Elinor Ostrom and the Bloomington School of Political Economy: Volume 2, Resource Governance.* Lanham, MD: Lexington Books.

Epstein, Graham, Abigail Bennett, Rebecca Gruby, Leslie Acton, and Mateja Nenadovic. 2014. "Studying Power with the Social-Ecological System Framework." In *Understanding Society and Natural Resources: Forging New Strands of Integration across the Social Sciences*, edited by Michael J. Manfredo, Jerry J. Vaske, Andreas Rechkemmer, and Esther A. Duke, 111–35. New York: Springer.

Feiock, Richard C., and John T. Scholz, eds. 2009. *Self-Organizing Federalism: Collaborative Mechanisms to Mitigate Institutional Collective Action Dilemmas.* New York: Cambridge University Press.

Gibson, Clark, Krister Andersson, Elinor Ostrom, and Sujai Shivakumar. 2005. *The Samaritan's Dilemma: The Political Economy of Development Aid.* New York: Oxford University Press.

Kiser, Larry L., and Elinor Ostrom. 1982. "The Three Worlds of Action: A Metatheoretical Synthesis of Institutional Approaches." In *Strategies of Political Inquiry*, edited by Elinor Ostrom, 179–222. Beverly Hills, CA: Sage.

McGinnis, Michael D., ed. 1999a. *Polycentric Development and Governance: Readings from the Workshop in Political Theory and Policy Analysis*. Ann Arbor: University of Michigan Press.

———, ed. 1999b. *Polycentricity and Local Public Economies: Readings from the Workshop in Political Theory and Policy Analysis*. Ann Arbor: University of Michigan Press.

———, ed. 2000. *Polycentric Games and Institutions: Readings from the Workshop in Political Theory and Policy Analysis.* Ann Arbor: University of Michigan Press.

———. 2011a. "An Introduction to IAD and the Language of the Ostrom Workshop: A Simple Guide to a Complex Framework." *Policy Studies Journal* 39(1): 163–77. Updated version: http://php.indiana.edu/~mcginnis/iad_guide.pdf.

———. 2011b. "Elinor Ostrom: Politics as Problem-Solving in Polycentric Settings." In *Maestri of Political Science*, vol. 2, edited by Donatella Campus, Gianfranco Pasquino, and Martin Bull, 137–58. Colchester, UK: ECPR Press.

———. 2011c. "Networks of Adjacent Action Situations in Polycentric Governance." *Policy Studies Journal* 39(1) (February): 45–72.

Mincey, Sarah, Miranda Hutten, Burnell Fischer, Tom Evans, Susan Stewart, and Jessica Vogt. 2013. "Structuring Institutional Analysis for Urban Ecosystems: A Key to Sustainable Urban Forest Management." *Urban Ecosystems* 16(3): 553–71.

North, Douglass C. 1990. *Institutions, Institutional Change and Economic Performance*. New York: Cambridge University Press.

Oakerson, Ronald J. 1992. "Analyzing the Commons: A Framework." In *Making the Commons Work: Theory, Practice, and Policy*, edited by Daniel W. Bromley et al., 41–59. San Francisco, CA: ICS Press.

Ostrom, Elinor. 1986a. "An Agenda for the Study of Institutions" *Public Choice* 48: 3–25.

———. 1986b. "Multiorganizational Arrangements and Coordination: An Application of Institutional Analysis." In *Guidance, Control, and Evaluation in the Public Sector*, edited by F. X. Kaufmann, G. Majone, and V. Ostrom, 495–510. Berlin and New York: de Gruyter.

———. 1989. "Microconstitutional Change in Multiconstitutional Political Systems." *Rationality and Society* 1(1) (July): 11–50.

———. 1990. *Governing the Commons: The Evolution of Institutions for Collective Action.* New York: Cambridge University Press.

———. 1992. *Crafting Institutions for Self-Governing Irrigation Systems*. San Francisco, CA: ICS Press.

———. 1999. "Institutional Rational Choice: An Assessment of the Institutional Analysis and Development Framework." In *Theories of the Policy Process*, edited by Paul A. Sabatier, 35–71. Boulder, CO: Westview Press.

———. 2005. *Understanding Institutional Diversity.* Princeton, NJ: Princeton University Press.

———. 2007. "Institutional Rational Choice: An Assessment of the Institutional Analysis and Development Framework." In *Theories of the Policy Process*, 2nd ed., edited by Paul A. Sabatier, 21–64. Boulder, CO: Westview Press.

———. 2010. "Beyond Markets and States: Polycentric Governance of Complex Economic Systems." *American Economic Review* 100(3) (June): 641–72.

———. 2011. "Background on the Institutional Analysis and Development Framework." *Policy Studies Journal* 39(1) (February): 7–27.

Ostrom, Elinor, with Michael Cox and Edella Schlager. 2014. "An Assessment of the Institutional Analysis and Development Framework and Introduction of the Social-Ecological Systems Framework." In *Theories of the Policy Process*, 3rd ed., edited by Paul A. Sabatier and Christopher M. Weible, 267–306. Boulder, CO: Westview Press.

Ostrom, Elinor, Roy Gardner, and James Walker, with Arun Agrawal, William Blomquist, Edella Schlager, and Shui-Yan Tang. 1994. *Rules, Games, and Common-Pool Resources*. Ann Arbor: University of Michigan Press.

Ostrom, Elinor, Clark Gibson, Sujai Shivadumar, and Krister Andersson. 2002. *Aid, Incentives, and Sustainability: An Institutional Analysis of Development Cooperation. Main Report*. Sida Studies in Evaluation #02/01. Stockholm: Swedish International Development Cooperation Agency (Sida).

Ostrom, Elinor, and Vincent Ostrom. 2004. "The Quest for Meaning in Public Choice." *American Journal of Economics and Sociology* 63(1): 105–47.

Ostrom, Elinor, Larry Schroeder, and Susan Wynne. 1993. *Institutional Incentives and Sustainable Development: Infrastructure Policies in Perspective*. Boulder, CO: Westview Press.

Ostrom, Vincent. 1991. *The Meaning of American Federalism: Constituting a Self-Governing Society*. San Francisco, CA: ICS Press.

———. 1997. *The Meaning of Democracy and the Vulnerability of Democracies: A Response to Tocqueville's Challenge*. Ann Arbor: University of Michigan Press.

———. 2011. *The Quest to Understand Human Affairs: Natural Resources Policy and Essays on Community and Collective Choice*, vol. 1. Edited by Barbara Allen. Lanham, MD: Lexington Books.

———. 2012. *The Quest to Understand Human Affairs: Essays on Collective, Constitutional, and Epistemic Choice*, vol. 2. Edited by Barbara Allen. Lanham, MD: Lexington Books.

Ostrom, Vincent, Charles M. Tiebout, and Robert Warren. 1961. "The Organization of Government in Metropolitan Areas: A Theoretical Inquiry." *American Political Science Review* 55: 831–42.

Sabetti, Filippo, and Paul Dragos Aligica, eds. 2014. *Choice, Rules, and Collective Action: The Ostroms on the Study of Institutions and Governance*. Colchester, UK: ECPR Press.

Sabetti, Filippo, Barbara Allen, and Mark Sproule-Jones, eds. 2009. *The Practice of Constitutional Development: Vincent Ostrom's Quest to Understand Human Affairs*. Lanham, MD: Lexington Books.

Simon, Herbert A. 1972. "Theories of Bounded Rationality." In *Decision and Organization: A Volume in Honor of Jacob Marshak*, edited by C. B. McGuire and Roy Radner, 161–76. Amsterdam: North Holland.

———. 1981. *The Sciences of the Artificial*. 2nd ed. Cambridge, MA: MIT Press.

Sproule-Jones, Mark, Barbara Allen, and Filippo Sabetti, eds. 2008. *The Struggle to Constitute and Sustain Productive Orders: Vincent Ostrom's Quest to Understand Human Affairs*. Lanham, MD: Lexington Books.

PART I

Implementing Institutional Analysis

1

Selections from Y673 Syllabus: Institutional Analysis and Development—Micro

ELINOR OSTROM

Preface

The central questions underlying this course are:

- How can *fallible* human beings achieve and sustain self-governing ways of life and self-governing entities as well as sustaining ecological systems at multiple scales?
- When we state that institutions facilitate or discourage effective problem solving and innovations, what do we mean by institutions and what other factors affect these processes?
- How do we develop better frameworks and theories to understand behavior that has structure and outcomes at multiple scales (e.g., household use of electricity affecting household budget and health as well as community infrastructure and investments and regional, national, and global structures and outcomes)?
- How can institutional analysis be applied to the analysis of diverse policy areas including urban public goods, water and forestry resources, and healthcare?

To address these questions, we will have to learn a variety of tools to understand how fallible individuals behave within institutions as well as how they can influence the rules that structure their lives. This is a particularly challenging question in an era when global concerns have moved onto the political agenda of most international, national, and even local governing bodies without recognizing the importance of the local for the global. Instead of studying how individuals craft institutions, many scholars are focusing on how to understand national and global phenomena. It is also an era of substantial political uncertainty as well as violence, terrorism, and disruption. Many of the problems we are witnessing today are due to a lack of understanding of the micro and meso levels that are essential aspects of global processes.

In our effort to understand self-governance, we will be studying the four "I's": individuals, incentives, institutions, and inquiry.

To understand processes at any level of organization, one needs to understand the *individuals* who are participants and the incentives they face. When we talk about "THE" government doing X or Y, there are individuals who hold positions in a variety of situations within "THE" government. We had better understand how individuals approach making decisions in a variety of situations given the incentives they face. Those *incentives* come from a variety of sources, but a major source, particularly in the public sector, are the rules of the game they are playing. *Institutions* include the rules that specify what may, must, or must not be done in situations that are linked together to make up a polity, a society, an economy, and their interlinkages. To understand this process, we must be engaged in an *inquiry* that will never end.

The settings we study are complex, diverse, multiscaled, and dynamic. Thus, we need to develop frameworks that provide a general language for studying these complex, multiscaled systems. And, we can learn a variety of theories (and models of those theories) that help us understand particular settings. We cannot develop a universal theory of actions and outcomes in all settings for all time. Thus, our task of inquiry is a lifelong task. And, the task of citizens and their officials is also unending. No system of governance can survive for long without commonly understood rules and rule enforcement. Rule enforcement relies on varying degrees of force and potential use of violence. Consequently, we face a Faustian bargain in designing any system of governance.

A self-governing entity is one whose members (or their representatives) participate in the establishment, reform, and continued legitimacy of the constitutional and collective-choice rules-in-use. All self-organized entities (whether in the private or public spheres) are to some extent self-governing. In modern societies, however, it is rare to find any entity whose members (or their representatives) have fashioned *all* of the constitutional and collective-choice rules that they use. Some rules are likely to have come from external sources. Many rules will have come from earlier times and are not discussed extensively among those using the rules today.

On the other hand, even in a totalitarian polity, it is difficult for central authorities to prevent all individuals from finding ways of self-organizing and creating rules of their own. Some of these may even be contrary to the formal laws of the totalitarian regime. Given that most modern societies have many different entities, let me rephrase the first question: How can fallible individuals achieve and sustain large numbers of small-, medium-, and large-scale self-governing entities in the private and public spheres?

We cannot thoroughly understand all of the diverse processes of self-governance in any semester-long or year-long course of study. How humans can govern themselves is a question that has puzzled and perplexed the greatest thinkers of the last several millennia. Many have answered that self-governance is impossible. In this view, the best that human beings can do is live in a political system that is imposed on them and that creates a predictable order within which individuals may be able to achieve a high level of physical and economic well-being without much autonomy. In this view, the rules that structure the opportunities and constraints facing individuals come from outside from what is frequently referred to as "the state."

For other thinkers, rules are best viewed as spontaneously emerging from patterns of interactions among individuals. In this view, trying to design any type of institution, whether to be imposed on individuals or self-determined, is close to impossible or potentially disastrous in its consequences. Human fallibility is too great to foretell many of the consequences that are likely to follow. Efforts to design self-governing systems, rather than making adaptive changes within what has been passed along from past generations, involve human beings in tasks that are beyond their knowledge and skills.

The thesis that we advance in this seminar is that individuals, who seriously engage one another in efforts to build mutually productive social relationships—and to understand why these are important—are capable of devising ingenious ways of relating constructively with one another. The impossible task, however, is to design *entire* social systems "from scratch" at one point in time that avoid the fate of being monumental disasters. Individuals who are willing to explore possibilities, consider new options as entrepreneurs, and to use reason as well as trial-and-error experimentation, can evolve and design rules, routines, and ways of life that are likely to build up to self-governing entities with a higher chance of adapting and surviving over time than top-down designs. It takes time, however, to learn from errors, to try and find the source of the error, and to improve one part of the system without generating adverse consequences elsewhere.

Successful groups of individuals may exist in simple or complex nested systems ranging from very small to very large. The problem is that in a complexly interrelated world, one needs effective organization at all levels ranging from the smallest work team all the way to international organizations. If the size of the group that is governing and reaping benefits is too small, negative externalities are likely to occur. Further, even in small face-to-face groups, some individuals may use any of a wide array of asymmetries to take advantage of others. Individuals who are organized in many small groups nested in larger structures—a polycentric system—may find ways of exiting from some settings and joining others. Or, they may seek remedies from overlapping groups that may reduce the asymmetries within the smaller unit. If the size of the group that is governing and reaping benefits is too large, on the other hand, essential information is lost, and further, the situation may again be one of exploitation.

Scale and complex nesting are only part of the problem. Another part has to do with how individuals view their basic relationships with one another. Many individuals learn to be relatively truthful, considerate of others, trustworthy, and willing to work hard. Others are opportunistic. Some approach governance as involving basic problem-solving skills. Some approach governance as a problem of gaining dominance over others. The opportunities for dominance always exist in any system of rule-ordering, where some individuals are delegated responsibilities for devising and monitoring conformance to rules and sanctioning rule breakers. Those who devise self-governing entities that work well only when everyone is a "saint" find themselves invaded by "sinners" who take advantage of the situation and may cause what had initially worked successfully to come unglued and fail.

Thus, the initial answer to the first question is: Self-governance is possible in a setting, if . . .

- most individuals share a common, broad understanding of the biophysical, cultural, and political worlds they face; of the importance of trying to follow general principles of trust, reciprocity, and fairness; and of the need to use artisanship to craft their own rules;
- most individuals have significant experience in small- to medium-sized settings, where they learn the skills of living with others, being responsible, gaining trust, being entrepreneurial, and holding others responsible for their actions;
- considerable autonomy exists for constituting and reconstituting relationships with one another that vary from very small to very

large units (some of which will be highly specialized while others may be general-purpose organizations);

- individuals learn to analyze the incentives that they face in particular situations (given the type of physical and cultural setting in which they find themselves) and to try to adjust positive and negative incentives so that those individuals who are most likely to be opportunistic are deterred or sanctioned.

The above is posed as a "possibility" not a determinate outcome. In other words, we view self-governing entities as fragile social artifacts that individuals may be able to constitute and reconstitute over time. A variety of disturbances are likely to occur over time. A key question is to what kind of disturbances is a self-organized governance system robust? We can make scientific statements about the kinds of results that are likely if individuals share particular kinds of common understandings, are responsible, have autonomy, possess analytical tools, and consciously pass both moral and analytical knowledge from one generation to the next. These are strong conditions!

With this view, small self-governing entities may exist as an enclave in the midst of highly authoritarian regimes. This may not be a stable solution, but self-governance may provide opportunities to develop productive arrangements for those who establish trust and reciprocity backed by their own willingness to monitor and enforce interpersonal commitments. If the macro structure is not hostile or even supports and encourages self-organization, what can be accomplished by smaller private and public enclaves can be very substantial. This is initially a bottom-up view of self-governance. Productive small-scale self-organization, however, is difficult to sustain over time in a larger political system that tries to impose uniform rules, operates through patron-client networks, or uses terror to sustain authoritarian rule. Having vigorous local and regional governments and many types of voluntary associations is part of the answer but not sufficient in and of itself.

Simply having national elections, choosing leaders, and asking them to pass good legislation is hardly sufficient, however, to sustain a self-governing society over the long run. Electing officials to national office and providing them with "common budgetary pools" of substantial size to spend "in the public interest" creates substantial temptations to engage in rent-seeking behavior and distributive politics. The central problem is how to embed elected officials in a set of institutions that generates information about their actions, holds them accountable, allows for rapid response in times of threat, and encourages innovation and problem solving. Solving such problems involves the design of a delicately balanced system. It requires decisions from sophisticated participants who understand the theory involved in constituting and reconstituting such systems and share a moral commitment to the maintenance of a democratic social order.

Now, what is the role of the institutional analyst in all of this? Well, for one, it is essential for those who devote their lives to studying the emergence, adaptation, design, and effects of institutional arrangements to understand a very wide array of diverse rules that exist in an equally diverse set of physical and cultural milieus. To understand how various rules may be used as part of a self-governing society, one has to examine how diverse rules affect the capacities of individuals to achieve mutually productive outcomes over time or the dominance of some participants over others. Eventually, one has to examine constellations of embedded institutional arrangements rather than isolated situations. And, one has to examine the short- and long-run effects of many different types of rules on human actions and outcomes. Further, one has to acquire considerable humility regarding exactly how precise predictions can be made about the effects of different rules on incentives, behavior, and outcomes achieved. Design of successful institutions may indeed be feasible. Designed institutions, which tend to generate substantial information rapidly and accurately and allow for the change of rules over time in light of performance, are more likely to be successful than those resulting from "grand designs" for societies as a whole.

To be an institutional analyst, one needs to learn to use the best available theoretical and data collection tools, while at the same time trying to develop even better theories and conducting further empirical studies that contribute to our theoretical understanding of self-governing systems. All tools have capabilities and limits. The task of the skilled artisan—whether an institutional theorist or a cabinetmaker—is to learn the capabilities and limits of relevant tools and how best to use a combination of tools to address the wide diversity of puzzles that one comes across in a lifetime of work.

Relevant tools are plentiful in the sense that we do have an extensive body of political, social, and economic theory that focuses on the impact of diverse rules on the incentives, behavior, and likely outcomes within different settings. These tools are limited, however, in that many of the most rigorous theories make questionable assumptions about both the individual and about the settings within which individuals find themselves. This can be problematic for explaining behavior in many settings. These explicit and often implicit assumptions may mask some of the deeper problems of sustaining democratic systems over time. Many of the difficult problems that human beings face in trying to develop and sustain democratic organizations are assumed away when one starts with assumptions that individuals have complete and perfect information and can make error-free calculations about expected consequences for themselves and no one else in complex, uncertain worlds.

Further, when assumptions are made that the structure of the situations facing individuals are fixed and cannot be changed by those in the situation, little effort is devoted to addressing how individuals affect their own situations. Yet, these same assumptions (full information and fixed structures) are useful when the analyst wants to examine the expected short-term outcomes of an institutional and physical setting, where the options available to individuals are narrowly constrained and where individuals have many opportunities to learn about the costs and benefits of pursuing diverse options. Learning which assumptions, theories, and models to use to analyze diverse institutional arrangements combined with diverse settings is an important aspect of the training of institutional analysts.

During this seminar, we will use a variety of theoretical tools. These will help us to understand the Institutional Analysis and Development (IAD) framework that we have been developing over many years at the Workshop as well as the more recent Program for Institutional Analysis of Social-Ecological Systems (PIASES) framework. The skilled institutional analyst uses a framework to identify the types of questions and variables to be included in any particular analysis. The artisan then selects what is perceived to be the most appropriate theory available given the particular questions to be addressed, the type of empirical evidence that is available or is to be obtained, and the purpose of the analysis. For any one theory, there are multiple models of that theory that can be used to analyze a focused set of questions. Choosing the most appropriate model (whether this is a mathematical model, a simulation, a process model, or the design for an experiment) also depends on the particular puzzle that an analyst wants to examine.

Further, there are multiple tools that are used in the conduct of research ranging from individual case studies, meta-analyses, large-N studies, laboratory and field experiments, GIS and remote sensing, agent-based models, and others. Institutional analysts respect all of these methods when used to understand human behavior in diverse settings. No scholar can use all of these methods well nor are they all appropriate for the study of all institutional settings, but it is important to learn more about diverse tools and their strengths and weaknesses for examining diverse research questions.

Objectives of the Seminar

Given the above background to the substantive focus of this seminar, let us try to present the central objectives for the semester as we see them. The objectives are:

- To understand the constraints and opportunities of human artisanship and entrepreneurship.

  If self-governance within any particular organizational setting is only a possibility and not a necessity, then students of self-governance need to understand the constraints on choice presented by the structure of a physical, biological, and social world at any particular point in time as well as the opportunities of using human insight, reason, persuasion, and vigilance to transform inherited structures.

- To learn how to use the IAD framework and the related SES framework for understanding the commonalities underlying entities that are often treated by diverse disciplines as fundamentally different things.

  Markets and states are frequently posed as opposite types of entities. Those who study the American Presidency or the American Congress sometimes view what they study as entirely different from European Parliamentary systems or some of the national systems of Africa or of Asia. We will instead use a common set of elements to analyze repetitive relationships within and across markets, hierarchies, local communities, private associations, families, churches, and across markets, hierarchies, local communities, private associations, families, churches, regional governments, national governments, multinational corporations, and international regimes.

- To learn some very basic elements of game theory as *one* of the theories that is consistent with the IAD framework and to gain some knowledge of simple games, but this is really a very basic introduction and not a course on game theory.

Game theory is emerging as one of the theoretical tools in heavy use across all of the social sciences (as well as in biology). Game theory is useful for the institutional analyst when trying to understand the patterns of outcomes that result from the operation of repetitive situations over time when the motivational structure of participants is clearly understood. It also provides a theoretical tool for analyzing what to expect when rules are changed. As will become obvious in the semester, there are also many perplexing issues that are not yet resolved both about the theory of games and its applications to the study of institutions. We will do some reading drawing more on an evolutionary perspective and how this perspective combined with game theory helps us understand some of the above issues.

- To recognize core problems that humans repeatedly face in a wide diversity of settings such as those involved in providing and regulating the use of public goods, common-pool resources, asymmetric information problems, adverse selection problems, moral hazard problems, aggregation of preferences problems, team coordination problems, principal-agent problems, and the problems of constituting complex orders under incomplete information.

  Learning how to recognize the key symptoms of the core problems that humans repeatedly face is essential for institutional analysts. Diagnosis of the source(s) of the problems involved in a simple or complex setting is necessary prior to effective advice about the types of rules, norms, and strategies that have a chance to improve on outcomes.

- To understand how polycentric political systems, including but not limited to federal ones, operate based on principles learned from this course.

  An irony exists in the contemporary world. This problem is at the heart of recent controversies about how to govern America and how to solve problems in the developing world. The recent policy focus on devolution in developing countries has emphasized shifting responsibility from national to state and local level. As this has been happening, the national governments have frequently continued to seek control but not implementation of many programs. One needs to dig into proposals for decentralization to see what is being devolved and HOW before one can even begin to evaluate these.

- To share with colleagues how to analyze diverse policy arenas.

- To understand the importance of respecting the assets and limits of diverse disciplines and core research methods that are used to undertake careful empirical studies of the institutions and their operations in diverse environments.

  Many of the theoretical questions of interest to an institutional analyst can be studied using individual case studies, meta-analyses of existing case studies, large-N field studies, formal theory, experimental research, and agent-based modeling. No one person can become an expert in all of these methods, but scholars need to overcome their suspicion of methods developed by others and recognize that learning cumulates faster and better if careful research has been undertaken with complementary research methods. One also needs to learn the limits of each method.

- To conduct an institutional analysis of an important and interesting puzzle relating to human behavior in a rule-ordered setting at a local, regional, national, or international domain.

Each enrolled student and visiting scholar will write a paper (for the Mini-Conference) that is an institutional analysis of a structured situation or linked set of situations that generate outcomes that are either puzzling, deemed inefficient, inequitable, unsustainable, or in need of change. It is also important to study situations that have generated productive outcomes and are worthy of emulation and to identify what aspects of the structure, and the human behavior within that structure, that has led to positive results.

Note

This chapter is a selection of the Political Science Y673 syllabus that Elinor Ostrom used in Fall 2011, pp. 1–7, Indiana University, Workshop in Political Theory and Policy Analysis. The complete syllabus is available online at https://ostromworkshop.indiana.edu/resources/archives/index.html.

2

An Institutional Framework for Policy Analysis and Design

Margaret M. Polski and Elinor Ostrom

This chapter applies the Institutional Analysis and Development (IAD) framework to policy analysis and design. The IAD framework is the collective product of the many and diverse social scientists who have participated in the Workshop in Political Theory and Policy Analysis over the past twenty-five years. The interdisciplinary nature of these collaborations, the training and interests of Workshop scholars cross every discipline in the social sciences and a number of disciplines in the physical sciences, has produced a tool that can be used to analyze and design policy interventions in a broad variety of political-economic situations. Whereas past descriptions of the IAD framework have focused on its use as a research method, in this chapter, we develop it as a tool for policy analysts who are evaluating policy effectiveness, initiating policy reform, or designing new policy interventions.[1] The chapter proceeds as follows. The first section defines and motivates the subject of institutional analysis and policy design. The second section provides a brief overview of the IAD framework. We then develop a systematic process for policy analysis and design in the third section. Finally, we provide some examples of policy applications.

Institutional Analysis and Policy Design

Institutions are everywhere, governing our lives in fundamental ways. Yet, until fairly recently, policy analysis has often ignored the role of institutions in political economic behavior. Public choice scholars are among the first analysts in the twentieth century to grapple systematically with the role of institutions in policy design.[2] Their analyses have been further invigorated by efforts over the past fifteen years to reintegrate the study of politics and economics as the interdisciplinary specialty of political economy. Variously known as public choice theory, social choice theory, and institutional economics, this work has led to a paradigmatic shift in policy analysis and design from supply-driven approaches, to institutionally driven approaches.[3] Mounting evidence from this work, applied to myriad public policy matters, suggests that policy work can be substantially improved if we include institutions in our analysis.[4]

Past oversight of the importance of institutions is due, in part, to the inherent difficulty of analyzing them. Conceptually, institutions are highly abstract and frequently invisible elements of the policy environment. Ostrom (1996b) identifies a number of challenges in this regard. First, the term "institution" is used in many ways. We define an institution as a widely understood rule, norm, or strategy that creates incentives for behavior in repetitive situations (Crawford and Ostrom 1995). Institutions may be formally described in the form of a law, policy, or procedure, or they may emerge informally as norms, standard operating practices, or habits. Alone or in a set of related arrangements, they are mechanisms for adjusting behavior in a situation that requires coordination among two or more individuals or groups of individuals (Hurwicz 1994). Because institutions are fundamentally invisible, shared concepts that exist in the minds and routines of participants in policy situations, we believe policy analysis must include a careful survey of how participants actually do things and why they do them one way rather than another.

Sometimes the terms "institution" and "organization" are used interchangeably. It is useful to draw a distinction between these two concepts. An organization can be thought of as a set of institutional arrangements and participants who have a common set of goals and purposes, and who must interact across multiple action situations at different levels of activity. Like institutions, organizations may be formally or informally constructed. Thus defined, the term organization includes, for example, legislatures, government agencies, multilateral organizations like the United Nations or the World Bank, nongovernmental organizations, colleges and universities, business enterprises, cooperatives, religious groups, clubs, social networks, clans, tribes, and families. Organizations are the product of human effort to order relations by removing uncertainty in repetitive interactions. All organizations (and many institutions) are formed subject to existing, higher-level institutions. For example, the organizational form of the US public corporation is prescribed by corporate and tax law. Corporate and tax law have been developed subject to the constraints of US constitutional law.

Another challenge for institutionally oriented policy analysis is complexity. Few policy situations are simple. Most involve knowledge from many different perspectives, activities are organized at multiple levels, and any given policy situation overlaps with other policy situations so that activities in one situation affect activities in another. No single discipline addresses all the issues that humans address when they interact in complex social situations. In order to understand what is actually going on in a policy area, as well as how things might proceed differently, it is important to incorporate input from multiple disciplines, multiple levels of activity, and multiple policy situations. One of the reasons for developing the IAD framework was to provide a common basis for integrating diverse policy elements and the work of diverse policy analysts.

A final challenge for policy analysts and designers is to avoid taking a "blueprint approach" (Korten 1980). When facing real policy imperatives, it is tempting to take a successful policy model as a kind of blueprint, and apply it broadly, designing new policies according to this blueprint. The problem with this approach is that the model or blueprint may not work in a different political-economic setting. In order to intelligently apply successful models, we must understand (1) the information and incentive structures inherent to the model, (2) the existing information and incentive structures in the policy situation in question, and (3) the fit between the model and policy setting. All policy situations are governed, for better or for ill, by institutional arrangements that are specific to the demands of a particular time, place, and people. These arrangements are deliberately crafted (or circumvented) by individuals and groups in order to make interaction more predictable by removing uncertainty and reducing risk. Policy reform that ignores an existing institutional context is doomed to failure.

In sum, institutions delimit capacity for social change. They are important precisely because they are intentional constructions that structure information and create incentives to act or not to act in a particular situation, thereby imposing constraints on the range of possible behavior and feasible reforms. Interacting with physical and cultural conditions, institutions create incentives for social behavior. This behavior generates observable patterns of interaction, which in turn produce policy outcomes. Hence, if we wish to evaluate, design, or reform policy, we must have a systematic way to analyze existing arrangements and to generate and compare alternatives. This brings us handily to a discussion of the IAD framework.

An Overview of the IAD Framework

The IAD framework is best viewed as a systematic method for organizing policy analysis activities that is compatible with a wide variety of more specialized analytic techniques used in the physical and social sciences. It does not replace other techniques, but provides a means to synthesize the work of multiple participants, including those who are directly involved in the policy situation and have an interest in policy outcomes. The IAD framework helps analysts comprehend complex social situations and break them down into manageable sets of practical activities. When applied rigorously to policy analysis and design, analysts and other interested participants have a better chance of avoiding the oversights and simplifications that lead to policy failures.

Figure 2.1 provides a schematic representation of the framework. After defining a policy question or problem, the focus of the analysis is on behavior in the action arena, which includes the action situation, and individuals and groups who are routinely involved in the situation (actors). One objective of the analysis is to identify factors in each of three areas that influence the behavior of individuals and groups in the policy situation: physical and material conditions, community attributes (culture), and rules-in-use. Two other objectives are to identify and evaluate patterns of interaction that are logically associated with behavior in the action arena, and outcomes from these interactions. This can be a very demanding task, even for very simple policy situations. However, more than twenty years of use by Workshop colleagues in all parts of the world investigating many different social questions, suggests that it is well worth the effort (see Applications section below).

Applying the IAD framework to policy analysis and design prompts us to think carefully about a wide assortment of issues that are important aspects of a particular policy problem. The more comprehensive and precise our analysis, the better hope we have of designing successful policy solutions. Many of these issues would be overlooked by technical analyses that consider a relatively narrow range of closely related factors. It also provides a means to incorporate diverse participants in policy analysis and design. Because the framework demands multiple disciplinary perspectives, it holds the potential to produce a very rich understanding of social situations. And in addition to providing the basis for more effective policy, this understanding can provide a firm foundation for building consensus for coordinated action. Now let us look at the process of institutional analysis using the IAD framework.

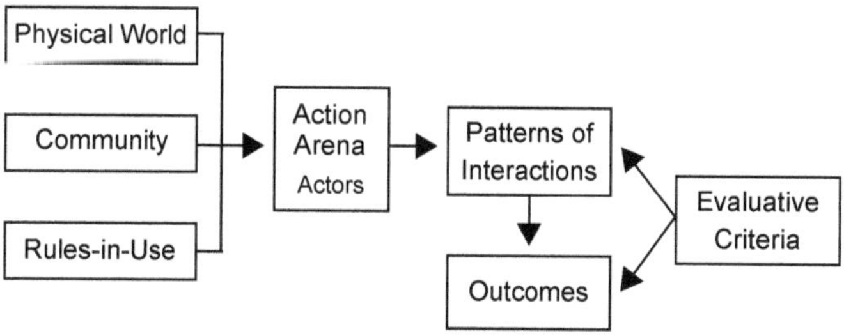

Figure 2.1. Institutional Analysis and Development framework.
Source: Adapted from Ostrom, Gardner, and Walker (1994, 37).

Using the IAD Framework for Policy Analysis and Design

Before we begin our analysis, we must first define a policy issue or objective as specifically as possible and decide how we will apply the IAD framework.

Step 1: Define the Policy Analysis Objective and the Analytic Approach

There are two ways to approach this task. The first approach involves using the framework as a diagnostic tool and working backwards through the flow diagram to reaffirm or revise policy objectives, evaluate policy outcomes, understand the information and incentive structure of a policy, or develop reform initiatives. This approach is best suited to analyzing well-established policy situations. We begin by isolating a specific policy issue or program, and specifying its objectives. We then observe some facts about outcomes of activity in the policy arena. The kinds of questions we ask include:

- What is happening in the policy arena?
- How do observed outcomes compare to policy objectives?
- Which outcomes are satisfactory? Which are not?
- Which outcomes are most important?

Focusing on a particular class of outcomes, we then identify relevant patterns of interaction. For example, key patterns of interaction in political-economic analyses typically include market structure, information flows, and the structure of political participation. Some questions we ask include:

- When are these outcomes occurring?
- Where are they occurring?
- Who is involved?

At this point, our backward-flowing diagnostic analysis leads us to specify the action arena, physical and material conditions, community attributes, and rules-in-use. We approach these analyses, which are described in more detail later in this section, by asking:

- How are policy outcomes occurring?

For example, imagine that we observe the following outcome of a publicly financed health care policy: costs have been increasing dramatically over the past five years and these costs are unsustainable given realistic assumptions about future public budgets. We would like to reform existing policy or create a complementary new policy that will balance the health care budget and still achieve other health care policy objectives. Focusing on the very general problem of rising costs, we narrow the analysis by making some further observations about patterns of interaction, asking which costs are rising most rapidly, when they are rising, and where they are rising. Data from this analysis leads to description of the policy action situation. We then deepen the analysis of the action situation by asking who is involved in generating rising costs; for example, who receives care, who makes decisions about giving care, who oversees health care service providers, and so on. Next, we ask detailed questions about how these costs are generated by investigating physical and material conditions, community conditions, and rules-in-use.

A second approach to defining a policy issue or objective and applying the IAD framework involves specifying a political-economic activity and then working forward rather than backward through the framework. So, for example, we might investigate infant health care. We would begin by describing the physical and material attributes of infant care, and proceed through community attributes, rules-in-use, a detailed analysis of the action arena, patterns of interaction, and outcomes. This approach is best suited to policy tasks that involve developing new policy initiatives, or comparing alternative policy designs. The same general questions used in a backward-flowing diagnostic analysis are useful in a prospective analysis.

In either approach, the analysis can be based on empirical observation of past and present events, hypothetical forecasts and simulations, or a combination of both. Naturally, we recommend that policy analysts take care to maximize the validity and reliability of their analyses by using generally accepted investigation procedures. Although we have organized this chapter following the approach of working forward through the framework, we do not favor one approach over the other. In fact, we have both sometimes analyzed the components of the framework in idiosyncratic order, depending upon the particular analytic circumstances we were facing. Our advice is to analyze each component in the order that makes the most sense for a particular policy analysis project.

Step 2: Analyze Physical and Material Conditions

Physical and material conditions often influence policy action situations and constrain institutional arrangements in important ways. When we refer to physical and material conditions, we mean the physical and human resources and capabilities related to providing and producing goods and services. These conditions include production inputs like capital, labor, and technology, as well as sources of finance, storage, and distribution channels. It is important to specify these conditions because they have significant implications for policy design, politics, and collective action, which are all critical aspects of the policy-making process. The kinds of questions we ask to determine the physical and material conditions associated with a particular policy activity include:

- Focusing on the good or service produced in the policy situation, what is the economic nature of the activity?
- How is this good or service provided?
- How is this good or service produced?
- What physical and human resources are required to provide and produce this good or service? What technologies and processes are required? What are storage requirements, and distribution channels?
- What is the scale and scope of provision and production activity?

Following standard economic theory, the economic nature of a good or service can be determined by two attributes: (1) the extent to which access to consumption can be controlled (excludability) and (2) the extent to which one person's consumption reduces the supply available to others (subtractability). High subtractability implies individual consumption; low subtractability implies that more than one person will consume the

Table 2.1. Determining the economic nature of a good or service

	High excludability	Low excludability
High subtractability	*Private*	*Common Pool*
Low subtractability	*Toll*	*Public*

good or service at the same time. High excludability implies that consumers will have difficulty consuming the good or service without contributing to its cost; low excludability implies that consumers may be able to "free-ride," consuming the good or service without contributing to the cost of provision or production (Olson 1965). This classification scheme is summarized in the matrix in Table 2.1, which shows four broad categories of goods and services: private, toll, common pool, and public.

Consumption of goods and services is more or less subtractable or excludable depending upon the physical characteristics of a good or service, available production technology, the scale and scope of activity, and other aspects of the production system including storage and distribution. Private goods and services do not have a public character: consumption is perfectly excludable and subtractable. However, many other goods and services do have a public character. Consider, for example, various forms of physical infrastructure. Metered energy, water, telecom, sanitation, and arterial roads are often classified as toll goods. This is because while many people can use these goods or services at once, there are production processes, control systems, and distribution systems that make it possible to physically control consumption access so that consumers contribute to the cost of provision and production.[5] Conversely, isolated roads are an example of a public good; they can be used by many people at once and one person's use does not subtract from another's. However, use is not easily observable, so it is costly to exclude those who benefit from using these roads but do not contribute to their cost. When this is the case, there is little incentive for users to contribute to building and maintaining these roads, and hence it can be difficult to develop and sustain them. Consumption of common-pool goods, like grazing lands, fisheries, and irrigation systems, poses yet another dilemma—one person's use reduces the supply available to others and it is difficult to physically control access. This combination of consumption and production characteristics means that these resources are easily destroyed, often to everyone's disadvantage.

Having identified the economic nature of the policy activity, we next differentiate production activities from provision activities. Production refers to all those activities that involve transforming inputs into outputs. Provision refers to activities associated with financing and distribution activities. For example, consider a policy to build and maintain a footpath between two villages through a remote grassland. The footpath is an example of a public good. It is costly to monitor and exclude others from using the path because it is in a remote area, so we say it has low excludability. It also has low subtractability: one person's use of the footpath does not diminish another person's use. In fact, the more people who use the path, the easier it is to maintain it. However, a public good presents a classic coordination dilemma. Every inhabitant of the area who has a reason to travel back and forth between the two villages benefits from a well-maintained path, yet it is difficult to act collectively to develop and sustain it. This problem can be exacerbated by the scale and scope of the activity: coordinating to provide and produce one relatively short path is easier than coordinating to provide and produce a very long path or multiple paths. So, absent some form of coordination to overcome the free-rider problem, it is unlikely that a footpath will be built and sustained without some form of intervention. This is where community attributes and rules come in to play, but we will defer these matters to subsequent sections.

Producing a footpath through a grassy area requires a scythe or some other piece of equipment to cut the grass, and competent labor to use the cutting equipment on the particular terrain. Providing a footpath involves noticing when it is time to cut the grass in order to properly maintain the path, making arrangements to cut the grass, and financing the cost. Production costs include the cost of purchasing and maintaining the cutting equipment, training and wages for the operator, and compensation for the opportunity cost of capital. Those who produce the footpath could also provide the footpath. For example, those who live in one village could form a cooperative association to provide and produce a footpath to the other village. Alternatively, the members of the village could provide the footpath, but hire someone in the neighboring village who has a sharp scythe to produce and maintain it. Or members of the two villages together could provide the footpath, hiring a private contractor who provides footpath services to a number of villages in the region to produce and maintain it.

As the foregoing example demonstrates, analyzing the economic nature of a policy activity and distinguishing between provision and production activities tells us quite a lot about which resources, capabilities, and coordination mechanisms are required to effectively implement a policy. This example also suggests that there is not just one way but many different ways to organize these activities. Which way is the “best” way will depend upon a number of circumstances that are specific to a particular time, place, and people. The IAD framework thus compels us to consider community attributes.

Step 3: Analyze Community Attributes

The attributes of a community that affect a policy action situation include the demographic features of the community, generally accepted norms about policy activities, the degree of common understanding potential participants share about activities in the policy area, and the extent to which potential participants’ values, beliefs, and preferences about policy-oriented strategies and outcomes are homogeneous. The kinds of questions we ask to determine the community attributes relevant to a policy action situation include:

- What knowledge and information do participants have about the relationship among policy-oriented strategies, actions, and outcomes?
- What are participants’ values and preferences with respect to strategies for achieving outcomes, as well as outcomes themselves?
- What are participants’ beliefs about the relationship among policy-oriented strategies, actions, and outcomes?
- What are participants’ beliefs about other participants’ strategy preferences and outcomes?

Investigating community and cultural attributes is notoriously difficult.[6] The validity and reliability of our conclusions are frequently controversial. Nevertheless, we believe it is imperative that policy analysts make an effort to understand the cultural context of policy activity as participants themselves understand it. The policy and development literatures are replete with examples of well-intended policy failures that were inconsistent with cultural norms and routines. If these kinds of inconsistencies can be discovered after the fact, it seems to us that they are potentially discoverable before policies are initiated if we carefully integrate sociological, anthropological, or social-psychological studies in the policy analysis process. Consider, for example, the complex set of community attributes that affect US business policy. Business educators aim to create a consistent business ethos to enhance business performance. They promote a shared understanding (norms, values, beliefs, preferences) among business professionals that management's first obligation is to maximize the market value of the company, subject to constraints imposed by its rather diverse constituency.[7] The performance measures used by the financial community to evaluate and compare business performance reflect and reinforce this ethos. These standards include revenue and earnings growth (overall, and within strategic business segments), control of operating expense, debt to equity ratios, return on investment, and whether current stock price overstates or understates fundamental business value.

While the norm of maximizing business market value appears to be widely shared by business academics, the business press, and professionally trained business people, a 1996 Yankelovich Partners poll shows that 51 percent of Americans think a business firm's first obligation is to its employees, and only 17 percent think shareholders deserve highest priority (Rosewicz 1996). Considering that most Americans are employed by business and better than 50 percent of all Americans currently own stock in business corporations, this contradiction has very interesting implications for policy that affects business incentives to balance competing demands by employees and stockholders. A policy analysis that fails to consider these different community attributes will be considerably weaker than one that is more complete.

Step 4: Analyze Rules-in-Use

The types of rules the IAD framework asks us to consider in an institutional analysis are closely linked to the elements of an action situation. They are the minimal but necessary set of rules that are needed to explain policy-related actions, interactions, and outcomes. As we will see in a subsequent section, the types of rules we consider correspond with the clusters of elements we analyze in the policy action situation (Figure 2.2). This makes sense when we recall that the focus of institutional analysis is on understanding the formal and informal rules that affect behavior in the action arena.

When we analyze rules-in-use in the action arena, we concentrate on the operating rules that are commonly used by most participants and on the sources of these rules, rather than on rules that can be articulated but are not widely observed. Taking a representative sample of the population engaged in the policy activity in question, we want to know what these

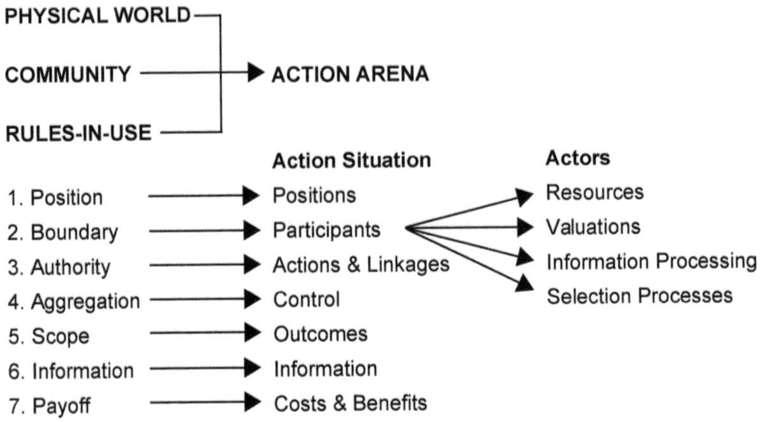

Figure 2.2. Relationship between rules-in-use and elements of the policy action arena.

rules are, the source of each of the rules, who observes them and why, and who does not observe them and why.[8] The seven types of rules we consider are: (1) position, (2) boundary, (3) authority, (4) aggregation, (5) scope, (6) information, and (7) payoff.

We have previously observed that rules are abstract phenomena. Let us look at a cursory example of an IAD analysis to illustrate how we analyze rules-in-use. Table 2.2 presents a contrived (and quite exaggerated) analysis of traffic policy in two types of metropolitan intersections, based on one of the author's subjective experience.

Position rules specify the set of positions or roles that participants assume in an action situation, and the number and type of participants who hold each position. In our example, we have drivers, pedestrians, a voluntary association (American Automobile Association), and traffic control officials. *Boundary rules* can be thought of as exit and entry rules: they specify which participants enter or leave positions and how they do so, for example, rules related to licensing drivers or becoming employed as a traffic control official. *Authority rules* specify the actions participants in given positions may take, such as the set of rules that governs what a traffic control officer may do when s/he stops a driver, or when one driver collides with another. *Aggregation rules* determine how decisions are made in an action situation. For example, a driver entering an intersection controlled by a traffic signal decides whether or not to proceed into the intersection based upon the color of the traffic light. *Scope rules* specify the jurisdic-

Table 2.2. IAD analysis of traffic policy in two types of metropolitan intersections

IAD domain	*Minneapolis*	*Boston*
Physical world	Four-way square intersection. Severe winter weather. Well-marked streets. Few potholes. Heavy traffic.	Four-way traffic circle. Moderate snow, ice, and rain. Poorly marked streets. Many potholes. Congested traffic.
Community	Homogeneous Communitarian	Heterogeneous Individualistic
Rules-in-use	Pedestrian has right-of-way. Otherwise, driver in intersection has right-of-way. No traffic signal. Drivers enter intersection when there is no one waiting in an opposing lane. Traffic control is a low priority for metro police. AAA campaign to encourage polite driving habits.	No pedestrians. Driver in outer lane of traffic circle has right-of-way. No traffic signal. Drivers simultaneously and continuously enter and exit traffic circle using all available lanes possible. Traffic control is a low priority for metro police. No AAA campaign.
Action arena	—	—
Patterns of interaction	Sequential queuing.	Chaotic queuing.
Outcomes	Average time through intersection, collisions, property damage, and so forth	

tion of outcomes that can be affected and whether these outcomes are or are not final. Traffic policy can cover all traffic intersections in a state, or it can apply to a more limited class of intersections. Similarly, a traffic control officer's citation can be made subject to appeal in traffic court. *Information rules* affect the amount and type of information available to participants in an action arena. For example, a rule that makes information about enforcement of traffic laws in an intersection available to drivers

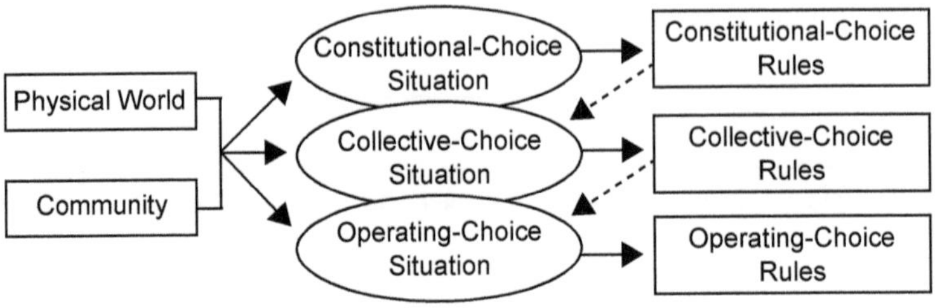

Figure 2.3. Rules and policy systems.

who routinely use the intersection could affect the way drivers behave. And last, but not least, *payoff rules* determine how costs and benefits are meted-out in the action arena. In our example, insurance rules, licensing rules, and traffic codes determine who bears the cost of driving violations in a traffic intersection and hence, the benefits of complying with different types of rules in the action situation.

We have briefly described and illustrated how we would use the IAD framework to analyze rules-in-use in a relatively simple policy action situation. But many policy questions involve complex systems of interaction. In these cases, we court policy failure if we limit analysis to single action arenas. While we cannot hope to fully develop a systemic institutional analysis in such a short exposition, we can briefly consider how the IAD guides us to approach it.

Analyzing Policy Systems

In addition to delving deeply into the factors that affect single action arenas, the IAD framework helps an analyst to organize and explain behavior in policy systems. Most policy situations are composed of multiple distinct but overlapping action arenas that are linked sequentially or simultaneously, and several levels of rules. Figure 2.3 depicts this complexity. For example, the system of banking regulation that has evolved over two centuries in the United States uses ten competing federal agencies, fifty state banking commissions, and fifty state insurance commissions to regulate ten different types of financial service enterprises operating in twenty regulation-defined markets related to borrowing, transactions management, and savings. Banks, consumers, and regulators use myriad competitive and cooperative strategies in policy action situations, including participating in financial services markets, organizing to take collective action, lobbying for private action, lobbying for legislative action, lobbying for executive action, lobbying for regulatory action, monitoring and enforcing regulation, legislating, and taking legal action. In order to understand banking policy, an analyst must link activity in many different action arenas, and consider rules at operating, collective-choice, and constitutional levels.

It is not always easy to identify relevant action arenas in large, complex policy systems. Continuing with our example of US banking policy, depending upon the policy question, one might need to analyze scores of action arenas involving banking, insurance, and investment brokerage firms, credit unions, the market for financial services, trade associations, public interest organizations, presidential commissions, interstate governmental commissions, several departments of the US Treasury, the Board of Governors of the Federal Reserve, the Department of Justice, the Federal Deposit Insurance Corporation, state banking commissions, state legislatures and legislative committees, federal legislatures and legislative committees, state and federal courts, the Supreme Court, and the Bank for International Settlements. The key is to continually narrow the policy question as much as possible. In systemic analyses, this winnowing process occurs as the analysis progresses. What we generally find is that the most relevant arenas readily emerge from a rigorous application of the IAD framework.

Analyzing Multiple Levels of Rules

Rules are frequently nested in other sets of rules that define how lower-level rules function. Whenever we address questions about policy change, we must distinguish three levels of rules that cumulatively affect the actions taken and outcomes obtained in any policy situation (Kiser and Ostrom 1982). The first level is the operating level. Operating rules affect participants' day-to-day decision making in specific political and economic settings. The second level is the collective-choice level. Collective-choice rules determine who is eligible to participate in activity affecting the operating level, and how operating rules may be changed. Similarly, constitutional rules determine who is eligible to participate in crafting collective-choice rules, and how these rules may be changed. At each level of analysis there can be one or more arenas in which different types of decisions made at that level will occur. The linkages among these rules and action arenas are diagramed in Figure 2.4.

Once again, we will use banking regulation to illustrate. Consider the levels of rules pertaining to the policy action situation in which banks operate branches in any state in the United States. In this example, the operating activity is branching across state lines. Until fairly recently, US banks were not permitted to make this decision. They could collect and analyze infor-

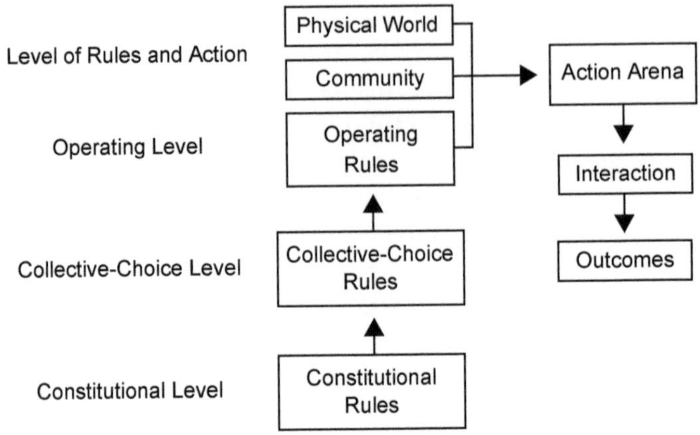

Figure 2.4. The linkages among levels of rules and IAD components.

mation about the possible effects of nationwide banking, formulate a corporate position, meet with other bank officials to strategize about change, and hire legislative lobbyists, but they could not legally branch throughout the United States. This was so because collective-choice rules specified that only state legislatures (who make the rules for state-chartered banks) and federal legislatures (who make the rules for nationally chartered banks) could decide whether banks could branch across state lines. Until passage of the Interstate Banking and Branching Efficiency Act of 1994, federal banking law deferred to the states on interstate branching. Hence, state and nationally chartered banks could only branch across state lines if states adopted permissive legislation. Under US constitutional rules, states cannot make rules on behalf of other states. But the US Congress can impose rules on the states, providing the rules do not violate states' constitutionally guaranteed rights. And so to understand policy change in this action situation, an analyst must consider the effects of rules at all three levels: operational, collective choice, and constitutional.

Step 5: Integrate the Analysis

As we previously indicated, the action arena is the focus of policy analysis and design—it is where the policy action is! The action arena is a conceptual space in which actors inform themselves, consider alternative courses of action, make decisions, take action, and experience the consequences of these actions. Who is present in this situation, the roles they play, the actions they take, and so on, are all affected by factors in the physical and material world, the community, and rules-in-use. The action arena has two aspects: the action situation, and the actors who interact in the action situation.

Action Situation

We integrate an IAD policy analysis by explaining behavior in terms of the following situational elements:

- What are the *positions* or roles that actors play in this situation?
- Who are the *participants*?
- What *actions* can participants take, and *how are actions linked to outcomes*?
- What is the level of *control* that each participant has over action in this situation?
- What *outcomes* are possible in this situation?
- What *information* about the action situation is available to participants?
- What *costs and benefits* do participants incur when they take action in this situation?

For example, when analyzing overharvesting from a common-pool resource (CPR), we need to know how physical and material conditions, community attributes, and rules encourage or discourage who and how many individuals use the resource system; what roles they play when they use it; what geographic region and which events in that region are affected by users' resource consumption; which types of harvesting processes and technologies are used; whether there are conservation measures such as open and closed seasons; whether users withdraw resources on their own initiative, confer with others, or obtain a permit; how much information users have about the condition of the resource and how their use and other users' use affects the resource; and what costs or benefits users incur if they overharvest. Recall that the economic nature of a CPR creates incentives for users to free-ride on the efforts of others to sustain the resource, which can lead to degradation (see Table 2.1). A growing body of empirical and theoretical research suggests that the likelihood of this occurring depends critically upon the fit among the physical and material conditions associated with providing and producing the resource, community attributes, and institutional arrangements. This work suggests that using the IAD framework to guide CPR policy analysis and design is a very sensible thing to do.[9]

Actors

In the IAD approach, it is very important to rigorously analyze the decision-making capabilities of actors in action arenas. This is accomplished by considering the following:

- Resources
- Valuations
- Information Processing
- Selection Processes

Actors' decision choices are often influenced by access to stocks of capital, labor, knowledge, technology, time, and social influence. These resources endow actors with the capacity to act unilaterally, bilaterally, or multilaterally, over short, medium, and long time horizons. This capacity fundamentally determines the relative strength of one actor or group of actors. The extent to which relative strength may be exercised to circumvent or change existing rules is itself a function of higher order institutional arrangements.

Valuations or preferences refer to what it is that an actor wishes to achieve in a given situation. Human values and preferences are the subject of considerable theoretical work in psychology, economics, and philosophy. An institutional analyst must either estimate from survey measurements or make intelligent assumptions about preferences in order to construct a model of decision behavior in the action arena.

We have already noted that decision making is affected by the quantity and quality of participants' information. Information processing, the processes used to incorporate information to make decisions about actions, is another element of this analysis. Consciously or unconsciously, we often assume that participants in a given policy situation are perfectly informed (or will take the trouble to become so), and that they use rational decision-making processes.[10] Many policy professionals are trained to assume that policy situations can be analyzed as constrained optimization problems. This sort of analysis often assumes that diverse participants have the same information, face no uncertainty, and can costlessly overcome innate individual differences, formulate mutually acceptable valuations, and assign probabilities for all inputs to the decision process. Further, that they can quickly and accurately make these calculations.

Most policy analysts recognize that these conditions are rarely met in the naturally occurring world, that strictly rational optimization will not occur, and that policy designs based on these assumptions will fail. In most policy settings, participants have differing amounts of information, endowments, experience, and processing capabilities. Uncertainty is rampant and preferences are often radically opposed. Search and negotiation impose substantial costs on coordination, problem solving, and decision making. These conditions mean that social behavior will have a strategic character as self-interested individuals square-off with those who have broader social objectives. While we believe that policies can and ought to be designed to encourage reconciliation of individual and group interests, as well as rational decision making, some policy situations are more conducive to this type of information processing than others. Hence, it is critical that policy analysts assess the capacity of participants to overcome those factors that contribute to opportunistic behavior in particular policy situations.

Finally, the selection criteria actors use to order and evaluate one action alternative with respect to another, is a related consideration. Again, one must consider the extent to which individual and group decision making is rational. And rationality is affected by a variety of sociopsychological factors including the availability of information, education levels, personality differences, nutrition, peer pressure, and so on. Selection criteria are particularly sensitive to the vagaries of the physical and material world, community attributes, and existing rules-in-use.

Step 6: Analyze Patterns of Interaction

Once the constraints of the physical and material world, community attributes, and rules-in-use are taken into consideration, patterns of interaction flow logically from the behavior of actors in the action arena. Patterns of interaction refer to the structural characteristics of an action situation and the conduct of participants in the resulting structure. In tightly constrained policy action situations with little or no uncertainty, participants have a limited range of strategies, and a policy analyst can make strong inferences and specific predictions about likely patterns of behavior. For example, when there is no limit on the number of people who use a common-pool resource, or the amount of harvesting activities they can undertake, and users do not have access to arenas in which to negotiate common resource management rules, we can safely predict that users will overharvest the resource and fully dissipate economic surplus (E. Ostrom, Gardner, and Walker 1994). Similarly, if bankers face intense competitive pressure, taxpayers guarantee deposits, and regulators relax supervision, we can expect to find an increase in the riskiness of bank lending (Polski 1996).

Unfortunately, most policy analysis situations do not generate such unambiguous patterns of interaction. Rather than make completely independent decisions, individuals may make their decisions within the context of community norms that dramatically change the structure of the situation. Or, they may meet with other stakeholders in the situation to solve problems. In the process, they may implement production innovations, or design new institutions and organizations. In these situations, participants often have a broader range of strategies. Further, these strategies can change over time as participants learn about the results of past actions. When examining these more open, less constrained situations, a policy analyst is forced to make weaker inferences about patterns of interaction. However, well-informed weak inferences can still provide important policy information. At times, it is possible to predict patterns that will not emerge. Narrowing the range of predictions is very helpful in policy design.

Step 7: Analyze Outcomes

Just as patterns of interaction flow logically from a rigorous IAD analysis, insight about outcomes flows logically from similarly well-founded observations about patterns of interaction. When we analyze outcomes, we are really analyzing the performance of a policy system. Hence, we need some kind of objective standard or principle for comparison. Sometimes, programs or policies provide these baselines. But in many cases, we must specify evaluative criteria as part of the policy analysis process. While there are many potential candidates, we briefly focus on six common concerns in political-economic analysis: economic efficiency, fiscal equivalence, redistributional equity, accountability, conformance to general morality, and adaptability.

Policy design must frequently consider how alternative policies affect participants' incentives to produce efficiently. An outcome is technically efficient if the marginal cost of producing a unit of output is equal to the price. From a social welfare perspective, an outcome is allocatively efficient if the marginal social benefit equals the marginal social cost. In a dynamic analysis, an outcome is efficient if the discounted present value of net benefits is maximized. A less strict but often acceptable efficiency standard is cost effectiveness—producing a good or service at the lowest possible cost. However, many policy issues do not lend themselves to strict economic evaluation because there are no readily observable market prices for some social goods or services, or because inputs to the production process cannot be precisely valued.

The concept of fiscal equivalence is one means to evaluate the equity of policy outcomes. Fiscal equivalence or proportionality means that those who benefit from a good or service bear the cost of providing it in equal measure to benefits received from it. Following this principle, those who derive greater benefits pay more than those who derive fewer benefits. Because perceptions about fiscal equivalence can affect consumers' willingness to contribute to developing and sustaining a policy initiative, there must be some way to estimate the value of costs and benefits that is acceptable to this group in order to implement fiscal equivalence as an evaluation device.

Another principle for evaluating the equity of policy outcomes is distributional equity. According to this principle, individuals contribute toward the cost of goods and services based upon their ability to pay for them. Depending upon the distribution of income in a society, progressive equity schemes may directly conflict with those based on the principle of fiscal equivalence. As with fiscal equivalence, evaluating outcomes on the basis of the principle of distributional equity requires the ability to convincingly estimate the value of costs and benefits.

Another common policy performance criteria is accountability. The key questions here are (1) the extent to which the policy context facilitates low-cost information sharing or transparency, (2) the relative capacity or skill of participants to evaluate the actions of others in the policy situation, and (3) the extent to which participants have ready access to mechanisms that permit them to monitor and sanction one another. If there are imbalances in any of these areas, accountability will be impaired. And without accountability, there is no check on opportunistic behavior.

In addition to accountability, one might also evaluate the extent to which the policy context fosters conformance to general morality.[11] Can participants harm each other and go undetected? If they do, do they obtain high payoffs? Are those who fail to conform to the rules or honor their commitments penalized? Can people trust each other to play by the rules?

Finally, one might wish to consider the extent to which the policy context encourages sustainability through innovation and adaptation in response to change. Sometimes existing policies impose rigidities. This is of course the basis for arguing against quota systems and other forms of tariffs and subsidies. In a more general sense, institutional systems based on general principles are often thought to permit greater adaptation than strictly codified institutional systems. Similarly, policy situations subject to greater local control might permit greater adaptation in some sets of circumstances.

Summary

We know this has been a rather quick tour of a complex analytic process. It may even seem a bit overwhelming. However, we can assure you that the IAD framework makes policy analysis and design easier, not more difficult. Followed rigorously, the end product will be comprehensible to a wide audience. Further, it can be used by a policy manager to design an inclusive and participatory policy analysis process. Following is a summary of the steps involved in conducting a policy analysis based on the IAD framework.

1. Define the policy analysis objective and specify the analytic approach

   What is happening in the policy arena?
   How do observed outcomes compare to policy objectives?
   Which outcomes are satisfactory? Which are not?
   Which outcomes are most important?
   When are these outcomes occurring?
   Where are they occurring?
   Who is involved?
   How are policy outcomes occurring?

2. Analyze physical and material conditions

   What is the economic nature of the policy activity?
   How is this good or service provided?
   How is it produced?
   What physical and human resources are required? What technologies and processes?
   What are storage requirements and distribution channels?
   What is the scale and scope of provision and production activity?

3. Analyze community attributes

   What is the size of the community and who is in it?
   What knowledge and information do members have?

What are members' values and preferences?
What are members' beliefs?
What are members' beliefs about other participants' strategy preferences and outcomes?
How homogeneous is the community?

4. Analyze rules-in-use

Position
Boundary
Authority
Aggregation
Scope
Information
Payoff

5. Integrate the analysis

Action Situation

What are the *positions* or roles that actors play in this situation?
Who are the *participants*?
What *actions* can participants take, and *how are actions linked to outcomes*?
What is the level of *control* that each participant has over action in this situation?
What *outcomes* are possible in this situation?
What *information* about the action situation is available to participants?
What *costs and benefits* do participants incur when they take action in this situation?

Actors

Resources
Valuations
Information Processing
Selection Processes

6. Analyze patterns of interaction

Structure of economic and political participation
Information flows

7. Analyze outcomes

   Efficiency
   Fiscal Equivalence
   Distributional Equity
   Accountability
   Conformance to General Morality
   Sustainability/Adaptability

Applications

In the early 1970s, when the IAD framework was first being developed, Workshop research colleagues were trying to understand how the diverse paradigms in political science affected the way we thought about public administration and metropolitan organization (see V. Ostrom and E. Ostrom 1971; E. Ostrom 1972; E. Ostrom and V. Ostrom 1986). Then, for a decade and a half, the framework was used as a foundation to conduct an extensive number of empirical studies of police service delivery in metropolitan areas (see E. Ostrom and Whitaker 1973; E. Ostrom, Parks, and Whitaker 1973, 1978; Parks and Ostrom 1981; Parks 1984, 1985; E. Ostrom 1975, 1985b; McIver 1978; McDavid 1974). During the past decade, the IAD framework has been used to analyze common-pool resources (see, e.g., E. Ostrom, Gardner, and Walker 1994), among many other policy issues.

In designing empirical studies using the IAD framework, a key question has always been the appropriate units and levels of analysis for any particular type of question (see Gregg 1974). For example, when Ostrom and Parks studied police services, the police department was only one of the units of analysis included in this work. Instead, they tried to understand who the actors were in diverse service situations such as immediate response services, homicide investigation, laboratory analysis, training, and communication services. They found different sets of actors involved in each of the service situations. In some, citizens as well as police officers as street-level bureaucrats were key participants. In others, they found participants from many different urban service agencies. They had to examine interorganizational arrangements to understand patterns of interaction and results. Using this perspective, they found highly structured patterns of relationships where others had found only chaos. The highest levels of police performance existed, for example, in those metropolitan areas where small-scale, immediate-response units worked along with large-scale investigatory, laboratory, and communication units (Parks 1985). Ongoing research by Parks in the Indianapolis area is providing strong evidence that many of the patterns observed in the 1970s and 1980s are still in evidence in the 1990s. In light of this extensive empirical research, we have a far better understanding of the patterns of metropolitan organization and local government (ACIR 1987, 1988; V. Ostrom, Bish, and E. Ostrom 1988; Oakerson and Parks 1988; Parks and Oakerson 1989; Stein 1990).

The second broad area in which the IAD framework has been extensively applied is the study of common-pool resources. In 1985, the National Academy of Sciences (NAS) organized a research panel on the study of common property (National Research Council 1985). Ronald Oakerson (1992) wrote a framework paper for the panel that was used in the organization of a series of case studies of how diverse peoples had devised institutional arrangements related to common-pool resources (see also Edwards and Steins 1998; Thomson, Feeny, and Oakerson 1992; E. Ostrom 1992a, 1992b). Oakerson's presentation of the framework has influenced an untold number of studies of common-property regimes in many diverse sectors in all regions of the world. A revised publication from this conference (Bromley et al. 1992) contains several case studies based on the framework. The intellectual productivity stimulated by the work of the NAS panel has led to the formation of an International Association for the Study of Common Property (IASCP). More than five hundred scholars attended the 1998 meeting of the association held in Vancouver, British Columbia, in June.

The IAD framework has now been used to develop three major databases related to the study of common-pool resources and diverse property regimes. The first "CPR Database" drew on the cases produced for the NAS panel and on the extremely large number of individual case studies that we discovered had been written by historians, sociologists, engineers, political scientists, anthropologists, and students of environmental science (Hess 1999).[12] We used the IAD framework overtly to create a structured database for appropriation and collective-choice arenas. Schlager (1990, 1994) and Tang (1991) studied approximately fifty inshore fisheries and irrigation systems, respectively, and were able to isolate key rules that were positively associated with higher performance levels. In *Governing the Commons*, Ostrom (1990) was able to draw on the framework and on an analysis of extensive case studies to examine the design principles that characterized robust, self-organized institutions for achieving sustainable resource use over very long periods of time.

A second database focuses entirely on irrigation systems and has been used to code more than 175 irrigation systems in Nepal (Benjamin et al. 1994). That database has enabled Workshop colleagues to test many theoretical propositions that have long influenced policy analysis and design (see Lam 1998; Schweik, Adhikari, and Pandit 1997; Lam, Lee, and Ostrom 1997; E. Ostrom 1994, 1996a; E. Ostrom, Lam, and Lee 1994; E. Ostrom and Gardner 1993). These studies challenged many of the empirical assumptions used by development specialists who have presumed that farmers are unable to self-organize and engage in costly collective action without the imposition of rules from external authorities (see also Thomson 1992). One study found that farmer-managed irrigation systems in Nepal are able to outperform agency-managed systems in regard to agricultural productivity when we have controlled for factors such as size of group, length of canal, and type of terrain (Lam 1998).

The third database is an integral part of the International Forestry Resources and Institutions (IFRI) research program, which is a major ongoing research program of the Workshop in Political Theory and Policy Analysis at Indiana University, and of the recently established Center for the Study of Institutions, Population, and Environmental Change (CIPEC). This program is designed to address knowledge and information gaps about how institutions affect the incentives of forest users and result in substantial levels of deforestation in some locations while forest conditions are improving in other locations. Six collaborative research centers have now been established in Bolivia, Ecuador, India, Kenya, Nepal, and Tanzania, Uganda, and several more will be established in future years (E. Ostrom and Wertime 1994; Jerrells and Ostrom 1995). In Uganda, Banana and Gombya-Ssembajjwe (2000) have shown in their initial studies that the only forests where deforestation is not extensive are where local institutional arrangements are viewed by local residents as legitimate and are monitored extensively. In their study of a *comuna* in Ecuador, Gibson and Becker (2000) have documented the importance of distance from a forest as it affects the costs that villagers would have to pay to actively monitor and enforce rules even when they have full authority to make and enforce their own rules. In India, Agrawal (2000) provides an empirical challenge to the presumption of many specialists that collective action becomes progressively more difficult as the size of the group increases from a very small face-to-face group. He shows that moderately sized villages are better able to generate the labor needed to protect local forests than are very small villages. Schweik (2000) has examined the geographic distribution of *Shorea robusta*, a highly valued species. He found that neither population density of the villages adjacent to the three forests he studied in Nepal nor predictions from optimal foraging theory adequately predict the spatial distribution of the species. The most robust explanation for the distribution of this species relates to the institutional rules that allow higher-caste villagers to access their "own" forests as well as forests located near villages where lower-caste villagers live but not vice versa.

In addition to these research programs, the IAD framework has also influenced a variety of other studies including those developing models of social-choice situations and then subjecting them to empirical tests in experimental laboratories (Herzberg 1986; Wilson and Herzberg 1987; Herzberg and Wilson 1988; Herzberg and Ostrom 1991). Other policy questions include rural infrastructure in developing countries (E. Ostrom, Schroeder, and Wynne 1993; Gerrard and Polski 1998a, 1998b); privatization processes (Walker 1994a, 1994b); development processes more generally (V. Ostrom, Feeny, and Picht 1993; Thomson 1992; Wunsch and Olowu 1995); constitutional dynamics in the American federal system (Jillson and Wilson 1994; V. Ostrom 1994, [1971] 1987) as well as in the Canadian federal system (Sproule-Jones 1993); linking local and global commons (McGinnis and Ostrom 1996; Keohane and Ostrom 1995); the East Asian financial crisis (Polski 1998); and banking runs and panics (Polski 1996). In addition, the IAD framework has influenced the analysis of a wide range of issues related to how institutions are organized for the provision and production of education, microcredit facilities, day care, primary health, fertilizer, and coffee. Empirical work has been carried on in Bangladesh, Bolivia, Brazil, Cameroon, Canada, China, Costa Rica, Ecuador, Ghana, Guatemala, Hong Kong, India, Indonesia, Ivory Coast, Liberia, Madagascar, Mali, Nepal, Nigeria, Norway, Poland, Russia, Sweden, Taiwan, Uganda, and the United States.

In closing, we summarize the general categories of policy analysis that Workshop colleagues have undertaken using the IAD framework:

1. Economic development issues including infrastructure, privatization, fiscal policy, credit allocation, health and human services, and resource management
2. Common-pool resource management including forests, fisheries, irrigation, water resources, and grazing
3. Local and metropolitan public services and governance
4. State/Regional/Provincial public services and governance
5. Federal public services and governance

6. Constitutional design
7. International relations

Further information, bibliographies, and research assistance are available on the Workshop website (https://ostromworkshop.indiana.edu).

Acknowledgments

We gratefully acknowledge helpful comments on prior drafts of this chapter from Henning Karcher and Charlotte Hess.

Notes

This chapter was originally a 1999 unpublished working paper from the Workshop in Political Theory and Policy Analysis at Indiana University. Figure 2.1 reprinted with the permission of the University of Michigan Press.

1. For discussions of the IAD framework as a tool for research and theoretical development, see, for example, Kiser and Ostrom (1982); Oakerson (1992); E. Ostrom (1985a, 1986, 1991, 1996a, 1996b); E. Ostrom, Gardner, and Walker (1994); and V. Ostrom, Feeny, and Picht (1993). Oakerson (1992) and Oakerson and Walker (1997) discuss the IAD framework as a policy analysis tool for common property and development policy issues.

2. For a survey of the early public choice literature on institutions, see E. Ostrom (1986).

3. For example, the 1997 World Annual Development Report (World Bank 1997) provides a comprehensive discussion of this change. An institutional approach has also provided the foundation for two recent international policy workshops sponsored by the World Bank: one on developing sustainable rural infrastructure (May 1997), and another on community participation in natural resource management (May 1998).

4. For summaries of the evidence, see E. Ostrom (1998b).

5. We note that providing and producing metered utilities requires a certain minimum scale, adequate investment capital, and particular sets of institutional arrangements to be politically and economically viable. It is widely believed that these conditions are not met in developing countries. However, a growing body of research and practical experience suggests that participatory institutional arrangements can provide a foundation for coordinating to meet these conditions where they might not otherwise be met. For experience pertaining to rural infrastructure, see Gerrard and Polski (1998a). Also see E. Ostrom (1990) on self-governed

common-pool resources, and E. Ostrom, Schroeder, and Wynne (1993) on infrastructure policies.

6. Thomson and Freudenberger (1997) provide a useful description of key community attributes, which includes historical factors such as population and settlement history and conflict history; social factors such as ethnicity and language, family structure, caste and other social divisions; economic factors such as livelihood strategies and stratification; and cultural beliefs.

7. In addition to stockholders, constituents include customers, suppliers, employees, other firms in the same industry, local, state, and federal government, and other members of the community who are affected by business actions.

8. Analyzing both compliance and noncompliance helps us to better understand the incentive structure in the action arena.

9. For a review of the CPR literature in the context of the IAD framework, see E. Ostrom (1996a).

10. Strict rationality implies perfect and complete information as well as the ability to accurately process this information in a logically consistent way. Weaker assumptions about information and information processing (bounded rationality) relax the restrictions of strict rationality.

11. We freely admit that specifying "general morality" is a slippery slope. Nevertheless, we are encouraged by empirical evidence that suggests that people in many different types of policy settings relentlessly struggle to develop and enforce generally acceptable moral standards.

12. Hess (1999) is a searchable and browsable bibliography on CD-ROM containing more than 22,500 citations on the multidisciplinary study of jointly owned or managed natural and man-made resources, from forests, fisheries, and irrigation systems to urban playgrounds, transportation systems, and the Internet. The references to this international literature include both theoretical works and case studies.

References

ACIR (Ronald J. Oakerson). 1987. *The Organization of Local Public Economies.* #A109. Washington, DC: Advisory Commission on Intergovernmental Relations.

ACIR (Ronald J. Oakerson, Roger B. Parks, and Henry A. Bell). 1988. *Metropolitan Organization: The St. Louis Case.* #M158. Washington, DC: Advisory Commission on Intergovernmental Relations.

Agrawal, Arun. 2000. "Small Is Beautiful, but Is Larger Better? Forest-Management Institutions in the Kumaon Himalaya, India." In *People and Forests: Communities, Institutions, and Governance*, ed. Clark Gibson, Margaret McKean, and Elinor Ostrom, 57–86. Cambridge, MA: MIT Press.

Banana, Abwoli Y., and William Gombya-Ssembajjwe. 2000. "Successful Forest Management: The Importance of Security of Tenure and Rule Enforcement in Ugandan Forests." In *People and Forests: Communities, Institutions, and Governance*, ed. Clark Gibson, Margaret McKean, and Elinor Ostrom, 87–98. Cambridge, MA: MIT Press.

Benjamin, Paul, Wai Fung Lam, Elinor Ostrom, and Ganesh Shivakoti. 1994. *Institutions, Incentives, and Irrigation in Nepal.* Burlington, VT: Associates in Rural Development.

Bromley, Daniel W., David Feeny, Margaret McKean, Pauline Peters, Jere Gilles, Ronald Oakerson, C. Ford Runge, and James Thomson, eds. 1992. *Making the Commons Work: Theory, Practice, and Policy*. San Francisco, CA: ICS Press.

Crawford, Sue E. S., and Elinor Ostrom. 1995. "A Grammar of Institutions." *American Political Science Review* 89(3): 582–600.

Edwards, Victoria M., and Nathalie A. Steins 1998. "Developing an Analytical Framework for Multiple-Use Commons." *Journal of Theoretical Politics* 10(3): 347–83.

Gerrard, Christopher D., and Margaret Polski. 1998a. *Local Actions, Better Lives: Decentralizing Rural Infrastructure Services*. Washington, DC: The Economic Development Institute of the World Bank.

———. 1998b. *Seizing the Opportunity, Meeting the Challenge: Institutional Reform for Sustainable Rural Infrastructure.* Washington, DC: The Economic Development Institute of the World Bank.

Gibson, Clark C., and Dustin C. Becker. 2000. "A Lack of Institutional Demand: Why a Strong Community in Western Ecuador Fails to Protect its Forest." In *People and Forests: Communities, Institutions, and Governance*, ed. Clark Gibson, Margaret McKean, and Elinor Ostrom, 135–62. Cambridge, MA: MIT Press.

Gregg, Phillip M. 1974. "Units and Levels of Analysis: A Problem of Policy Analysis in Federal Systems." *Publius* 4(4) (Fall): 59–86.

Herzberg, Roberta. 1986. "Blocking Coalitions and Policy Change." In *Congress and Policy Change*, ed. Gerald C. Wright, Leroy Rieselbach, and Larry Dodd, 201–22. New York: Agathon Press.

Herzberg, Roberta, and Vincent Ostrom. 1991. "Votes and Vetoes." In *The Public Sector—Challenge for Coordination and Learning*, ed. Franz-Xaver Kaufmann, 441–50. Berlin and New York: de Gruyter.

Herzberg, Roberta, and Rick Wilson. 1988. "Results on Sophisticated Voting in an Experimental Setting." *The Journal of Politics* 50(2): 471–86.

Hess, Charlotte. 1999. "A Comprehensive Bibliography of Common Pool Resources." CD-ROM. Bloomington: Indiana University, Workshop in Political Theory and Policy Analysis.

Hurwicz, Leonid. 1994. "Economic Design, Adjustment Processes, Mechanisms, and Institutions." *Economic Design* 1(1): 1–14.

Jerrells, Joby, and Elinor Ostrom. 1995. "Current Developments in a Relational Database for Biological and Social Science Research." Working Paper. Bloomington: Indiana University, Workshop in Political Theory and Policy Analysis.

Jillson, Calvin C., and Rick K. Wilson. 1994. *Congressional Dynamics: Structure, Coordination, and Choice in the First American Congress, 1774–1789*. Stanford, CA: Stanford University Press.

Keohane, Robert O., and Elinor Ostrom, eds. 1995. *Local Commons and Global Interdependence: Heterogeneity and Cooperation in Two Domains*. London: Sage.

Kiser, Larry L., and Elinor Ostrom. 1982. "The Three Worlds of Action: A Metatheoretical Synthesis of Institutional Approaches." In *Strategies of Political Inquiry*, ed. Elinor Ostrom, 179–222. Beverly Hills, CA: Sage.

Korten, David C. 1980. "Community Organization and Rural Development: A Learning Process Approach." *Public Administration Review* 40(5): 480–511.

Lam, Wai Fung. 1998. *Governing Irrigation Systems in Nepal: Institutions, Infrastructure, and Collective Action*. Oakland, CA: ICS Press.

Lam, Wai Fung, Myungsuk Lee, and Elinor Ostrom. 1997. "The Institutional Analysis and Development Framework: Application to Irrigation Policy in Nepal." In *Policy Studies and Developing Nations: An Institutional and Implementation Focus*, vol. 5, ed. Derick W. Brinkerhoff, 53–85. Greenwich, CT: JAI Press.

McDavid, James C. 1974. "Interjurisdictional Cooperation among Police Departments in the St. Louis Metropolitan Area." *Publius* 4(4) (Fall): 35–58.

McGinnis, Michael D., and Elinor Ostrom. 1996. "Design Principles for Local and Global Commons." In *The International Political Economy and International Institutions*, vol. 2, ed. Oran Young, 465–93. Cheltenham, UK: Edward Elgar.

McIver, John P. 1978. "The Relationship between Metropolitan Police Industry Structure and Inter-Agency Assistance: A Primary Assessment." *Policy Studies Journal* 7: 406–13.

National Research Council. 1986. *Proceedings of the Conference on Common Property Resource Management, April 21–26, 1985*. Washington, DC: National Academies Press.

Oakerson, Ronald J. 1992. "Analyzing the Commons: A Framework." In *Making the Commons Work: Theory, Practice, and Policy*, ed. Daniel W. Bromley et al., 41–59. San Francisco, CA: ICS Press.

———. 1992. "Democracy, Governance, and Institutional Analysis." In *Workshop on Democracy and Governance: Proceedings*. Burlington, VT: Associates in Rural Development.

Oakerson, Ronald J., and Roger B. Parks. 1988. "Citizen Voice and Public Entrepreneurship: The Organizational Dynamic of a Complex Metropolitan County." *Publius* 18 (Fall): 91–112.

Oakerson, Ronald J., and S. Tjip Walker. 1997. "Analyzing Policy Reform and Reforming Policy Analysis: An Institutionalist Approach." In *Policy Analysis Concepts and Methods: An Institutional and Implementation Focus*, ed. Derick W. Brinkerhoff, 21–52. Greenwich, CT: JAI Press.

Olson, Mancur. 1965. *The Logic of Collective Action: Public Goods and the Theory of Groups.* Cambridge, MA: Harvard University Press.

Ostrom, Elinor. 1972. "Metropolitan Reform: Propositions Derived from Two Traditions." *Social Science Quarterly* 53: 474–93.

———. 1975. "On Righteousness, Evidence, and Reform: The Police Story." *Urban Affairs Quarterly* 10(4): 464–86.

———. 1985a. "A Method of Institutional Analysis." In *Guidance, Control, and Evaluation in the Public Sector*, ed. Franz-Xaver Kaufmann, Giandomenico Majone, and Vincent Ostrom, 459–75. Berlin and New York: de Gruyter.

———. 1985b. "Racial Inequalities in Low-Income Central City and Suburban Communities: The Case of Police Services." In *Policy Implementation in Federal and Unitary Systems*, ed. Kenneth Hanf and Theo A. J. Toonen, 235–65. Dordrecht, the Netherlands: Martinus Nijhoff.

———. 1986. "An Agenda for the Study of Institutions." *Public Choice* 48(1): 3–25.

———. 1990. *Governing the Commons: The Evolution of Institutions for Collective Action.* New York: Cambridge University Press.

———. 1991. "A Framework for Institutional Analysis." Working Paper. Bloomington: Indiana University, Workshop in Political Theory and Policy Analysis.

———. 1992a. *Crafting Institutions for Self-Governing Irrigation Systems.* San Francisco, CA: ICS Press.

———. 1992b. "The Rudiments of a Theory of the Origins, Survival, and Performance of Common-Property Institutions." In *Making the Commons Work: Theory, Practice, and Policy*, ed. Daniel W. Bromley et al., 41–59. San Francisco, CA: ICS Press.

———. 1992c. "A Framework for Institutional Analysis." In *Workshop on Democracy and Governance: Proceedings*. Burlington, VT: Associates in Rural Development.

———. 1994. "Neither Market nor State: Governance of Common-Pool Resources in the Twenty-First Century." Lecture presented at the International Food Policy Research Institute, June 1, 1994.

———. 1996a. "Institutional Rational Choice: An Assessment of the IAD Framework." Paper presented at the 1996 Annual Meetings of the American Political Science Association, San Francisco, CA, August 29–September 1.

———. 1996b. "Incentives, Rules of the Game, and Development." In *Proceedings of the Annual World Bank Conference on Development Economics 1995*, 207–34. Washington, DC: World Bank.

———. 1998a. "A Behavioral Approach to the Rational Choice Theory of Collective Action." *American Political Science Review* 92(1): 1–22.

———. 1998b. "Institutional Analysis, Design Principles, and Threats to Sustainable Community Governance and Management of Commons." In *Law and the Governance of Renewable Resources: Studies from Northern Europe and Africa*, ed. E. Berge and N. C. Stenseth, 27–53. Oakland, CA: ICS Press.

———. 1998c. "The Institutional Analysis and Development Approach." In *Designing Institutions for Environmental and Resource Management*, ed. E. T. Loehman and D. M. Kilgour, 68–90. Northampton, MA: Edward Elgar.

Ostrom, Elinor, and Roy Gardner. 1993. "Coping with Asymmetries in the Commons: Self-Governing Irrigation Systems Can Work." *Journal of Economic Perspectives* 7(4): 93–112.

Ostrom, Elinor, Roy Gardner, and James Walker. 1994. *Rules, Games, and Common-Pool Resources.* Ann Arbor: University of Michigan Press.

Ostrom, Elinor, Wai Fung Lam, and Myungsuk Lee. 1994. "The Performance of Self-Governing Irrigation Systems in Nepal." *Human Systems Management* (14)3: 87–108.

Ostrom, Elinor, and Vincent Ostrom. 1986. "Analytical Tools for Institutional Design." In *Institutional Development: Improving Management in Developing Countries—Reports on a Seminar Series.* Washington, DC: American Consortium for International Public Administration.

Ostrom, Elinor, Roger B. Parks, and Gordon P. Whitaker. 1973. "Do We Really Want to Consolidate Urban Police Forces? A Reappraisal of Some Old Assertions." *Public Administration Review* 33: 423–32.

———. 1978. *Patterns of Metropolitan Policing.* Cambridge, MA: Ballinger.

Ostrom, Elinor, Larry Schroeder, and Susan Wynne. 1993. *Institutional Incentives and Sustainable Development: Infrastructure Policies in Perspective.* Boulder, CO: Westview Press.

Ostrom, Elinor, and Mary Beth Wertime. 1994. "IFRI Research Strategy." Working Paper. Bloomington: Indiana University, Workshop in Political Theory and Policy Analysis.

Ostrom, Elinor, and Gordon P. Whitaker. 1973. "Does Local Community Control of Police Make a Difference? Some Preliminary Findings." *American Journal of Political Science* 17(1): 48–76.

Ostrom, Vincent. [1971] 1987. *The Political Theory of a Compound Republic.* Lincoln: University of Nebraska Press.

———. 1994. *The Meaning of American Federalism: Constituting a Self-Governing Society.* San Francisco, CA: ICS Press.

Ostrom, Vincent, Robert Bish, and Elinor Ostrom. 1988. *Local Government in the United States.* San Francisco, CA: ICS Press.

Ostrom, Vincent, David Feeny, and Hartmut Picht, eds. 1993. *Rethinking Institutional Analysis and Development: Issues, Alternatives, and Choices.* 2nd ed. San Francisco, CA: ICS Press.

Ostrom, Vincent, and Elinor Ostrom. 1971. "Public Choice: A Different Approach to the Study of Public Administration." *Public Administration Review* 13: 203–16.

Parks, Roger B. 1984. "Linking Objective and Subjective Measures of Performance." *Public Administration Review* 44(2): 118–27.
———. 1985. "Metropolitan Structure and Systematic Performance: The Case of Police Service Delivery." In *Policy Implementation in Federal and Unitary Systems*, ed. Kenneth Hanf and Theo A. J. Toonen, 161–91. Dordrecht, the Netherlands: Martinus Nijhoff.
Parks, Roger B., and Ronald J. Oakerson. 1989. "Metropolitan Organization and Governance: A Local Public Economy Approach." *Urban Affairs Quarterly* 25(1): 18–29.
Parks, Roger B., and Elinor Ostrom. 1981. "Complex Models of Urban Service Systems." In *Urban Policy Analysis: Directions for Future Research*, ed. Terry N. Clark, 171–99. Beverly Hills, CA: Sage.
Polski, Margaret M. 1996. "An Institutional Analysis of U.S. Commercial Banking: Regulating Financial Risk in a Compound Republic." Working Paper. Bloomington: Indiana University, Workshop in Political Theory and Policy Analysis.
———. 1998. "Other People's Money: An Institutional Analysis of the East Asian Financial Crisis." Working Paper. Bloomington: Indiana University, Workshop in Political Theory and Policy Analysis.
Rosewicz, Barbara. 1996. "The Checkoff." *Wall Street Journal*, May 21.
Schlager, Edella. 1990. "Model Specification and Policy Analysis: The Governance of Coastal Fisheries." PhD diss., Indiana University.
———. 1994. "Fishers' Institutional Responses to Common-Pool Resource Dilemmas." In *Rules, Games, and Common-Pool Resources*, Elinor Ostrom, Roy Gardner, and James Walker, 247–66. Ann Arbor: University of Michigan Press.
Schweik, Charles M. 2000. "Optimal Foraging, Institutions, and Forest Change: A Case from Nepal." In *People and Forests: Communities, Institutions, and Governance*, ed. Clark Gibson, Margaret McKean, and Elinor Ostrom, 99–134. Cambridge, MA: MIT Press.
Schweik, Charles M., Keshav Adhikari, and Kala Nidhi Pandit. 1997. "Land-Cover Change and Forest Institutions: A Comparison of Two Sub-Basins in the Southern Siwalik Hills of Nepal." *Mountain Research and Development* 17(2): 99–116.
Sproule-Jones, Mark. 1993. *Governments at Work: Canadian Parliamentary Federalism and Its Public Policy Effects.* Toronto: University of Toronto Press.
Stein, Robert. 1990. *Urban Alternatives: Public and Private Markets in the Provision of Local Services.* Pittsburgh, PA: University of Pittsburgh Press.
Tang, Shui Yan. 1991. "Institutional Arrangements and the Management of Common-Pool Resources." *Public Administration Review* 51: 42–51.
Thomson, James T. 1992. *A Framework for Analyzing Institutional Incentives in Community Forestry.* Rome: FAO.
Thomson, James T., David Feeny, and Ronald J. Oakerson. 1992. "Institutional Dynamics: The Evolution and Dissolution of Common-Property Resource

Management." In *Making the Commons Work: Theory, Practice, and Policy*, ed. Daniel W. Bromley et al., 19–60. San Francisco, CA: ICS Press.

Thomson, James T., and Karen Schoonmaker Freudenberger. 1997. *Crafting Institutional Arrangements for Community Forestry.* Community Forestry Field Manual 7. Rome: FAO.

Walker, S. Tjip. 1994a. *Crafting a Market: A Case Study of USAID's Fertilizer Sub-Sector Reform Program.* Decentralization: Finance & Management Project Report. Burlington, VT: Associates in Rural Development.

———. 1994b. *Pitfalls of Privatization: A Case Study of the European Community's Programme Spécial d'Importation d'Engrais.* Decentralization: Finance & Management Project Report. Burlington, VT: Associates in Rural Development.

Wilson, Rick, and Roberta Herzberg. 1987. "Negative Decision Powers and Institutional Equilibrium: Experiments on Blocking Coalitions." *Western Political Quarterly* 40(4): 593–609.

World Bank. 1997. "The State in a Changing World." World Development Report. Washington, DC: World Bank.

Wunsch, James S., and Dele Olowu, eds. 1995. *The Failure of the Centralized State: Institutions and Self-Governance in Africa.* 2nd ed. San Francisco, CA: ICS Press.

3

Appendix A: The Institutional Analysis and Development Framework

ELINOR OSTROM, CLARK GIBSON, SUJAI SHIVAKUMAR, AND KRISTER ANDERSSON

This chapter is divided into four sections. The first section provides a basic overview of the IAD framework—its history and broad capabilities. The second section focuses on the core analytical construct we use in all analyses—the action arena composed of an action situation and actors that interact within it. How to examine patterns of interaction, outcomes, and the evaluation of outcomes is addressed in the third section. The fourth section digs into the contextual factors that affect all action situations by examining rules, physical and material conditions, and the general attributes of a community. The conclusion of the chapter focuses on the use of IAD in incentive analyses.

An Overview of the Institutional Analysis and Development Framework

Since its formation in 1973, Workshop scholars have developed a useful theoretical tool called the *Institutional Analysis and Development* (IAD) framework (Kiser and Ostrom 1982; Oakerson 1992; E. Ostrom, Gardner, and Walker 1994). The IAD framework has been used as the foundation for a large number of studies including those that (1) measured the impact of metropolitan-area governance structures on urban service delivery, (2) gauged how institutional incentives affect infrastructure sustainability in developing countries, (3) examined how diverse forms of organization affect irrigation system performance, and (4) explained how ecological conditions combined with institutional structure affect land use change dynamics (particularly changes in forest cover, extent, and composition) (see McGinnis 1999a, 1999b, 2000). It highlights the ways in which policy outcomes are jointly shaped by physical and material conditions, rules-in-use, and the attributes of community.[1]

A Tool for Studying Development Cooperation and Sustainability

The IAD framework serves as an appropriate tool to study development assistance and sustainability for several reasons. First, the IAD framework has a multidisciplinary origin. One cannot study development assistance processes drawing on one discipline alone. All of the social sciences—anthropology, economics, history, political science, and sociology—have developed important concepts and theories that are relevant for understanding why some development processes are sustainable while others wither away when external funds are no longer available. Sociologists are interested in value systems and how humans organize their relationships. Economists are concerned with the efficient use of resources. Anthropologists and historians have developed tools to analyze the context within which a situation is located. Political scientists tend to be focused on the power relationships among participants. IAD provides a more general language than the languages developed by any single social science discipline (but one compatible with all of them) needed to address development assistance puzzles.

Second, IAD presents a practical method for dealing with multiple levels of analysis. When individuals interact in repetitive settings, they may be in *operational* situations that directly affect the world, such as the construction of a power plant or the planting of an agricultural field. Alternatively, they may be making decisions at other levels of analysis that eventually impinge on operational decision-making situations. Elected officials in legislative or executive decision situations make some of these policy decisions. These policies or *collective choices* are themselves made within a set of *constitutional* rules that affect who will make policy decisions using what type of procedures. The nested structure of rules within rules, within still further rules, is a particularly difficult analytical problem to unravel for those interested in the study of institutions and incentives. IAD provides a way to communicate about processes that occur at all of these levels as required for a study of aid, incentives, and sustainability.

Third, IAD allows for investigation of configural processes. Configural processes are those where the relationship between two or more variables is dependent upon the values of at least one other variable. In other words, the final outcome of a configural process is not a simple additive process. Many of the causal processes related to the study of incentives are basically configural or interactive in nature. This is particularly the case with the rules that affect incentive structures. In order to predict and understand the effect of a change in one rule, one must frequently know the other rules in effect. The configural nature of rules makes institutional analysis a more difficult and complex enterprise than studies of phenomena that are strictly additive. IAD provides a framework for relating the complex configural processes found in development cooperation.

Frameworks, Theories, Models

The study of institutions and incentives depends on theoretical work undertaken at three levels of specificity: frameworks, theories, and models. *Frameworks* are metatheoretical schema that facilitate the organization of diagnosis, analysis, and prescription. The IAD framework provides a general list of the types of variables that should be used to analyze a relevant problem. In other words, the framework identifies the *universal* elements that studies of incentives need to include.

The development and use of *theories* enables the analyst to specify which elements of the framework are particularly relevant to specific kinds of puzzles and to make assumptions about these elements. After using the framework to ensure that the important questions are asked, an analyst needs to utilize theory to put the answers together, explain processes, and predict outcomes. Economic theory, game theory, the theory of complex adaptive systems, transaction cost theory, and theories of public goods and common-pool resources are all compatible with the IAD framework. We will make use of all of these theories from time to time within the body of this report. Game theory is a particularly useful tool for institutional analysis when it can be reasonably assumed that actors have a high level of common knowledge, the capability of processing information, and strategically choose actions to achieve the desired goods, as is illustrated in the technical appendix B by Gardner and Waller.

Models make precise assumptions about a limited set of parameters and variables and enable one to make precise predictions for a limited set of specific settings of relevant variables. Specific game theory models of several core processes involved in development assistance are presented in the technical appendix B.

Doing Institutional Analysis

When conducting an institutional analysis, the analyst needs to identify the arena that is of direct relevance to the problem being examined, the context that frames and affects that arena (including other relevant arenas), and the behavioral interactions and outcomes that are likely. The context of a situation provides the initial conditions or "the environment" that structures the efforts to achieve outcomes (Ashby 1960). It is within that context that an analyst can identify an action arena and its incentives. Actors facing these incentives interact and generate outcomes. The analyst may apply one or more evaluative criteria in addition to examining the likely set of outcomes that will be achieved. Sida has, for example, identified the evaluative criteria of *sustainability* as being of major interest in sponsoring this research effort and report. Other evaluative criteria that are frequently used in evaluating international assistance are efficiency, accountability, and equity (see discussion below and E. Ostrom, Schroeder, and Wynne 1993). At the broadest level, these elements of institutional analysis are related as shown in Figure 2.1.

When actually conducting a specific analysis, all of these elements are decomposed into finer and ever-finer categories of analysis. The *context* is set by configurations of physical conditions, rules-in-use, and the attributes of a community. In examining any kind of problem or puzzle, the analyst first needs to identify a relevant *action arena*, which is a complex conceptual unit containing one set of variables about an *action situation* and a second set of variables about an *actor*. An actor can be either a single individual or a group of individuals who have a regularized way of making decisions, such as a firm or a government (see Figure 2.2). The concept of an *action situation* helps the analyst isolate the immediate structure affecting a process so as to explain why particular outcomes tend to occur and potentially identify ways of reforming them.

The structure of an action situation is composed of the following sets of variables:

1. The set of actors;
2. The specific positions that are filled by the actors;
3. The set of actions that each actor in a position can potentially take;
4. The level of control that an actor has over this choice of actions;
5. The linkage of actions to a set of potential outcomes (the decision or game tree);

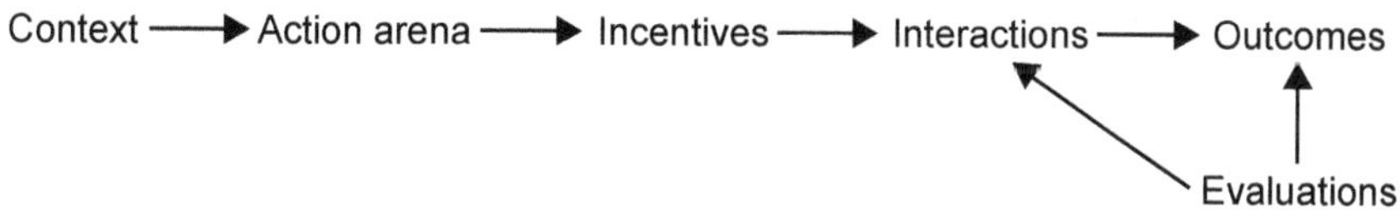

Figure 3.1. The most general elements of institutional analysis.

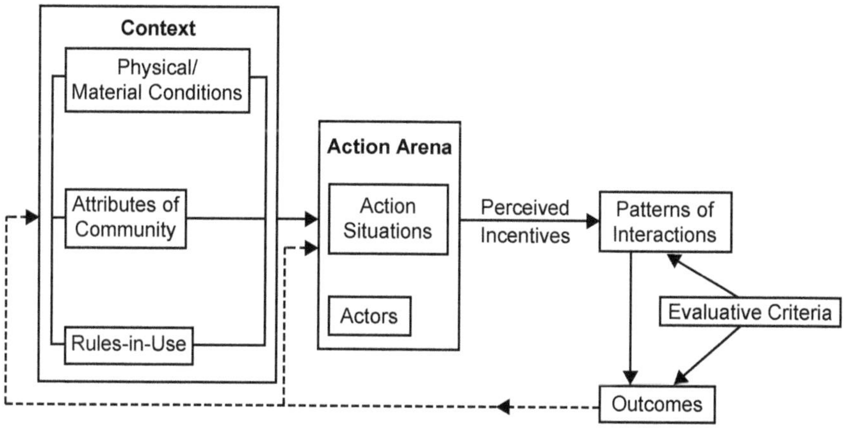

Figure 3.2. A framework for institutional analysis.

Source: Adapted from E. Ostrom, Gardner, and Walker (1994, 37).

6. The external costs and benefits assigned to actions and outcomes; and
7. The information that is available to each actor about a situation.

An action situation that occurs only once may generate different outcomes than one that is finitely or indefinitely repeated.

The *actors* in a situation can be characterized by four sets of variables:

1. The *resources* (time, energy, finances) that an actor brings to a situation;
2. The *internal valuation* that actors assign to actions and outcomes (including pride and shame);

3. The way actors acquire, process, retain, and use *knowledge* and *information*; and
4. The *processes* actors use to *select* particular courses of actions.

Before we discuss each of the above working parts of a particular action arena, it is important to mention that there are two additional and important steps to conducting an institutional analysis if one is interested in doing policy analysis and in recommending ways of improving the outcomes of a situation. First, besides learning about the structure of a particular action arena, the analyst wants to know the factors that affect the structure of the arena itself. To do so requires that one dig into the physical and material conditions that are involved, the specific rules being used to structure the arena, and the nature of the general community within which any particular arena exists. Second, one may want to examine how an arena is linked to others—and in the analysis of development assistance processes, both of these steps are important.

Having gained an overview of the IAD framework, we will now venture a little deeper into the basic elements and begin to unpack some of these into specific variables. The first part of section 2.2 is a discussion of the specific assumptions used about the "actor" in doing institutional analysis and the second part focuses on the components of an action situation. Then, we will examine the diverse set of evaluative criteria that can be used before examining the contextual variables involved in an institutional analysis.

Focusing on Actors and Action Situations

The Actor in a Situation

Definition of Actor and Action

The *actor* in a situation can be thought of as a single individual or as a group functioning as a corporate actor. The term *action* refers to those human behaviors for which the acting individual attaches a subjective and instrumental meaning. All analysts of micro behavior use an implicit or explicit theory of how individuals make decisions in order to derive inferences about the likely behavior of each actor in a situation (and, thus, about the pattern of joint results that may be produced). The analyst must make assumptions about what and how actors value; what resources, information, and beliefs they have; their information-processing capabilities; and the internal mechanisms they use to decide upon actions (or strategies involving plans for future actions to be taken) given the expected strategies of others.

Use of Full Information, *Homo Economicus* Model of Actors

For many problems, it is useful to accept the political economy view that an actor's choice of strategy in any particular situation depends on how he or she perceives and weighs the benefits and costs of various strategies and their likely outcomes. The most well-established model of the individual used in institutional analysis is *homo economicus*. The *homo economicus* model frequently involves the assumptions that actors have complete and well-ordered preferences, complete information, unlimited computational capability, and that they maximize the net value of expected returns to themselves.

All of these assumptions are controversial and their empirical validity is being challenged on many fronts (see, e.g., Camerer and Thaler 1995; Bowles 1998; Bowles and Gintis 1993). These assumptions are, however, extremely useful for analyzing situations in which considerable competition exists and when the competitive process generates survivors whose behavior is consistent with these assumptions. For field settings that approximate this kind of competition, these theories generate empirically confirmed predictions. Further, these assumptions can be used analytically—in game theoretic and other microinstitutional models—to generate specific and testable conclusions. These assumptions are also useful when one is interested in knowing what results to expect when individuals are shortsighted and competitive. The formal models of problematic situations, on which our discussions in chapter 3 are largely based, use this model of the individual. It is the base model initially used by most political economists to capture the core incentives of a particular situation.

Need for a Broader Conception of Individual Behavior

Once the stark features of a situation are understood, many institutional analysts prefer to use a broader conception of individual actors. For example, some scholars stress that perceived costs and benefits should include the time and resources devoted to establishing and maintaining relationships (Williamson 1979), as well as the value that individuals attach to establishing a reputation for being reliable and trustworthy (Breton and Wintrobe 1982). Many of the situations of interest in understanding collective-action problems are uncertain, complex, and lack the selective pressure and information-generating capabilities of a competitive market. Therefore, one can substitute the assumption of bounded rationality—that persons are intendedly rational but only limitedly so—for the assumptions of perfect information and utility maximization used in axiomatic choice theory (see Simon 1965, 1972; Williamson 1985; E. Ostrom, Gardner, and Walker 1994, chap. 9).

Information search is costly, and the information-processing capabilities of human beings are limited. Individuals, therefore, often must make choices based on incomplete knowledge of all possible alternatives and their likely outcomes. With incomplete information and imperfect information-processing capabilities, all individuals may make mistakes in choosing strategies designed to realize a set of goals (V. Ostrom 1986). Over time, however, they can acquire a greater understanding of their situation and adopt strategies that result in higher returns. Reciprocity may develop rather than strictly narrow, short-term pursuit of self-interest (Hyden 1990; Oakerson 1993).

Not all individuals in an interaction have access to the same information. Literacy makes available to some individuals much more information than to others. The contribution of any one individual to a joint undertaking is often difficult for others to judge. When joint outcomes depend on multiple actors contributing inputs that are costly and difficult to measure, incentives exist for individuals to behave opportunistically (Williamson 1975). Opportunism—deceitful behavior intended to improve one's own welfare at the expense of others—may take many forms, from the inconsequential, and perhaps unconscious (e.g., shirking), to a carefully calculated effort to defraud others with whom one is engaged in ongoing relationships. The opportunism of individuals who may say one thing and do something else further compounds the problem of uncertainty in a given situation. Moreover, the level of opportunistic behavior that may occur in any setting is affected by the norms and institutions used to govern relationships in that setting, as well as by attributes of the decision environment itself. Boundedly rational individuals may learn from the institutional setting in which they find themselves how to make reciprocity work for them over time or how to act opportunistically so as to achieve more than others in the same situations. Different types of individuals learn from situations which strategies pay off in the long run.

Using a Fallible Learner Model

More broadly, one could assume that individuals calculate benefits and costs but do so as *fallible learners*. Fallibility and the capacity to learn can thus be viewed as assumptions of a more general theory of the individual (Simon 1985, 1997; V. Ostrom 1987). Fallible learners can, and often do, make mistakes. Mistakes are, in fact, essential for learning to occur (Ashby 1960). Whether incentives encourage people to learn from these mistakes, or to continue to make the same mistakes forever, depends on the particular institutional setting. And, whether incentives encourage the adoption of a reputation for being reliable and trustworthy or the seeking out of short-term benefits without taking into account the effect on longer-term patterns of interactions, also depends largely on the rules structuring particular situations.

Viewing actors as fallible learners within specific institutional arenas leads to the conclusion that the institutional arrangements that individuals use in governing and managing problematic situations offer different incentives and opportunities to learn. In some settings, incentives lead them to repeat the mistakes of the past or to seek only short-term advantages. In these settings, individuals learn to become more opportunistic over time. In other settings, actors learn quickly from their past actions and can adopt more effective strategies over time. They may learn the importance of a reputation as a trustworthy participant and norms of behavior that, when adopted by most participants, leave them all better off. Further, in all cases, the repertoire of institutional design principles known to individuals and their past experience in crafting their own rules also affect their capacity to change their institutions in order to improve learning and other outcomes when faced with repeated failures.

When fallible, learning individuals interact in frequently repeated and simple situations, it is possible to model them as if they have complete information about the relevant variables for making choices in those same situations. In highly competitive environments, mentioned above, we can also assume that the individuals who survive the selective pressure of the environment, act as if they are maximizers of a key variable associated with survival in that environment (e.g., profits or fitness) (Alchian 1950; Dosi and Egidi 1987). When individuals face a relatively simple decision situation where institutions generate accurate information about the variables relevant to a particular problem, that problem can be adequately represented as a straightforward, constrained maximization problem.

Variation in Internal Norms Adopted

Game theorists tend to assume that actors are, in addition to having complete information, narrowly selfish and do not adopt any internal norms that would constrain their maximizing of personal gain. Actors who enter and succeed in highly competitive situations can be modeled successfully using this narrow conception of individual morality. However, in many settings other than highly competitive markets for strictly private goods, actors vary in regard to the extent to which they care for others' well-being and in terms of their personal commitment to keeping promises and honoring forms of reciprocity extended to them (E. Ostrom 1998). Even within private profit-making firms, individuals need to establish reputations for being trustworthy. Cultural norms developed within firms reduce problems of shirking and untrustworthy behavior (Kreps 1990).

Assuming variation in the types of norms that guide individual behavior adds substantial complexity to formal models. Recent work drawing on evolutionary theory has begun to provide some analytical tools that can be used to manage this complexity (Güth 1995; Boyd and Richerson 1985). What is most important, however, is to recognize that humans are capable of adopting norms about the actions that they must, must not, or may choose to take. Given this capacity for reflection and choice of personal norms, groups that develop a shared understanding of the "do's and don'ts" that they all agree to follow are able to deal more effectively with many of the collective-action problems discussed in chapter 3. Designing rules that enhance the likelihood that actors may come to know one another, interact at least occasionally on a face-to-face basis, detect when others fail to conform to group rules and norms, and encourage learning about the importance of shared norms, greatly increases the sustainability of collective action (E. Ostrom 2000).

The Fallible Learner in Development

Individuals in society, whether within the developing or developed countries of the world, behave for the most part within the bounds of some indigenous institutional framework. Though we rarely reflect consciously on this, whether we, as fallible learners, learn from our mistakes or keep repeating them depends on whether the particular institutional settings that we find ourselves in are suited to the problems we face.

The appropriateness of these institutional settings for development, in turn, depends on the repertoire of design principles we possess and on our own past experience in crafting rules to adapt to contemporary challenges. Indigenous institutions contain a wide variety of normative prescriptions that are expressed in ways resonant to us in our own social context. As such, they help to constitute an adaptive community of understanding, and, in this way, contribute to the wealth of social capital.

While such institutions have enabled groups to solve collective-action problems in the past, they may not necessarily (1) be applied to new situations in socially beneficial ways or (2) be legal in a contemporary setting.

Further, they may have been perverted over time for partisan purposes, through negligence, or as a result of misunderstandings by external authorities. Negative outcomes can result when institutions fail as a result. In developing countries, aid projects and programs frequently address the manifestations or outcomes of such institutional failures. However, interventions by a foreign donor introduce additional rules and constraints to the action arena. These often reflect institutional understandings formed within the cultural context of the donor's own community. New rules and constraints are necessarily interpreted, however, by the developing country learner within the context of his or her own indigenous institutional context.

Unless external aid initiatives build on existing institutional understandings and hence "improve" them in terms of their ability to overcome particular collective-action problems, indigenous learning will not occur or the lessons learned may hinder rather than promote development. Any resolution to the underlying problem will not be sustained. Indeed, ownership in aid takes meaning when individuals confronting a collective-action problem are poised to modify an institutionalized system of incentives by drawing on past learning to encourage new learning and resulting changes in the structure of incentives they face. Ominously, however, aid can erode or undermine local social capital when the rules and constraints that come along with it are placed carelessly in inappropriate interaction with other elements within the local structure of social capital. When this happens, social capital is destroyed, learning is inhibited, and the developing society is left poorer for the aid it has received.

An Action Situation

The term *action situation* refers to an analytic concept that enables an analyst to isolate the immediate structure affecting a particular process of interest in order to explain emergent regularities in human action and results. In order to improve patterns of interactions and outcomes obtained, one needs a deeper understanding of processes that generate them. Through institutional analysis, we can attempt, by changing the structure of interaction, to improve on the pattern of outcomes.

The common set of variables used to describe the structure of an action situation within a particular environmental context includes:

1. the set of actors;
2. the specific positions to be filled by actors;

3. the set of allowable actions and their linkage to outcomes;
4. the potential outcomes that are linked to individual sequences of actions;
5. the level of control each actor has over choice;
6. the information available to actors about the structure of the action situation; and
7. the costs and benefits—which affect perceived incentives—assigned to actions and outcomes.

Also affecting individual strategies is whether a situation will occur once, a known finite number of times, or indefinitely. When explaining actions and cumulated results within the framework of an action arena, these variables are the "givens" that one works with to describe the structure of the situation. These are also the common elements used in game theory to construct a formal game.

A Common-Pool Resource Action Situation—An Illustration of the IAD Approach

A frequent collective-action situation found in all countries is that of a set of users harvesting from a local natural resource such as a forest, an irrigation system, or a fishery. Common-pool resources can be overused, congested, and even destroyed. Garrett Hardin (1968) paints a grim picture to characterize the "tragedy of the commons," thought by many observers to occur whenever multiple actors jointly use a single common-pool resource. In explaining how, Hardin asks us to "picture a pasture open to all." He then sets out an institutional structure where each herder has an incentive to keep more animals on the commons:

> Adding together the component partial utilities, the rational herdsman concludes that the only sensible course for him to pursue is to add another animal to the herd. And another. . . . But this is the conclusion reached by each and every rational herdsman sharing a commons. Therein lies the tragedy. Each man is locked into a system that compels him to increase his herd without limit—in a world that is limited. Ruin is the destination towards which all men rush, each pursuing his own best interest in a society that believes in the freedom of the commons. (Hardin 1968, 1244)

While the metaphor of the commons is a particularly dramatic picture, field research has identified many common-pool resources where the users of the resource have developed rather effective rules for governing and managing it over time. The particulars of any specific harvesting situation differ dramatically from one location to another and one cannot tell simply from the outside whether a resource is actually being harvested in a sustainable manner or whether overharvesting is occurring. Determining what kinds of problems exist in the use of local resources is of major concern when adopting policies, as it is possible to create new institutions for governing and managing common-pool resources that end up destroying existing systems that have functioned relatively well for long periods of time.

We apply the IAD framework to common-pool resource problems to help make the framework more understandable (see also appendix B). We have chosen to illustrate the IAD framework with a situation frequently confronting development assistance agencies. In one of the projects that we examine in chapter 9, for example, related to developing sustainable forests in Orissa, India, a core part of the problem is helping participants to overcome the incentives they face in common-pool resource problems. Solving forestry problems have been a major activity in the portfolio of Sida and other development agencies. This has become even more important as deforestation is a core problem leading to global warming. In addition to forestry problems, development agencies are coping with helping to improve the governance and management of inshore fisheries, grazing lands, and irrigation systems. It should be pointed out that the basic issues related to *natural* common-pool resources also relate to common-pools created within organizations. Government budgets are obviously one of the largest common-pool resources of importance in development assistance. The IAD framework helps improve policy analysis by identifying the minimal set of questions that an analyst would need to ask in order to *begin* an examination of a common-pool resource situation (see E. Ostrom, Gardner, and Walker 1994; E. Ostrom, Schroeder, and Wynne 1993). Answers to the following questions are needed before analysis:

- *The Set of Actors*: Who and how many individuals withdraw resource units (e.g., timber, water, or fish) from this resource system in an environmental context?
- *The Positions*: What positions exist (e.g., members of a forest users' committee or an irrigation association, guards, officers of an association, others)?
- *The Set of Allowable Actions*: Which types of harvesting technologies are used? (e.g., Are chainsaws authorized for harvesting tim-

ber or only hand implements? Are there open and closed seasons? Is there a rotation system for water or fishing times? Are some species off limits? Is there an upper or lower size limit to the resource units harvested?)

- *The Potential Outcomes*: What chain of events links actions to outcomes? How do actions link to the sustainability of a resource? What kinds of actions would lead to the destruction of the resource?
- *The Level of Control over Choice*: Do users take the above actions on their own initiative or do they confer with others? (e.g., Before entering the forest to cut fodder, does a user obtain a permit?)
- *The Information Available*: How much information do users have about the condition of the resource itself, about other users' cost and benefit functions, about how their actions cumulate into joint outcomes? Do users know what actions other users (or their officials) are taking currently or have taken in the past?
- *The Costs and Benefits of Actions and Outcomes*: How costly are various actions to each type of user, and what kinds of joint and individual benefits can be achieved as a result of various group outcomes?

Predicting Outcomes within an Action Arena

Depending upon the analytical structure of a situation and the particular assumptions about the actor used, the analyst makes strong or weak inferences about results. In tightly constrained, one-shot, action situations under conditions of complete information, where participants are motivated to select particular strategies or chains of actions that jointly lead to stable equilibria, an analyst can frequently make strong inferences and specific predictions about likely patterns of behavior and outcomes. Gardner and Waller (appendix B) illustrate how specific conclusions can be reached in well-specified game theoretical models.

When no limit exists on the number of users harvesting from a common-pool resource or on the amount of harvesting activities they undertake, for example, one can develop a mathematical model of an open-access, common-pool resource (see, e.g., E. Ostrom, Gardner, and Walker 1994). When the net benefits of harvesting to each entrant increase for the initial set of resource units sought and decrease thereafter, each appropriator acting independently tends to make individual decisions that jointly yield a deficient (but stable) equilibrium. The tragedy of the commons will occur in such a situation. A model of an open-access, common-pool resource generates a clear prediction of a race to use up the resource leading to high social costs. Both field research and laboratory experimental research strongly support the predictions of overuse and potential destruction of open-access, common-pool resources where appropriators do not share access to collective-choice arenas in which to change the open-access structure they face (E. Ostrom, Gardner, and Walker 1994). But, as we discuss below, many common-pool resources are managed in a sustainable way by local users who have devised rules-in-use to counteract the perverse incentives stemming from the nature of the resource itself.

Many action arenas, however, do not generate such unambiguous results. Instead of completely independent decision making, individuals may be embedded in communities where initial norms of fairness and conservation may change the structure of the situation dramatically. Within these situations, participants may adopt a broader range of strategies. Further, they may change their strategies over time as they learn about the results of past actions. The institutional analyst examining these more open, less-constrained situations makes weaker inferences and predictions on the patterns of outcomes that forecast greater variation in the likely result from a particular type of situation.

In field settings, one can assume that helping individuals to engage in face-to-face discussions will increase the probability of improved outcomes, but there are many historical factors that also affect this likelihood. Even weak inferences about likely results have an importance in specifying general tendencies. At times, it is possible to predict what will *not* occur. Predictions of impossibilities are very useful when contemplating reforms.

In field settings, it is hard to tell where one action arena starts and another stops. Life continues in what appears to be a seamless web as individuals move from home to market to work (action situations typically characterized by reciprocity, by exchange, or by team problem-solving or command). Further, within arenas, choices of actions *within* a set of rules as contrasted to choices *among* future rules are frequently made without recognizing that the level of action has shifted. So, when a "boss" says to an "employee," "How about changing the way we do X?," and the two discuss options and jointly agree upon a better way, they have shifted from taking actions *within* previously established rules to making decisions *about* the rules structuring future actions. In language of the IAD framework, they have shifted from an operational arena to a collective-choice arena.

Evaluating Outcomes

In addition to predicting outcomes in terms of the events that transpire as a result of the actions of participants, the institutional analyst may also evaluate the outcomes that are being achieved as well as the likely set of outcomes that could be achieved under alternative institutional arrangements. Evaluative criteria are applied to both the outcomes and the processes of achieving outcomes. While there are many potential evaluative criteria, let us briefly focus on those most frequently used in institutional analysis: (1) economic efficiency, (2) equity through fiscal equivalence or through redistribution or a search for just remedies, (3) accountability, (4) conformance to general morality, and (5) adaptability. Given that we have been asked to examine the effect of incentives on the sustainability of development assistance, we will ask how these evaluative criteria are themselves linked to sustainability.

Economic Efficiency

Efficiency is a criterion for evaluating the relationship between the benefits produced by a set of actions as contrasted to the costs of these actions. To be minimally efficient, the benefits must be greater than the costs. Maximal efficiency is achieved when no other option will produce a greater positive difference between benefits achieved and costs borne. The concept of efficiency plays a central role in studies estimating the benefits and costs or rates of return to investments, which are often used to determine the economic feasibility or desirability of public policies. When considering alternative institutional arrangements, therefore, it is crucial to consider how revisions in the rules affecting participants will alter their perceived incentives, their behavior and, hence, the allocation of resources.

Equity

There are three principal methods for assessing equity: (1) fiscal equivalence—or the relationship between individuals' contributions and the benefits they derive and (2) redistributional equity—or the long-term opening up of resources to the poor, and (3) equitable solutions to a conflict.

- *Fiscal Equivalence*: Fiscal equivalence is a criterion for evaluating the equity of the formula used to assign the costs of creating goods and benefits to those who benefit from these goods (Olson 1969). A fundamental assumption underlying much of contemporary life—

and, particularly in an exchange economy—is that those who benefit from a service should bear the major burden for financing that service. Perceptions of fiscal equivalence, or a lack thereof, affect the willingness of individuals to contribute toward the development and maintenance of public facilities that generate public benefits. On the other hand, in many poor countries, if fiscal equivalence were the only criterion of equity applied, many poor people would not be eligible to receive needed goods and services.

- *Redistributional Equity*: As an alternative criterion of equity, redistributional equity asks whether those who are the poorest in a particular setting receive sufficient goods and services that they can improve their condition over time. Some public facilities may be created primarily to achieve redistributional equity so that essential goods and services are made available to those who are the most needy. Thus, although efficiency would dictate that scarce resources be used where they produce the greatest net benefit, equity goals may temper this objective, resulting in the provision of facilities that benefit particularly needy groups. Likewise, redistributional objectives may conflict with the goal of achieving fiscal equivalence.

- *Equitable Conflict-Resolution Remedies*: Concepts of equity are also involved when actors deal with conflicts. Having available open and relatively low-cost confliction-resolution mechanisms allows participants in ongoing conflict situations to seek out equitable solutions so that long-term conflicts do not disrupt productive arrangements.

Accountability

In a democratic polity, officials should be accountable to citizens concerning the development and use of public facilities and natural resources. This is the principle of *res publica*. Accountability is a criterion applied to the pattern of interactions rather than to the outcomes of a process. Without accountability and openness, actors can engage successfully in the various opportunistic behaviors. Concern for accountability need not conflict greatly with efficiency and equity goals. Indeed, achieving efficiency requires that information about the preferences of citizens be available to decision makers, as does achieving accountability. Institutional arrangements that effectively aggregate or make transparent this information assist in realizing efficiency at the same time that they serve to increase accountability and promote the achievement of redistributional objectives.

Conformance to General Morality

Do the procedures used or the outcomes achieved conform to the general norms held in a society or by the individuals who are most involved in a situation? If rules seem unfair or appear to result in unfair outcomes, such rules are unlikely to be observed and followed for long. Thus, this evaluative criterion needs especially to be used in the design of a new project and in explaining situations that are faltering. Any situation that involves voluntary compliance over a long period of time is likely to be evaluated as involving procedures and outcomes that are consistent to the general norms accepted in that society.

Adaptability

Finally, unless institutional arrangements are able to respond to ever-changing environments, the sustainability of investments and resources is likely to suffer. Rural areas of developing countries are often faced with natural disasters and highly localized special circumstances. If an institutional arrangement is too inflexible to cope with these unique conditions, it is unlikely to last. For example, centrally controlled infrastructure projects are sometimes unable to respond to local emergencies due to rigid procedures and a lack of information about the conditions existing in diverse service areas.

Trade-Offs among Evaluative Criteria

Trade-offs among these criteria are often necessary. It is particularly difficult to choose between the goals of efficiency and of redistributional equity. The trade-off issue arises most explicitly in considering alternative methods of funding public projects. Economically efficient pricing of the use of an existing resource or facility should reflect only the incremental maintenance costs and any external or social costs associated with its use. This is the well-known, efficiency-pricing principle that requires that prices equal the marginal costs of usage.

The principle is especially problematic in the case of goods with *nonsubtractability* attributes—such as with the generation of new knowledge. When the goods involved are nonsubtractive, one person's gaining a benefit from using the good does not subtract from the availability of that good to others. In such instances, the marginal cost of another user utilizing the good is zero; hence, the efficient price is also zero. Zero user prices, however, require that all sources of resource mobilization are tax-based, which induces other kinds of perverse incentives and potential inefficiencies given that funds are extracted from individuals without their being able to withhold payment for nonperformance. Evaluating how institutional arrangements compare across overall criteria is quite a challenge. Analytical examination of the likely trade-offs between intermediate costs is valuable in attempting to understand comparative institutional performance (see E. Ostrom, Schroeder, and Wynne 1993, chap. 5).

Further, how these frequently used criteria in the evaluation of public programs are themselves related to sustainability needs to be examined rather closely. Obviously, a donor-funded program or project that is not considered efficient, in the sense that benefits exceed costs, is immediately suspect in regard to its sustainability. When the most important overall goal is poverty reduction, however, some projects that are not immediately efficient, but do benefit the needy (and would be evaluated positively in regard to redistribution), may be considered sustainable so long as those who would pay for the activities after donor funds are withdrawn are deeply committed to the goal of redistribution. A donor may contribute to the construction of a major infrastructure project in the first place due to its own commitment to redistribution (from its taxpayers to the poorest in the recipient country). It is hard to imagine how such a project would be sustainable in the long run, however, if operating costs are not assigned roughly in proportion to those who receive benefits from the continuing operation of the project.

Further, indigenous practices that may seem on the surface to be wasteful in terms of time or effort, may be sustainable if they simultaneously satisfy other criteria such as conformity to local traditions or perceptions of fairness. Time spent in deciding various aspects about a project, if they lead to an agreement that most perceive as fair and appropriate, may add to the social capital of those involved by re-enforcing the legitimacy of shared norms as well as the long-term sustainability of the project. Given the importance of solving information problems discussed in chapter 3, some indigenous practices are very effective in sharing information about the input of all participants even though it would be possible to design a more efficient practice if solving information problems was not so difficult.[2]

As we will see below, one of the most difficult problems facing donors is finding ways of shifting the support of an ongoing project from revenue provided by the donor to revenue provided by the beneficiaries. The criterion of accountability is clearly related to sustainability. Ensuring that (1) funds are used for the purposes they were allocated, (2) corrupt practices are revealed, and (3) procedures for reviewing practices are institutionalized, are all necessary conditions for any investment to be sustained over the long run.

The Context of Human Action

We have now completed a brief overview of the working parts of an institutional analysis applied to any particular action arena. Underlying the conceptualization of action arenas are implicit assumptions about the *rules-in-use* individuals use to order their relationships, about attributes of *states of the world and their transformations*, and about the *nature of the community* within which the arena occurs. Rules, states of the world, and the nature of the community all jointly affect the types of actions that individuals can take, the benefits and costs of their attributes to these actions and resulting outcomes, and the likely outcomes achieved.

The Concept of Rules

In the IAD framework, we use the term "rules" rather than the term "institutions" since the latter term is frequently used to refer to organizations as well as to the rules that individuals use within and across organizational boundaries. Rules are shared understandings among those involved that refer to enforced prescriptions about what actions (or states of the world) are *required*, *prohibited*, or *permitted*. All rules are the result of implicit or explicit efforts to achieve order and predictability among humans by creating classes of persons (positions) who are then required, permitted, or forbidden to take classes of actions in relation to required, permitted, or forbidden states of the world (Crawford and Ostrom 1995; V. Ostrom 1991). Some of these positions are the agreed-upon enforcers of the rules themselves and have the power to coerce conformance. In a democratic society, rule enforcers must follow agreed-upon procedures for the enforcement of rules. In an authoritarian society, enforcement may be quite arbitrary. In studying these development assistance processes, one needs to ask where the rules that individuals use in given action situations originate.

In an open and democratic governance system, there are many sources of the rules that individuals use in everyday life. In many instances, individuals may legally self-organize in voluntary associations and craft their own rules of interaction. There are also formal rule-making processes—laws and regulations are apt to be passed by central, regional, local, and special units of government. Within private firms and voluntary associations, individuals are authorized to adopt many different rules regarding who is a member of the firm or association, how profits (benefits) are to be shared, and how decisions will be made. Even each family constitutes its own rule-making body or is organized in relation to a patriarchal or matriarchal extended family.

Many of the multiple layers of rules are written down on paper in literate societies. Many rules, however, emerge as individuals work together to figure out solutions to commonly faced problems. For example, colleagues in a work team craft their own rules when they say to one another: "How about if you do A in the future, and I will do B, and before we ever make a decision about C again, let's both discuss it and make a joint decision." In a democratic society, problem-solving individuals do this all the time. They also participate in less fluid decision-making arrangements, including elections to select legislators.

Working rules may also come about "informally" to serve illegal or immoral purposes. For instance, institutional arrangements among politicians, allowing them to behave as organized bandits (McGuire and Olson 1996) and prey on the citizenry, do not promote the overall prosperity of societies. In some bureaucracies, officials have set the price that they must be paid by an applicant in order to receive a position in the bureaucracy (Wade 1985). Here, the rules by which positions are to be purchased are well known, as are the rewards and punishments for observing or violating these (usually illegal) rules and norms. Although such rules and norms create incentives that promote cooperation and coordination within the rent-seeking bureaucracy, the corruption and ineptitude sponsored by this institution inhibit the development of the larger society (de Soto 2000).

When doing institutional analysis, we attempt first to understand the working rules that individuals use in making decisions. Working rules are the set of rules to which participants make reference when asked to explain and justify their actions to fellow participants. While following a rule may become a "social habit," it is possible to make participants consciously aware of the rules they use to order their relationships. Individuals can consciously decide to adopt a different rule and change their behavior to conform to such a decision. Over time, behavior in conformance with a new rule may itself become habitual (see Shimanoff 1980; Toulmin 1974; Harre 1974).[3]

Once we understand the working rules, we can attempt to understand where those rules come from. In a system governed by a "rule of law," the general legal framework in use will have its source in actions taken in constitutional, legislative, judicial, and administrative settings augmented by decisions taken by individuals in many different particular settings. In other words, the rules-in-form are consistent with the rules-in-use (Sproule-Jones 1993). In a system that is not governed by a "rule of law," citizens actively attempt to evade many formal laws and the officials in the system may also seek ways of evading formal law.

Rule-following or conforming actions are not as predictable as biological or physical behavior explained by scientific laws. All rules are formulated in human language. As such, rules share problems of lack of clarity, misunderstanding, and change that typify any language-based phenomenon (V. Ostrom 1980, 1997). Words are always simpler than the phenomenon to which they refer. The acceptance of rules represents a type of Faustian bargain (V. Ostrom 1996). Someone is given the authority to use coercion in order to increase the general good.

The stability of rule-ordered actions is dependent upon the shared meaning assigned to words used to formulate a set of rules. If no shared meaning exists when a rule is formulated, confusion will exist about what actions are required, permitted, or forbidden. Regularities in actions cannot result if those who must repeatedly interpret the meaning of a rule within action situations arrive at multiple interpretations. Because "rules are not self-formulating, self-determining, or self-enforcing" (V. Ostrom 1980, 342), it is human agents who formulate them, apply them in particular situations, and attempt to enforce them. Even if shared meaning exists at the time of the acceptance of a rule, transformations in technology, in shared norms, and in circumstances more generally change the events to which rules apply. "Applying language to changing configurations of development increases the ambiguities and threatens the shared criteria of choice with an erosion of their appropriate meaning" (V. Ostrom 1980, 342).

What rules are important for institutional analysis? Myriad specific rules are used in structuring complex action arenas. Anyone attempting to define a useful typology of rules must be concerned that the classification is more than a method for imposing superficial order onto an extremely large set of seemingly disparate rules. The way we have tackled this problem using the IAD framework is to classify rules according to their impact on the elements of an action situation.

Rule Configurations

A first step toward identifying the working rules can be made, then, by overtly examining how working rules affect each of the variables of an action situation (see above). A set of working rules that affect these variables should constitute the minimal but necessary set of rules needed to explain actions and results based on the working rules used by actors to order their relationships within an action arena. Because states of the world and their transformations and the nature of a community also affect the structure of an action situation, working rules alone never provide a sufficient explanation of outcomes.

Seven types of working rules can be said to affect the structure of an action situation. These are: *entry and exit rules*, *position rules*, *scope rules*, *authority rules*, *aggregation rules*, *information rules*, and *payoff rules*. The cumulative effect of these seven types of rules affects the seven elements of an action situation.

Entry and exit rules affect the number of *actors*, their attributes and resources, whether they can enter freely, and the conditions they face for leaving. Position rules establish *positions* in the situation. Authority rules assign sets of *actions* that actors in positions at particular nodes must, may, or may not take. Scope rules delimit the *potential outcomes* that can be affected and working backwards, the actions linked to specific outcomes. Authority rules, combined with scientific cause and effect relationship of the world being acted upon, determine the shape of the decision tree—the *action-outcome linkages*. Aggregation rules affect the level of *control* that an actor in a position exercises in the selection of an action at a node. Information rules affect the *knowledge-contingent information sets* of actors. Payoff rules affect the *benefits and costs* that will be assigned to particular combinations of actions and outcomes and establish the objective benefits and costs of action. These expected, objective benefits are perceived by actors as incentives or deterrents. The set of working rules is a *configuration* in the sense that the effect of a change in one rule may depend upon the other rules-in-use.

Let us return to the example of conducting an analysis of a common-pool resource situation discussed earlier. Now we will focus on a series of questions that are intended to help the analyst get at the rules-in-use that help structure a situation. Thus, to understand these rules, one would begin to ask questions such as:

- *Entry and Exit Rules*: Are the users from this resource limited to local residents; to one group defined by ethnicity, race, caste, gender, or family structure; to those who win a lottery; to those who have obtained a permit; to those who own required assets (such as a fishing birth or land); or in some other way limited to a class of individuals that is bounded? Is a new actor allowed to join a group by some kind of entry fee or initiation? Must a user give up rights to harvest upon migrating to another location?

- *Position Rules*: How does an actor move from being just a "member" of a group of appropriators to someone who has a specialized task, such as a water distributor-guard?
- *Scope Rules*: What understandings do the users and others have about the authorized or forbidden geographic or functional domains? Do any maps exist showing who can appropriate from which region? Are there understandings about resource units that are "off-limit" (e.g., the historical rules in some sections of Africa that particular *acacia* trees could not be cut down even on privately owned land)?
- *Authority Rules*: What understandings do users have about mandatory, authorized, or forbidden harvesting technologies? For fishers, must net size be of a particular grossness? For forest users, must they use some cutting tools and not others? What choices do various types of monitors have related to the actions they can take?
- *Aggregation Rules*: What understandings exist concerning the rules affecting the choice of harvesting activities? Must certain actions require permission from, or agreement of, others prior to taking the action?
- *Information Rules*: What information must be held secret and what information must be made public?
- *Payoff Rules*: How large are the sanctions that can be imposed for breaking any of the rules identified above? How is conformance to rules monitored? Who is responsible for sanctioning nonconformers? How reliably are sanctions imposed? Are there any positive rewards offered to appropriators for any actions they can take? (e.g., Is someone who is an elected official relieved of labor duties?)

The problem for the field researcher is that many rules-in-use are not written down. Many of the rules-in-use are not even conceptualized by participants as rules. Therefore, the field researcher cannot simply be a survey worker asking a random sample of respondents about their rules. In settings where the rules-in-use have evolved over long periods of time and are understood implicitly by participants, obtaining information about rules-in-use requires spending time in a site and learning how to ask non-threatening, context-specific questions about rule configurations.

Physical and Material Conditions (The Nature of the Good)

While a rule configuration affects all elements of an action situation, some of the variables of an action situation are strongly affected by attributes of the physical and material world. What actions are physically possible, what outcomes can be produced, how actions are linked to outcomes, and what is contained in the actors' information sets are affected by the physical world being acted upon in a situation. The same set of rules may yield entirely different types of action situations depending upon the types of events in the world being acted upon by participants.

The attributes of states of the world and their transformation are explicitly examined when the analyst self-consciously asks a series of questions about how the world being acted upon in a situation affects the outcomes, action sets, action-outcome linkages, and information sets in that situation. The relative importance of the rule configuration and states of the world in structuring an action situation varies across different types of settings. The relative importance of working rules to attributes of the world also varies dramatically within action situations considered to be part of the public sector.

For example, rules define and constrain the way legislators vote more than attributes of the world. Voting can be accomplished by raising hands, by paper ballots, by calling for the ayes and nays, by marching before an official counter, or by installing computer terminals for each legislator on which votes are registered. However, in regard to organizing communication within a legislature, attributes of the world strongly affect the available options. The principle that only one person can be heard and understood at a time in any one forum strongly affects the capacity of legislators to communicate effectively with one another (see V. Ostrom 1987). Size of deliberative bodies is an important variable affecting intelligible communication. The larger the size, the greater the threat to human understanding.

Certain configurations of physical and material factors play an especially important role in institutional analysis. We discuss private and public goods, common-pool resources, and natural monopolies below.

Private Goods

Attributes, frequently used to distinguish the particular nature of goods and services, help us to analyze the mechanisms for their provision, production, and allocation. Private goods are those where the cost of excluding potential beneficiaries from access to a good or service is relatively low, and where one person's consumption subtracts from the corpus of goods available. Examples of private goods include agricultural commodities as well as consumer durables such as refrigerators and automobiles. The production of all private goods involves some combination of fixed costs (those incurred in creating the facility needed to produce the good) and marginal costs (those incurrent in the day-to-day production of an increment of the good). Private goods differ from one another rather substantially in regard to the relationship of their fixed costs of production versus the marginal costs of production. Arrangements for exchange within markets provide the context for the efficient provision and production of private goods (see any basic textbook on microeconomics).

Here, those who seek and sell private goods and services engage in quid pro quo relationships. In a well-functioning market, producers and suppliers respond to the demands made by consumers in the marketplace. Competition among producers increases their efficiency and this generates goods at lower cost to consumers. When market processes are well-ordered, donors are less involved in supporting projects related to strictly private goods, with the possible exception of those that require very large initial investments.

Natural Monopolies

Many private goods do not involve large investments in fixed costs before units of the good can be produced. Others require extremely large initial investments. Goods such as electricity and water not only require a large investment in plant and facilities but also a large investment in the facilities that connect individual households and industrial plants to the source of electricity or water. If there were to be direct competition for final consumers between two producers of water or electricity, each producer would need to replicate the extensive service lines that connect central facilities to final consumption units. Thus, instead of competition between private producers leading to economies, competition greatly increases the total costs of production and thus the cost of the services for consumers. Goods and services that have these characteristics are called "natural" monopolies. "A market has a natural monopoly if one firm can produce the total output of the market at lower cost than several firms could" (Perloff 1999, 394). Many donor-assisted projects are designed to help in the initial financing, construction, and maintenance of energy or other infrastructure projects that have the structure of natural monopolies (see chapters 9 and 10 for brief case studies of such projects in India and Zambia).

Excludability, Free-Riding, and Public Goods

When it is very difficult or costly to exclude beneficiaries from a good once it is produced, it is frequently assumed that such a good must be provided and produced by governmental agencies, rather than by private firms in a competitive market (Weimer and Vining 1999; Riker and Ordeshook 1973). Goods that are characterized by difficulties in exclusion, but where one person's consumption does not subtract from the level of the good available to others, are called *public goods*. Knowledge, national defense, and protection of the air we breathe are typical examples of public goods.

When the benefits of a good are available to a group, whether or not members of the group contribute to the provision of the good, that good is characterized by problems with excludability. Where exclusion is costly, those wishing to provide a good or service face a potential free-rider problem—a type of collective-action problem, discussed more generally in chapter 3 (Olson 1965). Individuals who gain from efforts to rid the atmosphere from pollutants, for example, may not wish to contribute to the costs of higher fuel, more expensive cars, or other necessary inputs, hoping that others will bear the burden. This is not to say that all individuals will free ride whenever they can. A strong incentive exists to be a free rider in all situations where potential beneficiaries cannot easily be excluded for failing to contribute to the provision of a good or service.

When it is costly to exclude individuals from enjoying benefits, private, profit-seeking entrepreneurs, who must recoup their investments through quid pro quo exchanges, have few incentives to provide such services on their own initiative. Provision of a good involves finding out the demand for it, finding a way of financing the production of that good, arrangement for production, and allocating the good to consumers (V. Ostrom, Tiebout, and Warren 1961). Production of a good can be undertaken by a public agency or by a for-profit or not-for-profit private firm that contracts with a public agency making provision decisions relying on the power to tax or other nonexchange mechanisms for mobilizing resources. Government agencies, private firms, and NGOs are all involved in delivering development assistance.

Public sector provision of goods and services with excludability problems raises additional problems in determining preferences and in organizing finances. When exclusion is low-cost to the supplier, preferences are revealed as a result of many quid pro quo transactions. Producers learn about preferences through the consumers' willingness to pay for various goods offered for sale. Where exclusion is difficult, designing mechanisms that honestly reflect beneficiaries' preferences and their willingness to pay is complex, regardless of whether the providing unit is organized in the public or the private sphere.

In very small groups, those affected are usually able to discuss their preferences and constraints on a face-to-face basis and to reach a rough consensus. In larger groups, decisions about public goods are apt to be made through mechanisms such as voting or the delegation of authority to public officials. The extensive literature on voting systems demonstrates how difficult it is to translate individual preferences into collective choices that adequately reflect individual preferences (Arrow 1951; Shepsle 1979; Buchanan and Tullock 1962).

Another attribute of some goods with excludability problems is that, once they are provided, consumers may have no choice whatsoever as to their level of consumption. An example is public spraying for insect control. If an individual does not want this public service to be provided, there are even stronger incentives not to comply with a general tax levy. Thus, compliance with a broad financing instrument may, in turn, depend upon both the legitimacy of the public-choice mechanism used to make provision decisions and the value of the goods provided by these mechanisms to those who are taxed for their provision.

Subtractability of the Flow and Common-Pool Resources

Another set of problematic goods and services are common-pool resources that yield benefits where exclusion is difficult and each person's use of a resource system subtracts units of that resource from a finite total available for harvesting. The withdrawal of a quantity of water from an irrigation canal, for example, by one farmer means that there is that much less water for anyone else to use. Most agricultural or urban uses of water are highly subtractive. Similarly, the cutting down of trees for timber or the extraction of firewood from a local forest is also highly subtractive. When the use of a flow of services by one individual subtracts from what is available to others and when the flow is scarce relative to demand, users will be tempted to try—that is, face incentives—to obtain as much as they can of the flow for fear that it will not be available later.

Effective rules are required if scarce, fully subtractive service flows are to be allocated in a productive way. Charging prices for subtractive services obviously constitutes one such allocation mechanism. Sometimes, however, it is not feasible to price services. In these instances, if other allocation rules do not limit who can use and how much use is authorized, some individuals will be able to grab considerably more of the subtractive services than others, thereby leading to inefficient uses of the flow and creating high levels of conflict among users.

Allocation rules also affect the incentives of users to maintain a common-pool resource, as well as to use the subtractable flow efficiently. In regard to an irrigation system, for example, farmers located at the tail end of an irrigation system that lacks effective allocation rules have little motivation to contribute to the maintenance of that system. They will only occasionally receive their share of water given that the farmers at the head end have no restrictions on their use. Similarly, farmers located at the head end of such a system are not motivated to provide maintenance services voluntarily because they will receive disproportionate shares of the water whether or not the system is well maintained (E. Ostrom 1996).

Consequently, for common-pool resources whose flows are highly subtractive, institutional arrangements related to the allocation of the flow of services are intimately tied to the sustainability of the resource. It is highly unlikely that aid projects can achieve sustainability without careful attention to the efficiency, fairness, and enforceability of the rules specifying who can appropriate how much of the service flow, at what times and places, and under what conditions. Furthermore, unless responsibilities are linked in a reasonable fashion to benefits obtained, the beneficiaries themselves will resist efforts to insist that they take responsibilities.

Many of the collective-action problems that so pervade the political economies of developing countries are the result of a lack of appropriate institutions designed to facilitate the provision, production, distribution, and allocation of goods produced by natural monopolies, public goods, and common-pool resources.

Attributes of the Community

A third set of variables that affect the structure of an action arena relates to the community. The attributes of a community that are important in affecting the structure of an action arena include the norms of behavior generally accepted in the community, the level of common understanding potential participants share about the structure of particular types of action arenas, the extent of homogeneity in the preferences of those living in a community, and the distribution of resources among those affected. The term *culture* is frequently applied to this bundle of variables. At times, external advisors look at all communities within a developing country as an undifferentiated group rather than recognizing the substantial differences in the cultural endowments of diverse groups (see Kottak 1990).

Groups, for example, differ substantially in regard to their capabilities for managing a common-pool resource efficiently and sustainably. When the users of a common-pool resource share a common set of values and interact with one another in a multiplex set of arrangements, the probability of their developing adequate rules and internal norms to govern resources is much greater than that of larger groups or highly heterogeneous groups without shared norms (Taylor 1987). The importance of building a reputation for keeping one's word is important in such a community. The cost of developing monitoring and sanctioning mechanisms is relatively low. If the users [of] a resource come from many different communities and are distrustful of one another, the task of devising and sustaining effective rules is substantially increased. Thus, the particular norms that are accepted, the homogeneity or heterogeneity of the groups involved, and the history of conflict on diverse issues are important contextual factors in any given situation.

Linking Action Arenas

Having outlined the components of action arenas and the contexts that define them, in this section we move to a consideration of the ways in which different action arenas are linked together. Whereas the concept of a "single" arena may include large numbers of participants and complex chains of action, most of social reality is composed of multiple arenas linked simultaneously or sequentially.

When individuals wish to intervene to change the outcomes achieved in socially constructed realities to guide (or control) participants toward a different pattern of results, they do so by attempting to change the rules individuals use to order their interactions within particular types of action arenas. Some interesting and important institutional arrangements for coordinating complex chains of actions among large numbers of actors involve multiple organizations competing with one another according to a set of rules.

Markets are the most frequently studied institutional arrangements that achieve coordination by relying primarily on rule-governed, competitive relationships among organizations (Bowles 1998). Rule-governed competition among two or more political parties is considered by many analysts to be an important requisite for a democratic polity. Less studied, but potentially as important a means for achieving responsiveness and efficiency in producing public goods and services, are arrangements that allow rule-ordered competition among two or more potential *producers* of public goods and services (McGinnis 1999a, 1999b).

Multiple Levels of Analysis

Besides multiple and nested action arenas at any one level of analysis, nesting of arenas also occurs across several levels of analysis. All rules are nested in another set of rules that define how the first set of rules can be changed. The nesting of rules within rules at several levels is similar to the nesting of computer languages at several levels. What can be done at a higher level will depend on the capabilities and limits of the rules (or the software) at that level and at a deeper level. Whenever one addresses questions about *institutional change*, as contrasted to action within institutional constraints, it is necessary to recognize the following:

1. Changes in the rules used to order action at one level occur within a currently "fixed" set of rules at a deeper level.
2. Changes in deeper-level rules usually are more difficult and more costly to accomplish, thus increasing the stability of mutual expectations among individuals interacting according to a set of rules.

It is useful to distinguish three levels of rules that cumulatively affect the actions taken and outcomes obtained in any setting (Kiser and Ostrom 1982). *Operational rules* directly affect day-to-day actions made by the actors in any setting. *Collective-choice rules* affect operational activities and results through their effects in determining who is eligible and the specific rules to be used in changing operational rules. *Constitutional-choice rules* affect operational activities and their outcomes in determining who is eligible and the rules to be used in crafting the set of collective-choice rules that in turn affect the set of operational rules (see Siegan 1994; Buchanan and Tullock 1962; Shugart and Carey 1992).

At each level of analysis there may be one or more arenas in which the types of decisions made at that level will occur. In the government and management of a local resource, for example, some of the operational rules are made locally, some are derived from laws passed at a regional level (if present), and others are adopted at a national collective-choice (or constitutional-choice) level. The units usually correspond to multiple geographic domains. In collective-choice and constitutional-choice situations, activities involve prescribing, invoking, monitoring, applying, and enforcing rules (Lasswell and Kaplan 1950; Oakerson 1994). The concept of an "arena" as described earlier does not imply a formal setting, but can include such formal settings as legislatures and courts. Policy making (or governance) regarding the rules that will be used to regulate operational-level choices is usually carried out in one or more collective-choice arenas. Federal systems of governance necessarily imply multiple layers of governance.

Using IAD for Incentive Analysis

To conduct a thorough institutional analysis in a particular field setting, the analyst can use the broad IAD framework to identify relevant questions that need to be answered in order to understand the structure of a particular situation and the underlying contextual variables creating that structure. We have provided illustrative questions in this chapter for beginning to examine one type of situation that is often at the core of a development assistance project—common-pool resource situation. No single list of questions, however, will fit any and all situations involved in complex development assistance programs. The task is to try to understand who the actors are, how they came to be in this situation, and the characteristics that they share (or do not share) that affect their perceptions of the situation and each other. In addition to understanding the actions they can take and how these are linked to outcomes, the institutional analyst pays particular attention to the information available to actors (in terms of completeness and distribution) and to the benefits and costs assigned to different actions. The analyst is trying to understand the structure of the situation as viewed by the participants. All these factors enter into the perception of incentives by actors.

It is the identification of the perceived incentives that leads the analyst to generate hypotheses about expected patterns of interactions and resulting outcomes. If the analyst finds that the behavior actually observed in a situation is similar to that expected from the analysis, the analyst has generated a sufficient explanation. If the resulting behavior is different, the analyst has missed one or more crucial variables that impinge on actors' incentives and thus on their interactions with one another. Some field settings are so complex that it takes several iterations to understand the context and the existing situation. Thus, an institutional analysis of a particular project would involve a relatively detailed and precise analysis of how the various working parts of a situation fit together and the resulting motivational and informational problems that may exist or have been solved by the way individuals have structured the rules they are using or the norms that are generally shared by the community.

Institutional analysis is also used to examine more general types of situations that are repeatedly found in most societies. Here the effort is not to understand the specific structure of a particular situation, but rather to understand the incentives that may exist in a large number of situations that share the broad outlines of the "stylized" situation. Knowing the general structure of a diverse set of situations can be useful to a policy analyst investigating a potential project or evaluating an existing one. The analyst can immediately ask whether or not an existing situation has a known structure and thus a set of likely outcomes prior to the advent of donor assistance. Then the important question is how donor assistance changes the incentives toward, or away from, a sustainable and productive set of outcomes.

Notes

This chapter was originally published in *Aid, Incentives, and Sustainability: An Institutional Analysis of Development Cooperation—Main Report*, Sida Studies in Evaluation #02/01 (Stockholm, Sweden: Swedish International Development Cooperation Agency [Sida]), pp. 273–300, http://www.sida.se). Figure 3.2 reprinted with the permission of the University of Michigan Press.

1. A similar framework was used by Alexis de Tocqueville (1945) in *Democracy in America*, as his first three chapters of volume 1 clearly lay out.
2. An example of this are the many practices used by irrigators or fishers that have been criticized as economically inefficient when analysis is conducted assuming full information. When the information-generating aspects of the indigenous institution are examined, however, many indigenous institutions are evaluated differently as having solved some of the problems that have limited the sustainability of other institutions in similar settings due to missing or asymmetric information (see E. Ostrom 1990).
3. The capacity of humans to use complex cognitive systems to order their own behavior at a relatively subconscious level makes it difficult for empirical researchers to ascertain what the working rules for an ongoing action arena may be.

References

Alchian, Armen A. 1950. "Uncertainty, Evolution, and Economic Theory." *Journal of Political Economy* 58(3): 211–21.
Arrow, Kenneth. 1951. *Social Choice and Individual Values*. 2nd ed. New York: Wiley.
Ashby, W. Ross. 1960. *Design for a Brain: The Origin of Adaptive Behavior*. 2nd ed. New York: Wiley.

Bowles, Samuel. 1998. "Endogenous Preferences: The Cultural Consequences of Markets and Other Economic Institutions." *Journal of Economic Literature* 36: 75–111.

Bowles, Samuel, and Herbert Gintis. 1993. "The Revenge of Homo Economicus: Contested Exchange and the Revival of Political Economy." *Journal of Economic Perspectives* 7(1): 83–102.

Boyd, Robert, and Peter J. Richerson. 1985. *Culture and the Evolutionary Process*. Chicago, IL: University of Chicago Press.

Breton, Albert, and Ronald Wintrobe. 1982. *The Logic of Bureaucratic Conduct: An Economic Analysis of Competition, Exchange, and Efficiency in Private and Public Organizations*. Cambridge, UK: Cambridge University Press.

Buchanan, James M., and Gordon Tullock. 1962. *The Calculus of Consent: Logical Foundations of Constitutional Democracy*. Ann Arbor: University of Michigan Press.

Camerer, Colin, and Richard H. Thaler. 1995. "Anomalies: Ultimatums, Dictators, and Manners." *Journal of Economic Perspectives* 9(2): 209–19.

Crawford, Sue E. S., and Elinor Ostrom. 1995. "A Grammar of Institutions." *American Political Science Review* 89(3): 582–600.

de Soto, Hernando. 2000. *The Mystery of Capital: Why Capitalism Triumphs in the West and Fails Everywhere Else*. New York: Basic Books.

Dosi, Giovanni, and Massimo Egidi. 1987. "Substantive and Procedural Uncertainty: An Exploration of Economic Behaviours in Complex and Changing Environments." Paper prepared at the International Workshop on Programmable Automation and New Work Modes, Paris, April 2–4.

Güth, Werner. 1995. "An Evolutionary Approach to Explaining Cooperative Behavior by Reciprocal Incentives." *International Journal of Game Theory* 24: 323–44.

Hardin, Garrett. 1968. "The Tragedy of the Commons." *Science* 162: 1243–48.

Harre, R. 1974. "Some Remarks on 'Rule' as a Scientific Concept." In *Understanding Other Persons*, edited by T. Mischel. Oxford, UK: Basil Blackwell.

Hyden, Goran. 1990. "Reciprocity and Governance in Africa." In *The Failure of the Centralized State: Institutions and Self-Governance in Africa*, edited by James Wunsch and Dele Olowu, 245–69. Boulder, CO: Westview Press.

Kiser, Larry, and Elinor Ostrom. 1982. "The Three Worlds of Action: A Metatheoretical Synthesis of Institutional Approaches." In *Strategies of Political Inquiry*, edited by Elinor Ostrom, 179–222. Beverly Hills, CA: Sage.

Kottak, Conrad P. 1990. "Culture and Economic Development." *American Anthropologist* 92(3): 723–31.

Kreps, David M. 1990. "Corporate Culture and Economic Theory." In *Perspective on Positive Political Economy*, edited by James E. Alt and Kenneth A. Shepsle, 90–143. New York: Cambridge University Press.

Lasswell, Harold D., and Abraham Kaplan. 1950. *Power and Society: A Framework for Political Inquiry*. New Haven, CT: Yale University Press.

McGinnis, Michael D., ed. 1999a. *Polycentric Governance and Development: Readings from the Workshop in Political Theory and Policy Analysis*. Ann Arbor: University of Michigan Press.

———, ed. 1999b. *Polycentricity and Local Public Economies: Readings from the Workshop in Political Theory and Policy Analysis*. Ann Arbor: University of Michigan Press.

———. 2000. *Polycentric Games and Institutions: Readings from the Workshop in Political Theory and Policy Analysis*. Ann Arbor: University of Michigan Press.

McGuire, Martin, and Mancur Olson. 1996. "The Economics of Autocracy and Majority Rule: The Invisible Hand and the Use of Force." *Journal of Economic Literature* 34: 72–96.

Oakerson, Ronald J. 1992. "Analyzing the Commons: A Framework." In *Making the Commons Work: Theory, Practice, and Policy*, edited by Daniel W. Bromley et al., 41–59. San Francisco, CA: ICS Press.

———. 1993. "Reciprocity: A Bottom-Up View of Political Development." In *Rethinking Institutional Analysis and Development: Issues, Alternatives, and Choices*, edited by Vincent Ostrom, David Feeny, and Hartmut Picht, 141–58. San Francisco, CA: ICS Press.

———. 1994. "The Logic of Multi-Level Institutional Analysis." Paper presented at the Workshop on the Workshop conference, Indiana University, Workshop in Political Theory and Policy Analysis, Bloomington, June 15–19.

Olson, Mancur. 1965. *The Logic of Collective Action*. Cambridge, MA: Harvard University Press.

———. 1969. "The Principle of 'Fiscal Equivalence': The Division of Responsibilities among Different Levels of Government." *American Economic Review* 59(2): 479–87.

Ostrom, Elinor. 1990. *Governing the Commons: The Evolution of Institutions for Collective Action*. New York: Cambridge University Press.

———. 1996. "Incentives, Rules of the Game, and Development." In *Proceedings of the Annual World Bank Conference on Development Economics 1995*, 207–34. Washington, DC: World Bank.

———. 1998. "A Behavioral Approach to the Rational Choice Theory of Collective Action." *American Political Science Review* 92(1): 1–22.

———. 2000. "Collective Action and the Evolution of Social Norms." *Journal of Economic Perspectives* 14(3): 137–58.

Ostrom, Elinor, Roy Gardner, and James M. Walker. 1994. *Rules, Games, and Common-Pool Resources*. Ann Arbor: University of Michigan Press.

Ostrom, Elinor, Larry Schroeder, and Susan Wynne. 1993. *Institutional Incentives and Sustainable Development: Infrastructure Policies in Perspective*. Boulder, CO: Westview Press.

Ostrom, Vincent. 1980. "Artisanship and Artifact." *Public Administration Review* 40: 309–17.

———. 1986. "A Fallabilist's Approach to Norms and Criteria of Choice." In *Guidance, Control, and Evaluation in the Public Sector*, edited by Franz-Xaver Kaufmann, Giandomenico Majone, and Vincent Ostrom, 229–49. Berlin and New York: de Gruyter.

———. 1987. *The Political Theory of a Compound Republic: Designing the American Experiment*. 2nd ed. Lincoln: University of Nebraska Press.

———. 1991. *The Meaning of American Federalism: Constituting a Self-Governing Society*. San Francisco, CA: ICS Press.

———. 1996. "Faustian Bargains." *Constitutional Political Economy* 7: 303–8.

———. 1997. *The Meaning of Democracy and the Vulnerability of Democracies: A Response to Tocqueville's Challenge*. Ann Arbor: University of Michigan Press.

Ostrom, Vincent, Charles M. Tiebout, and Robert Warren. 1961. "The Organization of Government in Metropolitan Areas." *American Political Science Review* 55(4): 831–42.

Perloff, Jeffrey M. 1999. *Microeconomics*. Reading, MA: Addison Wesley.

Riker, William H., and Peter C. Ordeshook. 1973. *An Introduction to Positive Political Theory*. Englewood Cliffs, NJ: Prentice Hall.

Shepsle, Kenneth A. 1979. "The Role of Institutional Structure in the Creation of Policy Equilibrium." In *Public Policy and Public Choice*, edited by Douglas W. Rae and Theodore J. Eismeier, 249–83. Beverly Hills, CA: Sage.

Shimanoff, Susan B. 1980. *Communication Rules: Theory and Research*. Beverly Hills, CA: Sage.

Shugart, Matthew, and John M. Carey. 1992. *Presidents and Assemblies: Constitutional Design and Electoral Dynamics*. Cambridge, UK: Cambridge University Press.

Siegan, Bernard H. 1994. *Drafting a Constitution for a Nation or Republic Emerging into Freedom*. 2nd ed. Fairfax, VA: George Mason University Press.

Simon, Herbert A. 1965. *Administrative Behavior: A Study of Decision-Making Processes in Administrative Organization*. New York: Free Press. Originally published in 1947.

———. 1972. "Theories of Bounded Rationality." In *Decision and Organization: A Volume in Honor of Jacob Marschak*, edited by C. B. McGuire and Roy Radner, 161–76. Amsterdam: North Holland.

———. 1985. "Human Nature in Politics: The Dialogue of Psychology with Political Science." *American Political Science Review* 79: 293–94.

———. 1997. *Models of Bounded Rationality: Empirically Grounded Economic Reason*. Cambridge, MA: MIT Press.

Sproule-Jones, Mark. 1993. *Governments at Work: Canadian Parliamentary Federalism and Its Public Policy Effects*. Toronto: University of Toronto Press.

Taylor, Michael. 1987. *The Possibility of Cooperation*. New York: Cambridge University Press.

Tocqueville, Alexis de. 1945. *Democracy in America*. 2 vols. Ed. Phillips Bradley. New York: Alfred A. Knopf. First published in 1835 and 1840. .

Toulmin, S. 1974. "Rules and Their Relevance for Understanding Human Behavior." In *Understanding Other Persons*, edited by T. Mischel. Oxford, UK: Basil Blackwell.

Wade, Robert. 1985. "The Market for Public Office: Why the Indian State is Not Better at Development." *World Development* 13(4): 467–97.

Weimer, David L., and Aidan R. Vining. 1999. *Policy Analysis: Concepts and Practice*. 3rd ed. Upper Saddle River, NJ: Prentice-Hall.

Williamson, Oliver E. 1975. *Markets and Hierarchies*. New York: Free Press.

———. 1979. "Transaction Cost Economics: The Governance of Contractual Relations." *Journal of Law and Economics* 22(2): 233–61.

———. 1985. *The Economic Institutions of Capitalism*. New York: Free Press.

4

The IAD Framework in Action: Understanding the Source of the Design Principles in Elinor Ostrom's Governing the Commons

MICHAEL D. MCGINNIS

The Institutional Analysis and Development (IAD) framework should be understood as a starting point for analysis of complex policy situations. This framework, which is most closely associated with the work of Elinor Ostrom, a corecipient of the 2009 Nobel Memorial Prize in Economic Sciences, has been shaped by contributions from many of her large community of collaborators. This framework has undergone a series of transformations, and even after Ostrom's untimely death in 2012, it continues to undergo significant changes, transformations, and extensions to new topics (see Kiser and Ostrom 1982; Ostrom 1989, 2007, 2010, 2011; Oakerson 1992; Ostrom, Gardner, and Walker 1994; Ostrom and Ostrom 2004; McGinnis 2011a; Cole, Epstein, and McGinnis 2014).

This chapter is based on notes that I distributed to graduate students in my seminars on Institutional Analysis and Development in previous years. These notes are intended to serve as a guideline to anyone first trying to apply the abstract concepts and analytical tools included in this framework to a detailed study of some specific policy problem or concern.

Overview of Steps in Analysis

1. Decide if your primary concern is *explanation of a puzzle* (Why does outcome X occur in cases like Y, but not in cases like Z?) or *policy analysis* (What is likely to happen if current policy A were

replaced by policy B? What would need to be done in order to implement B?).

2. Summarize two to three plausible *alternative explanations* for why this outcome occurs, or why your preferred outcome has not been realized; express each explanation as a *dynamic process*.
3. *Identify the focal action situation(s)*, the one (or a few) arena(s) of interaction that you consider to be most critical in one or more of these alternative explanations.
4. *Systematically examine categories of the IAD framework* to identify and highlight the most critical (1) actors in positions, (2) rules-in-use, (3) attributes of relevant communities, (4) types of goods involved and biophysical dynamics, (5) evaluative criteria, and (6) feedback loops and sources of learning in these focal action situations.
5. *Follow the information* flow in each of these focal action situations. What sources of information are available to which actors under which circumstances, and what might prevent them from using that information to change the outcomes that result?
6. *Locate adjacent action situations* that determine the contextual categories of the focal action situation, that is, outcomes of adjacent situations in which collective actors are constructed and individual incentives shaped, rules are written and collective procedures established, norms are internalized and other community attributes are determined, goods are produced and inputs for production are extracted from resource systems (that may need replenishment), and where evaluation, learning, and feedback processes occur.
7. *Select those adjacent action situations* that are critical for distinguishing among alternative explanations, and repeat steps 4 and 5 (and if necessary, step 6) for those action situations.
8. *Compare and contrast the ways these linked and nested action situations are interrelated in the processes emphasized by each of your alternative explanations.* Do the same actors write, implement, and enforce rules? How do outcomes of other action situations shape processes of information flow and evaluation in the focal action situation(s)? Which incentives or values of actors are reinforced or undermined by outcomes of these action situations?
9. *Identify the most critical steps for more detailed analysis*, by isolating components of adjacent action situations that determine the context currently in place in the focal action situation(s), and that if changed would result in fundamental changes in outcomes. But remember that if you change one contextual factor in one action

situation, then you must also incorporate all relevant changes in closely related action situations. (Ceteris paribus is more complicated in institutional analysis!)

10. Draw upon principles of research design or evaluative research to *select cases* for further analysis by whatever *methods* are best suited to that purpose. *Follow relevant conventions when writing up your conclusions*; DO NOT describe this process of discovery in detail.

Example of Application to Community-Based Management of Resource Commons, as Exemplified in Elinor Ostrom's *Governing the Commons*

Ironically, Elinor Ostrom makes only a passing reference to the IAD framework in her best-known and her most highly influential book, *Governing the Commons* (1990). In later books, especially *Understanding Institutional Diversity* (2005), she dove into the details of this framework as an analytical perspective, but since *Governing the Commons* was designed (successfully!) to reach a wide and diverse audience of scholars, practitioners, and non-specialists, the analytical apparatus that provided the foundation for the conclusions she summarizes in that book remain hidden from the reader. But those of us who had the good fortune to get to know her closely can see the influence of the IAD framework permeating throughout her writings, in this book and elsewhere.

It's safe to say that scholars who are selected for Nobel prizes tend to see more deeply into the core foundations of the things they study, and the thought processes they have used to arrive at their unique insights are infused with a heavy dose of creativity and subtlety. This makes it impossible for others to fully understand how they arrived at their conclusions, even once we have come to understand the implications of their discoveries.

Ostrom identified a set of eight Design Principles that she described as characterizing those instances of community-based resource management regimes that managed to stand the test of time, proving resilient to the many vagaries of environmental, political, and demographic shocks and transformations. Even she found it difficult to express how she managed to arrive at these insights, which she always framed as not being the end point of analysis, but instead as a set of conjectures that needed to be subjected to further analysis, elaboration, and revisions.

Below I suggest a way in which these design principles can be understood as emerging from Ostrom's engagement with the complexity of her case studies, with her thought processes being shaped, in a fundamental sense, by the categories and relationships expressed in the form of the IAD framework. I am not claiming that this is the actual process through which she reasoned her way to these conclusions, and any effort to make such a demonstration would have to be undertaken by an expert in intellectual history or biography. But I am confident that these principles can be understood as emerging, in a natural sense, from the repeated application of the foundational principles of the IAD framework.

The remainder of this chapter consists of my effort to illustrate how we might understand the conclusions that Elinor Ostrom articulated in *Governing the Commons*, if we go through the exercise of implementing the steps stated above in the context of the case materials that formed the empirical foundation for her research on this topic. I present this exercise in the form of observations and interpretations of the implications of each of the ten steps identified above as the steps needed to fully implement an institutional analysis along the lines of the IAD framework, properly understood.

Before diving into these steps, however, I feel it necessary to reassure any reader who might be intimidated by the magnitude of the analytical task summarized here to remember that this particular research project was so comprehensive and influential as to merit the highest forms of praise (as signified by her Nobel). Even those of us who do not pretend to be able to operate at that same level can make effective use of at least some of the steps identified here, as we strive to make our own contributions to the existing store of knowledge on important policy matters.

1. Decide if your primary concern is *explanation of a puzzle* (Why does outcome X occur in cases like Y, but not cases like Z?) or *policy analysis* (What is likely to happen if current policy A were replaced by policy B? What would need to be done in order to implement B?).

Research Puzzle: Garrett Hardin concluded that all commons are doomed to exhaustion, unless managed by a central authority or divided up into private parcels, yet many such commons persist for very long periods of time. How can that happen?
Policy Concern: What can be done to improve the sustainability of common-pool resources? Can similarly successful processes occur in different ways under diverse ownership schemes and governance arrangements?

Note: Elinor Ostrom was a firm believer in the importance of research design as the foundation for good research in the social sciences. She routinely taught our introductory graduate seminar for first-year students as a review of alternative forms of research design, and this example has inspired me to make it clear that students interested in either primarily academic research or in more practical policy analysis can feel equally welcome in applying this form of institutional analysis. The Workshop in Political Theory and Policy Analysis that Elinor and Vincent Ostrom established at Indiana University in 1973 was widely known for its unique ability to combine scientific rigor and policy relevance within the scope of each of its many research programs. Few of us will be able to be equally successful in both academic and policy arenas of discourse, but I am convinced that the IAD framework can help clarify and deepen our lines of argument in either context.

2. Summarize two to three plausible *alternative explanations* for why this outcome occurs, or why your preferred outcome has not been realized; express each explanation as a *dynamic process*.

   A. *Hardin's tragedy of the commons explanation* (1968) is based on the presumptions that (1) individual resource users will extract more resources in order to maximize their own returns, but (2) any such resource is limited and must be replenished by processes that are themselves limited, and that (3) if no one takes responsibility for matching the overall level of extraction to the carrying capacity of that resource, then the result will be overuse and collapse of the resource. However, this tragic outcome can be avoided if the common resources are privatized or managed by a central authority. In effect, Hardin distinguishes among three alternative governance models:

      1. *Tragedy of the (open access) commons*: Resource levels are determined by exogenous forces, and since no one has taken responsibility to replenish resources or maintain relevant infrastructure, eventually any uncoordinated efforts will prove to be insufficient to avoid collapse.
      2. *Privatized commons*: Individual property owners manage and maintain their own private property in a cost-efficient manner, but need not be concerned about anything beyond that. In this model, the commons will become a market.

3. *Centrally managed commons*: Rules for use and maintenance of resources are set and enforced by external actors, and local herders respond to those incentives, provided they are adequately enforced. If these managers are sufficiently competent, the resource should be sustainable (if that is their goal).

B. Ostrom (1990) demonstrates that communities of resource users can, in some circumstances, devise and enforce rules limiting their own extraction levels and maintenance activities, and that these efforts may be successful in maintaining sustainable access to that resource over long periods of time. However, in other circumstances, Hardin's tragic conclusion may well apply. In effect, Ostrom adds a fourth possible model of resource management, namely,

4. *User-managed commons*: All (or most) of the rules for use and maintenance of resources are set and/or enforced by local users, and under certain conditions this arrangement may turn out to be sustainable.

3. *Identify the focal (or core) action situation(s)*, the one (or a few) arena(s) of interaction that you consider to be most critical in one or more of these alternative explanations.

A. *Appropriation* of resource, combined with its natural renewal or replenishment.
B. *Maintenance* of resource, including artificial replenishment and any infrastructural improvements.
C. *Rule-making*, the collective process of formulating rules and procedures for individual participation in appropriation and maintenance activities.
D. *Monitoring* of how closely actual appropriation and maintenance activities satisfy applicable rules and procedures, *and sanctioning* rule violators.

Other related action situations are considered below, but these four are the most fundamental ones for this setting. The first two—appropriation and maintenance—might be assigned an even more importance than the other two, because there is no need for monitoring and sanctioning if there are no rules, and because appropriation and maintenance may occur in the total absence of rules. However, for all practical purposes, it is not possible to imagine an entirely ruleless social setting, especially if rules are allowed to be informal in nature.

Note: Ostrom, Gardner, and Walker (1994) clearly differentiate between the appropriation and provision dilemmas in their game models of common-pool resource (CPR) situations. They use the term "provision" to encompass all replenishment and maintenance activities because this part of the CPR situation corresponds to a public good, at least for members of the user group. When they move to setting up experimental versions of this generic model, they, as the experimenters, make the rules that the participants must follow, as well as any rules concerning how those participants may select different types of monitoring and sanctioning regimes. Even in this very abstracted version of a generic CPR situation, all four of these action situations are deeply interconnected.

4. *Systematically examine categories of the IAD framework* to identify and highlight the most critical (1) actors in positions, (2) rules-in-use, (3) attributes of relevant communities, (4) types of goods involved and biophysical dynamics, (5) evaluative criteria, and (6) feedback loops and sources of learning in these focal action situations.

   A. *Appropriation*: Actors (users) may extract resource units from common-pool resource system for personal use (consumption, exchange, or production), and each of them may or may not follow rules on level, time, and technology of extraction, may or may not be closely connected to each other in a tight community, and may or may not be able to observe information on quality and quantity of resource available for use.
   B. *Maintenance*: Actors (users and/or others) may or may not contribute time, money, and/or effort to collective activities to replenish resource and/or to construct and maintain infrastructure for resource extraction, may or may not follow rules on level, time, and technology of effort, may or may not be closely connected to each other in a tight community, and may or may not be able to observe information on quality and quantity of resource available for use.
   C. *Rule-making*: External authorities and/or local actors may or may not participate in formulating formal or informal specifications of who has legitimate access to a resource system, as well as limitations on level, time, and technology of extraction.

Rule-makers may or may not be the same people as those who appropriate or maintain resources, and are generally not able to directly observe compliance with the rules they have written.

D. *Monitoring and sanctioning*: Those actors who can directly or indirectly observe appropriation and maintenance activities and determine if relevant rules have been violated and then decide whether to impose sanctions on rule violators, may or may not be same people as those who appropriate or maintain resources or who write these rules.

Notes:

- *Evaluative processes* (involving individuals, organizations, or informal groups) can take place in any of these settings, and evaluations may occur before, during, or after the making and implementation of any of the key decisions being made in each of those action situations. For some cases, these evaluations can be treated as if they take place in separate action situations, while in other cases the evaluation step is too closely associated with decision-making or implementation for such separation to be analytically useful.
- In some situations, the same set of actors may play dominant roles in all four of the core action situations. In such an "idealized" situation of a *user group* as a *self-governing community*, those who appropriate resources are also responsible for replenishing or maintaining that resource, as well as making and enforcing rules on both appropriation and maintenance, and on the way these rules are written and outcomes evaluated. Such "perfect isolation" is hard to imagine in most sectors of a modern political economy, but many of the cases considered in *Governing the Commons* provide a reasonable approximation to this convergence of the actor sets active in all four of these core action situations.

5. *Follow the information flow* in each of these focal action situations. What sources of information are available to which actors under which circumstances, and what might prevent them from using that information to change the outcomes that result?

    - *Evaluation* requires access to information, which may or may not be available to local actors or external rule-makers in a timely fashion.

- Information may or may not be available in a *timely* manner. Appropriators and those involved in maintenance activities should be able to observe short-term variation in resource availability, but some changes may occur more quickly or more abruptly than they can monitor and evaluate incoming information. Also, actors may not have extensive records on longer-term trends or on the system's viability as a whole; systemic conditions and resource availability may change more quickly than they can adjust their behavior.
- Rules tend to change more slowly than the individual choices of appropriators and those involved in maintenance. This disjuncture may lead to significant lags between the emergence of new challenges and the community's eventual response.

6. *Locate adjacent (or supplemental) action situations* that determine the contextual categories of the focal action situation, that is, outcomes of adjacent situations in which collective actors are constructed and individual incentives shaped, rules are written and collective procedures established, norms are internalized and other community attributes are determined, goods are produced and inputs for production are extracted from resource systems (that may need replenishment), and where evaluation, learning, and feedback processes occur.

Note: The term "adjacent action situations" is drawn from McGinnis (2011b), but the basic idea that there would be multiple action situations operating simultaneously was included in the IAD framework from the very beginning (see, e.g., Ostrom 1986, 1989).

- *Constitutive processes*: One important function not explicitly identified in the list above is the *construction of collective actors* who have the authority to act, or whose members act as if they have such authority. In constitutive processes, formal organizations or more informal groups capable of making a common decision are designed and/or established and responsibility is allocated to occupants of specified "positions" for actions related to appropriation, maintenance, rule-making, monitoring, sanctioning, and evaluation. This process of constitutional choice can also set limits on the types of rule changes that are acceptable, and who can participate in making such changes. These processes are typically dominated by legally defined formal authorities, with rules on what constitutes a viable organization set by both legal strictures and widespread social expectations.

- *Dispute resolution*: Action situations in which disputes among any of the actor types engaged in focal action situations are brought to some resolution. The criteria taken into account in arriving at some resolution may vary widely across situations. Actors directly involved in dispute resolution may include authorities specially designated with responsibilities for arbitration, adjudication, and so forth, as well as other authorities or social leaders who resolve disputes as part of their other roles. An especially relevant concern is whether or not these "dispute deciders" take into account the interests of the community as a whole in their evaluation of disputes arriving at disputes, or if they rely exclusively on arguments made on behalf of the parties most directly involved in that dispute.
- *Knowledge*: New scientific knowledge is typically generated by researchers not directly involved in focal activities. However, indigenous communities have access to substantial bodies of local knowledge that may or may not be consistent with current scientific findings. Either (or both) systems of knowledge may be drawn upon in evaluative settings. Scientific experts are often most influential in the rule-making process through which formal authorities set standards or impose limitations.
- *Market conditions*: Resource units extracted from a common pool may be used as inputs to production processes, consumed directly, and/or exchanged for other resources or rights. The economic value of resource units may vary widely, depending on trends in any of the markets to which these resources are connected, including markets that may be distant from the place of extraction. Consumer demand plays a critical role in all markets, but so do the decisions of producers and intermediaries.
- *Political regime changes*: Victories by new leaders or political parties or regimes may result in fundamental changes in the rules governing the types of organizations or informal groups that are authorized or allowed to make decisions regarding appropriation, maintenance, rule-making, monitoring, sanctioning, and forming new collective entities. All this may all be subject to more fundamental laws or rules determined in more formal governance settings, such as provincial or national government agencies or

international treaties. This setting tends to be dominated by public officials in normal times, but there are also situations of a more revolutionary character in which non-traditional actors wrest power through illegal means.

- *Cultural and demographic change*: Driven primarily by exogenous changes in livelihoods and cultural trends, these are unlikely to be directly manipulable by any actors, especially in the short term. In some settings, these changes may reflect subtle influences on local practices driven by longer-term tendencies driven by globalization. Religious and ethnic differences can often be used to greatly intensify the emotional flavor of otherwise mundane conflicts over access to resources.

7. *Select those adjacent action situations* that are critical for distinguishing among alternative explanations, and repeat steps 4 and 5 (and if necessary, step 6) for those action situations.

    - Analysis of many, especially smaller-scale, common-pool resource extraction regimes can be completed with little or no explicit reference to any of these supplemental action situations adjacent to the focal action situations. This was the case for most of the studies reviewed by Ostrom. The exception was the Southern California groundwater example examined in chapter 6 (see discussion below).

8. *Compare and contrast the ways these linked and nested action situations are interrelated in the processes emphasized by each of your alternative explanations*. Do the same actors write, implement, and enforce rules? How do outcomes of other action situations shape processes of information flow and evaluation in the focal action situation(s)? Which incentives or values of actors are reinforced or undermined by outcomes of these action situations?

    - In *Hardin's tragedy of the (open-access) commons*, only the appropriation and natural replenishment action situations are explicitly considered. He does not allow for effort directed toward resource maintenance or rule-making, and thus there is no need for monitoring or sanctioning. Individual appropriators may monitor resource conditions, but will often respond to lowered returns by increasing their extraction levels.

1) Hardin made reference to exogenous forces such as market pressures or demographic changes that would be included in some of these supplemental action situations.
2) Ostrom admitted that some common-pool resource systems do fall victim to the tragedy of the commons dynamic identified by Hardin. Her analysis of the four core action situations helps clarify what would be needed for either of his policy proposals to be able to successfully cope with these challenges.

- In a *centrally managed commons*, the rule-making function is undertaken by official authorities, who may write rules regarding both appropriation and maintenance. These rules are likely to be based on the recommendations of outside experts instead of those familiar with local conditions. Special monitors may be hired, which raises the problem of making sure they have the right incentives to monitor and punish rule violations, rather than accepting bribes or other inducements to overlook violations.
  1) *Any central authority* would need regular access to real-time accurate information on the extent to which resource users follow the rules enacted by this authority. Ostrom's findings suggest that *local monitors* would be needed to make externally imposed rules be effective.
  2) Central authorities are likely to be highly dependent on non-local experts for advice on setting quotas and other limits and for implementation of most monitoring and enforcement activities.

- In a *privatized commons*, appropriation and maintenance activities would be undertaken by each private owner separately, perhaps in conjunction with other owner/users. Exchange of extracted resources would be governed by contract law and other provisions of market regulation.
  1) Responsibility for monitoring and sanctioning would typically fall upon police and courts.
  2) Externally driven market dynamics would be an especially important consideration for this case.

- After extensive efforts to estimate regression and other statistical models, Ostrom concluded that all of the long and enduring institutions in her cases satisfied eight *design principles*, that is,

(1) clear resource and social boundaries, (2) broad participation in writing rules, (3) these rules were both appropriate for local conditions and had consequences that balanced costs and benefits in a way that was deemed fair by participants, (4) behavior was regularly monitored, (5) graduated sanctions were imposed for rule violations, (6) easily accessible and reasonably costly procedures were available for disputes to be resolved, (7) different tasks could be organized by multiple teams, and (8) higher authorities conveyed at least a minimal level of autonomy to local communities in the making and enforcement of rules.

- In most of the cases of long and enduring institutions for *community-based management* of common-pool resources discussed in Ostrom's *Governing the Commons*, essentially *the same set of actors is directly involved in all four focal action situations.*

Note: Don't overlook chapter 6 of *Governing the Commons*, in which Elinor Ostrom returns to the case study that was her doctoral dissertation (Ostrom 1965).

- Technically, this case does not fit the definition of a simple common-pool resource, but can be more accurately described as *local public goods*. This suggests that the design principles may apply more generally than only to situations in which some group asserts collective ownership over a specific set of resources.
- *The example of groundwater governance in Southern California involved a diverse array of organizational actors at multiple levels of aggregation. Critical contributions were made by actors operating in constitutive, judicial, scientific processes (occurring in adjacent or supplemental action situations!)*
  - Scientific experts in *USGS* clarified the danger of saltwater incursion, and the consequent need for concerted action to avoid this outcome. These efforts greatly facilitated local cooperation.
  - A new law empowered groups to establish new entities, with taxing authority, and allowed to run programs like freshwater infusion.
  - *Users used courts to impose constraints on themselves, by setting up special water districts*, which restricted use and levied taxes, and resolved disputes over details.

- Raymond Basin actors negotiated an agreement based on *mutual prescription* (proportional cutbacks), holdouts challenged in court, lost, appealed, lost again.
- West Basin Water Association established, sued in 1945, city of Hawthorne as holdout, decided upon proportional cutbacks, and courts forced holdouts to comply.
- Combined West-Central Basins District Authority formed to limit pumping, replenish water levels, inject freshwater barrier.
- *Watermaster* played critical role in all legal agreements—source of information and dispute resolution, but not enforcement or sanctioning.

- *In sum, new institutions were built by an incremental, sequential, self-transforming process of learning and joint discussions, within a supportive regime of state law (home-rule).* Scientific experts and courts often play critical roles in clarifying details and in establishing and enforcing complex agreements for water use and replenishment. Finding the right balance of small- and large-scale operations is critical.

9. *Identify the most critical steps for more detailed analysis*, by isolating components of adjacent action situations that determine the context currently in place in the focal action situation(s), and that if changed would result in fundamental changes in outcomes. But remember if you change one contextual factor in one action situation, then you must also incorporate all relevant changes in closely related action situations. (Ceteris paribus is more complicated in institutional analysis!)

- *Monitoring* turned out to play a surprisingly important role in much of Ostrom's analysis. This means that *evaluation of any policy reform cannot be complete without careful consideration of the means though which these new rules will be monitored, and who will be responsible for conducting and overseeing this monitoring.*

1) When locally constructed irrigation systems are replaced by large-scale and more technically advanced systems, the *lack of direct community involvement* in constructing and maintaining this system can undermine any sense of community ownership of that system, and thereby lead to poor perfor-

mance of technical systems, compared to smaller-scale systems requiring regular repair and maintenance.

2) Policies to restrict resource extraction in *protected areas* tended to be effective if and only if local citizens were given meaningful incentives to directly participate in the monitoring of these restrictions. This result remained relevant for different kinds of governance arrangements, suggesting that processes of monitoring may be more consequential than organizational form or the particular status of parks or protected areas.

- It may be useful to more carefully investigate interconnections between pairs or triples of core or supplemental action situations. Specifically, processes of *resource extraction and replenishment/maintenance* are very closely related, and it may be critical that the same actors are involved in both sets of activities. Otherwise, it is difficult to give those involved in the former activities the appropriate incentives to complete the latter. For example, in some cases of irrigation systems, those farmers located at the head end of the system were much less dependent on the system's maintenance than were those at the tail end of the system, and this kind of *asymmetry* must be taken into consideration in the design and operation of a sustainable irrigation system.

- *Each of these design principles can be interpreted as attributes of one or more of the core and supplemental action situations identified above.* In effect, then, these design principles imply conditions on the operation of the focal action situations as well as a few of the adjacent action situations noted above.
  1) clear boundaries would have to occur as a consequence of constitutive processes;
  2) not all forms of rule-making will include wide participation;
  3) appropriation and maintenance rules need to be congruent with local conditions and values;
  4) monitoring should be done by monitors responsible to the core users;
  5) sanctioning should be applied in a graduated fashion;
  6) evaluative processes for the resolution of disputes should be widely available and at a reasonable cost in time and effort;

7) constitutive processes should be able to be carried out relatively easily, thus generating multiple limited-task teams; and
8) the organizations that emerge from constitutive processes need to be recognized as legitimate by higher authorities.

- Subsequent research has highlighted other contributing factors that were also present in most of the cases examined by Ostrom, specifically, of *leadership*, *a shared concern for long-term outcomes*, *access to timely information*, and *trust and reciprocity norms*. These additional requirements can be grounded in core and supplementary processes if
  1) effective leadership is demonstrated in all action situations, a condition that could be described as distributed leadership;
  2) long-term concerns are incorporated in dispute resolution and other evaluative processes;
  3) information is available in a timely fashion for all monitoring and evaluative processes; and
  4) trust and reciprocity norms are reinforced by participation in most or all of these processes.

- Many of the conditions in Ostrom's list of eight design principles tend to be more easily realized in *tightly-knit communities of users whose livelihoods are critically dependent on the continued availability of particular resources* than they can be in larger and more technically complex sectors of a modern political economy. It may well be that these unusual cases enabled Ostrom to identify these underlying patterns, which might have been more difficult to isolate in more complex settings.
  1) For example, in close-knit dependent communities, it may be very difficult for rule violations to remain unnoticed, and social exclusion can be a powerful disincentive to continuing to commit these violations. Members of resource-dependent groups tend to automatically adopt the long-term perspective and leadership/stewardship imperatives that Hardin presumed could only be provided by market discipline or dispassionate social planners.
  2) Extension of these conditions to highly technical systems cannot be assumed to be easily accomplished. Instead, each design principle (or facilitating condition) would need to be

explicitly interpreted in terms of specific aspects of that particular policy sector. For example, natural leaders are likely to emerge from the dense social interactions of tightly-knit communities, and these interactions can be effective generators of trust and reciprocity norms. In other policy sectors, identification of leaders and development of basic trust among competing stakeholders may prove to be very difficult and contentious tasks.

- These correspondences suggest that the Design Principles may turn out to be only the tip of the iceberg. *Each core action situation is associated with one or more of the design principles, but only some of the supplemental processes are covered in that list.* This implies that some characteristics of core or supplemental processes might also be stipulated as having important effects on sustainability. Further investigation into these processes may provide a tentative guide for identification of other critical factors.

10. Draw upon principles of research design or evaluative research to *select cases* for further analysis by whatever *methods* are best suited to that purpose. *Follow relevant conventions when writing up your conclusions*; DO NOT describe this process of discovery in detail.

- Ostrom's analysis was based on *multiple methods*: a systematic comparison of existing case studies, supplemented by new field research as well as innovative use of game models and laboratory experiments (see Poteete, Janssen, and Ostrom 2010). But, as noted above, the set of case studies considered was dominated by relatively small, resource-dependent communities.
- *Governing the Commons* is located within a broader research program that occupied Elinor Ostrom throughout her long and distinguished career, and that this research program has by no means reached the end of its productive life. Researchers working in this tradition continue to make important new contributions, related to the following factors.
    - The strongest evidence comes from studies with clear research designs allowed for direct comparisons between similar cases. Among the best examples are:

        - Comparisons of agency- and farmer-managed irrigation systems in Nepal (Lam 1998).
        - Comparisons of protected forests in similar ecological settings but managed under different types of property rights (Chhatre and Agrawal 2008).
        - Remote images of the boundaries of protected areas, some of which show sharp demarcations between ecological conditions under different regimes and other boundaries that are more difficult to see (Ostrom and Nagendra 2006).
    - Different combinations of biophysical conditions, cultural predilections, and rules-in-use will construct fundamentally different settings for all of the key processes of appropriation, maintenance, rule-making, and monitoring and sanctioning, as well as the supplemental action situations identified above.

- All focal and supplemental action situations are *dynamic*, and the feedback processes most critical for each remain a promising subject for future analysis. In particular, more attention could be devoted to understanding processes of *learning* at the individual, group, and organizational levels and their interactions. Of particular importance is consideration of the *time scales* at which endogenous changes and exogenous shocks operate in dynamic resource systems.
- Any investigation of all relevant *threats to sustainability* posed by changes in any of these adjacent action situations would have to be more elaborate. Each of these supplementary action situations are driven by dynamic forces unrelated to local changes. Prices for natural resources are notoriously dependent on the vagaries of distant market forces, national political authorities often have the power and the incentive to ignore or displace locally formulated arrangements, previously isolated regions may, through no fault of their own, become enmeshed in processes of multinational business expansion or geopolitical competition among global powers, and the multifaceted phenomenon of globalization can disrupt long-established traditions of social, cultural, economic, and political arrangements.
- When analyzing proposals to cope with the complexities of *global climate change*, Ostrom (2012) emphasized that many different positive and negative externalities can be realized at all levels of aggregation from neighborhoods to the world as a whole. Thus,

groups at all levels need to be involved in devising and monitoring practices that can contribute to this overall effort. A full representation of the detailed structure of such a multilevel and polycentric package of policy proposals remains a topic for future research.

Treating the Design Principles and IAD as an Inexhaustible Source of Useful Questions

I would like to conclude this chapter by highlighting one of my most gratifying moments as a scholar, which was triggered by reading little more than a passing reference to a personal communication I made to Elinor Ostrom, as a comment on a draft of one of her papers. The paper in question ended up making it into the final chapter of Ostrom's most extended presentation of her foundational theoretical perspective in *Understanding Institutional Diversity*. I would like to quote Elinor Ostrom in some detail on our exchange on this topic.

> At a recent colloquium where the design principles were discussed, Mike McGinnis made an interesting observation drawing broadly on the work of Herbert Simon. He noted that Simon has repeatedly stressed the complexity of designing humanly engineered systems whether they be computers, road networks, or institutional arrangements. In *The Sciences of the Artificial* (1981), Simon specifically argues that no humanly designed, complex system can be fully planned to achieve optimal performance. Rather, he stressed that all complex systems must be built up from simpler components. Simon does point out that where one begins a search to improve the performance of a complex system, however, makes a substantial difference in the quality and speed of the search process (see also H. Simon, 1972, 1995, 1999).
>
> My own conclusion related to the impossibility of doing a *complete* analysis of a complex, adaptive system is, of course, strongly influenced by the work of Simon, as well as our research on coupled social-ecological systems. So, one way of thinking about the practical implications of the design principles is as a beginning point for conducting a broad search for appropriate means of solving problems. One can translate the design principles into a series of questions that could be asked when thinking about improving the sustainability of a common-pool resource system. For local appropriators, a rough translation of the first six design principles into a set of initial questions would be:

> 1. How can we better define the boundaries of this resource, and of the individuals who are using it, so as to make clear who is authorized to harvest and where harvesting is authorized?
> 2. How can we clarify the relationship between the benefits received and the contributions to the costs of sustaining this system?
> 3. How can we enhance the participation of those involved in making key decisions about this system?
> 4. Who is monitoring this system and do they face appropriate incentives given the challenge of monitoring?
> 5. What are the sanctions we are authorizing and can they be adjusted so that someone who makes an error or a small rule infraction is sufficiently warned so as to ensure longer-term compliance without our trying to impose unrealistic sanctions?
> 6. What local and regional mechanisms exist to resolve conflicts arising over the use of this resource?
>
> The seventh and eighth principles are targeted at a higher level of governance. They could be translated as:
>
> 7. Are there functional and creative efforts by local appropriators to craft effective stewardship mechanisms for local resources that should be recognized?
> 8. How do we create a multiple-layer, polycentric system that can be dynamic, adaptive, and effective over time?
>
> These are not, of course, the only questions appropriators and officials should ask in an effective design process, but they can be thought of as a good beginning. (Ostrom 2005, 270–71; original emphasis)

I am proud to report that these questions had their origins in a memo I wrote to Elinor Ostrom in the form of comments on an earlier version of the analysis she presents in this book. She changed the detailed wording of some of the questions I sent her, but I fondly remember her expression of gratitude for helping her come up with a better way to encapsulate this part of the complex argument she was trying to make. When she and Vincent Ostrom were alive, we exchanged those kinds of memos on a routine basis, and I sorely miss those exchanges.

Finally, I leave it as an exercise for the reader to translate these questions into forms best suited for application to the factors they deem most important for understanding the research puzzle or policy concern that serves as the focus on their own work. I hope the steps outlined in this chapter will prove as helpful in their work as they have been in mine.

Note

An earlier (and much shorter) version of this chapter was prepared for distribution to graduate students in Political Science Y673, dated August 25, 2012, and posted on the author's personal website. It has not been previously published in print. This version was revised on July 4, 2016.

References

Chhatre, Ashwini, and Arun Agrawal. 2008. "Forest Commons and Local Enforcement." *Proceedings of the National Academy of Sciences* 105(36): 13286–91.

Cole, Daniel H., Graham Epstein, and Michael D. McGinnis. 2014. "Toward a New Institutional Analysis of Social-Ecological Systems (NIASES): Combining Elinor Ostrom's IAD and SES Frameworks." Indiana Legal Studies Research Paper No. 299; Indiana University, Bloomington, School of Public & Environmental Affairs Research Paper No. 2490999. Available at SSRN: http://ssrn.com/abstract=2490999.

Hardin, Garrett. 1968. "The Tragedy of the Commons." *Science* 162(3859): 1243–48.

Kiser, Larry L., and Elinor Ostrom. 1982. "The Three Worlds of Action: A Metatheoretical Synthesis of Institutional Approaches." In *Strategies of Political Inquiry*, edited by Elinor Ostrom, 179–222. Beverly Hills, CA: Sage.

Lam, Wai Fung. 1998. *Governing Irrigation Systems in Nepal: Institutions, Infrastructure, and Collective Action*. Oakland, CA: ICS Press.

McGinnis, Michael D. 2011a. "An Introduction to IAD and the Language of the Ostrom Workshop: A Simple Guide to a Complex Framework." *Policy Studies Journal* 39(1): 163–77. Updated version at http://php.indiana.edu/~mcginnis/iad_guide.pdf.

———. 2011b. "Networks of Adjacent Action Situations in Polycentric Governance." *Policy Studies Journal* 39(1): 45–72.

Oakerson, Ronald J. 1992. "Analyzing the Commons: A Framework." In *Making the Commons Work: Theory, Practice, and Policy*, edited by Daniel W. Bromley et al., 41–59. San Francisco, CA: ICS Press.

Ostrom, Elinor. 1965. *Public Entrepreneurship: A Case Study in Ground Water Basin Management*. PhD diss., University of California, Los Angeles.

———. 1986. "Multiorganizational Arrangements and Coordination: An Application of Institutional Analysis." In *Guidance, Control, and Evaluation in the Public Sector*, edited by F. X. Kaufmann, G. Majone, and V. Ostrom, 495–510. Berlin and New York: de Gruyter.

———. 1989. "Microconstitutional Change in Multiconstitutional Political Systems." *Rationality and Society* 1(1): 11–50.

———. 1990. *Governing the Commons: The Evolution of Institutions for Collective Action.* New York: Cambridge University Press.

———. 2005. *Understanding Institutional Diversity.* Princeton, NJ: Princeton University Press.

———. 2007. "Institutional Rational Choice: An Assessment of the Institutional Analysis and Development Framework." In *Theories of the Policy Process*, 2nd ed., edited by Paul A. Sabatier, 21–64. Boulder, CO: Westview Press.

———. 2010. "Beyond Markets and States: Polycentric Governance of Complex Economic Systems." *American Economic Review* 100(3): 641–72.

———. 2011. "Background on the Institutional Analysis and Development Framework." *Policy Studies Journal* 39(1): 7–27.

———. 2012. "Nested Externalities and Polycentric Institutions: Must We Wait for Global Solutions to Climate Change before Taking Actions at Other Scales?" *Economic Theory* 49(2): 353–69.

Ostrom, Elinor, Roy Gardner, and James Walker, with Arun Agrawal, William Blomquist, Edella Schlager, and Shui-Yan Tang. 1994. *Rules, Games, and Common-Pool Resources*. Ann Arbor: University of Michigan Press.

Ostrom, Elinor, and Harini Nagendra. 2006. "Insights on Linking Forests, Trees, and People from the Air, on the Ground, and in the Laboratory." *Proceedings of the National Academy of Sciences* 103(51): 19224–31.

Ostrom, Elinor, and Vincent Ostrom. 2004. "The Quest for Meaning in Public Choice." *American Journal of Economics and Sociology* 63(1): 105–47.

Poteete, Amy, Marco Janssen, and Elinor Ostrom. 2010. *Working Together: Collective Action, the Commons, and Multiple Methods in Practice.* Princeton, NJ: Princeton University Press.

Simon, Herbert A. 1972. "Theories of Bounded Rationality." In *Decision and Organization: A Volume in Honor of Jacob Marschak*, edited by C. B. McGuire and Roy Radner, 161–76. Amsterdam: North Holland.

———. 1981. *The Sciences of the Artificial*. 2nd ed. Cambridge, MA: MIT Press.

———. 1995. "Near Decomposability and Complexity: How a Mind Resides in a Brain." In *The Mind, the Brain, and Complex Adaptive Systems*, edited by Harold J. Morowitz and Jerome L. Singer, 25–44. Reading, MA: Addison-Wesley.

———. 1999. "The Potlatch between Political Science and Economics." In *Competition and Cooperation: Conversations with Nobelists about Economics and Political Science*, edited by James Alt, Margaret Levi, and Elinor Ostrom, 112–19. New York: Russell Sage Foundation.

PART II

Polycentricity in Regional Public Economies

5

Public Economy Organization and Service Delivery

Elinor Ostrom and Vincent Ostrom

New York City's recent financial plight dramatizes the problem many cities have in financing the delivery of urban public services. Changes in institutional arrangements that may increase the capacity of large center cities to finance and deliver an efficient and equitable level of public services are being considered.

Some proposals ask the federal government to assume a larger proportion of the financing, particularly welfare and other social services. Others recommend that the financial base of center cities be extended through governmental consolidation. Still others propose dramatically different reforms including an increase in government fragmentation by creating small-scale units of government within the center city itself.

Consideration of these and many other proposals is particularly important for those concerned about the future of Southeastern Michigan (SEM). Detroit has recently faced considerable financial difficulty. The level of governmental fragmentation is high in the metropolitan area. As of 1972, there were 241 local governmental units in the three-county metropolitan area. Eighty-eight different municipalities served a population of more than four million people—or one general-purpose government for each 47,768 residents. However, the variation in size of local governmental units was considerable. Thirty-four of the municipalities served communities of less than 5,000 residents. Twenty-five municipalities served communities that ranged from 5,000 to 24,999 residents, and 27 municipalities served communities with more than 25,000 residents (1972 Census of Governments, vol. 1, table 19).

Decision makers in the Detroit area are faced with the consideration of changing the organization of governmental units as one means of increasing both the efficiency and equity of urban services delivery. However, a key question is whether a decrease (or an increase) in governmental fragmentation will affect financial capability to deliver equitable and efficient urban services.

The question cannot be answered without a well-developed and empirically based theory of institutional analysis and design. For years, conventional theories have been based on untested hypotheses about the relationship between the size and fragmentation of local governmental units on the one hand, and the efficient and equitable delivery of urban services on the other. This has been challenged in the past twenty years by a growing number of economists and political scientists who have made considerable advances both theoretically and empirically. Their work has not yet produced a completed, accepted, and empirically validated theory of institutional analysis and design. The basic elements have, however, been worked out, and considerable empirical investigation supports hypotheses derived from this theoretical tradition.

In this chapter, we will first provide a basic overview of this developing theory of institutional analysis. Any theory has its own language, and to understand it, one must understand the basic terms. Thus, we shall first define and discuss some elemental concepts that are essential for understanding the approach. Then we will examine some opportunities and problems of complex structures, and, last, examine some implications of this approach for the SEM area.

The Nature of Goods

Within the last two decades, an extensive literature has developed on the characteristics that distinguish public or collective goods from private or individual ones. *Exclusion* and *jointness of use* are two essential defining characteristics, and our discussion shall use them to distinguish among four types of goods and services.

Exclusion

Exclusion has long been identified as a necessary characteristic for goods and services to be supplied under market conditions. Exclusion occurs when potential consumers can be denied goods or services unless they meet the terms and conditions of a vendor. Conversely, a consumer is at liberty to refuse to do business with any particular vendor, and to enter into transactions with a vendor of his choice. Where exclusion is feasible, a consumer can maintain an arm's-length relationship with vendors or producers of private goods and services. If both consumer and vendor agree, goods or services are supplied at a price. A quid pro quo exchange occurs: the consumer acquires the good and the seller acquires the value specified.

Where exclusion is infeasible, anyone can derive benefits from the good as long as nature or the efforts of others supply it. The air we breathe can be viewed as a good supplied by nature where exclusion is infeasible. A view of a building—whether seen as a good or a bad—is supplied by the efforts of others and is not subject to exclusion in normal circumstances. Where exclusion is infeasible, a consumer will not have the option to maintain an arm's-length relationship and bears whatever advantage or disadvantage is associated with events that can be conceived as either goods or bads.

Where exclusion is feasible, consumers face the problems of the marketplace. If they have the resources necessary, they may obtain the good in exchange for a price. Moreover, those with few monetary resources are less able to influence production decisions about exclusionary goods than those with greater monetary resources. If tastes are similar, consumers are apt to find goods readily available. Where exclusion is difficult or impossible, private entrepreneurs will usually not supply such goods because they cannot derive revenue from doing so, and consumers must find alternative ways of obtaining them.

Jointness of Use or Consumption

Another attribute of goods or services pertains to what we shall call *jointness of use or consumption*. It exists when consumption by one person does not preclude the use or consumption of a good by another. But where the use of a good *does* foreclose its use (or enjoyment) by others, we may say that consumption is completely "subtractable." A piece of bread, for example, when consumed by one person is not available for consumption by another, that is, it is completely "subtractable."

Yet few, if any, joint-consumption goods are perfectly nonsubtractable. Most joint-consumption goods are instead subject to *partial* subtractability. At certain thresholds of supply, the use or consumption of a good by anyone subtracts *in part* from its use and enjoyment by others. With increased demand, and given thresholds of supply, congestion begins to occur. Each further increase impairs the use of that good for each person in the community of users. Highways, for example, become subject to congestion where the addition of more motorists causes delays and inconveniences. Fire protection, another joint-consumption good, may deteriorate when a finite firefighting force experiences a high rate of demand.

A Typology Using Exclusion and Jointness of Use

Both exclusion and jointness of use are independent characteristics that vary in degree rather than being all-or-none characteristics. Both characteristics of goods can be arrayed in relation to one another as shown in Table 5.1. For purposes of analysis, both characteristics have been arrayed into two classes showing their extreme values. Jointness of consumption is arrayed into *individual uses* that are highly subtractable and *joint uses* that are nonsubtractable, or where one person's use interferes with others' use. Exclusion is shown as being either *feasible* or *infeasible*. Exclusion is technically infeasible where no practical technique exists for either packaging a good or controlling access by a potential user. Exclusion may also be economically infeasible where the costs of exclusion are too high to justify the effort.

By using these two attributes arrayed in a simple matrix, four types of goods can be described: private goods, toll goods, common-pool resources, and public goods. Market arrangements can be used to deliver either private or toll goods, that is, where exclusion is feasible. In the case of toll goods, a price is charged for access, but the good is used in common. With toll goods, special problems arise from jointness of use, as in a theater, where the conduct of one user may add to or detract from the enjoyment of others. The value of the good depends both on the quality of the good produced and upon the way it is used by a community of consumers.

In the case of common-pool resources, exclusion may be difficult or infeasible in the sense that many users or consumers cannot be denied access. But use by any one consumer precludes use of that fixed quantity of good by others. Each pumper in a groundwater basin, for example, consumes water that is alternative to its use by all other pumpers. Each fish or ton of fish taken by any one fisherman precludes any other fisherman from taking those same fish. Yet no basis may exist for excluding fishermen from access to fish in the ocean. Once appropriated, water can be dealt with as a toll good supplied to those having access to a distribution system, or fish can be dealt with as a private good.

Table 5.1. Types of goods

Exclusion	*Individual use*	*Joint use*
Feasible	Private goods: Bread, shoes, automobiles, haircuts, books, and so forth	Toll goods: Theaters, nightclubs, telephone service, toll roads, cable TV, library, and so forth
Infeasible	Common-pool resources: Water pumped from a groundwater basin, fish taken from an ocean, crude oil extracted from an oil pool	Public goods: Peace and security of a community, national defense, mosquito abatement, air pollution control, fire protection, weather forecasts, public TV, and so forth

The broad range of services rendered by governmental agencies may cover all different types of goods and services. The food supplied to schoolchildren at no charge is an example of a private good. It is potentially subject to exclusion and involves no jointness of use. But its consumption may create *consumption externalities* that have the characteristics of a public good. Most government services are of the public good, toll good, or common-pool resource variety. Public goods are rarely supplied without access to some instrumentality (such as a government), but this is not necessarily the case for toll goods and common-pool resources. Variations among these different types of goods affect the types of problems consumers face.

Moving from a simple division of private and public goods to a typology involving four types of goods increases our understanding of the range of problems encountered by users. For some analysis, this increase in the complexity of conceptual analysis is all that is necessary to increase our explanatory powers. However, two other attributes of goods are important for understanding some public sector problems. These are measurement and coproduction.

Measurement

Since most private goods can be packaged, they are usually relatively easy to measure; comparisons and computations are easy to make. However, even some private goods are difficult to measure. The services of a psychiatrist, for example, are usually consumed individually and exclusion is feasible. However, such services are difficult to measure. Since someone pays a price, we can compute the "value" of the output by adding together the fees so charged, but the product is usually defined in terms of the hours of activity. This measure is like using the total number of hours of labor by a wheat farmer to calculate the value of the product instead of the number of bushels of wheat produced.

While the difficulty of measuring output varies among private goods and services, the problem grows immensely in regard to the other types of goods. Qualitative measures such as road surface condition and traffic delay rates can be used to measure important characteristics of goods subject to joint consumption. Qualitative measures cannot be added in the same way as quantitative measures. One cannot simply add up traffic delay rates for an entire metropolitan area like one can add up total bushels of wheat produced. One must compute averages and/or measures of dispersion. Averages mask considerable variation in quality. Measures of dispersion provide information about the extent of variation, but do not allow one to get some measure of the total good produced.

Consequently, no simple calculations can be made to measure the output of public goods. One is forced to rely on estimates of total output derived from multiple indicators and proxy measures. By using several indicators for public good output, weak measures of performance can be developed even though direct measurement of output is not feasible. Some of the indicators of performance may relate to units of input (i.e., number of teachers with university degrees, teacher-pupil ratios, number of hours devoted to particular tasks, and so forth). Such indicators can be controlled by those who allocate resource input. Relying upon any *single* indicator of performance that is a measure of input means that consumers are totally dependent for measures of performance on actions that producers can control. If the input is not directly related to desired output, the performance rating could be high, but the "real" quality of the product may be very low.

Coproduction

The dominant model of the production process is a factory where input factors are combined to produce output. Only the production firm is involved in making goods. Hence, output occurs without efforts on the part of consumers. This model is appropriate for thinking about producing a wide variety of goods. However, it is not an appropriate model for thinking about the production of many services, particularly those in the public sector. Many services require high levels of coproduction. Coproduction may be defined as the inputs and activities of citizens that affect the quality of services delivered. Without the participation of children and their parents, schools cannot educate. Fire prevention requires that citizens adopt strategies in their everyday life that reduce the danger of fire, report fires when they occur, and attempt to reduce loss by taking the right actions at the time of a fire. Crime prevention depends as much on citizen actions as it does on police actions. Little can be done about crime or suspicious circumstances if they are not reported.

Transferring the factory model to the production of services in the public sector adversely affects the level of coproduced services. Thus, when individuals believe that fire or police departments are solely responsible for fire or crime, then consumers make less investment in their own activities and pay a disproportionately high cost as a consequence. Institutional arrangements that decrease individual sense of responsibility for what occurs also reduce the level of coproduction undertaken by consumers (Newman 1972). As we will discuss in a later section, many consumer problems in the public sector stem from a failure to recognize the importance of coproduction.

Attributes of Goods and Their Consequences

Goods that (1) are subject to joint use or consumption, (2) are not amenable to exclusion, (3) are difficult to measure, and (4) require large elements of coproduction pose serious problems in human organization. If a pure public good is supplied by nature or the efforts of others, all are free to take advantage of the good since no one can be excluded from its enjoyment. A cost-minimizing individual is motivated to take advantage of whatever is freely available and will not contribute a proportionate share of the effort to supply a pure public good. So long as the rules are strictly voluntary, some individuals will hold out or act as free riders, and if some are successful, others will follow suit. Voluntary efforts will *fail* in the supply of public goods. In small groups, individuals may account for each other's efforts and apply social coercion so that each person assumes a share of the burden. But large groups are less successful in coping with the provision of public goods shared by a whole community. Each person's share of the total cost may seem so insignificant that each can hold out with greater impunity. Thus, recourse to coercion by levying taxes to prevent holdouts is more important in larger groups than in smaller, face-to-face ones.

Coercive sanctions are necessary for the operation of a public economy if it is to produce and deliver a wide variety of goods and services. But coercion and governmental organization do not guarantee the delivery of optimal amounts of public goods and services. Instruments of coercion can be used to deprive those not in power and make them worse off rather than better off. Governmental institutions permit majorities to impose decisions on those in the minority. Majority decisions can at times represent significant costs to the minority. And, at times, well-organized minorities can dominate governmental decisions and impose costs on the majority. Governmental institutions can become instruments of tyranny where the powerful dominate the allocation of goods in a society to the detriment of others.

The Organization of Public Economies in Metropolitan Areas

Nonexclusion and joint consumption, when coupled with difficulty of measurement and the need for coproduction, pose substantial problems for organizing public economies in metropolitan areas. Given the wide diversity of preferences of different individuals living in metropolitan areas as well as the variety of different goods, it is not an easy task to devise patterns of organization to surmount the difficulties discussed above.

The most important difficulty occurs in organizing the consumption side related to public goods. Governments, like households, are consumers of public goods and should be viewed generally as *collective-consumption units*. We will first discuss the problems of organizing effective collective-consumption units. Next we will turn to a discussion of ways of organizing *production units* including both governmental and private agencies. A particular governmental unit may simultaneously be both a collective-consumption unit and a production unit. Or, alternatively, a particular government may operate only as a collective-consumption unit and contract with private firms or other governments to produce public goods for its citizens.

Collective-Consumption Units

In the organization of collective-consumption units, arrangements need to be made for levying assessments, taxes, or user charges on beneficiaries in order to supply funds for jointly used goods or services and to avoid the problem of the holdout refusing to pay for benefits received. For example, some forms of private organizations have the authority to levy compulsory assessments on their members. Homeowners' improvement associations, condominiums, and some cooperatives are often organized so that anyone buying a house in a subdivision or a unit in an apartment complex is required in their deed to become and remain members so long as they own the house or apartment. The bylaws of homeowners' improvement associations or condominiums provide for the election officers to act on behalf of members. These bylaws usually authorize the levy of assessments as an equivalent of a tax to provide joint services and facilities used in common by the residents.

Each person acquiring property in the subdivision or condominium voluntarily agrees to pay assessments and be bound by the terms of the bylaws as a part of the purchase contract. All other purchasers are required to do so as well. With unanimity about the appropriateness of bylaws and their assessing authority assured, no single resident can hold out and derive benefits from joint endeavors without paying a proportionate share of the costs. When effectively organized, homeowners' improvement associations, housing cooperatives, and condominiums can provide police protection, recreation services, public works, and other benefits for their member-consumers.

Where property rights have already been vested, and a group desires to procure services for their benefit, the problem of dealing with potential holdouts usually requires some form of governmental organization, such as a municipal corporation or a special public service district, as a substitute for the unanimous consent of property owners or residents. A large number of special districts have been organized in SEM including the Huron-Clinton Metropolitan Authority, the Southeastern Michigan Transportation Authority, and a number of hospital, water, sanitation, and soil conservation districts. An alternative might be the creation of a special assessment or improvement district within an established unit of government to finance a special service for a particular neighborhood or community of potential beneficiaries. Each of these public instrumentalities has the authority, under the terms of its charter, to tax and employ criminal sanctions to enforce its rules and regulations.

The problems of measuring public goods must also be considered. Where the income received for selling a private good conveys information about the demand for that good, taxes collected under the threat of coercion say little about the demand for a public good or service. It indicates only that taxpayers would rather pay taxes than go to jail. Obviously, an alternative mechanism must be created; something that will articulate and aggregate consumer demands into collective choices that reflect their preferences for a quantity and/or quality of public goods or services.

An appropriately constituted collective-consumption unit would include within its jurisdiction most of the relevant beneficiaries who share a common interest in the joint good or service, and would exclude those who do not. The collective-consumption unit would be empowered to make decisions without requiring unanimity, in order to eliminate holdouts. It would hold a limited monopoly on the *consumption side*.

Decisions about how to organize collective-consumption units may best be thought of as constitutional decisions. While we frequently think of constitutional decisions involving only nation-states and occurring infrequently, constitutional decision making about collective-consumption units in metropolitan areas is an ongoing process. Charter revision committees and state legislatures frequently make constitutional-level decisions about the voting rules to be used, the form of representation, allowable taxes, and tax rates. Such rules provide the mechanisms for articulating demand when market mechanisms are not available for translating individual demands into decisions about the level of services to be provided.

All constitutional decision making involves some level of conflict. Since individual preferences differ, it is impossible to design collective-consumption units that can operate without generating conflict. In fact, a collective decision-making unit with procedural rules that enable conflict to be easily articulated will probably operate more effectively in the long run than one that suppresses it. Citizen-consumers gain a voice through conflict. Markets can operate with much articulated conflict because of the alternatives available to consumers. Collective-consumption units make decisions that jointly affect all those within the unit. Unless all happen to agree in their preferences for services, some will be disappointed by the decisions made.

Production Units

Production units put together the factors of production-yielding goods and services. Production units require a manager to assume entrepreneurial responsibility to bring together factors of production, organize them, and monitor the performance of a production team.

Table 5.2. Collective-consumption units and production units in a public economy

Collective-consumption unit	*Production unit*
Generally, a government that aggregates and articulates the demands of its constituents	May be a unit of government; a private, profit-making firm; a not-for-profit institution; or a voluntary association
Has coercive power to obtain funds to pay for public services and to regulate consumption patterns	Aggregates factors of production and produces goods to the specification of a collective-consumption unit
Pays producers for delivering public goods	Receives payment from collective-consumption unit for delivering public goods
Receives complaints and monitors performance of production unit	Supplies information to collective-consumption unit about costs and production possibilities

Organizing consumption in a public economy can be distinguished from organizing the production. We refer to the one as "provision"; the other as "production" (V. Ostrom, Tiebout, and Warren 1961). Some general characteristics of collective-consumption units and production units are summarized in Table 5.2.

A collective-consumption unit may supply a public good or service through its own production unit. In this case, the collective-consumption and production unit would serve the same population. Yet the constitution of the two units is essentially separable. The chief executive or city council representing the collective-consumption unit bargains with managers of production units (i.e., police chiefs, bureau heads, and so forth) to secure an appropriate supply of public goods and services. Newspapers are filled with accounts of such negotiations. They frequently stress the conflict of interest between production units and those who represent the interests of citizens as consumers. Nevertheless, this is a common occurrence, typified by a municipality with its own police, fire, or street-maintenance department.

As an alternative to organizing its own production unit, a collective-consumption unit might contract with a private vendor. In that case, public officials would translate decisions about the quantity or quality of public goods or services into specifications. These would then be used to secure bids from potential vendors, state the terms and conditions for contractual arrangements, and establish standards for assessing performance. The collective-consumption unit would also need to employ its own manager as a purchasing agent. He would receive information about costs and production possibilities from potential vendors, negotiate and contract with vendors, receive service complaints from consumers, and monitor vendors' performance in delivering services. The collective-consumption unit would operate as a "provider" or "buyer" of the service; and the private vendor as the "producer" or "supplier." A variety of municipal services in the United States, including street sweeping, snow removal, solid waste collection and disposal, fire and police protection, engineering services, planning services, and construction of public works, among others, are supplied by private vendors.

A third option is to establish standards of service that apply to all residents of a community and let each household decide which private vendor should supply the service. A number of vendors may be franchised, or anyone who wished to do business under the terms and conditions specified by the collective-consumption unit might be allowed to conduct a business. Solid waste collection is a good example. These services are highly individualized and possess only a limited degree of joint consumption, readily taken care of by applying common standards to all households and vendors.

Voucher systems represent a fourth option. By collecting taxes, one assures that each contributes his proportionate share of the burden. A voucher is then made available to each household so that it can decide among alternative producers and service packages. If applied to educational services, for example, a voucher would be issued for each eligible person. Decisions about the type of school and curriculum would be left to the family rather than to school authorities alone. Services amenable to voucher arrangements have characteristics associated with private and toll goods where others are also benefited by individual consumption. Community contributions to each individual's education are justified by this broader benefit. Vouchers have been used for housing (rent-supplement vouchers), health services (Medicaid can be considered a form of health voucher), and for food (food stamps). These services, while usually considered a private good, are like education in that others may benefit from consumption externalities.

As a fifth possibility, a collective-consumption unit could also contract with a production unit, organized by a different unit of government. Many municipalities, acting as collective-consumption units, contract with other municipalities—or some other unit of government—to supply, for example, police services, fire services, water storage and transmission services, specialized educational services, and library services. More than two-thirds of the citizens served in the Detroit Metro Water Department in 1977, for example, lived in communities that have chosen not to produce their own water and contract with the Water Board. (The pricing policies of the Detroit Water Department are discussed in detail in Andrea Long's chapter in this volume.)

A sixth way of organizing production occurs when a collective-consumption unit relies upon its own production unit or bureau to supply some components of a service, but relies upon other consumption and production units for others. Its own production unit may draw on other producers to supply it with factors of production, serve as a purchasing agent to procure and monitor the delivery of supplemental services, or function as a joint producer supplying a mix of services rendered by the joint effort of multiple production teams.

Options for obtaining public services are summarized in Table 5.3.

Public Service Industries

As we consider the options for organizing collective-consumption and production units, a number of possibilities become apparent. Each citizen-consumer is not served by "the government," but, rather, by a variety of public service industries, each composed of collective-consumption units serving as providers. Production units serve as suppliers for some types of closely related public goods or services, jointly consumed by people in a community.

Such a system may have many autonomous units of government that overlap substantially among multiple levels of government. Several private enterprises and voluntary associations may function as integral parts of public service industries. Each citizen-consumer participates in multiple consumption units organized around diverse communities of interest through overlapping levels of government, and is served by an array of different public and private producing units supplying any particular bundle of public goods or services.

We can then think of the public sector being composed of many public service industries including police, education, water, fire protection, welfare, health service, transportation, and so forth. The government component in some industries (the police, for example) is proportionately larger

Table 5.3. Options for obtaining public services

A government that serves as a collective-consumption unit may obtain the desired public goods by:	*Example*
Operating its own production unit	A city with its own fire or police department
Contracting with a private firm	A city that contracts with a private firm for snow removal, street repair, or traffic-light maintenance
Establishing standards of service and letting each consumer select a private vendor and purchase service	A city that licenses taxis or refuse collection firms
Issuing vouchers to families and permitting them to purchase service from any authorized supplier	A jurisdiction that issues food stamps, rent vouchers, or education vouchers, or operates a Medicaid program
Contracts with another government unit	A city that purchases tax assessment and collection services from a county government unit, sewage treatment from a special sanitary district, and special vocational education services from a school board in an adjacent city
Produces some services with its own unit, and procures other services from other overlapping jurisdictions and from private firms	A city with its own police patrol force that purchases laboratory services from the county sheriff, joins with several adjacent communities to pay for a joint dispatching service, and pays a private ambulance firm to provide emergency medical transportation

than others, such as health services or transportation. But most public service industries have important private components.

Each industry is characterized by distinctive production technologies and types of services rendered. These permit operational arrangements to be coordinated within an industry, and allow for substantial independence between industries. The water industry, for example, is based on technologies that facilitate collaboration among many agencies operating at different levels of government and among both public and private interests. The technologies in the water industry are easily distinguishable from the police or the education industry. A water industry serving any particular area normally includes large-scale water production agencies like the US Corps of Engineers, which operates dams and large water-storage facilities; intermediate producers like metropolitan water districts and county water authorities, which operate large aqueducts and intermediate storage facilities; and municipal water departments, water service districts, mutual water companies, or private water utility companies that operate terminal storage facilities and retail distribution systems. The quality and cost of water delivered at the tap, as well as the facilities available for recreation, navigation, flood control, and related uses will depend on the joint operation of many different governments, agencies, and firms functioning in a water industry.

Some Opportunities of a Complex Structure

Conventional wisdom alleges that overlapping jurisdiction leads to wasteful and inefficient duplication of functions. Thus, presumably, efficiency can be increased by eliminating overlapping government jurisdictions. Yet we know that efficiency can be realized in a market economy only if a number of firms serve the same market; overlapping service areas and duplicate facilities are necessary for the maintenance of competitive forces.

Can similar forces operate in a public economy? If they can, they would need to be coordinated through patterns of interorganizational arrangements rather than patterns of hierarchical control alone. The structure of interorganizational arrangements may create important economic opportunities and have elements of self-regulation. We will discuss some of these opportunities before turning to a discussion of some of the problems involved in complex structures.

Obtaining the Advantage of Diverse Scales for Consumption and Production

In a world where goods subject to joint consumption vary from household size to global proportions, it is necessary to provide collective-consumption and production units of different sizes, thus realizing what is called "diverse economies-of-scale." Tastes for public goods, like those for private goods, vary considerably. Some people like to live in neighborhoods where the streets are constantly filled with activity. Others prefer relatively quiet streets devoted only to low-density residential use. Some wish to invest heavily in sidewalks and streets. Others desire to live in areas without sidewalks and minimal investment in local roads. Some like brightly lit streets, while others do not. For diverse preferences to be achieved, radically different production strategies of local public goods are required. The creation of a very large city that attempts to provide a uniform set of local public goods or services throughout its domain imposes high deprivation costs on all those whose preferences do not match the "uniform standard" applied.

Where heterogeneous preferences for public services exist, advantage can be gained by having relatively small collective-consumption units. As long as the unit can articulate preferences for its own constituency and has access to a reasonably equitable distribution of income, it can specify the mix of services preferred, procure an appropriate supply, and pay for them. In this case a small collective-consumption unit might contract with large production units to obtain those goods that are more economically produced by larger units. Smaller production units could provide other goods more efficiently produced at a small scale. Each takes advantage of diverse scale considerations in both the consumption and production of a public good or service.

Another circumstance may exist where the relevant collective-consumption unit is large but efficient production is realized on a smaller scale. The appropriate consumption unit for users of interstate highways in the United States, for example, is probably a national unit. This national unit functions as a provisioner by developing appropriate specifications and financial arrangements for procuring interstate highway services. However, varying climatic and geographic conditions over a large continental area are such that the production and maintenance services can be more efficiently supplied by smaller organizations. Thus, the US Department of Transportation acts as a buyer of interstate highway services from state highway departments and private contractors that act as the principal production units.

The proportioning of diverse consumption and production possibilities in a complex public economy will not occur automatically. It requires a conscious pursuit of relative advantages by those affected. An awareness that bigger or smaller isn't necessarily better must precede a search for the *combinations* that generate the highest user satisfaction for given expenditures of efforts. Substantial improvements can be made in most metropolitan areas to take advantage of the diverse scale of consumption and production units already available, as well as to create new enterprises of varying scales to fulfill currently unmet levels of demand.

Competition, Bargaining, and Cooperative Efforts

If each collective-consumption unit has potential access to several production units and is prepared to consider alternative options in arranging for the supply of a public good or service, the relationships between collective-consumption units and production units will take on the characteristics of a bargaining relationship. The bargaining in this case is *not* between producers and individual consumers. Such efforts will usually fail. The opportunity for bargaining, instead, arises in the relationships among *collective-consumption units* and *production units*.

If potential producers include an array of private vendors and public agencies, an opportunity exists for bargaining to procure public goods or services at lowered costs. The opportunity for bargaining among collective-consumption units and production units also creates incentives on the part of the parties involved to increase levels of information and to develop indicators of performance.

Bargaining may also occur in a noncompetitive situation where multiple production units may be able to gain a joint benefit by coordinating their actions with one another. Various police agencies may, for example, have mutual aid or joint operating agreements to provide back-up service whenever emergencies arise and all personnel are otherwise committed. Peak-load capabilities may be maintained by drawing on reserves in other departments rather than requiring all departments to meet peak-load demands from their own reserves. Without competitive pressures, bargaining among public producers may involve collusion against the general public.

These joint efforts may be extended to organizing supplemental public or private enterprises to supply a variety of indirect services such as crime laboratories, police training academies, and joint dispatching services. Where high levels of interdependency have developed through cooperative arrangements, collective-consumption and production units can be expected to develop routine organizational arrangements to reduce bargaining costs. These arrangements often take the form of a voluntary association with regularly scheduled meetings, with officials to set meeting agendas and to arrange for the organization and presentation of pertinent information. Many of these voluntary associations of collective-consumption and production units may be formally organized with bylaws and membership fees, or assessments to cover the cost of a small permanent secretariat that organizes information, implements decisions, and engages in entrepreneurial activities on behalf of the association.

Some Problems Affecting Relationships among Collective-Consumption Units and Production Units in Public Service Industries

The special characteristics of public goods generate a number of difficulties that affect relationships within public service industries, especially in the relationship between collective-consumption and production units. Market arrangements characteristically involve financial transactions. Consumers pay directly for what they get. This is not usually the case in the public sector, and the result, quite often, is service delivery without satisfactory information about demand or user preference. Inequitable service delivery is always a further possibility. Where jointness of consumption is accompanied by partial subtractability, special problems may also arise in regulating patterns of use among diverse consumers. One use may, in the absence of regulation, seriously impair the value of the good or service for another. Moreover, many of the agreements among collective-consumption and production units in a public sector are based on unanimity. But any one unit may adopt a holdout strategy, resulting in considerable conflict among units. Each of these problems—(1) financing, (2) equitable service delivery, (3) regulating patterns of use, and (4) conflict and conflict resolution—pose difficulties in the relationships between collective-consumption and production units. Satisfactory performance in public service industries will depend on finding constructive resolutions to these problems.

Finance

In market relationships, the decision to buy any particular good or service automatically entails a consideration of foregone opportunities. The price expressed in money terms is the equivalent of all other goods and services that could be purchased with the same amount of money. A decision to buy a particular good or service reflects a willingness to forego all other opportunities for which that money could have been used. In a market system, an expression of demand always includes reference to what is foregone as well as what is purchased.

In the public sector, the articulation of preferences often fails to take account of foregone opportunities. The service is, after all, simply available for the taking. We might think that taxes could indicate user preference. But the mode of taxation may have few or no relationships to the service being supplied. Furthermore, individuals may function in many different communities of users. Neighborhood residents who commute elsewhere to work may have different demands for police services than those who do not commute. Commuters are interested in the level of policing both where they live and where they work. Unless collective-consumption units are properly constituted to give voice to user preferences, much essential information may be lost.

Because most public goods and services are financed through a process of taxation involving no choice, optimal levels of expenditure are difficult to establish. The provision of public goods can be easily over- or underfinanced. Public officials and professionals may have higher preferences for some public goods than the citizens they serve. Thus they may allocate more tax monies to these services than would the citizens being served had they a voice in the process. Underfinancing can occur where many of the beneficiaries of a public good are not included in the collective-consumption units financing the good, even though they might be willing to help pay their fair share. Financing any particular public good or service may thus require contributions from more than one collective-consumption unit.

Public education, for example, is of primary benefit to the families whose children are being educated. However, substantial benefits to others located within the same state and within the nation may result from having a good educational system in each locality. Thus, financing education may best be achieved through a combination of resources from local, state, and national sources. However, funding a school system directly from several tax sources may make the school system less sensitive to the diverse interests of the different families who directly receive educational services. The use of a voucher system to finance at least a major portion of public education would increase the relative voice of the family units choosing the school or schools that educate their children.

Working out financial arrangements between collective-consumption units and production units is one of the most difficult problems faced by entrepreneurs in the public economy. Without market prices and market transactions, the act of paying for a good generally occurs at a time and place far from the act of consuming the good; individual costs are widely separated from individual benefits. Yet a principle of fiscal equivalence—that those receiving the benefits from a service pay the costs for that service—should apply in the public economy just as it applies in a market economy. Costs must be proportioned to benefits if people are to have any sense of economic reality. Otherwise, beneficiaries may assume that public goods are free, that money in the public treasury is "the government's" money, and that no opportunities are foregone in spending that money. When this happens, the foundations of a democratic society are threatened. The alternative is to adhere as closely as possible to the principle of fiscal equivalence and to proportion taxes as closely as possible to benefits received.

Where charges can be appropriately levied on individual beneficiaries, user charges or use taxes can substantially alleviate the problems associated with rationing the use of a joint good when partial subtractability results in potential congestion costs. Highway construction and maintenance services, highway police patrols, and other services for motorists could, for example, be charged against gasoline taxes rather than other forms of general taxation. User charges or use taxes lead beneficiaries to calculate the cost of a service against the value of a marginal use. Criminal sanctions need not be the principal means to regulate the use of a public good or service that is freely available to all users, if user charges can more appropriately proportion use to supply.

Equitable Service Delivery

Designing institutions to equitably deliver goods and services that are difficult to measure and jointly consumed by individuals having little choice regarding their consumption is an extraordinarily difficult task. Further, considerable disagreement exists on a definition for equity; many are used in common discourse, and even involve contradictory approaches to the concept. What one person calls equitable, another classifies as inequitable. When one comes to put terms used in different definitions into operation in a local public economy, the possibility for serious disagreement grows still larger. Attempts to measure the unmeasurable cannot help but produce considerable discord over the indicators used.

Those concerned with the relationship between the way local government units are structured and equitable services are delivered have focused on several key issues. One is related to the division of metropolitan areas into a large number of separate taxing zones. By allowing more than a single governmental jurisdiction within a metropolitan area, the wealthy may be able to escape to the jurisdictions that operate primarily as tax shelters, and may avoid contributing tax funds to the center city. Many feel that this is unjust, for the wealthy themselves use center-city facilities and have some obligation to pay for them.

To the extent that the facilities used by most individuals in a metropolitan area are financed only by the tax base of the center city, fragmentation allows both corporate and personal wealth to flee center-city tax rates. In a complex urban public economy, including overlapping units of various sizes, it is possible to design arrangements that reduce the number of free riders. The costs of building and maintaining facilities serving an entire metropolitan area should be borne by collective-consumption units encompassing as much of that area as possible. County and regional units have been designed in some metropolitan areas to finance sewer and water systems, major transportation networks, air pollution control, cultural facilities located in the center city, airports, and many others. For example, the Wayne County Road Commission operates the Detroit Metropolitan Airport.

In some metropolitan areas, center-city residents (as well as residents of incorporated suburbs) help fund the services that primarily benefit residents of unincorporated county territory. The county sheriff's office is usually funded from a general tax assessed on all property in a county. The county is an appropriate unit for financing that aspect of the sheriff's activities related to jail and the court, which benefit residents throughout the county. However, sheriffs frequently provide local police and other urban services in the unincorporated portions of the county. A major part of the costs should be borne by the residents of the unincorporated areas. Assessing a special tax on unincorporated land to support county services delivered primarily to unincorporated parts of the county corrects this inequity. Thus, increasing the number of taxing zones within a metropolitan area may actually reduce the burden on center-city taxpayers.

The wealthy, some argue, have a moral obligation to the poor left behind in the center city. But metropolitan areas are too small to be effective units for achieving significant redistribution; and any attempt to do so at this level places that area at a competitive disadvantage. If industry and wealthier individuals do not feel their tax dollars are yielding sufficient benefits, they can easily move outside the center city. No matter how large the boundaries of a center city become, far more territory exists outside its boundaries. Federal and state governments, however, have the potential for being far more effective in devising and administering progressive taxes on personal and corporate wealth. Policies of redistribution—to be effective—must take place at the national level. The costs of exit at this level are substantial, and no area within the nation is placed at a competitive disadvantage.

Reducing the number of individual units within a metropolitan area, it is argued, will lead to a more uniform level of service. Many proposals for large-scale consolidation of governmental units serving metropolitan areas are based on an assumption that increased equity will result by expanding the tax base. This will ensure that the wealthy suburbanites pay for essential services needed by the poor. No evidence is available indicating that this actually happens in large cities. Instead of uniform service delivery to all neighborhoods, large cities are themselves characterized by substantial differences in the quality and quantity of services delivered to different neighborhoods. A study made in Oakland, California, found that considerable variation existed in the distribution of schools, streets, and libraries to different neighborhoods. The patterns were *not* the same for all three services. Nor was it easy to decide whether the distributions were equitable; the standard selected substantially affects how one judges performance. As the authors of the study stated:

> Consider two parents looking at current allocations in the Oakland school system. A well-to-do parent might look at the present allocation of funds and suggest that, if anything, it overfavored poor neighborhoods. Student/teacher ratios are lowest in the low-income schools; these schools have specialists and extra supplies purchased with federal funds. By contrast, the richest schools have somewhat larger classes, fewer specialists, and practically no teacher aids. . . . Thus the well-to-do parent concludes that the system is biased in favor of the poor.
>
> A poor, or minority, citizen might come to a much different conclusion. He might acknowledge that dollar expenditures per pupil were higher in the poorest schools; yet he might feel that expenditures are a poor measure of outcomes. He could argue that a more appropriate measure of outcomes would be reading ability on standardized tests, that as long as poor children are reading at lower levels than rich children (which is currently true) the allocation of resources favoring the low-income schools is insufficient. (Levy, Meltsner, and Wildavsky 1974, 243)

A study conducted in the Chicago metropolitan area found that the Chicago Police Department, with fourteen times the financial resources allocated to three poor, black neighborhoods, was not able to perform any more effectively than two poor, black, and independent city police departments serving small communities in the southern portion of Cook County (E. Ostrom and Whitaker 1974). Poor neighborhoods receiving "services" that are not tailored to their needs may not be better off when increased resources are allocated. In large collective-consumption units, residents of poor neighborhoods may have even less voice about levels and types of services desired than they do in smaller-sized collective-consumption units. Increasing the size of the smallest collective-consumption unit may not help solve problems of redistribution.

The problem of achieving equitable service delivery in a metropolitan context has been raised in a number of court cases in recent years. In some cases, municipalities were required by a court to pave streets and provide other services to a neighborhood in which black residents predominated and where service levels were grossly maldistributed (Hawkins v. Town of Shaw [Mississippi], 457 F. 2nd 1286). However, the effects of court decisions in the field of education may not be as beneficial to the poor and disadvantaged as those who brought the cases had hoped. The school finance cases have been based on two questionable assumptions. First, it has been assumed that the poverty level of the children in a school district is closely correlated with the district's resource base (Rodriguez et al. v. San Antonio Independent School District et al., 1972, 377 F. Supp. 280 [W.D. Tex]). Since nearly one-half of the property tax base in most school districts is nonresidential property, whether the school district has a high or low tax base depends largely on the type of commercial, industrial, agricultural, or other land uses in the area. Wealthy residential school districts frequently have a lower tax base than districts with substantial industry and a poor, residential population. Whether school district wealth is related to individual wealth must be determined empirically in each individual setting. While tax resources and personal income were found to be positively correlated at a county level (Harrison 1974), this is too aggregated a level to undertake the analysis. As the size "of the unit under analysis becomes smaller, the land uses within the units become more specialized. Divergencies between wealth as measured by total taxable property and family income become more predominant" (Bish 1976, 85). The cost of undertaking research at the school district level is quite high so that few studies have been conducted. However, in California, a study was conducted to examine the association between school district wealth and family income. No such association was found for elementary, secondary, or unified school districts (Cox 1975). It has also been assumed that education is directly related to levels of expenditure (Serrano v. Priest, 1971, 95 Cal. Rptr. 601). However, most empirical research in the field has not supported this assumption (Averch et al. 1972, but also see Sommers and Wolfe 1977). The chapter by William Neenan in this volume contains an in-depth discussion of school finance structure in SEM.

Regulating Patterns of Use

The characteristics of partial subtractability of consumption imply that increased use at any given threshold of supply may impair the value of a good or service for other users. As congestion occurs, as more users take advantage of available facilities, parks or streets decline in value to each user. Where multiple uses occur, one pattern of use may drive out other patterns of use. The use of a waterway to discharge wastes, for example, may exclude its use for recreation. If the costs of opportunities foregone are not taken into account, as some uses drive out others, a serious erosion in the qualities of public life can occur.

Jointness of use under conditions of partial subtractability may require rules for ordering patterns of use to reduce potential conflict in the community. If rules are to be effective, mechanisms for their enforcement must be available. The delivery of public goods and services under these conditions depends on proportioning supply to demand with rules that account both for the conditions of supply and the patterns of use. Unless those rules account for varying patterns of use and supply conditions in discrete circumstances, they are likely to become serious impediments to joint well-being. Heavy use of city streets for through traffic may, for example, impair their use by local residents in patronizing local businesses.

These conditions may require an especially close coordination between production and consumption units. The delivery of service by a producer needs to occur where patterns of use are regulated to gain optimal advantage of the available services and facilities. Regulating patterns of use becomes one of the critical consumption tasks performed by collective-consumption units. This is why authority to enforce rules and regulations by recourse to criminal sanctions is usually assigned to governmental instrumentalities responsible for procuring a public good or service. Collective-consumption units must assume primary responsibility for regulating and enforcing patterns of use. Yet those regulations are meaningful only in light of discrete demand and supply conditions. Modifying supply conditions may alter the regulation and enforcement problems.

Even among government agencies, producing a service is frequently separated from regulating and enforcing its patterns of use. Agencies responsible for policing the use of streets and highways, for example, are separate from those responsible for constructing and maintaining them. Nevertheless, producers in a public service industry must be aware that services subject to joint use involve sensitive problems in proportioning supply to use and in regulating patterns of use. Otherwise, problems of congestion and conflicts among users can erode public services and degrade community life.

Conflict and Resolution

Most arrangements between and among collective-consumption and production units are maintained under a rule of unanimity. A rule of unanimity can always be threatened by the presence of a holdout. One collectivity may find it advantageous to hold out and enjoy the benefits from the joint actions of others without assuming its proportionate share of the costs. If some collective-consumption or production units hold out successfully, others will follow suit, and cooperative arrangements will fail. An erosion in welfare will occur for everyone concerned. Holding out may lead some units to respond with threats or counterthreats. Unless constrained by the availability of institutions for adjudicating and resolving conflicts, threats and counterthreats can escalate into violence.

A highly fragmented political system *without* substantial overlap among the many jurisdictions is especially vulnerable to this form of institutional failure frequently called "Balkanization." With overlapping units of government, conflicts among governments at any one level may be resolved by recourse to the decision-making arrangements at a higher level. Such arrangements are inherent in federal systems of government. The critical feature is the availability of legal, political, and constitutional remedies to the parties injured as a consequence of costs generated by governmental action.

Courts have played an especially important role in resolving conflicts among independent agencies and firms operating in a public economy. In California, where contracting for public services has the greatest competitive pressure, county grand juries have assumed a continuing responsibility for monitoring the operation of intergovernmental contracts. Inappropriate use of tax funds by public agencies functioning as contract producers would transfer service costs to the public treasury of the producing agency rather than the treasury of the benefitting community. Tax funds, inappropriately used, might also subsidize public producers. These subsidies would drive out private enterprises even though they might be more efficient in rendering a comparable quality of public service. Grand juries with jurisdiction to inquire into the discharge of public trust by state and local agencies can maintain the integrity of market-like relationships and encourage competitive pressure in a public economy.

Without appropriate mechanisms for resolving conflicts and monitoring the operation of a public service economy, contracting can be an instrument for political corruption. Contracts with firms that are the chosen instruments of political bosses have long been used in some states to milk public treasuries, supply the coffers of political machines, and create private fortunes.[1] No system of economic relationships will perform well without appropriate public policies and institutions to enforce these policies.

Conflict arises when someone believes he is being harmed by another's action. Thus, conflict is as important an indicator of potential economic losses as the red ink on a balance sheet. Mechanisms for conflict resolution contribute to economic welfare when they right wrongs and restructure arrangements so that everyone is left better off or, at least, unharmed.

But to maintain a system open to conflict and conflict resolution, the participating parties must have autonomous legal status with authority to sue and be sued, and to take independent decisions that advance a set of interests. If public economies are to gain the advantage of bargaining relationships and voluntary cooperation in producing and consuming public goods, they must maintain arm's-length relationships and must have available to them institutions that can adjudicate conflicts among parties with equal standing in law. Adjudication does not occur in the absence of equal legal standing. Subordinates obey rather than cooperate.

Questions and Implications for the Detroit Metropolitan Area

What does this approach imply for those interested in organizing and financing the delivery of urban public goods and services in the SEM metropolitan area? Since this approach does not prescribe one best way to organize metropolitan areas, one cannot describe an ideal organizational model. We can, however, identify key questions to be asked by policy makers. Answers to these questions may enable them to identify those aspects of current organization that might need reform. These questions include:

- Does the current organization of collective-consumption units adequately represent the diverse interests of citizens in the area?
- Does the current organization of production units include a mix of public and private firms of various scales of production?
- Are mechanisms available for increasing the direct relationship of financing to goods and services received?

- Have institutional arrangements that encourage coproduction of services by local residents been developed?
- What mechanisms exist for effective conflict resolution among different agencies in public service industries?
- What efforts can be made to get federal and state governments to take on greater responsibility for redistribution policies?

Each of these questions will be discussed below.

Does the Current Organization of Collective-Consumption Units Adequately Represent the Diverse Interests of Citizens in the Area?

Are collective-consumption units in the Detroit area organized to deal with public goods having different scales of effects? What units aggregate citizen preferences for services with widespread effects throughout the area such as air pollution, transportation facilities, industrial location and development, traffic flow on major arteries, and large-scale water and sewage transmission and treatment? Are there sufficient large-scale collective-consumption units to enable citizens throughout the area to have a voice in planning those facilities that jointly affect them? Do they have a share in financing these facilities? (See Andrea Long's discussion in this volume of SEMCOG's rocky history for a partial answer to some of these questions.)

What units aggregate citizen preferences regarding more localized public goods and services such as maintaining playgrounds, street cleaning, trash removal, snow removal, problems of abandoned housing, rodent and insect control, and other localized goods? Do citizens living within the city of Detroit and the other jurisdictions in the SEM metropolitan area have a voice in the supply of localized public goods and services in their neighborhoods?

What capabilities do collective-consumption units have to join forces, to establish and fund enterprises affecting some of them but not the entire region? Can municipalities enter a joint agreement to finance a sewage treatment plant or undertake a watershed management program benefiting a subportion of the metropolitan area bigger than the smallest collective-consumption units? Or, can a particular portion of a county or municipality create a defined "zone of benefit" or an assessment district within its boundaries and establish a governing and financing authority, primarily of benefit to that zone? In California, for example, County Flood Control

Districts can create zones of benefit within their boundaries to finance a water conservation project benefiting only a small section of the county. Some relatively sophisticated groundwater management plans involving the use of flood waters to replenish groundwater basins have been partially funded with taxes collected through this type of instrumentality.

Does the Current Organization of Production Units Include a Mix of Public and Private Firms of Various Scales of Production?

Is there sufficient potential competition among producers of different public services that collective-consumption units have some bargaining leverage with production units? Or, are collective-consumption units forced to create their own monopolistic government bureaus without options available to them when that bureau delivers inferior services at high costs? As labor unions become a more potent force in delivering local public services, the collective-consumption unit's option of purchasing services from another agency may also increase the bargaining power of production unit managers. It is hard to resist demands for major increases in pension plans and other fringe benefits (whose impact is delayed) when a service can be produced only by the employees of a particular government bureau. Weakness at the bargaining table may have increased some of the financial strains felt by many major US cities. The external pressure of potential substitute producers is an important force not only in dealing with public service unions but also in decreasing the general organizational slack that results from any production unit holding a monopoly position.

Are Mechanisms Available for Increasing the Direct Relationship of Financing to Goods and Services Received?

As discussed above, increasing the relationship between financing and service received is always a difficult problem in the public sector. But relying on a limited number of taxes, imposed without attempts to relate tax revenue to services performed, makes all involved think of the local public treasury as one fund subject to raiding. If one group does not raid the treasury for special purposes, others will. A competitive race to see who can get the largest share of a fixed asset is not the type of incentive system that one would consciously design to increase the quality of decisions made about the allocation of joint resources. And yet, this is the type of incentive system that has emerged in many metropolitan areas due to the lack of efforts to tie revenue sources to services received.

But there are other possibilities. Region-wide gasoline taxes can help finance traffic control on major local arteries. Parking decals can be sold to those who regularly commute to work and park in downtown areas. This would help to finance road and street repair in the central business district and other facilities as well. Water and sewage charges should cover the full marginal costs of transmission and distribution so that property taxes are not supporting an inefficient use of water. If a particular neighborhood petitions to improve their local streets or sidewalks—and is willing to pay a substantial portion of the costs—special short-term property taxes could be assessed. Police departments could charge for many of the services they perform such as bank escort service for local businesses, burglar alarms installed at police headquarters, vacation checks for residents, and special details assigned to parades, funerals, and sporting events. It is not necessary to cover all costs fully, but without some charge no one has any incentive to conserve their demands for free public services.

User charges that are higher during peak periods of use would also lead individuals to decrease their demands on those joint facilities subject to congestion. Lower bus fares during off-peak hours, water rates favoring large-scale users who build in-house storage facilities and obtain their water from utilities at off-peak periods, and electricity rates that are lower for off-peak water heating, would all help to reduce problems of peak load, and would assess a higher rate to those contributing to congestion.

Contracting arrangements between local governments and either private or public producers also increase the information available to public decision makers about the cost of particular services. When a producer must justify the cost of the services being provided in a competitive bidding situation, the producer will keep more effective records about costs and activity levels. City managers acting as purchasing agents have an opportunity to tailor contracts reflecting preferred levels of public services.

Have Institutional Arrangements That Encourage Coproduction of Services by Local Residents Been Developed?

The out-of-pocket costs of service delivery are substantially less if citizens are motivated to act as effective coproducers. Do any facilities exist to create general-purpose neighborhood organizations throughout the region? Such facilities could provide a forum for information exchange among neighborhood organizations, staff help for organizations in the early stages of formation, facilities for reproducing local newsletters and other forms of communication to members, and recognition of the essential role that these organizations can play in the local public economy of a metropolitan area. The Neighborhood Watch program, fostered by the National Sheriff's Association, has had a positive impact on the number of suspicious circumstances reported and the general level of cooperation between local citizens and their police agencies. Well-organized parent-teacher associations can encourage parents to take a more active role in supervising the type of education made available to their children, and in supplementing the activities of school employees by volunteering their activities in the classroom and at home. Neighborhood clean-up campaigns, organized by citizens with the active help of city agencies, are far more effective than either citizens or agencies undertaking such campaigns on their own. Citizens may themselves clean up vacant lots if they can be assured that their efforts to stop future dumping will be backed up by official governmental activity.

What Mechanisms Exist for Effective Conflict Resolution among Different Agencies in Public Service Industries?

Do these mechanisms exist, and are they invoked as soon as potential interests are adversely affected so that joint decisions can be taken in light of knowledge about differences in perspectives? Do agencies have sufficient arm's-length relationships that articulated conflict may lead to genuine communication rather than a solution dominated by the most powerful agency involved? Are there judicial remedies available that may enable public and private agencies to work out mutually agreeable solutions in the shadow of the court? Do associations of local government officials such as a regional police chiefs' association, a juvenile officers' association, a city managers' association, a water engineers' association, a town clerks' association, an assessors' association, and so forth, exist that encourage public officials holding similar positions to know their counterparts in other agencies in the region? While such associations serve largely social and professional interests, they are also the meeting ground to discuss joint problems encountered by members of the same public service industry. Where such groups are active, considerable state and local legislation has been drafted by ad hoc committees to solve joint problems faced by local units of government.

What Efforts Can Be Made to Get Federal and State Government to Take On Greater Responsibility for Redistribution Policies?

Major metropolitan areas need to join forces to make federal and state governments accept primary responsibility for redistribution efforts. Many federal social service programs of the past have been advertised as efforts to achieve redistribution but have not accomplished their aim. Federal urban renewal programs, originally sold as efforts to provide better housing for the poor, have instead moved the poor out of well-established patterns of life to clear valuable inner-city land for commercial and middle- to upper-income housing. The War on Poverty programs did not produce many jobs for the target population.

While state governments are not as effective for redistribution as the federal government, metropolitan areas should at least ensure that state taxes collected in the metropolitan area find their way back in the form of services. An issue of recent concern in Detroit has been the lack of services provided by the Michigan State Highway Patrol. The Highway Patrol provided services primarily in rural areas, while a substantial source of state funds comes from urban areas. Highway patrols in many other states patrol all major freeways crossing metropolitan areas. This frees the local county and municipal forces for duty elsewhere in the metropolitan area.

William Neenan, in his chapter in this volume on "Fiscal Relations between State of Michigan and Southeastern Michigan," analyzes the impact of state and federal grants on local revenues. He concludes that per capita state and federal grants have increased more rapidly in recent years and that the cities with the largest ratio of poor residents—Detroit and Pontiac—received the highest percentage increases.

Many other questions could, of course, be asked. However, we hope that this preliminary list helps illustrate the usefulness of the approach discussed in this chapter. The mere presence of relatively complex governmental arrangements in a metropolitan area does not constitute evidence about the relative efficiency or equity of service delivery. Complex systems possess both opportunities and difficulties in achieving efficient and equitable local public service delivery. To exploit the opportunities takes self-conscious efforts on the part of local decision makers to increase the bargaining possibilities within the system, to foster coproduction of local services by those served, to increase the correspondence between funds collected and services delivered, and to maintain effective conflict-resolution mechanisms in a system of overlapping jurisdictions.

Acknowledgments

The authors wish to thank Robert L. Bish, John McIver, William Neenan, Stephen L. Percy, Larry Platt, Louis Weschler, and Gordon Whitaker for their helpful comments and suggestions on an earlier version of this chapter. Part of the research contained in this chapter was funded by the National Science Foundation (Research Applied to National Needs Division) under Grant #GI–43949. The authors gratefully acknowledge this support. Any findings, inferences, views, or opinions expressed herein are, however, those of the authors and do not necessarily reflect the views of the National Science Foundation.

Notes

This chapter was originally published in *Financing the Metropolis*, edited by Kent Mathewson and William B. Neenan (New York: Praeger, 1980), pp. 63–101.

1. The Indiana Department of Motor Vehicles, for example, contracts out its licensing operation to the county chairmen or other party officials of the political party controlling the office of governor. The party official derives fees from this contract service to finance political operations. In the absence of competitive pressure from other vendors, it is most doubtful that this form of contracting enhances efficiency.

Bibliography

Altshuler, Alan A. 1970. *Community Control: The Black Demand for Participation in Large American Cities*. New York: Pegasus.

Averch, Harvey A., Stephen J. Carroll, Theodore S. Donaldson, Herbert J. Kiesling, and John A. Pincus. 1972. *How Effective is Schooling? A Critical Review and Synthesis of Research Findings*. Prepared for President's Commission on School Finance, R–956–PCSF/RC. Santa Monica, CA: Rand Corporation.

Barzel, Yoram. 1969. "Two Propositions on the Optimal Level of Producing Public Goods." *Public Choice* 6: 31–37.

Bish, Robert L. 1976. "Fiscal Equalization through Court Decisions: Policy-Making without Evidence." In *The Delivery of Urban Services: Outcomes of Change*, edited by Elinor Ostrom, 75–102. Beverly Hills, CA: Sage.

Bish, Robert L., and Hugh O. Nourse. 1975. *Urban Economics and Policy Analysis*. New York: McGraw-Hill.

Bish, Robert L., and Vincent Ostrom. 1973. *Understanding Urban Government: Metropolitan Reform Reconsidered.* Washington, DC: American Enterprise Institute for Public Policy Research.

Bish, Robert L., and Robert Warren. 1972. "Scale and Monopoly in Urban Government Services." *Urban Affairs Quarterly* 8: 97–120.

Boskin, M. J. 1973. "Local Government Tax and Product Competition: The Optimal Provision of Public Goods." *Journal of Political Economy* 78: 203–10.

Breton, Albert. 1974. *The Economic Theory of Representative Government*. Chicago, IL: Aldine-Atherton.

Buchanan, James M. 1970. "Public Goods and Public Bads." In *Financing the Metropolis*, edited by John P. Crecine, 51–71. Beverly Hills, CA: Sage.

Buchanan, James M., and Gordon Tullock. 1962. *The Calculus of Consent: Logical Foundations of Constitutional Democracy*. Ann Arbor: University of Michigan Press.

California Governor's Task Force on Local Government Reform. 1974. *Public Benefits from Public Choice*. Sacramento, CA: Governor's Office.

Cox, Millicent Ann. 1975. "Equality in California School Finance: Impact of Alternatives on Taxpayers." Working Paper No. 20. Los Angeles: University of Southern California, Center for Public Affairs.

Crozier, Michel. 1964. *The Bureaucratic Phenomenon*. Phoenix Books ed. Chicago, IL: University of Chicago Press.

Dales, J. H. 1968. *Pollution, Property, and Prices*. Toronto: University of Toronto Press.

Elazar, Daniel J. 1971. "Community Self-Government and the Crisis of American Politics." *Ethics* 81: 91–106.

Gregg, Phillip M. 1974. "Units and Levels of Analysis: A Problem of Policy Analysis in Federal Systems." *Publius* 4: 59–86.

———. 1975. *Problems of Theory in Policy Analysis*. Lexington, MA: Lexington Books.

Hamilton, Alexander, John Jay, and James Madison. [1788] n.d. *The Federalist*. New York: The Modern Library.

Harrison, R. 1974. "What Now After San Antonio Independent School District v. Rodriguez? Electoral Inequality and the Public School Finance Systems in California and Texas." *Rutgers Camden Law Journal* 5: 191–217.

Hirsch, Werner. 1964. "Local versus Areawide Urban Government Services." *National Tax Journal* 17: 331–39.

———. 1968. "The Supply of Urban Public Services." In *Issues in Urban Economics*, edited by Harvey S. Perloff and Lowdon Wingo Jr., 435–75. Baltimore, MD: Johns Hopkins Press.

Hochman, Harold M., ed. 1976. *The Urban Economy*. New York: Norton.

Kotler, Milton. 1969. *Neighborhood Government: The Local Foundations of Community Life*. Indianapolis, IN: Bobbs-Merrill.

Landau, Martin. 1969. "Redundance, Rationality, and the Problem of Duplication and Overlap." *Public Administration Review* 29: 346–58.

Levy, Frank, Arnold J. Meltsner, and Aaron Wildavsky. 1974. *Urban Outcomes: Schools, Streets, and Libraries*. Berkeley: University of California Press.

Lindblom, Charles E. 1955. *Bargaining: The Hidden Hand in Government*. Research Memorandum 1434–RC. Santa Monica, CA: Rand Corporation.

———. 1965. *The Intelligence of Democracy: Decision Making through Mutual Adjustment*. New York: Free Press.

Long, Norton E. 1970. "Rigging the Market for Public Goods." In *Organizations and Clients: Essays in the Sociology of Service*, edited by William R. Rosengren and Mark Lefton. Columbus, OH: Charles E. Merrill.

Martin, Dolores Tremewan. 1976. "The Institutional Framework of Community Formation: The Law and Economics of Municipal Incorporation in California." PhD diss., Virginia Polytechnic Institute and State University.

Mishan, E. J. 1969. "The Relationship between Joint Products, Collective Goods, and External Effects." *Journal of Political Economy* 77: 329–48.

Mushkin, Selma, ed. 1972. *Public Prices for Public Products*. Washington, DC: Urban Institute.

McKean, Roland N. 1965. "The Unseen Hand in Government." *American Economic Review* 55: 496–506.

Newman, Oscar. 1972. *Defensible Space: Crime Prevention through Urban Design*. New York: Macmillan.

Niskanen, William A., Jr. 1971. *Bureaucracy and Representative Government*. Chicago, IL: Aldine-Atherton.

Olson, Mancur. 1969. "The Principle of 'Fiscal Equivalence': The Division of Responsibility among Different Levels of Government." *American Economic Review* 59: 479–87.

Ostrom, Elinor. 1971. "Institutional Arrangements and the Measurement of Policy Consequences: Applications to Evaluating Police Performance." *Urban Affairs Quarterly* 6: 447–75.

———. 1972. "Metropolitan Reform: Propositions Derived from Two Traditions." *Social Science Quarterly* 53(3): 474–93.

———. 1975. "On Righteousness, Evidence, and Reform: The Police Story." *Urban Affairs Quarterly* 10(4): 464–86.

Ostrom, Elinor, and Roger B. Parks. 1973. "Suburban Police Departments: Too Many and Too Small?" In *The Urbanization of the Suburbs*, edited by Louis H. Masotti and Jeffrey K. Hadden, 367–402. Beverly Hills, CA: Sage.

Ostrom Elinor, Roger B. Parks, and Gordon P. Whitaker. 1973. "Do We Really Want to Consolidate Urban Police Forces? A Reappraisal of Some Old Assertions." *Public Administration Review* 33: 423–33.

———. 1974. "Defining and Measuring Structural Variations in Interorganizational Arrangements." *Publius* 4(4): 87–108.

Ostrom, Elinor, and Dennis C. Smith. 1976. "On the Fate of 'Lilliputs' in Metropolitan Policing." *Public Administration Review* 36(2): 192–200.

Ostrom, Elinor, and Gordon P. Whitaker. 1973. "Does Local Community Control of Police Make a Difference? Some Preliminary Findings." *American Journal of Political Science* 17: 48–76.

———. 1974. "Community Control and Governmental Responsiveness: The Case of Police in Black Communities." In *Improving the Quality of Urban Management*, edited by David Rogers and Willis Hawley, 303–34. Beverly Hills, CA: Sage.

Ostrom, Vincent. 1968. "Water Resource Development: Some Problems in Economic and Political Analysis of Public Policy." In *Political Science and Public Policy*, edited by Austin Ranney, 123–50. Chicago, IL: Markham.

———. 1969. "Operational Federalism: Organization for the Provision of Public Services in the American Federal System." *Public Choice* 6(1): 1–17.

———. 1971a. *The Political Theory of a Compound Republic: A Reconstruction of the Logical Foundations of American Democracy as Presented in* The Federalist. Blacksburg: Virginia Polytechnic Institute, Center for Study of Public Choice.

———. 1971b. *Institutional Arrangements for Water Resource Development.* PB207–314. Springfield, VA: National Technical Information Service.

———. 1973. "Can Federalism Make a Difference?" *Publius* 3(2): 197–238.

Ostrom, Vincent, and Elinor Ostrom. 1965. "A Behavioral Approach to the Study of Intergovernmental Relations." *Annals of the American Academy of Political and Social Science* 359: 137–46.

———. 1971. "Public Choice: A Different Approach to the Study of Public Administration." *Public Administration Review* 31(2): 302–16.

Ostrom, Vincent, Charles M. Tiebout, and Robert Warren. 1961. "The Organization of Government in Metropolitan Areas: A Theoretical Inquiry." *American Political Science Review* 55(4): 831–42.

Pennock, J. Roland. 1959. "Federal and Unitary Government: Disharmony and Frustration." *Behavioral Sciences* 4: 147–57.

Perlstadt, Harry. 1975. "Voluntary Associations and the Community: The Case of Volunteer Ambulance Corps." *Journal of Voluntary Action Research* 4: 85–89.

Polanyi, Michael. 1951. *The Logic of Liberty: Reflections and Rejoinders*. Chicago, IL: University of Chicago Press.

Pommerehne, Werner W., and Bruno S. Frey. 1977. "Public versus Private Production Efficiency in Switzerland: A Theoretical and Empirical Comparison." In *Comparing Urban Service Delivery Systems: Structure and Performance*, edited by Vincent Ostrom and Frances Pennell Bish, 221–42. Beverly Hills, CA: Sage.

Savas, E. S. 1974. "Municipal Monopolies versus Competition in Delivering Urban Services." In *Improving the Quality of Urban Management*, edited by Willis D. Hawley and David Rodgers. Beverly Hills, CA: Sage.

Savas, E. S., and S. Ginsburg. 1973. "The Civil Service: A Meritless System?" *The Public Interest*, no. 32 (Summer): 70–85.

Shields, Currin V. 1952. "The American Tradition of Empirical Collectivism." *American Political Science Review* 46: 104–20.

Sommers, Anne A., and Barbara L. Wolfe. 1977. "Do Schools Make a Difference?" *American Economic Review* 67: 639–52.

Stigler, George S. 1962. "The Tenable Range of Functions of Local Government." In *Private Wants and Public Needs: Issues Surrounding the Size and Scope of Government Expenditure*, edited by Edmund S. Phelps. New York: Norton.

Stinson, Thomas F., and Jerome K. Stam. 1976. "Toward an Economic Model of Volunteerism: The Case of Participation in Local Government." *Journal of Voluntary Action Research* 5: 52–60.

Tiebout, Charles M. 1956. "A Pure Theory of Local Expenditures." *Journal of Political Economy* 64(5): 416–24.

Tolley, G. S. 1969. *The Welfare of Economics of City Bigness*. Urban Economics Report No. 31. Chicago, IL: University of Chicago.

Tullock, Gordon. 1965. *The Politics of Bureaucracy*. Washington, DC: Public Affairs Press.

———. 1969. "Federalism: The Problem of Scale." *Public Choice* 6: 19–29.

———. 1970. *Private Wants, Public Means: An Economic Analysis of the Desirable Scope of Government*. New York: Basic Books.

Warren, Robert. 1964. "A Municipal Services Market Model of Metropolitan Organization." *Journal of the American Institute of Planners* 30(3): 193–204.

———. 1966. *Government in Metropolitan Regions: A Reappraisal of Fractionated Political Organization*. Davis: University of California, Institute of Governmental Affairs.

———. 1970. "Federal-Local Development Planning: Scale Effects in Representation and Policy Making." *Public Administration Review* 30: 584–95.

Weschler, Louis F., and Robert Warren. 1970. "Consumption Costs and Production Costs in the Provision of Antipoverty Goods." Paper presented at the 66th Annual Meeting of the American Political Science Association, Los Angeles, CA, September 8–12, 1970.

Whitaker, Gordon P., and Stephen D. Mastrofski. 1976. "Equity in the Delivery of Police Services." Police Services Study Technical Report T–29. Bloomington: Indiana University, Workshop in Political Theory and Policy Analysis.

Wildavsky, Aaron. 1966. "The Political Economy of Efficiency." *Public Administration Review* 26: 292–310.

———. 1976. "A Bias toward Federalism: Confronting the Conventional Wisdom on the Delivery of Governmental Services." *Publius* 6: 95–120.

Wolozin, Harold. 1975. "The Economic Role and Value of Volunteer Work in the United States: An Exploratory." *Journal of Voluntary Action Research* 4: 23–42.

6

Metropolitan Governance and Institutional Collective Action

Richard C. Feiock

Metropolitan regions have emerged as perhaps the dominant economic and social units in global society (Katz 2000; Scott 2001; Feiock, Moon, and Park 2008). The organization of governance and public authority in metropolitan areas is a long standing and contentious issue in urban politics and public administration. Fragmentation of policy making among multiple governmental units diminishes problems of concentrated powers and can promote competition and innovation, but it also imposes inefficiencies, as decisions by one governmental unit impose positive and negative externalities on others.

Urban service delivery decisions must confront scale and externality problems and other transaction risks that are exacerbated by the fragmented patterns of local governments that provide customized mixes of public goods to suit the taste of the local constituency. Costs and conflicts from fragmentation are acute in metropolitan areas because authority is fragmented horizontally among competing local governments as well as vertically among overlapping specialized federal, state, and local agencies.

The Institutional Collective Action Perspective

Institutional collective action (ICA) problems arise directly from the delegation of service responsibilities to a multitude of local governments and authorities. Fragmentation creates diseconomies of scale, positive and negative externalities, and common property resource problems. Collaborative responses to the ICA problems facing local governments, agencies, and concerned stakeholders produce joint gains, but these gains are often not sufficient to stimulate the ICA necessary for local actors to create these mechanisms.

The ICA framework draws insights from actor-centered (Scharpf 1997) and institutional analysis and development (Ostrom 1990) frameworks by extending theories of contracting and collective action among individuals to institutional actors such as cities, counties, government agencies, and other organizations (Bickers and Stein 2004; Feiock 2004; Scholz and Feiock 2007). Recent work incorporates concepts from agency and social network theories into the ICA approach and extends it to a broad set of collective decisions relating to urban service provision (Feiock 2007; Feiock and Scholz 2009) and to regional management of natural resources (Lubell et al. 2002; Schneider et al. 2003; Scholz, Berardo, and Kile 2008).

Only individuals are capable of action, yet individuals often act in the name of a group or organization. Thus, it is meaningful to investigate collective action among composite actors defined by position, authority, and aggregation rules (Ostrom 2005). These rules solve the problem of matching empirically observable individual behavior with the institutionally defined unit of reference on whose behalf action is taken. For example, mayors and councils have the ability to conclude legally binding agreements for their cities and state, or federal agency officials have specified authority to commit the agency to contracts or agreements. ICA implies capability for intentional action above the level of individuals. This requires us to focus on interactions between and within institutional units. Principal agent problems arise from difficulties in aggregating preferences of members of the institutional unit and preference divergence between members and representatives authorized to negotiate collective agreements (Feiock 2007). The capacity for strategic action in collective-choice situations depends on the extent of preference integration among members of the composite unit and capacity for conflict resolution when preferences diverge.

This chapter describes the ICA framework, outlines its application to the study of governance arrangements in metropolitan areas, and discusses its implications for theories of regional governance. To apply the ICA framework to study problems of fragmentation and resultant decision externalities, we first need to specify a policy arena that identifies the actors and the nature of the collective problem they face. For example, a horizontal collective-action problem arises if the governments are too small to efficiently produce on their own a service each government wishes to provide or if production of the service produces externalities that spill across jurisdiction boundaries. Vertical collective-action problems occur between actors at different levels in the design of programs or decision process when more than one level of government pursues similar policy objectives simultaneously such as economic development. Functional collective-action problems are defined by the connectedness of services, policies, and resource systems because externalities occur between functional areas as well as governmental units. For example, land use development and regulation decisions will likely have consequences for natural resources, transportation, economic development, and other specialized policy arenas across the region.

From our perspective, a policy arena is composed of formal policy-making venues with statutory authority to make policy decisions enforceable by the government, formal rules about participation and decision processes in each venue, and policy actors who are concerned with these policies. Externally imposed rules combine with the underlying collective problem to determine the specific incentives facing each actor. If we assume that institutional actors select the available strategy that most enhances their (generally short-term) interests, in the absence of mitigating institutions, the collective-action problem dictates that the outcome of individual decisions will lead to collectively inefficient decisions. These mitigating institutions constitute the solution mechanisms or tools of regional governance.

The urban politics and public administration literatures have focused primarily on establishment of regional governments or authorities as the mechanism for solving horizontal collective-action problems in metropolitan regions. Instead, we argue that there are an array of mechanisms that vary in the extent to which self-organization is evident in their creation and use. Understanding the role of these mechanisms in enhancing the general welfare beyond what would occur in their absence is perhaps the most important contribution of ICA analysis to the study of regional governance.

The next section outlines the tools of regional governance and classifies them by their focus on collective or network relationships and the autonomy retained by local government units. The role of self-organization within each of these mechanisms is then identified and the transaction costs barriers to the emergence of these regional governance institutions are reviewed. The concluding discussion identifies the limitations of self-organizing mechanisms and develops a research agenda to investigate the emergence, evolution, and performance of these regional governance institutions.

The Tools of Regional Governance

Feiock and Scholz (2009) suggest that the range of institutions that have emerged to mitigate regional ICA problems can be best understood according to the degree of autonomy the mechanisms afford local actors. In addition, the tools vary with regard to whether they focus on collective multilateral relationships or on individual bilateral exchange in networks. Figure 6.1 depicts six general categories of mechanisms classified by whether the focus is on collective or individual choice and whether the coordination mechanism allows individual units to act autonomously to enter or exit relationships. The upper portion of the vertical dimension reflects relationships that are multilateral, with decisions made collectively. The lower half reflects relationships that are networks of individual choices by local units to enter into bilateral exchange. The horizontal dimension captures the nature of the regional coordination mechanism. Forms to the left rely on the exogenous resources and authority of higher-level governments or other exogenous organizations. To the middle along this dimension, local units delegate some level of authority by voluntarily entering into organizations or contractual arrangements that bind themselves to some degree but rely on mutual consent. To the right side, relationships are informal and coordination is enforced by embedded social, economic, and political relationships rather than formal authority.

The types of regional governance tools vary from regional authorities in the upper-left quadrant that resolves the ICA problem by centralizing decision authority over the involved area, to informal policy networks in the lower-right quadrant that rely exclusively on social embeddedness to coordinate decisions while preserving the autonomy of the involved policy actors.

Centralized institutions and hierarchy are not the only way of resolving local ICA problems. As Ostrom (1990) argued in *Governing the Commons*, locally evolved self-governing institutions that are adapted to specific local circumstances may provide more effective resolution of collective-action problems than central intervention in many circumstances. The institutions that Ostrom studied focused primarily on dilemmas in relatively sparse institutional settings, but a similar argument applies to our concern with dilemmas in the complex institutional settings of metropolitan governance for global city regions (Scott and Storper 2003).

This approach builds on the New Regionalist emphasis on the economic and environmental interconnectedness of metropolitan regions by emphasizing voluntary cooperation rather than top-down governmental

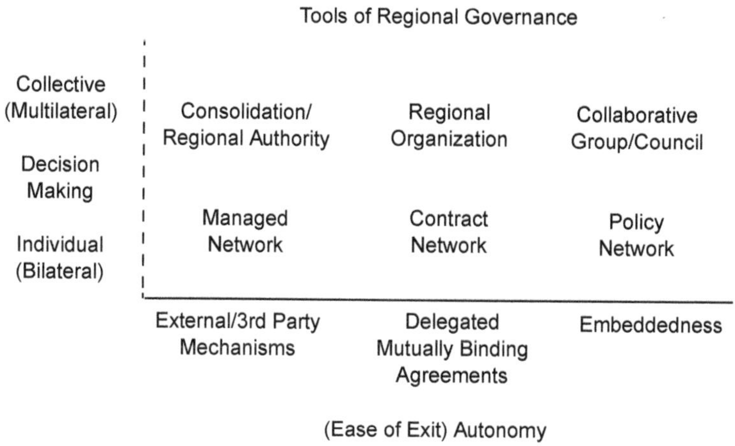

Figure 6.1. Tools of regional governance.

mechanisms to promote regional coordination among the fragmented local entities (Orfield 1997; Barnes and Ledebur 1998; Peirce 1993; Katz 2000; Foster 2001; Stephens and Wikstrom 2000). Self-organizing institutional solutions to ICA problems potentially offer several advantages over mandated institutional solutions. By preserving the autonomy of the actors in a given arena, self-organizing institutions avoid the inevitable political conflicts involved in revoking existing authority from local governments or specialized agencies. By generally requiring consent of all members, self-organizing institutions enhance the search for mutually advantageous resolution of ICA problems and reduce the conflicts that arise when majorities can impose solutions on unwilling minorities. By ensuring sufficient flexibility for rules, procedures, and exchanges to be decided locally, self-governing institutions can customize these rules to best fit the local conditions and specific ICA situations. To the extent that self-governing institutions contribute to local social capital, the resolution of one ICA can provide the basis for resolving unrelated ICAs in the same region as well. Figure 6.1 shows the six categories of regional governance mechanisms.

Regional Authorities

When governments and agencies in federalist systems encounter collective problems due to fragmentation, higher-level institutions have the authority to resolve the problems by changing the geographic or functional jurisdictions to internalize the externalities. For example, a consolidated government internalizes unconsidered impacts within broad metropolitan boundaries by uniting multiple local governments into a consolidated metropolitan general-purpose government.

Special districts provide a less obtrusive means of internalizing unconsidered impacts over a broad geographic area for a specific function. Regional authorities can be created and imposed by higher-level governments. For example, many states use regional-level special districts to mitigate the horizontal problem of metropolitan service provision for geographic consolidation of services such as planning, resource management, schools, or emergency services (Mullin 2008; Farmer 2008; Andrew 2006). Yet even these centralized mechanisms can have some element of self-organization. The consent of voters is often necessary for the creation of consolidated governments, and some regional districts can be formed by voluntary actions of the underlying governments.

Despite arguments that the creation of regional authority promotes rational and efficient urban policy, efforts at city-county consolidation have been unsuccessful in the vast majority of cases in the United States. The failures of consolidation efforts are attributed to political conflict and the availability of alternative, less costly coordination mechanisms (Carr and Feiock 2004). The political and administrative costs of creating regional governments limit the scope of consolidation and special district solutions to a narrow range of ICA problems. Existing agencies and government units generally resist their loss of authority. The larger units gain efficiencies in production, but frequently at the cost of reducing the ability of local units to vary the provision of services to reflect different local preferences.

Managed or Coordinated Networks

Managed networks encompass a set of mechanisms that are designed or coordinated by third parties such as state or federal governments, nonprofit organizations, or private producers of public goods. Often, these take the form of managed or designed service networks in which a higher-level government provides funding and mandates the formation of collaborative relations among local governmental actors or designates a lead agency or organization to manage and coordinate intergovernmental service provision (Provan and Kenis 2008). An extensive literature had developed in public administration focused on these managed service implementation networks (Bardach 1998; Milward and Provan 2000; Mandell 2001; Meier and O'Toole 2001; Agranoff and McGuire 2003; Graddy and Chen 2006).

Although less recognized in the literature, nonprofit and for-profit producers may also seek to manage and coordinate interlocal public service provision (Boris and Steuerle 1999; Galaskiewicz 1985; Feiock and Andrew 2006; Shrestha and Feiock 2006). A network of private contracts operates as a regional coordination mechanism if there is a natural monopoly and local governments contract with a single organization (or small set of organizations). A monopoly provider can set a standard level and quality of service that reduces coordination costs, achieves regional scale economies in production, and promotes uniformity of services across the region. Shrestha and Feiock report that third-party coordination through relational contracts is most likely for services with low transaction risk such as refuse collection. Intergovernmental contract network coordination is most likely for services with moderate transaction risks, such as parks and recreation services, and coordination through integration in a regional government authority is most likely for goods with high transaction risks, such as water and law enforcement.

Regional Organizations

The focus of regional organizations is collective and multilateral, rather than bilateral. Their creation and activities are often based on federal and state laws. Regional organizations take on a variety of forms. Although they are sometimes established as government agencies, such as Florida's Regional Planning Councils, they can also take the form on a nonprofit organization, such as The Tampa Bay Partnership, which coordinates and supports local government development activities in a six-county region. Local governments participate in regional organizations while maintaining some (in some cases all) of their independence and autonomy. These institutions facilitate collective responses to manage regional problems across jurisdictions, but are self-organizing to the extent that members participate at will and must approve the council's activities. Even when they are constructed as a government agency, these organizations generally have limited authority to force local units to do what they do not want to do. The specific policy actions that regional organizations take are the product of bargaining and the available mechanisms of collective choice (Gerber and Gibson 2006). Thus, even though a formal institution has been created, the forces of both cooperation and competition remain, and its operation remains reliant on self-organizing.

The most common forms of residual government organizations in the United States are regional councils of governments, metropolitan planning organizations, and regional partnership organizations. Regional councils are voluntary associations of elected public officials from most or all of the governments of a metropolitan area that provide services to their member governments and often engage in multiple functions such as comprehensive planning, economic and community development, land use, and services for the elderly (Stephens and Wikstrom 2000).

Metropolitan planning organizations are regional organizations designed to manage the federal transportation issues in metropolitan areas by allocating federal funds. They are structured as voluntary associations, and in many instances, an existing council of governments constitutes the metropolitan planning organization (Weiner 1997). Nevertheless, federal highway funds are linked to participation, so local government involvement is less than entirely voluntary, even though local governments play a direct role in their governance.

Regional partnerships are multilateral associations of diverse actors often including both public and private organizations. For example, regional economic development partnerships have become an increasingly popular approach to organizing regional economic development efforts (Feiock, Steinacker, and Park 2009). Development partnerships are an "alliance formed by local governments, often with the help of private sector firms and nonprofit organizations, which has a mission of enhancing the economy of a multijurisdictional area" (Olberding 2002, 253). Watershed partnerships are another example of regional partnership institutions that collectively address water-related issues at the watershed level, relying on collaborative participation by governmental and nongovernmental actors (Lubell et al. 2002).

Contract Networks

Contract networks link individual units through joint ventures, interlocal agreements, and service contracts that require the consent of those involved. Thus, this set of governance tools preserves the autonomy of local actors while providing a formalized mechanism for resolving externality issues of concern to the parties. Contract networks link local governments in legally binding agreements, but because agreements often overlap multiple activities, they may also be supported by norms of reciprocity (Thurmaier and Wood 2002). Andrew (2006) argues that contractual ties developed locally produce general patterns of regional integration, as bilateral ventures, agreements, and contracts create a unique formation of contractual ties at the macro level.

The Coase (1960) Theorem suggests that contracting can provide a voluntary solution to externality problems. If transaction costs are sufficiently low, rational parties can achieve a Pareto-efficient outcome through voluntary bargaining. The voluntary nature of the transaction guarantees that only outcomes where all participants benefit will be undertaken. Therefore, a necessary condition for a cooperative agreement is that it produces joint gains across the actors involved, either directly or through compensatory payments from the winners to the other participants. Application of Coase's work to intergovernmental contracts suggests that under the right conditions (low transaction costs), local governments can negotiate agreements to capture spillover effects from services and growth (Ostrom 1990; Weber 1998; Lubell et al. 2002). When the actions of one jurisdiction impose costs on others, say through approval of a commercial development that will increase traffic congestion in a neighboring city, compensation could be negotiated for the negatively affected jurisdiction. However, the second necessary condition for a successful Coasian bargain to be reached is that the transaction costs to achieve the outcome are sufficiently low so that they do not outweigh the sum of the benefits provided.

A contractual arrangement between two institutional actors constitutes a dyadic relationship. If each unit also participates in other agreements with other actors, together, the dyadic relations form a macro-level regional governance structure that comprises a set of actors in a social network (see Thurmaier and Wood 2002). Over time, embedded relationships with other local governments accumulate into a regional network that invests the reputation and reciprocity of information in the reliability and competencies of prospective partners (Gulati and Gargiulo 1999).

Collaborative Groups and Councils

Collaborative groups are informal associations or multilateral agreements among local actors that provide mechanisms for information exchange, program coordination, and joint action. Informal group decisions can take the form of collectively reinforced shared understandings and expectations that, although only socially enforced, are binding. For example, in the Milwaukee metro region, local development officials informally agreed to inform one another when a firm currently operating in one jurisdiction approached another regarding location incentives to move (Steinacker and Feiock 2003). Working group coordination can also take the form of more routinized interactions through professional associations or community conferences (LeRoux 2007). For example, the city managers of coastal communities in the southern portion of Tampa Bay meet over lunch each month to share ideas, information, and informally coordinate actions. In each case, collective decisions rely on mutual consent absent any formal authority or enforcement mechanism (Oakerson 1999).

Policy Networks

The institution that provides the greatest local autonomy is informal policy networks (Heclo 1978). Network interactions mitigate governance costs by fostering norms of trust and reciprocity among institutional actors and may help identify partners where defection is less likely. Opportunities for repeated face-to-face interactions among institutional actors may be especially important for norms of trust and reciprocity to develop at levels required for cooperative agreements to form (Axelrod 1984).

Often, policy networks complement and reinforce other mechanisms. Just as formal market institutions are embedded in social relationships that provide critical support to the markets (Granovetter 1985) and just as formal organizations can function despite design flaws because of the informal organization (Scott 1995), so too can the more formal regional governance structures rely on informal, self-organized relationships among authorities for performance and stability to buffer the system from changing demands. Formal authority structures are defined in statute, whereas informal network structures emerge unplanned from interactions among institutional actors. Informal networks coordinate complex decisions within the formal structure. They preserve full local autonomy and require no formal authority, although federal and state programs can influence their development (Schneider et al. 2003).

Ostrom warns that self-governing institutions can face limitations and difficulties both in creation and in maintenance. The role of consensus and flexibility increases the decision costs even when agreements can be reached and limits the kinds of conflicts that such institutions are capable of resolving. In particular, problems involving distributive conflict or enforcement problems pose difficult challenges for emerging or existing self-organizing institutions.

We know very little about the dynamics of how self-organizing regional governance mechanisms emerge and operate in the relatively dense, fragmented institutional setting of US metropolitan regions. A transaction-cost perspective helps identify underlying problems and the factors that shape the costs and benefits of creating and maintaining the tools of regional governance.

Regional Governance: Context and Transaction Costs

Networks and collective governance mechanisms may solve problems that transcend local political boundaries, but they reflect the participants' political and economic interests, so problems of conflict and negotiations remain, even after an institution is adopted (Gerber and Gibson 2006). Information and bargaining costs, agency problems, and enforcement difficulties present barriers to self-organizing regional governance.

The Nature of the ICA Problem

The various regional governance tools described above as solution mechanisms for addressing ICA problems reflect the underlying collective problem and the specific incentives facing each actor. The governance preference of local government actors will depend on the nature of the problem as well as transaction costs they face. If the problem is simply one of coordination, as is often the case with service delivery issues, local governments may seek to coordinate decisions around central actors through participation in regional organizations or forming formal and informal or contractual networks that link to key actors that possess critical information or form weak-tie relationships (Shrestha 2008; Feiock and Lee 2008).

Alternatively, where local actors confront high-risk cooperation dilemmas with the potential for other governments to act opportunistically, they may seek the mechanism based on external authority or seek clustered reciprocal or strong-tie network relationships. Trust, mutuality, and reputations that are manifestations of closely connected networked relationships facilitate collective action (Coleman 1988; Putnam 2000; Granovettor 1985; Lubell et al. 2002). The extent to which an ICA problem requires coordination and efficient transmission of information or cooperation and the building of reputations and trust thus lead to alternative mechanisms to achieve ICA (Scholz and Berardo 2007; Feiock and Scholz 2009).

Coordination to achieve economies of scale motivate regional collaborations because each participant benefits. Nevertheless, when a large infrastructure investment is needed, the transaction risks from specific assets create cooperation risks and problems that can preclude collaborative agreements and generate demand for creation of regional authorities to internalize risk. Even in areas such as emergency response in which economies of scale can be generated from pooling individual capacities rather than from infrastructure investments, there are still transaction costs in determining compliance with the agreement and punishment strategies if there is defection. Contract or policy network interactions that tie responses to actions in one policy area to those in other policy areas or across time help members identify partners that are less likely to defect and build an enforcement structure to reduce the transaction costs.

Intergovernmental externalities pose a cooperation dilemma rather than a coordination dilemma in which successful collective action is less likely because participants' incentives are in conflict. Solving the problem may benefit those adversely affected by the externality but not the externality generators (Steinacker 2004). This suggests that compensation or coercion might be necessary to see a behavior change. Although such agreements might be reached through bilateral bargaining, this solution is hindered by distribution and agency costs if the externality producer has the dominant bargaining position.

The threat of an imposed regional authority solution may lead the negative externality producer to be willing to accept a more equitable division of the benefits from cooperation if it changes expectations about the likely alternative outcome. Strong ties to the third-party enforcers through a network increase the credibility of this threat, and strong ties among local governments can increase their lobbying force when appealing to these enforcement agents.

Transaction Costs

The challenge for self-organized solutions in these contexts is to overcome the transaction cost barriers faced by individual actors. The next sections describe specific sources of transaction costs in regional governance.

Transaction costs need to be kept low for benefits to exceed the costs of collective action (Feiock 2007). This means that the ability of local officials to self-organize is tied to state-level rules, the transaction characteristics of goods, the spatial and demographic characteristics of institutional units, and their internal political structure.

State-Level Rules

The existing set of state statutes and case law—the externally imposed rules—determines not only the specific authority of each venue in each arena but also the strategies available to each of the actors in individual efforts to avoid negative externalities and capture positive externalities. Incentives and entitlements vary tremendously across states, sometimes encouraging and at others undermining collaborative governance mechanisms. For example, contractual agreements between municipalities are sometimes subject to a higher degree of bureaucratic oversight than contractual relationships with the private sector. State tax and revenue restrictions determine the revenue impacts for government that results from collective policy decisions (Bowman and Pagano 2004). Boundary laws are also important, because if incorporation is difficult and annexation is easy, cities have increased bargaining leverage with neighboring communities (Feiock and Carr 2001).

Transaction Characteristics of Goods

Two extensively analyzed characteristics of service are asset specificity and measurement difficulty in exchange (Williamson 1981). Integrative mechanisms such as contracts and interlocal agreements may require the parties to make transaction-specific investment to complete an exchange. Some transaction-specific investments cannot easily be deployed in alternative uses. Asset specificity arises when transaction-specific investments are largely nondeployable to alternative uses (Williamson 1991). Asset specificity may require agreements to be customized to the specific needs of the parties requiring mutual adaptation to complete the exchange. Dependency between transacting parties increases as the relation-specific investment becomes more and more customized (Williamson 1991).

Likewise, measurement difficulty arises when the outcome or the process of the transaction is not easily evaluated. Even writing of an agreement becomes difficult. Developing cooperative agreements is especially problematic for services whose outputs are not tangible or whose production is complex. Effective monitoring requires quantitative measures of outcomes or appropriate level of activity by a service provider, but metering or monitoring the quantity and/or quality of output or benefits of a service can be difficult and costly.

The articles by Andrew and Carr et al. in this issue extend and elaborate how collaborative risks in addressing ICA problems are influenced by asset specificity and measurement difficulty. In high-asset specificity transactions, local governments contract with other governments rather than private producers and form bridging ties with only a few popular or high-status actors. In transactions where service qualities are difficult to measure, local governments form bonding ties with partners of their existing partners to pool resources and reduce commitment risks (Andrew 2006).

Characteristics of Communities and Regions

Shared borders increase exposure to positive and negative externalities and lock neighbors into repeat play that provides opportunities for mutual assurances that each government will contribute to the provision of the collective good (Miller 1992). Homogeneity of preferences, both within units and across units, is salient to the development of partnerships as well as the selection of network partners. Homophily (preference for similarity) and the advantages of common policy preferences ease the relationship between homogeneous units, particularly when credible commitments are important. For public officials that are the bargaining agents for their governments, knowledge that counterparts in other jurisdictions represent similar constituencies signals similar political and economic interests. Demographic homogeneity suggests that there will not be political and economic power asymmetries that advantage one of the parties and create problems for negotiating fair divisions of benefits. Homogeneity within units, not just between units, is important, because it reduces agency costs for officials negotiating interlocal agreements on behalf of citizens. It is more difficult to aggregate preferences and hold agents accountable in heterogeneous communities. Thus, we expect that intraorganizational and intrajurisdictional homogeneity will increase the likelihood of self-organizing institutions.

Political Structures

Electoral institutions shape the information available and the incentives faced by government officials. Administrators and elected officials each participate in contract and policy networks, but they differ in bargaining resources and institutional position (Feiock and Lee 2008; Matkin and Frederickson 2009). For example, institutional separation of politics and administration through an appointed manager is claimed to "reduce information costs associated with policy making in a complex environment" (Krueger and McGuire 2005: 11) and to constrain risks of opportunistic behavior by both elected and appointed leaders (Feiock 2004; Miller 2000).

The career ambitions of managers lead them to seek to capture a portion of the benefits of local government activity, particularly when those activities produce efficiency gains. City managers can use the tangible success represented by service efficiencies to advance their careers, usually by finding better-paying positions in larger and wealthier communities (Stein 1990; Feiock and Clingermayer 2004; McCabe et al. 2008). Local elected officials with ambition for higher office use intergovernmental relations to promote themselves to a larger constituency. Progressively ambitious politicians engage in regional and intergovernmental collaboration to claim credit for services provided to individuals beyond their current constituencies (Bickers and Stein 2004).

A city or county council functions as a veto player, because council approval is typically necessary to ratify agreements (Tsebelis 2002). Gerber and Gibson (2006) argue that the underlying political dilemma associated with regional governance is that local officials need to give up some authority to achieve regional coordination, but they may then be held accountable for regional policies that are contrary to the preferences of their local constituents. Even if there are citywide benefits from collaboration, district representatives may be unwilling to delegate control of decisions regarding the scope and location of projects if it means a loss of the ability to direct benefits to their district constituencies. Taken together, the higher-level rules, the transaction properties of goods, the characteristics of communities, and existing political structures shape the transaction costs of regional collaboration.

Discussion

Can voluntary collaborations among local governments provide solutions to the regional problems confronting metropolitan areas? Solutions to fragmented authority are often imposed by statute and are designed and coordinated by a higher-level government or third party. The fragmentation and institutional complexity found in metropolitan areas makes the imposition of standardized solutions difficult or even impossible. The ICA framework instead focuses on different types of mediating institutions that are more self-governing in nature.

Self-organizing solutions to regional problems are typically seen as limited, because fragmentation is assumed to preclude integrated responses to interjurisdictional problems. Much of the literature portrays local governments as incapable of overcoming their social, economic, and political differences to address policy spillover problems (Lowery 2000; Olberding 2002; Downs 1994; Katz 2000). Informal groups and contract or policy networks are viewed as ad hoc solutions or a procedural rather than a political approach to metropolitan governance (Andrew 2006). Recent empirical evidence strongly refutes these assumptions and suggests that self-organizing governance mechanisms can and do coordinate decisions in many policy arenas.

Nevertheless, even if self-organization can effectively address horizontal collective-action problems, critics point to functional collective-action problems that are profound in metropolitan areas because residential sorting and segregation have resulted in asymmetries in service preferences, resources, and political power (Lowery 2000). Asymmetries that cumulate across issues can produce cumulative disadvantage to some areas of a metropolitan region.

One advantage of solutions based on regional general-purpose government authority is the potential to address these functional collective-action problems by authoritatively integrating policies across policy or service areas as well as places. Externalities arise among services and policy arenas, not just among governmental units. Because networks and collaborative groups are typically specific to a single service, they might exacerbate rather than solve the problems of fragmentation, by pushing costs or problems on to other policy arenas. For example, cooperative agreements on economic development will have implications for local transportation and land use regulation decisions (Hawkins 2007). Thus, policy networks may be subject to many of the criticisms directed to special district governance (Carr 2006).

If effective regional governance requires a holistic approach rather than acting on individual services and issue areas in isolation, self-organizing solutions cannot address every type of intergovernmental problem (Steinacker 2004). But holistic and integrated regional governance may still be possible in a self-organizing governance system. Autonomous governments take into account multiplex relations when judging pros and cons of intergovernmental exchange, because they have multiple responsibilities and live and conduct business in a multiplex relational environment. The very setting encourages them to think, appreciate, and use networks of cross-policy compensatory mechanisms to reduce transaction risks and to maximize utility.

Contract and policy networks constitute a macro-level regional governance structure that comprises a set of actors in a social network (Thurmaier and Wood 2002; Feiock and Scholz 2009). Local actors are able to enter or exit agreements and craft customized conditions without special review by a single superior coordinating agency. The transaction risks of agreements in one service area can be mitigated if they are embedded in broader multiplex service relationships. Local governments reduce the transaction costs of contracting by paying attention not just to a potential partner's individual characteristics but also by considering the relational characteristics of the partner within the broader network of intergovernmental relationships. Individual agreements are bargained within the broader pattern of agreements and contractual relationships. Thus, risks and other transaction costs associated with contractual exchanges can be reduced when these exchanges are embedded in other relationships (Granovetter 1985).

The ICA framework can help us understand the strengths, possibilities, and limitations of self-organizing organizations and networks among local government units in ways that provide practical insights for policy design. We may be able to learn better design principles for statutorily imposed regional authorities or managed networks by observing the structures that emerge as local units negotiate customized solutions to their problems. By the same token, the policy design principles in externally imposed and third-party approaches may provide insights to increase the likelihood that self-organizing solutions will develop and improve the performance of emergent structures.

Our broader goal is to advance a research agenda that clarifies the strengths and limitations of the full spectrum of regional governance institutions for resolving specific ICA problems (Feiock and Scholz 2009). Institutional mechanisms such as contract and policy networks, collaborative groups, and certain types of regional organizations involve a great degree of autonomy and self-organization by the actors involved, but they are less well understood than the more centralized coordination mechanisms. Social network analysis provides a valuable tool to test hypotheses about the emergence and evolution of self-organizing regionalism. For example, in the natural resource management policy arena, a study of all US watersheds found that watershed partnerships emerged where the benefits of coordination were highest and the costs of developing and maintaining the partnership were lowest (Lubell et al. 2002). The National Estuary Program significantly increased the size, and integration of policy networks and self-organized collaboration was greatest for network participants having extensive, wide-ranging contacts, not those with more transitive, overlapping relationships commonly associated with social capital and cooperation (Schneider et al. 2003; Scholz, Berardo, and Kile 2008; Scholz and Berardo 2007). Insights drawn from these studies have informed the study of regional land use, economic development, and service delivery (Feiock 2004).

In the land use and economic development arenas, survey-based investigation of the conditions under which contract networks emerge confirms that both the attributes of actors and relations among them contribute to the explanation of how and why local governments decide to collaborate (Berardo and Feiock 2007). Feiock, Steinacker, and Park (2009) report that a city's demographic similarity with neighbors and centrality in the social networks of local actors increase the likelihood of joint ventures. Spatial proximity also contributes to interdependencies that safeguard cooperative action and provide a larger opportunity set of reliable partners from which to develop new ventures. Both strong-tie networks of frequent interaction among cities and participation in weak-tie associational networks increased the likelihood of development collaboration. These results suggest that collaborative groups that provide venues for local government and other organizations to interact build networks and social capital that contribute to the emergence of self-organizing solutions to metropolitan problems.

Investigations of regional integration in service delivery through intergovernmental contracts report that transaction characteristics of various services influence cities' collaboration choices in a manner consistent with predictions that actors choose governance mechanisms in a transaction-cost minimizing way (Shrestha 2008). Analysis of the structure of individual agreements as a social network yields evidence that the evolution of collaborative networks over time is shaped by interactions between service type and network structure. Andrew (2006) applies a similar social network methodology to analyze patterns of binding intergovernmental contracts and more adaptive interlocal agreements in four metropolitan regions in Florida. In each case, local governments choose partners of their partners for new contracts to reduce risks of opportunism. This emergent pattern of voluntary self-organizing networks extends the ability of local governments to resolve their service provision problem.

Advocates of both fragmentation and consolidation have promoted their favored governance mechanism generally. Rather than advocating this unitary approach, the ICA framework argues that the potential for effective metropolitan governance is contingent on the nature of collective problems and contextual factors that influence the transaction costs of negotiating, monitoring, and enforcing agreements among local government units. Thus, it not only suggests the potential for voluntary regionalism but also its limitations. Where transaction cost barriers to ICA are substantial, self-organizing solutions may not be possible, and reliance on third parties and creation of regional governments may be more efficacious. Despite their prevalence, we know very little about the capabilities and dynamics of self-organizing mechanisms when confronted with ICA problems, especially problems spanning multiple policy fields. In extant research, the ICA problems imposed on the actors is defined by specific problems and the venues and formal rules in that specific policy arena. Future work can extend this analysis by considering externalities across different venues and policy arenas in analyzing the solution mechanisms that actors develop to cope with ICA problems. The ultimate objective of these efforts is a theory or regional governance to provide a richer explanation of who governs and how.

Acknowledgments

An earlier version of this chapter was presented at the 2007 annual meeting of the American Political Science Association. I wish to thank John Scholz for his input and comments on the earlier version. This chapter is based on work supported by the DeVoe Moore Center Program in Local Governance at Florida State University and the National Science Foundation (Grant No. 030799). Any opinions, findings, and conclusions or recommendations expressed in this chapter are those of the author and do not necessarily reflect the views of the National Science Foundation.

Note

This chapter was originally published in *Urban Affairs Review* 44(3) (January 2009): 356–77. Reprinted with the permission of Sage Publications.

References

Agranoff, Robert, and Michael McGuire. 2003. *Collaborative Public Management: New Strategies for Local Governments*. Washington, DC: Georgetown University Press.

Andrew, Simon A. 2006. "Institutional Ties, Interlocal Contractual Arrangements, and the Dynamic of Metropolitan Governance." PhD diss., Florida State University.

Axelrod, Robert. 1984. *The Evolution of Cooperation.* New York: Basic Books.

Bardach, Eugene. 1998. *Getting Agencies to Work Together: The Practice and Theory of Managerial Craftmanship.* Washington, DC: Brookings Institution.

Barnes, William R., and Larry C. Ledebur. 1998. *The New Regional Economies: The U.S. Common Market and the Global Economy.* Thousand Oaks, CA: Sage.

Berardo, Ramiro, and Richard C. Feiock. 2007. "Intergovernmental Networks and the Permeability of Land Use Decisions to Development Demands." Paper presented at the annual meeting of the Southern Political Science Association, New Orleans, LA, January.

Bickers, Kenneth, and Robert M. Stein. 2004. "Interlocal Cooperation and the Distribution of Federal Grant Awards." *The Journal of Politics* 66(3): 800–22.

Boris, Elizabeth T., and C. Eugene Steuerle. 1999. *Nonprofits and Government: Collaboration and Conflict.* Washington, DC: Urban Institute Press.

Bowman, Ann, and Michael A. Pagano. 2004. *Terra Incognita: Vacant Land and Urban Strategies.* Washington, DC: Georgetown University Press.

Carr, Jered B. 2006. "Local Government Autonomy and State Reliance on Special District Governments: A Reassessment." *Political Research Quarterly* 59(3): 481–92.

Carr, Jered B., and Richard C. Feiock. 2004. *City-County Consolidation and Its Alternatives: Reshaping the Local Government Landscape.* Armonk, NY: M. E. Sharpe.

Coase, Ronald. 1960. "The Problem of Social Cost." *Journal of Law and Economics* 3(1): 1–44.

Coleman, James S. 1988. "Social Capital in the Creation of Human Capital." *American Journal of Sociology* 94: 95–120.

Downs, Anthony. 1994. *New Visions for Metropolitan America.* Washington, DC: Brookings Institution.

Farmer, Jayce L. 2008. "Institutional Collective Action and Special Purpose Governments: Special District Formation and Regional Governance." PhD diss., Florida State University.

Feiock, Richard C., ed. 2004. *Metropolitan Governance: Conflict, Competition, and Cooperation.* Washington, DC: Georgetown University Press.

———. 2007. "Rational Choice and Regional Governance." *Journal of Urban Affairs* 29(1): 47–63.

Feiock, Richard C., and Simon A. Andrew. 2006. "Understanding the Relationship between Nonprofit Organizations and Local Governments." *International Journal of Public Administration* 29(10): 759–69.

Feiock, Richard C., and Jered B. Carr. 2001. "Incentives, Entrepreneurs, and Boundary Change: A Collective Action Framework." *Urban Affairs Review* 36: 382–405.

Feiock, Richard C., and James Clingermayer. 2004. "City Managers as Residual Claimants." Paper presented at the annual meeting of the Southeastern Conference for Public Administration, Charlotte, NC, October.

Feiock, Richard, and In-Won Lee. 2008. "Informal Collaboration Networks for Resolving Economic Development Problems in Metropolitan Regions." Paper presented at the Networks in Political Science Conference, Cambridge, MA, June.

Feiock, Richard C., M. Jae Moon, and Hyung Jun Park. 2008. "Is the World 'Flat,' or 'Spiky'? Rethinking the Governance Implications of Globalization for Economic Development." *Public Administration Review* 68(1): 24–35.

Feiock, Richard C., and John Scholz, eds. 2009. *Self-Organizing Federalism: Collaborative Mechanisms to Mitigate Institutional Collective Action Dilemmas*. New York: Cambridge University Press.

Feiock, Richard C., Annette Steinacker, and Hyung Jun Park. 2009. "Institutional Collective Action and Economic Development Joint Ventures." *Public Administration Review* 69(2): 256–70.

Foster, Katherine. 2001. *Regionalism on Purpose.* Boston, MA: Lincoln Institute of Land Policy.

Galaskiewicz, Joseph. 1985. *Social Organization of an Urban Grants Economy: A Study of Business Philanthropy and Nonprofit Organizations.* Orlando, FL: Academic Press.

Gerber, Elisabeth R., and Clark C. Gibson 2006. "Balancing Competing Interests in American Regional Government." Paper presented at the Program in American Democracy Speaker Series, Notre Dame University, February.

Graddy, Elizabeth A., and Bin Chen. 2006. "Influences on the Size and Scope of Networks for Social Service Delivery." *Journal of Public Administration Research and Theory* 16(4): 533–52.

Granovetter, Mark. 1985. "Economic Action and Social Structure." *American Journal of Sociology* 91(3): 481–510.

Gulati, R., and M. Gargiulo. 1999. "Where Do Interorganizational Networks Come From?" *American Journal of Sociology* 104(5): 1439–93.

Hawkins, Christopher V. 2007. "Local Government Joint Ventures." Working paper, University of North Texas.

Heclo, Hugh. 1978. "Issue Networks and the Executive Establishment." In *The New American Political System*, edited by Anthony King, 87–101. Washington, DC: American Enterprise Institute.

Katz, Bruce, ed. 2000. *Reflections on Regionalism.* Washington, DC: Brookings Press.

Krueger, Skip, and Michael McGuire. 2005. "A Transaction Costs Explanation of Interlocal Government Collaboration." Paper presented at the 8th National Public Management Research Conference, Los Angeles, CA, September.

Leach, William D., Neil W. Pelkey, and Paul Sabatier. 2002. "Stakeholder Partnerships as Collaborative Policy-Making." *Journal of Policy Analysis and Management* 21(4): 645–70.

LeRoux, Kelly. 2007. "Councils of Government and Nonprofit Community Conferences." Working paper, Wayne State University.

Lowery, David. 2000. "A Transaction Costs Model of Metropolitan Governance: Allocation vs. Redistribution in Urban America." *Journal of Public Administration Research and Theory* 10: 49–78.

Lubell, Mark, Mark Schneider, John Scholz, and Mihriye Mete. 2002. "Watershed Partnerships and the Emergence of Collective Action Institutions." *American Journal of Political Science* 46: 148–63.

Mandell, Myrna P. ed. 2001. *Getting Results through Collaboration: Networks and Network Structures for Public Policy and Management.* Westport, CT: Quorum Books.

Matkin, David S. T., and H. George Frederickson. 2009. "Metropolitan Governance: Institutional Roles and Interjurisdictional Cooperation." *Journal of Urban Affairs* 31(1): 45–66.

McCabe, Barbara, Richard C. Feiock, James Clinger, and Christopher Stream. 2008. "Turnover among City Managers: The Role of Political and Economic Change." *Public Administration Review* 68(2): 380–87.

Meier, Kenneth J., and Laurence J. O'Toole. 2001. "Managerial Strategies and Behavior in Networks: A Model with Evidence from U.S. Public Education." *Journal of Public Administration Research and Theory* 11(3): 271–94.

Miller, Gary. 1992. *Managerial Dilemmas: The Political Economy of Hierarchy.* New York: Cambridge University Press.

———. 2000. "Above Politics: Credible Commitment and Efficiency in the Design of Public Agencies." *Journal of Public Administration Research and Theory* 10: 289–327.

Milward, H. B., and K. G. Provan. 2000. "How Networks are Governed." In *Governance and Performance: New Perspectives*, edited by Carolyn J. Heinrich and Lawrence E. Lynn, 283–62. Washington, DC: Georgetown University Press.

Mullin, Megan. 2008. *Governing the Tap.* Cambridge, MA: MIT Press.

Oakerson, Ronald J. 1999. *Governing Local Public Economies: Creating the Civic Metropolis.* Oakland, CA: ICS Press.

Olberding Julia C. 2002. "Diving into the 'Third Waves' of Regional Governance Strategies: A Study of Regional Partnerships for Economic Development in U.S. Metropolitan Areas." *Economic Development Quarterly* 16: 251–72.

Orfield, Myron. 1997. *Metropolitics: A Regional Agenda for Community and Stability.* Washington, DC: Brookings Institution.

Ostrom, Elinor. 1990. *Governing the Commons: The Evolution of Institutions for Collective Action.* New York: Cambridge University Press.

———. 2005. *Understanding Institutional Diversity.* Princeton, NJ: Princeton University Press.

Peirce, Neal R. 1993. *Citistates: How Urban America Can Prosper in a Competitive World.* Washington, DC: Seven Locks Press.

Provan, Keith G., and Patrick Kenis. 2008. "Modes of Network Governance: Structure, Management, and Effectiveness." *Journal of Public Administration Research and Theory* 18(2): 229–52.

Putnam, Robert D. 2000. *Blowing Alone: The Collapse and Revival of American Community.* New York: Simon & Schuster.

Scharpf, Fritz. W. 1997. *Games Real Actors Play: Actor-Centered Institutionalism in Policy Research.* Boulder, CO: Westview Press.

Schneider, Mark, John Scholz, Mark Lubell, Denisa Mindruta, and Matthew Edwardsen. 2003. "Building Consensual Institutions: Networks and the National Estuary Program." *American Journal of Political Science* 47(1): 143–58.

Scholz, John T., and Ramiro Berardo. 2007. "Collective Action and Self-Organizing Policy Networks: Solving Coordination and Cooperation Problems in Estuaries." Unpublished manuscript, Florida State University.

Scholz, John T., Ramiro Berardo, and Bradley Kile. 2008. "Do Networks Enhance Cooperation? Policy Communities, Issue Networks, and Joint Environmental Projects." *Journal of Politics* 70(2): 393–406.

Scholz, John T., and Richard C. Feiock. 2007. "Self-Organizing Federalism: Voluntary Coordination in Metropolitan Areas." Paper presented at the workshop on Networks and Coordination of Fragmented Authority, Tallahassee, FL, February.

Scott, Allen J. 2001. *Global City Regions: Trends, Theory, Policy.* Oxford, UK: Oxford University Press.

Scott, Allen J., and Michael Storper. 2003. "Regions, Globalization, Development." *Regional Studies* 37(6/7): 579–93.

Scott, W. Richard. 1995. *Institutions and Organizations.* Thousand Oaks, CA: Sage.

Shrestha, Manoj. 2008. "Decentralized Governments, Networks and Interlocal Cooperation in Public Goods Supply." PhD diss., Florida State University.

Shrestha, Manoj, and Richard C. Feiock. 2006. "The Network Structure of Interlocal Cooperation for Water Related Services." Paper presented at the Midwest Political Science Association meetings, Chicago, IL, April.

Stein, Robert M. 1990. *Urban Alternatives: Public and Private Markets in the Provision of Local Services.* Pittsburgh, PA: University of Pittsburgh Press.

Steinacker, Annette. 2004. "Game Theoretical Models of Metropolitan Cooperation." In *Metropolitan Governance: Conflict, Competition and Cooperation,* edited by Richard C. Feiock, 46–66. Washington, DC: Georgetown University Press.

Steinacker, Annette, and Richard C. Feiock. 2003. "A Bargaining Framework for Local Development Policy Choices." Paper presented at the annual American Political Science Association meetings, Philadelphia, PA, August.

Stephens, G. Ross, and Nelson Wikstrom. 2000. *Metropolitan Government and Governance: Theoretical Perspectives, Empirical Analysis, and the Future.* Oxford, UK: Oxford University Press.

Thurmaier, Kurt, and Curtis Wood. 2002. "Interlocal Agreements as Social Networks: Picket Fence Regionalism in Metropolitan Kansas City." *Public Administration Review* 62(5): 585–98.

Tsebelis, George. 2002. *Veto Players: How Political Institutions Work.* Princeton, NJ: Princeton University Press.

Weber, Edward P. 1998. *Pluralism by the Rules: Conflict and Cooperation in Environmental Regulation.* Washington, DC: Georgetown University Press.

Weiner, Edward. 1997. *Urban Transportation Policy in the United States: A Historical Overview.* Washington, DC: US Department of Transportation.

Williamson, Oliver E. 1981. "The Economics of Organization: The Transaction Cost Approach." *American Journal of Sociology* 87(3): 548–77.

———. 1991. "Comparative Economic Organization." *Administrative Science Quarterly* 36: 269–96.

7

Structuring Institutional Analysis for Urban Ecosystems: A Key to Sustainable Urban Forest Management

Sarah K. Mincey, Miranda Hutten, Burnell C. Fischer, Tom P. Evans, Susan I. Stewart, and Jessica M. Vogt

More than 50 percent of the world's population now lives in urban areas and that figure is projected to increase to 60 percent by 2025 (Wu 2008). Increasing urban populations rely on urban forests that provide important positive externalities through ecosystem services. These services—public goods—include clean air and water; energy conservation; carbon storage and sequestration; cooler and more regulated air temperatures; wildlife habitat; recreational opportunities; social, physical, and psychological well-being; and economic stimuli (Bolund and Hunhammar 1999; McPherson et al. 1997; McPherson 2006; Nowak and Dwyer 2000; Wolf 2004, 2005). Yet, a decline in urban forest structure and related function in the United States has been noted (Nowak and Walton 2005; Wu 2008; Nowak and Greenfield 2012), elevating the importance of research to understand how the interactions between people, their institutions, and the biophysical environment affect the sustainability of urban natural resources. Such research facilitates the current focus on developing sustainable cities (Grove 2009) and is a key future focus in urbanization and human dimensions of global environmental change (IHDP 2010).

To date, there has been extensive work developing tools to evaluate coupled human-environment system dynamics in urban ecosystems. Along with comprehensive ecological assessments of vegetative and faunal populations (the ecology *in* cities approach), these methods have included survey instruments to understand how decision making by individual landowners, non-governmental organization stakeholders, and government actors at different scales affect ecological dynamics in urban environments (the ecology *of* cities approach) (Grove 2009). This work has developed particularly robust methods for linking landowner attributes to landscape outcomes on discrete spatial partitions (Pickett, Cadenasso, and Grove 2008), effectively applying analytical approaches from landscape ecology to urban contexts (Wu 2008). Much of this interdisciplinary research has been accomplished by urban ecologists and social scientists; their multi-method approach has been to study urban ecosystems as coupled social-ecological systems (SESs) in which biophysical and social systems, including human institutions, interact.

However, while frameworks for analyzing human institutions have been applied to many predominantly rural SES domains (e.g., fisheries, forests, irrigation networks), there has been less work formalizing institutional dimensions for the study of social-ecological dynamics in urban systems. To be clear, there have been empirical studies of institutions—the rules and norms that influence human decision making and action (Ostrom 1990)—in urban systems, but a formal structure for institutional analysis has not been developed for urban ecosystem research. While urban ecology's Human Ecosystem Framework includes "institutions" as a social ordering mechanism, among its applications, the use and meaning of the term has been varied. Therefore, given the considerable significance of institutions to sustainable management of community forests (Gibson, McKean, and Ostrom 2000) that are akin to urban forests (Nilsson, Konijnendijk, and Randrup 1999),[1] an exciting opportunity exists for cross-disciplinary fertilization of institutional analysis from rural SESs to urban ecosystems.

More in-depth and structured analysis of institutions in urban SESs promises to help answer why and how individuals are incentivized to conserve or remove urban trees—an imperative question for declining urban forests. While a strong thread of policy analysis exists in urban systems, additional structure is needed for long-term and cross-site analyses to develop the depth of understanding cumulated in rural systems through structured institutional analysis. Herein, we propose a clear definition of "institutions" and a structure for institutional analysis in urban ecosystems through a general institutional framework (Ostrom 1990, 2005). We demonstrate the use of this analytical framework by articulating unique institutional contexts found in urban systems and present approaches for characterizing those institutions and their interactions with urban actors and the resource by considering the management of a specific urban forest type, street trees.

Background on the Problem

Urban forests are coupled SESs composed of biophysical components (trees and associated vegetation) and social components, and like other SESs, are complex and adaptive, involving multiple subsystems as well as being embedded in larger systems. SES sustainability is related to both ecological resilience and engineered robustness, the latter being particularly significant for urban forests because they are, in part, engineered by humans (Anderies, Janssen, and Ostrom 2004; Zipperer et al. 1997). A robust SES is able to maintain some desired system characteristic despite changes in the behavior of its components parts, circumstances that contribute to long-enduring or sustainable systems overall (Anderies, Janssen, and Ostrom 2004). Dwyer, Nowak, and Noble (2003) argue it is the provision of ecosystem services (public goods) over space and time that constitutes sustainable urban forests.

Sustaining ecosystem services from an urban forest means developing a robust population of trees and associated vegetation across the myriad of subsystems that compose the larger system; street trees, park trees, treed preserves, and private parcels constitute some of the subsystems to be managed. Trees are one resource within these subsystems, and can be considered a stock from which a flow of goods and ecosystem services are obtained (see Lant, Ruhl, and Kraft 2008). Because important ecosystem services are provided via functioning urban forests, and a loss in urban forest structure leads to a loss in function (Nowak et al. 2008), sustainable urban forests are managed for maintenance of structure that does not forfeit long-term or distributional provision of ecosystem services (McPherson 2006). Thus, a number of structural management challenges facing urban forest managers have been empirically explored including maintenance of a sustainable tree population via tree relative age-distribution, native and diverse species distribution, tree condition, as well as aggregate canopy cover at the scale of interest and equitable distribution of canopy cover across spatial scales (Clark et al. 1997).

Because urban forests are human-engineered systems, their structural robustness lies in the collective actions of individuals. Humans at various scales or "subsystems" from households to city blocks to neighborhoods to governments are part of an urban ecosystem and make decisions that are integral to sustaining it (Grove 2009; Roy Chowdhury et al. 2011). Therefore, urban forest management is polycentric and involves operational-level (or on-the-ground) actors as well as policymakers that influence urban planning, land use, and development. For instance, city governments are frequently charged with managing "the" urban forest and its canopy cover. While governments may produce a portion of city trees, they rely heavily on tree production from individual private-property parcels that contain the majority of urban trees (Clark et al. 1997).

This scenario may be partly responsible for the noted decline in urban forest structure as few incentives exist for private individuals to produce public goods at levels that are socially optimal. For instance, since there is no effective market for ecosystem services, property owners often manage land and resources for outputs traded in extant markets (e.g., housing development) at the expense of natural capital (e.g., trees) and the flow of functional public benefits (ecosystem services that generally have no market). Related, the incentive for actors to rely on the provision of others without contributing themselves is known as the free-rider problem. If an individual pays to plant or maintain a tree, other individuals benefit as much as the investor without incurring costs. Further, an investor, acting alone, is likely to argue that one individual's efforts may make little to no difference in "the big picture" provision of ecosystem services. However, involving other individuals to avoid this dilemma is costly in terms of transaction time and effort to facilitate collective action for the sustainable provision of services.

For solutions to these social dilemmas, coordinated strategies of action that define how a community provides for, produces, and manages public goods are required involving rules and norms among actors or resource users in a given situation (Ostrom, Gardner, and Walker 1994). But for many decades, scholars argued that the appropriate institutions to solve such social dilemmas were property rights alone. More specifically, they argued for privatization (and market solutions) or government command and control, disregarding community management based on the theory that humans are exclusively rational egoists and do not collectively act for the public good as Hardin (1968) defined in "The Tragedy of the Commons." But clearly, markets do not always exist where needed—there is no functional market for ecosystem services—and government command and control can fail to incentivize socially beneficial actions, particularly when the target resource setting is as complex and "institutionally thick" as an urban forest (see Hardy and Koontz 2010). Moreover, humans do not always act as rational egoists but are boundedly rational—able to follow norms and rules and learn and adapt to collectively organize institutional arrangements of resource management (Ostrom 2005). From this perspective, institutions "change incentives to enable fallible humans to overcome social dilemmas" (Ostrom

2005, 125). Thus, regardless of tenure regimes, successful institutions in the forms of rules-in-use can help to establish sustainable systems (Moran 2005). Alternatively, misguided institutions can do more harm than good unless there is a coherent understanding of the nature of the resource itself (Ostrom, Gardner, and Walker 1994), a real concern in the relatively new field of urban ecology where policy prescriptions abound (Young and Wolf 2006). In either case, institutions appear as a key for integrating social and ecological analyses.

Yet, institutions have received less attention and scrutiny in urban forest management and urban ecosystems research despite recent emphasis on interdisciplinary or integrated research for environmental questions and problems that cut across traditional disciplinary boundaries—arguably the case for urban ecosystem sustainability. Wake (2008) argues that natural and social scientists of the twenty-first century must address societal needs in new and synthetic ways with integrative attitudes to solve contemporary problems. As in response, Lowe, Whitman, and Phillipson (2009) track a myriad of recent interdisciplinary efforts pointing to the relatively new and supportive perspective of ecologists that people are a part of nature (and thus, ecology) rather than apart from it. In fact, the "ecology of cities" approach, accepted by many urban ecologists, frames urban ecology in this light. And yet, Grove (2009) argues that we understand very little about the dynamics of urban ecosystem services and human preferences over space and time. In other words, the incentives (based on institutions) that structure human decisions and actions linking community characteristics and biophysical outcomes are not well understood. This failure to cumulate institutional understanding is arguably related to uncommon language among disciplines at work in urban ecosystem sustainability (discussed in the following section). Nonetheless, discovering why and how individuals and collective associations of individuals through various social subsystems are incentivized to conserve or remove urban trees is therefore, in part, an *institutional* inquiry—distinct from a more general social inquiry—because institutions are tools that influence the incentives of humans thereby affecting their decisions and actions. They are an important link for integrating social and ecological phenomenon. Moreover, urban environments are prone to rapid change through their emergent properties in response to institutions (Benvie 2005). Thus, to explore the sustainability of urban forests or any urban ecosystem resource, institutions must be well defined and institutional analysis must be undertaken to understand the dynamics affecting resource decision making.

Defining Institutions

Failure to cumulate institutional understanding in urban ecosystems, let alone other disciplines, is arguably related to variation in definitions among disciplines. In fact, this is a general problem in interdisciplinary work; Michalos (1997, 222) points to an inability to "get a generally accepted ontology" for the integration of social, economic, and environmental indicators of sustainability. Not surprisingly, competing definitions of "institutions" exist both within and among different academic disciplines even though the idea of institutions dates to Giambattista Vicco's 1725 *Scienza Nuova* (Ostrom 2005; Hodgson 2006). While the term commonly refers to organizations or entities, its academic focus has been governing forces and the majority of these explanations can be placed within two approaches: institutions-as-equilibria and institutions-as-norms/rules.

Scholars that advocate an institutions-as-equilibria study how stability emerges from mutually understood actor preferences as well as optimizing behavior (Menger 1963; Hayek 1945, 1967; Schotter 1981; Riker 1980; Calvert 1995). Proponents of this approach view stable behavior patterns (equilibrium) as a form of institutions. Calvert (1995, 18) finds "there is, strictly speaking, no separate animal that we can identify as an institution . . . institution is just a name we give to certain parts of certain kinds of equilibrium." This approach has been critiqued by a number of new institutional economics (NIE) scholars since the definition does not account for the foundations or underpinnings of stable outcomes that tease out different levels of equilibria like "shared advice based on prudence, shared obligations based on normative judgements, and shared commitments based on rules created and enforced by a community" (Crawford and Ostrom 1995, 583).

The institutions-as-norms/rules approach, supported by NIE scholars, argues that behavior patterns are grounded in what a society believes is both correct and improper behavior given a certain stimulus (Lewis 1969; Ullmann-Margalit 1977; Coleman 1988). The study of institutions should not solely be the study of equilibria but go "beyond immediate means-end relationships to analyze the shared beliefs of a group about normative obligations" (Crawford and Ostrom 1995, 583). This approach stresses that not only norms, but rules such as public policies or laws structure institutions (Hohfeld 1913; Commons 1986; Shepsle 1975, 1979, 1989; Shepsle and Weingast 1984, 1987; Plott 1986; Oakerson and Parks 1988; North 1986, 1990; Ostrom 1986; Ostrom, Gardner, and Walker 1994; Ostrom 1980; Williamson 1985; Knight 1992). Actions outside what a rule proscribes or requires are likely to be discouraged due to sanctions and punishments.

NIE scholars that utilize the Institutional Analysis and Development (IAD) framework originally developed by Kiser and Ostrom (1982) further distinguish between rules, norms, and shared strategies as different kinds of institutions. From this perspective, rules are institutional prescriptions for behavior that require, prohibit, or permit some action or outcome *and* include sanctions (an "or else" statement) if a rule is not abided. Rules can be as formal as law or as informal as common knowledge, so long as the rule also entails an "or else" clause (Ostrom 2005). The focus is more specifically on "rules-in-use" as rules followed in practice are not always the same as written rules, resulting in variable outcomes. Norms are the values that "individuals place on actions or strategies in and of themselves, not as they are connected to immediate consequences" (Ostrom 1990, 35); they are institutional prescriptions for behavior *without* defined sanctions that can be just as important as rules in constraining human behavior due to fear of social censure (Ostrom 1990, 2005). Shared strategies are even less formal as they do not include defined sanctions *or* an operator that "forbids" or "requires" or "permits" an action; instead, strategies are taken by actors based in part on their knowledge of norms and rules.

Institutions in Urban Ecosystem Research

Within their extensive empirical work that considers biophysical qualities and social characteristics of urban communities, urban ecologists have argued that "institutions" are components of urban ecosystems (Grove 2009); yet, given the interdisciplinary nature of urban ecology, a term that truly denotes social-ecological analyses, it is not surprising that some inconsistency exists within the field on how to incorporate this human component into frameworks for urban ecology[2] (McDonnell and Pickett 1993). While urban ecology scholars recognize institutions are related to behavior patterns and that institutions can take both formal and informal forms, they draw largely from the institutions-as-equilibria approach, and do not always define "rules" or "norms." This points to a difficulty in basing new institutional analysis in urban ecology on existing work, and highlights the rationale for drawing from the extensive institutional research in rural social-ecological systems and to build upon those urban studies that have utilized more structured institutional analysis.

A number of frameworks, such as the Human Ecosystem Framework (for an example, see www.beslter.org/one_pagers/pdf/the_human_ecosystem.pdf), have emerged in urban ecology that link human and natural systems (Boyden 1977; Blood 1994; Pickett et al. 1994, 1997; Machlis, Force, and Burch 1997; Grove 2009). These frameworks aim to account for connectivity issues and dynamics that govern social-ecological system outcomes. Among them, the prevalence and clarity of "institutions" varies. Those that include institutions frequently embed them as minor exogenous factors. More significantly, variation exists in the definition of institutions. For example, some scholars state that institutions are "rules of the game" and "play a key role in the adjustments or adaption of cities to changing conditions" (Grove 2009, 287; Burch and DeLuca 1984). However, what is meant by "rules" is not clearly stated. Institutions are also commonly described broadly as "dynamic solutions to universal needs, including health, justice, faith, commerce, education, leisure, government, and sustenance" (Grove 2009, 288; Machlis, Force, and Burch 1997), or inclusive of "kinship, economy, religion, polity, governance, and education" (Beddoe et al. 2009). Such broad definitions, while arguably appropriate for framing scholarship, make institutions difficult to operationally incorporate into empirical analysis.

Without a working definition of institutions, difficulty arises in conducting cumulative and comparative institutional analyses that otherwise have the potential to yield robust policy prescriptions for sustaining trees and related resources in urban ecosystems. This situation may be the reason for the relative scarcity of empirical analysis clearly linking institutional nuances with urban SES outcomes. Yet, surprisingly, Young and Wolf (2006) find urban ecology literature increasingly engaged in policy prescriptions; nearly three quarters of the papers analyzed specified the set of actors best positioned to effect change but without clarity on how institutions were evaluated within the studies.

Examples of empirical institutional research undertaken in urban ecological studies include analysis outside of the United States. In Stockholm, Sweden, urban green areas that are managed by local user groups have been studied to explain what norms and rules support ecological systems within different landscapes and governance regimes (Colding, Lundberg, and Folke 2006; Barthel, Colding, and Folke 2005; Ernstson, Sorlin, and Elmquist 2008). Without explicit analysis of how institutions vary across governance regimes, researchers conclude that "the incorporation of locally managed lands, and their stewards and institutions, into co-management designs holds potential for improving conditions for urban biodiversity [. . .]" (Colding, Lundberg, and Folke 2006, 237). Researchers in China link institutions with outcomes and have noted that where legal regulations are not enforced or understood by local people, urban forests have been destroyed (Ye 1997 in Li et al. 2005). Similarly, Nagendra and Gopal (2011) infer that the lack of consistent and publicly available tree policies in Bangalore, India, may be partly responsible for declining tree diversity within city parks.

Within the United States, Long Term Ecological Research (LTER) sites situated in Phoenix, Arizona and Baltimore, Maryland, have facilitated a number of studies that link lawn/parcel vegetation management with social variables, legacies, and institutions offering contributions to understanding this previously unexplored component of the urban forest. While these studies have found institutions to be influential factors apart from more general social variables, they stop short of fully exploring them through structured institutional analysis. Larson et al. (2009) have examined lawn management in Phoenix to understand how social and cultural norms and legacies impact urban landscapes. Martin, Peterson, and Stabler (2003) analyzed how municipal ordinances and home ownership rules shape unique grass-scapes while Jenkins (1994) identified how internalized social censure plays a role in compelling residents to conform to local lawn standards. According to Robbins and Sharp (2003), aesthetic norms and the fear of neighborhood sanctions are among key drivers affecting front yard maintenance. Larsen and Harlan (2006) explore the power of homeowner association (HOA) rules in influencing front yard landscapes in Phoenix and predict their increasing importance as legal prescriptions for landscape management. In Baltimore, building codes that required minimum set-backs from streets and zoning laws that forbade mixed-use development were determined to be important factors that contributed to residential developments of "seas of green grass" (Boone et al. 2009). Access to green areas—an issue of environmental justice—was impacted by institutional legacies in Baltimore; a neighborhood association that promoted tree planting and a past covenant that reserved properties for white occupancy-only led to racially biased access to trees within the city (Buckley 2010).

Other researchers, through complimentary work, have argued for in-depth empirical institutional analysis in urban ecosystems. Stewardship mapping and spatial social network analysis in New York, New York, is currently characterizing social groups that manage urban forests, with a focus on collective action and social networking (USDA Forest Service 2009). In fact, Tidball et al. (2010) purport that post-9/11 resilience (a concept linked to sustainability) within New York City communities was obtained in part by community civic ecology strategies, and argue that SES resilience should be studied not only in rural communities but in urban areas that are vital to global sustainability. Research is also being conducted in Chicago, Illinois, to connect institutions of urban forest restoration groups to potential biodiversity outcomes utilizing a well-developed research program, the International Forestry Resources and Institutions (IFRI) program (see http://www.umich.edu/~ifri/) (Lynne Westphal, personal communication, March 5, 2010). In this case, researchers have made the clear connection between rural and urban institutional analysis and are working to adapt the program's protocols, developed in rural sites, to urban social-ecological systems.

Urban forest ecology and management, arguably a subdiscipline of urban ecology, recognizes the importance of institutions in managing urban trees, but bases many widely accepted policy prescriptions on best practices espoused by certification programs such as Arbor Day Foundation's Tree City USA or the enduring "Model of Urban Forest Sustainability" (Clark et al. 1997; Van Wassenaer and Kenney 2010). For example, both define a sustainable urban forest as one governed by a municipal tree care ordinance, a formal institutional arrangement. Clearly, recognition exists that policy is an important tool for sustaining urban forests by adjusting human incentives and actions, but the rich array of institutional types and structures are not well enumerated or studied within the field. Only a handful of empirical works (McPherson 2001; Conway and Urbani 2007; Zhang et al. 2009) consider urban tree care ordinances in detail.

The IAD framework, which we suggest is useful for urban SES institutional analysis, has rarely been applied in urban ecosystem studies, although a few exceptions are notable. Benvie (2005) demonstrated that the presence of institutional design principles (see Ostrom 1990) supported successful adaptive management via collective efforts of resource users in a degraded and declining urban water outlet channel, the Las Vegas Wash. Additionally, a recent comparative study of rural and urban collaborative watershed groups utilized the IAD framework and concluded that urbanites took advantage of the institutional nature of urban areas to strengthen and add to top-down local policies protecting the watersheds; while the rural watershed group was equally successful, they utilized more bottom-up institutional approaches, encouraging landowners to engage in voluntary institutional arrangements including conservation easements (Hardy and Koontz 2010). This analysis found that urbanites compared to their rural counterparts incurred higher transaction costs in terms of sharing information, coordinating activities, and coming to agreement on management strategies due to the relatively large number of urban actors and overlapping urban jurisdictions. Such a social dilemma might not otherwise have been empirically uncovered without structured institutional analysis. This previous research lays the groundwork upon which we build our case for further use of the IAD framework.

Common Institutions Influencing Urban Forest Ecosystems

Clearly, urban forestry and urban ecosystem researchers have acknowledged the role of institutions in their field, thus these settings are well suited for more structured institutional analysis given their biophysical and social complexity and the important role that both formal and informal rules play in land use decisions that have the potential to produce public goods or "bads." Specifically, urban forests are fragmented into a multifaceted matrix of property rights and management strategies subject to a myriad of actors and their associated governance regimes. Within many cities, the majority of private property parcels and their trees are owned and managed by individuals, while some private parcels exist under shared ownership and management, and numerous public property parcels are owned and managed by public entities but often heavily used by the general public. Each of these various governance and use regimes is impacted by diverse and nested institutions given the urban context—a context that Hardy and Koontz (2010) reference as institutionally complex. For instance, municipal zoning laws can influence the area available for urban trees, while these institutions are authorized by state policies. Even federal urban forest management strategies are encouraged through state governments and at local levels through funding from the US Forest Service's State and Private Forestry arm that supports urban and community forestry.

Beyond the complexity of urban property rights, there are numerous, frequently encountered institutions directly related to and impacting urban forest management at the finest scale of management, the private residential parcel (Figure 7.1). Municipalities design urban forest conservation codes such as the requirement to obtain a permit to remove trees (even privately owned ones) above a certain size, the maintenance of a percentage of original canopy cover amidst private development, or tree planting requirements within the public right-of-way adjacent to private parcels. Besides municipal code, cities often enter into agreements with developers during

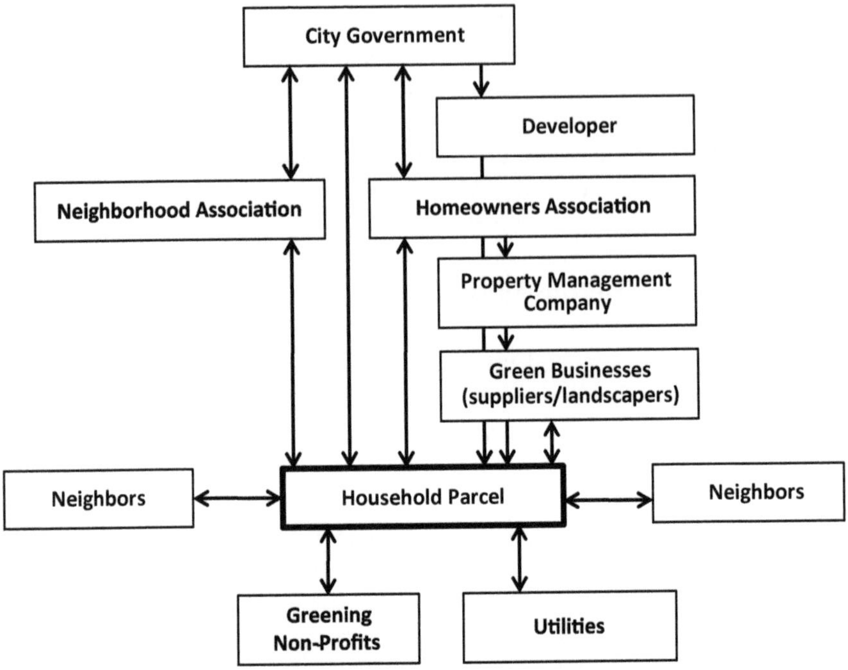

Figure 7.1. Common actors and types of institutional arrangements affecting action situations related to urban household land and tree management. Solid lines represent formal institutions or rules while dashed lines represent informal institutions, or norms/strategies. Arrows indicate the primary direction of institutional influence.

planning stages that establish conservation easements or tree preservation easements, which may then become covenants of the development and can be enforced or forgotten by the city, homeowners associations, or neighborhood associations. Thus, the macro-level force of development legacies, as they have been called (Larsen and Harlan 2006), may be altered by subsequent governance forces. For instance, collective residential associations often create their own institutions in terms of bylaws that affect the species that are planted, dead tree removal, or even the acceptable height of vegetation. Moreover, utility easements and their related institutions may overlap with any one of these previously mentioned arrangements. To add even more complexity, informal institutions—norms and strategies—can be quite significant in urban forest management, often incentivizing "popular" landscaping species (also affected by tree nurseries or private industry-landscape contractors) or management strategies—even poor ones, including tree-topping or monoculture plantings. Green non-profits and advocacy organizations may play a role by attempting to influence strategies and norms related to tree management.

Clearly, the nature of the urban forest in terms of governance and institutions is quite complex, facilitating heterogeneous outcomes at the parcel and neighborhood scale across urban landscapes. Unless a community—individual actors, associations, and governments—has established institutions that operate across scales (from parcels to neighborhoods and city-wide) to incentivize sustainable management of urban trees, it may struggle to influence the structure of the urban forest as a whole and its functional provision of ecosystem services. Moreover, unless urban ecosystem researchers have carefully considered institutional forces at play within a research site, their policy prescriptions have the potential to misguide solutions and do more harm than good.

The Institutional Analysis and Development (IAD) Framework and Lessons from Its Application

A wealth of institutional analyses that can be adapted to urban ecosystems research have been undertaken largely in *rural* social-ecological systems by building upon the IAD framework developed by Kiser and Ostrom (1982). Through this framework, Munger (2010) finds resolution by an exact definition of institutions as rules, norms, and shared strategies that constrain human behavior, each in precise ways (as previously detailed). The importance of institutional analysis in sustaining natural resources is made clear from this perspective: institutions are not minor, embedded components of social systems, but, along with characteristics of the physical world and the community of resource users, are top-tier variables that structure the context in which humans make decisions and act (Ostrom 2005). In fact, from research in numerous *rural* systems, Ostrom (1990) utilized institutional analysis to categorize institutional characteristics, or design principles, associated with long-enduring natural resource management communities that have proven robust across multiple sectors and over time (Cox, Arnold, and Villamayor Tomás 2010). In these systems, in-depth institutional analysis has determined how institutions shift individual incentives and actions, directly affecting sustainable outcomes.

This precise perspective of institutions within the context of the IAD framework (Figure 7.2) links attributes of the *physical world* (the resource

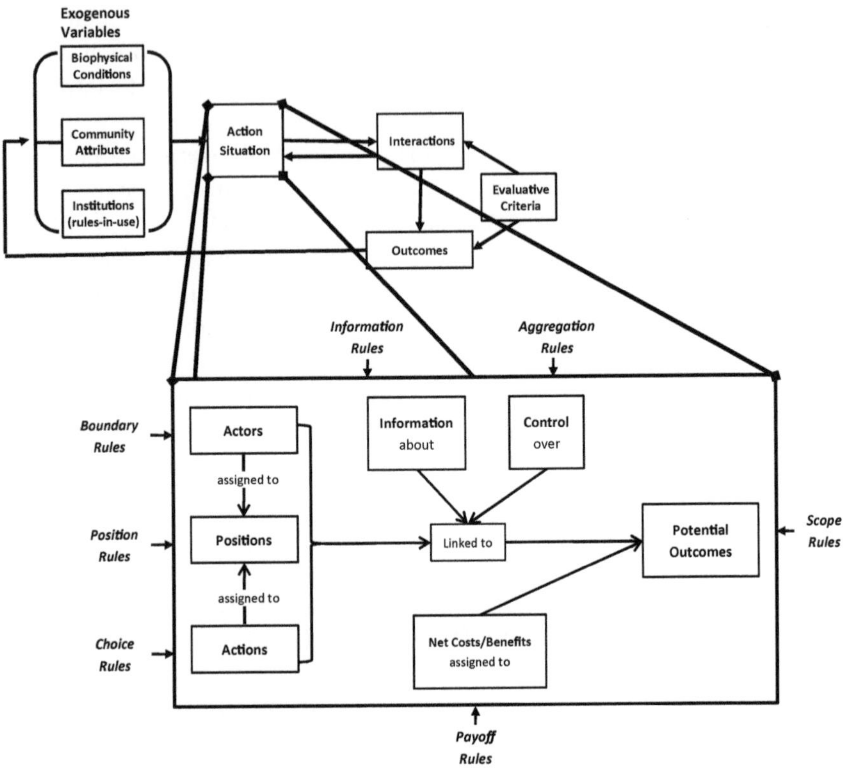

Figure 7.2. The IAD framework in the background and the inner-workings of an action situation in the foreground. The rules influencing the action situation's component parts are listed around its boundary.

Source: Adapted from Ostrom (2005, 189).

system and resource units), a *community of users*, and the *rules-in-use by that community* as the exogenous variables that incentivize and constrain *actors* in an *action situation*, ultimately leading to *outcomes* (Ostrom 2005). As suggested, an action situation is a setting where two or more individuals are faced with a set of potential actions that jointly produce outcomes representing a snapshot in time in which exogenous variables are held fixed for analysis (Ostrom 2005)[3]; an example includes users of a natural resource managing resource units, such as a forestry agency managing a forest for timber products. "Management" is a broad term for a number of actions related to governance. Ostrom, Tiebout, and Warren (1961) and McGinnis (2011) define key tasks (or individual action situations) that indicate an effective system of governance—the *provision* for, *production* of, and *consumption* of goods/services, *financing* activities, *rule-making* and *monitoring* related to goods/services, *sanctioning* rule-breakers, *dispute resolution mechanisms*, *information dissemination*, and *coordination* among all relevant actors. Each of these tasks defines an individual action situation that could be modeled in the IAD framework and for which a set of rules apply.

Within an action situation, actors (individuals or entities) are assigned to positions through which they choose to act in light of information, the control they have over action-outcome linkages, and the benefits and costs assigned to actions and outcomes (Figure 7.2). Each of these variables is affected by institutions. Position rules define the main role or position an actor can take (in the case of forest management, the position could be a "forest manager"), boundary rules define how actors are eligible for this position and how they enter and exit it, choice rules define the allowable actions that actors can take, and information rules affect the level of information available to actors, affecting their decisions among actions. In addition, aggregation rules define whether a single participant or multiple participants must make decisions in the case that multiple actors hold the same position; payoff rules assign rewards or sanctions to actions, and scope rules define allowable outcomes (see further details in Ostrom 2005). This framework clearly "serves to remind us that each actor's preferences, as well as the choice options available to them, are determined by the institutional arrangements" (McGinnis 2011, 2).

This approach further defines institutional arrangements as three nested layers of rules: constitutional, collective choice, and operational rules (Ostrom 1990). Operational rules govern day-to-day activities (e.g., "The forest manager may not cut down any standing tree or else he/she must pay a fine equivalent to the value of the tree"). Collective-choice rules determine how operational-level rules are set or changed (e.g., "The forest trustees must meet annually to review rules related to tree management; rules must be presented to trustees and voted upon utilizing a majority-rule procedure"). Likewise, constitutional rules determine how collective-choice rules are set and changed. Typically, the rules in place in a situation of operational choice are assumed to be determined at the collective-choice level and collective-choice (or policy) actions are governed by rules at the constitutional level; however, adjacent operational action situations impact one another and can be impacted by multiple processes of collective-choice or constitutional interactions (e.g., increased *financing* may lead to increased *production* of a good/service while both management activities can arise from the same operational level) (McGinnis 2011). In addition, actors move between levels—if a day-to-day operational tactic is failing, actors utilize collective-choice rules to make changes to operational rules. For instance, if *monitoring* of tree removal has not been effective at preserving a forest for the provision of ecosystem services (the outcome of interest), forest managers and concerned forest users (actors) may act in a collective-choice arena to adjust rules defining who operationally monitors the forest and the qualification they must have (boundary rules) and the tactics they use to monitor (choice rules).

The IAD framework has been utilized empirically in a myriad of seemingly disparate settings—across fisheries, forests, and irrigation networks, for example (Ostrom, Gardner, and Walker 1994)—and through these studies, design principles (theories) (Ostrom 1990) were built upon the IAD framework that demonstrate key characteristics that yield sustainable SESs. Many of these principles relate directly to institutions and provide reliable theory to be tested in urban systems: (1) resource users must be able to communicate; (2a) boundaries of the resource and (2b) the roles of the resource users must be clear; (3a) rules governing the use of the good must fit the local needs and conditions and (3b) benefits are proportional to inputs; (4) individuals affected by the rules can modify the rules; (5) external authorities respect the rights of users to devise rules; (6a) monitoring of the resource occurs and is undertaken by users and (6b) monitoring of the users occurs; (7) a graduated system of sanctions is used for rule breakers; and (8) a system of nested enterprises and institutions are necessary for complex resource systems (Ostrom 1990, 2005; Cox, Arnold, and Villamayor Tomás 2010). Although arising largely from *rural* resource management studies, the design principles have recently been deemed useful for analysis of collective resource management in *urban* settings (Benvie 2005).

Empirical work has confirmed the importance of these institutional characteristics and the IAD framework to important research findings. For instance, Chhatre and Agrawal (2009) used data on eighty forest study sites in ten countries to show that greater rule-making autonomy at the local level is associated with greater carbon storage and livelihood benefits, outcomes that facilitate sustainability. Another study found that for 220 forest communities, regular, institutionalized monitoring was significantly and positively correlated with forest condition (Gibson et al. 2005). Although not in the realm of social-ecological systems research, the framework was also utilized in urban studies related to the provision of policing as a public good in Chicago and Indianapolis (Ostrom and Baugh

1973; Ostrom, Parks, and Whitaker 1974), which is not dissimilar from the concept of the provision of ecosystem services, as both are essential public goods in urban communities.

Application of Institutional Analysis to Urban Forest Ecosystems

As a concrete illustration of the application of this kind of institutional analysis to urban ecosystem management, consider one subsystem of the urban forest: street trees. In Figures 7.3 and 7.4, we demonstrate operational and collective-choice action situations affecting the managed structure of a city's street trees.[4] Typically, in the United States, street trees are frequently defined formally in a city's municipal code as the trees in the public right-of-way (PROW). The PROW is also generally described in city code as land beyond the surface of the road pavement to some distance measured from the center of public streets. As described above, municipal governments and adjacent private property owners are generally responsible for the maintenance of street trees in accordance with broad city goals like public safety and aesthetics, or specific aims to plant all available tree spaces. Such information is generally included in code, as well. For example, some cities require adjacent property owners to obtain a permit to remove, plant, or prune trees in the PROW even if the responsibility of its maintenance is relegated to the adjacent property owner while its ownership is relegated to the city. These institutions in city code constitute operational-level rules (Figure 7.3), impacting the day-to-day management of street trees.

These operational rules are often recommended by tree commissions or boards to executive councils or administrators for enactment in accordance with collective-choice (Figure 7.4) and constitutional rules that determine policymaking and its procedure. For example, city ordinances frequently define that a city tree board write legislation regarding operational management of city trees, that a city council consider that legislation and take public comment regarding it, amend it as necessary, and vote to reject or pass it as city code.

Unfortunately, perverse incentives and unintended outcomes may result from such common urban forestry institutions meant to aid in the management of street trees and may be linked to the general decline of urban forests, causal links that may not be empirically derived without structured institutional analysis. The failed governance task in this exemplary circumstance is the *production* of healthy street trees (an action situ-

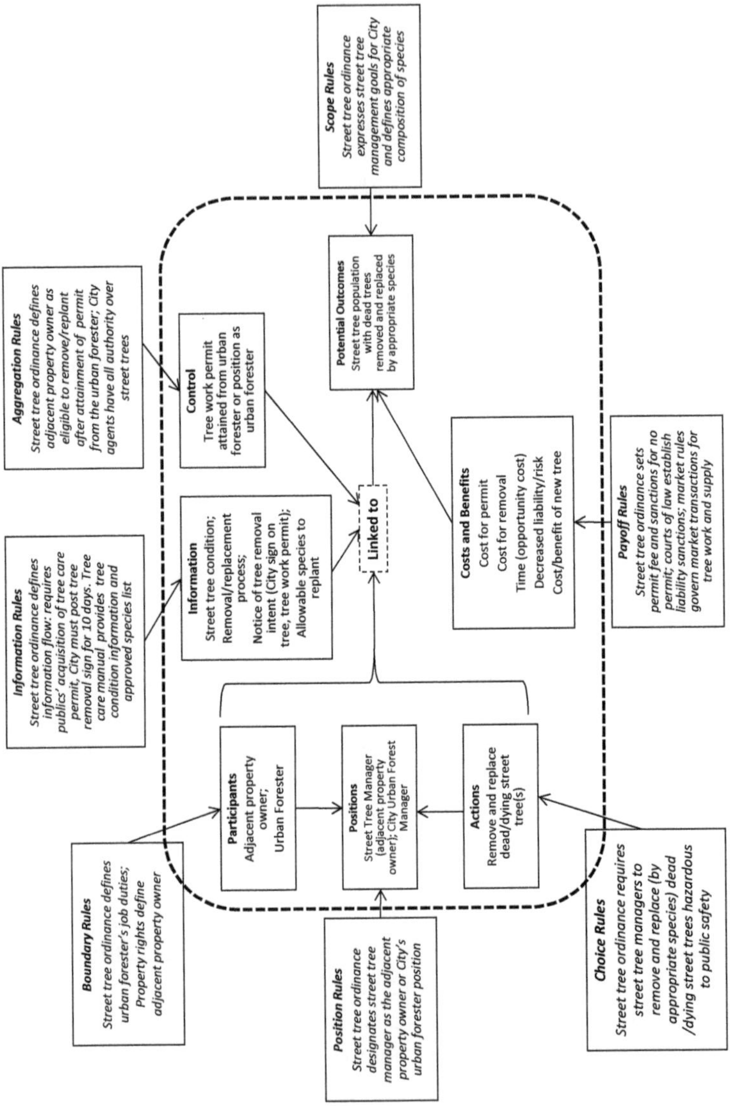

Figure 7. 3. The institutions impacting the inner workings of an action situation related to operational-level street tree management, specifically, street tree removal and replacement. Adjacent property owners are responsible for street trees but may only take action to remove or replace them when they are dead or dying and after attainment of a tree work permit from the City's urban forester. City foresters may remove or replace street trees but most post signage of the intent for the public unless the situation constitutes an emergency.

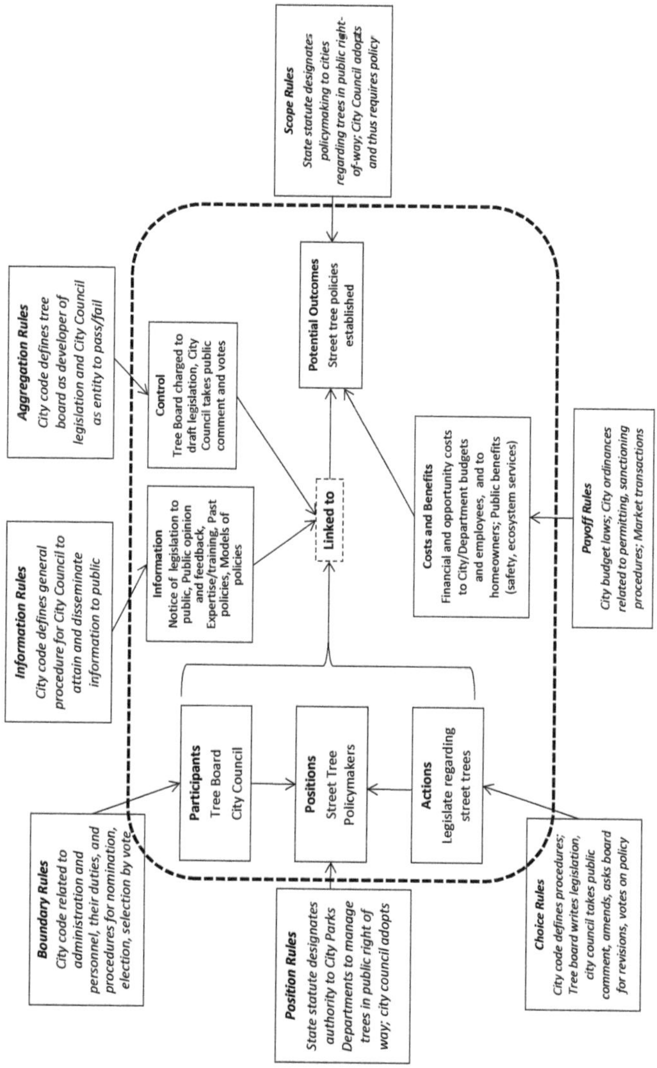

Figure 7.4. The institutions impacting the inner working of an action situation related to collective choice or policy-making regarding street tree management. State statute designates city parks departments (inclusive of urban forester) as responsible for street trees in the public right-of-way (PROW). Cities generally turn over legislative development to tree boards or commissions where parks department employees have one or more seats. The tree board is further composed of volunteer experts that develop street tree management legislation. Draft legislation is then presented to City Council for public feedback, requests for revisions, and ultimately, voting.

ation), which requires urban forest managers (defined by *position rules*) to remove dead or dying trees (with a permit) and replant appropriate species (defined by *choice rules*); the main actors involved are adjacent property owners and urban foresters (*boundary rules*).

Fischer and Steed (2008) argue that the definition of street trees is often unclear to the general public, as is the role of adjacent property owners in their management; attempts to clarify the definition of a street tree, particularly by defining it in the PROW, have led to increased confusion because PROW definitions are embedded in municipal code, which is often unclear or less accessible to the general public. Thus, *information rules* impact the production of street trees, as well. Moreover, when ownership is claimed by the public municipality but management responsibilities are assigned to the adjacent property owner, increased confusion arises about which entity (adjacent property owner or city) is responsible, indicting *aggregation rules*.

If a permit is required of the adjacent property owner to manage trees in the PROW, *payoff rules* are imposed and often increase transaction costs for the actor (in this case, in terms of time and potentially money spent obtaining the permit). If only particular species of street trees are allowed to be planted, *scope rules* are imposed. If municipal code is unclear, unknown, or unjustified, actors may not understand the benefits of street trees and cannot consider all the costs of not obtaining a permit to remove and plant trees (potentially including legal sanctions that are classified as *payoff rules*). Thus all benefits and costs are not weighed within the action situation, potentially resulting in inappropriate removal or planting of the wrong species of street tree in the PROW and/or the absence of a tree in a plantable space.

As mentioned, many action situations are influenced by actors within adjacent action situations, as is the case in the above scenario. Even if urban tree production arrangements are understood, outcomes are affected by adjacent action situations including *monitoring* and *sanctioning* related to street tree management. In fact, these adjacent action situations often fail to feed positively into the action of street tree production: limited urban forestry staff (as is commonly the case resulting from *financing* action situations) or uninformed neighbors may be unable to *monitor* street trees, and thus, do not *sanction* rule-breakers, adjusting their costs and benefits (*payoff rules*) in the production of street trees. Why follow a rule to plant or maintain a tree in the PROW if there is no cost to breaking the rule, but there is a cost to following it (the cost of the tree, the cost of the time and effort to obtain a permit and to plant, and so forth)?

As demonstrated through this specific example, institutional failure can arise from a variety of nuanced rules that structure an action situation, and likewise, can be resolved by understanding the specific sources of incongruence between policies and outcomes. Thus, in-depth institutional analysis is required to determine the relevant variables influencing the probability of sustainable actions in street tree management. However, to be clear, we do not mean to suggest that adjacent property owners can never sustainably manage street trees; rather, with clarified institutions (e.g., improved information rules about the location of PROW trees through informative mailers, for instance), incentives may be adjusted to allow for optimal street tree management from households. In fact, a major lesson from institutional analysis in rural resource management scenarios is that no particular form of tenure or governance regime is more successful than another (Moran 2005). Tucker (2009) argues that it is the local context, including history, political economy, social relationships, and biophysical characteristics that establish the appropriate tenure for resource management. Thus there are most certainly scenarios in which well-structured institutions allow for sustainable street tree management by adjacent households. Moreover, because street trees and their associated rules and norms are only one component of an urban forest and its many management policies and strategies, this example underscores that sustainability, as Clark et al. (1997) argue, can only be achieved in comprehensive urban forest management if policies and institutions are well crafted and respected and are considered across scales, space, and time. More importantly, it points to the fact that structured, repeatable analysis is required of institutional arrangements in order for urban forestry and urban ecosystems scholars to empirically derive a deeper understanding of the roles institutions play in sustaining (or distressing) urban ecosystems and to appropriately advise on policy prescriptions.

Conclusion

There has been much work to test several human ecosystem frameworks and develop a better understanding of urban ecology through institutional exploration (McIntyre et al. 2000). While institutions are recognized as integral to the study of urban ecosystems, theoretical and empirical analysis has been limited in both urban ecology and urban forest management. We argue that the lack of research is not indicative of institutions' relative importance in urban ecological systems; rather, it appears to stem from a lack of clarity regarding how institutions should be defined and analyzed.

This has prevented cumulative and comparative research regarding the role of institutions in sustaining urban ecosystems. Urban ecologists and urban forest management researchers could benefit from applying a working definition of institutions that uniquely defines rules, norms, and strategies, by recognizing the nested nature of operational, collective-choice, and constitutional institutions, and by applying the IAD framework to urban SESs such as urban forest systems. Although the IAD framework has not often been applied to urban SESs, it is an ideal paradigm to extend to the urban ecology field given its proven usefulness in understanding the relative role of institutions amidst social and biophysical factors in rural SES sustainability (Hardy and Koontz 2010). Research framed in this manner has provided a foundation of institutional design principles (Ostrom 1990) that work as hypotheses when extended to urban ecosystem research.

A recent study by Wolf and Kruger (2010) determined that urban forestry professionals, academics, and agency-based managers desire a policy-based research agenda to help determine adequate policy, code, and regulations for urban forest management. By detailing the role of institutions in the sustainable management of urban forests, we hope to offer direction for analysis in urban ecosystems research that will meet this need and facilitate a key future focus—institutional analysis—in urbanization and human dimensions of global environmental change (IHDP 2010). Opportunity exists for cross-disciplinary fertilization of institutional analysis from rural SESs to urban ecosystems and promises to help answer why and how individuals and their collective associations are incentivized to conserve or remove urban trees.

Acknowledgments

This research was funded in part by Indiana University's School of Public and Environmental Affairs Sustainability Grant, and Indiana University's Center for Research in Environmental Science (CRES) Sustainability Grant. The first author was also supported by The Garden Club of America Zone VI Fellowship in Urban Forestry. The authors would like to thank Kerry Krutilla, Michael McGinnis, Michael Cox, and Elinor Ostrom for their reviews of this manuscript.

Notes

This chapter was originally published in *Urban Ecosystems* 16(3) (2013): 553–71. Reprinted with the permission of Springer Science+Business Media. Figure 7.2 reprinted with the permission of Princeton University Press.

1. According to Sanesi, Gallis, and Kasperidus (2011, 35), "The term 'Community forestry' (CF) includes all the forest management types that provide both economic and social goals, under the control (or property) of a local community or larger social group. CF management is often set in a larger ecological landscape with other land uses." Urban forests, set in a landscape of variable land use, also include forest management that provides economic and social benefits that are largely controlled by the local community as the majority of the urban forest is privately owned (Clark et al. 1997).

2. It is important to emphasize here that institutions have been studied in urban areas in general; the urban planning and smart-growth literature emphasize policy solutions, such as zoning and urban growth boundaries, as tools for sustainable development (see Duany, Speck, and Lydon 2009). Our point is that in-depth institutional analysis is underutilized and seldom linked to understanding ecological outcomes in research framed as "urban ecosystem" or "urban forest management research," in particular.

3. This does not mean that the IAD framework cannot address rapidly changing circumstances. The framework assumes that the action situation is a holon, "[a] nested subassembly of part-whole units in complex adaptive systems" (Ostrom 2005, 11). Holons cannot be reduced to stand alone, but can be dissected for analysis to composite holons that allow for explanations at multiple levels and various spatial and temporal scales. Thus, in a rapidly changing environment for which urban systems are often characterized, iterative analyses may be required, particularly as outcomes may quickly influence and change the exogenous variables that must be fixed to determine outcomes.

4. As presented in the figures, the action situations produce *optimal* outcomes, however, we outline textually the potential for suboptimal outcomes given theoretical disconnects between exogenous rules and actual components of the action situations.

References

Anderies, J. M., M. Janssen, and E. Ostrom. 2004. "A Framework to Analyze the Robustness of Social-Ecological Systems from an Institutional Perspective." *Ecology and Society* 9(1): 18.

Barthel, S., J. Colding, and C. Folke. 2005. "History and Local Management of a Biodiversity-Rich, Urban, Cultural Landscape." *Ecology and Society* 10(2): 10.

Beddoe, R., R. Costanza, J. Farley, E. Garza, J. Kent, I. Kubiszewski, et al. 2009. "Overcoming Systemic Roadblocks to Sustainability: The Evolutionary Redesign of Worldviews, Institutions, and Technologies." *PNAS* 106: 2483–89.

Benvie, S. 2005. "A Case for Using Adaptive Platforms in the Development and Implementation of Urban-Centered Adaptive Management Plans." *Urban Ecosystems* 8: 285–311.

Blood, E. 1994. "Prospects for the Development of Integrated Regional Models." In *Integrated Regional Models: Interactions between Humans and Their Environment*, edited by P. Groffman and G. Likens, 145–52. New York: Chapman and Hall.

Bolund, P., and S. Hunhammar. 1999. "Ecosystem Services in Urban Areas." *Ecological Economics* 29: 293–301.

Boone, C. G., M. L. Cadenasso, J. M. Grove, K. Schwarz, and G. L. Buckley. 2009. "Landscape, Vegetation Characteristics, and Group Identity in an Urban and Suburban Watershed: Why the 60s Matter." *Urban Ecosystems* 13: 255–71.

Boyden, S. 1977. "Integrated Ecological Studies of Human Settlements." *Impact of Science on Society* 27: 159–69.

Buckley, G. 2010. "America's Forest Legacy: A Century of Saving Trees in the Old Line State." Santa Fe, NM: Center for American Places.

Burch, W., Jr., and D. DeLuca. 1984. *Measuring the Social Impact of Natural Resource Policies*. Albuquerque: New Mexico University Press.

Calvert, R. 1995. "Rational Actors, Equilibrium, and Social Institutions." In *Explaining Social Institutions*, edited by J. Knight and I. Sened, 57–94. Ann Arbor: University of Michigan Press.

Chhatre, A., and A. Agrawal. 2009. "Trade-Offs and Synergies between Carbon Storage and Livelihood Benefits from Forest Commons." *PNAS* 106(42): 17667–70.

Clark, J. R., N. Matheny, G. Cross, and V. Wake. 1997. "A Model of Urban Forest Sustainability." *Journal of Arboriculture* 23(1): 17–30.

Colding, J., J. Lundberg, and C. Folke. 2006. "Incorporating Green User Groups in Urban Ecosystem Management." *Ambio* 35: 237–44.

Coleman, J. 1988. "Free Riders and Zealots: The Role of Social Networks." *Sociological Theory* 6: 52–57.

Commons, J. R. 1986. *Legal Foundations of Capitalism*. Madison: University of Wisconsin Press.

Conway, T. M., and L. Urbani. 2007. "Variation in Municipal Urban Forestry Policy: A Case Study of Toronto, Canada." *Urban Forestry and Urban Greening* 6: 181–92.

Cox, M., G. Arnold, and S. Villamayor Tomás. 2010. "A Review of Design Principles for Community-Based Natural Resource Management." *Ecology and Society* 15(4): 38.

Crawford, S., and E. Ostrom. 1995. "A Grammar of Institutions." *American Political Science Review* 89: 582–600.

Duany, A., J. Speck, and M. Lydon. 2009. *The Smart Growth Manual*. Columbus, OH: McGraw-Hill.

Dwyer, J. F., D. Nowak, and M. Noble. 2003. "Sustaining Urban Forests." *Journal of Arboriculture* 29(1): 49–55.

Ernstson, H., S. Sorlin, and T. Elmquist. 2008. "Social Movements and Ecosystem Services." *Ecology and Society* 13: 39.

Fischer, B. C., and B. Steed. 2008. "Street Trees: A Misunderstood Common Pool Resource." In *International Society of Arboriculture: 84th Annual Conference and Trade Show, St. Louis, Missouri*. Champaign, IL: International Society of Arboriculture.

Gibson, C. C., K. Andersson, E. Ostrom, and S. Shivakumar. 2005. *The Samaritan's Dilemma: The Political Economy of Development Aid*. New York: Oxford University Press.

Gibson, C. C., M. McKean, and E. Ostrom. 2000. *People and Forests: Communities, Institutions, and Governance*. Cambridge, MA: MIT Press.

Grove, J. M. 2009. "Cities: Managing Densely Settled Social-Ecological Systems." In *Principles of Ecosystem Stewardship: Resilience-Based Natural Resource Management in a Changing World*, edited by F. S. Chapin, G. Kofinas, and C. Folke, 281–94. Dordrecht, the Netherlands: Springer.

Hardin, G. 1968. "The Tragedy of the Commons." *Science* 162: 1243–48.

Hardy, S. D., and T. Koontz. 2010. "Collaborative Watershed Partnership in Urban and Rural Areas: Different Pathways to Success?" *Landscape and Urban Planning* 95: 79–90.

Hayek, F. A. 1945. "The Use of Knowledge in Society." *American Economic Review* 35: 519–30.

———. 1967. *Studies in Philosophy, Politics and Economics*. Chicago, IL: University of Chicago Press.

Hodgson, G. 2006. "What are Institutions?" *Journal of Economic Issues* 40: 1–25.

Hohfeld, W. 1913. "Some Fundamental Legal Concepts as Applied in the Study of Primitive Law." *Yale Law Journal* 23: 16–59.

IHDP (International Human Dimensions Programme). 2010. *Urbanization and Global Environmental Change Project*. IHDP web page, http://www.ihdp.unu.edu/article/read/ugec.

Jenkins, V. 1994. *The Lawn: A History of an American Obsession*. Washington, DC: Smithsonian Institution Press.

Kiser, L., and E. Ostrom. 1982. "The Three Worlds of Action: A Metatheoretical Synthesis of Institutional Approaches." In *Strategies of Political Inquiry*, edited by Elinor Ostrom, 179–222. Beverly Hills, CA: Sage.

Knight, J. 1992. *Institutions and Social Conflict*. New York: Cambridge University Press.

Lant, C. L., J. Ruhl, and S. Kraft. 2008. "The Tragedy of Ecosystem Services." *BioScience* 58(10): 969–74.

Larsen, L., and S. Harlan. 2006. "Desert Dreamscapes: Residential Landscape Preference and Behavior." *Landscape and Urban Planning* 78(1–2): 85–100.

Larson, K., D. Casagrande, S. Harlan, and S. Yabiku. 2009. "Residents' Yard Choices and Rationales in a Desert City: Social Priorities, Ecological Impacts, and Decision Tradeoffs." *Environmental Management* 44: 921–37.

Lewis, D. K. 1969. *Convention: A Philosophical Study*. Cambridge, MA: Harvard University Press.

Li, F., R. Wang, X. Liu, and X. Zhang. 2005. "Urban Forest in China: Development Patterns, Influencing Factors, and Research Prospects." *International Journal of Sustainable Development & World Ecology* 12: 197–204.

Lowe, P., G. Whitman, and S. Phillipson. 2009. "Ecology and the Social Sciences." *Journal of Applied Ecology* 46(2): 297–305.

Machlis, G., J. Force, and W. Burch Jr. 1997. "The Human Ecosystem Part I: The Human Ecosystem as an Organizing Concept in Ecosystem Management." *Society and Natural Resources* 10: 347–67.

Martin, C., K. Peterson, and L. Stabler. 2003. "Residential Landscaping in Phoenix, Arizona, U.S.: Practices and Preferences Relative to Covenants, Codes, and Restrictions." *Journal of Arboriculture* 29: 9–16.

McDonnell, M., and S. Pickett. 1993. *Humans as Components of Ecosystems: The Ecology of Subtle Human Effects and Populated Areas*. New York: Springer.

McGinnis, M. 2011. "Networks of Adjacent Action Situations in Polycentric Governance." *Policy Studies Journal* 39(1): 51–78.

McIntyre, N., K. Knowles-Yanez, and D. Hope. 2000. "Urban Ecology as an Interdisciplinary Field: The Differences in the Use of 'Urban' between Social and Natural Sciences." *Urban Ecosystems* 4: 5–24.

McPherson, E. G. 2001. "Sacramento's Parking Lot Shading Ordinance: Environmental and Economic Costs of Compliance." *Landscape and Urban Planning* 57(2): 105–23.

———. 2006. "Urban Forestry in North America." *Renewable Resources Journal* 24(3): 8–12.

McPherson, E. G., D. Nowak, G. Heisler, S. Grimmond, C. Souch, R. Grant, and R. Rowntree. 1997. "Quantifying Urban Forest Structure, Function, and Value: The Chicago Urban Forest Climate Project." *Urban Ecosystems* 1: 49–61.

Menger, C. 1963. *Problems of Economics and Sociology: (Untersuchungen über die Methode der Socialwissenschaften und der politischen Oekonomie insbesondere)*. Edited by L. Schneider. Translated by F. J. Nock. Champaign: University of Illinois Press.

Michalos, A. C. 1997. "Combining Social, Economic, and Environmental Indicators to Measure Sustainable Human Well-Being." *Social Indicators Research* 40: 221–58.

Moran, E. 2005. "Human-Environment Interactions in Forest Ecosystems: An Introduction." In *Seeing the Forest and the Trees: Human Interactions in Forest Ecosystems*, edited by E. Moran and E. Ostrom, 3–22. Cambridge, MA: MIT Press.

Munger, M. 2010. "Endless Forms Most Beautiful and Most Wonderful: Elinor Ostrom and the Diversity of Institutions." *Public Choice* 143: 263–68.

Nagendra, H., and D. Gopal. 2011. "Tree Diversity, Distribution, History and Change in Urban Parks: Studies in Bangalore, India." *Urban Ecosystems* 14(2): 211–23.

Nilsson, K., C. Konijnendijk, and T. Randrup. 1999. "Urban Forestry: Where People Meet Trees." In *Community Forestry—A Change for the Better: Conference Proceedings, December 7–8, 1999, London*, edited by T. Heeley, 28–31. Cheltenham, UK: Forestry Commission and the Countryside Agency.

North, D. C. 1986. "The New Institutional Economics." *Journal of Institutional and Theoretical Economics* 142: 230–37.

———. 1990. *Institutions, Institutional Change and Economic Performance*. New York: Cambridge University Press.

Nowak, D. J., D. Crane, J. Stevens, R. Hoehn, J. Walton, and J. Bond. 2008. "A Ground-Based Method of Assessing Urban Forest Structure and Ecosystem Services." *Arboriculture & Urban Forestry* 34: 347–58.

Nowak, D. J., and J. Dwyer. 2000. "Understanding the Benefits and Costs of Urban Forest Ecosystems." In *Urban and Community Forestry in the Northeast*, edited by J. Kuser. New York: Plenum.

Nowak, D. J., and E. J. Greenfield. 2012. "Tree and Impervious Cover Change in U.S. Cities." *Urban Forestry & Urban Greening* 11: 21–30.

Nowak, D. J., and J. Walton. 2005. "Projected Urban Growth (2000–2050) and Its Estimated Impact on the US Forest Resources." *Journal of Forestry* 103: 383–89.

Oakerson, R., and R. Parks. 1988. "Citizen Voice and Public Entrepreneurship: The Organizational Dynamic of a Complex Metropolitan County." *Publius* 18: 91–112.

Ostrom, E. 1986. "An Agenda for the Study of Institutions." *Public Choice* 48: 3–25.

———. 1990. *Governing the Commons: The Evolution of Institutions for Collective Action*. New York: Cambridge University Press.

———. 2005. *Understanding Institutional Diversity*. Princeton, NJ: Princeton University Press.

Ostrom, E., and W. H. Baugh. 1973. *Community Organization and the Provision of Police Services*. Beverly Hills, CA: Sage.

Ostrom, E., R. Gardner, and J. Walker. 1994. *Rules, Games, and Common-Pool Resources*. Ann Arbor: University of Michigan Press.

Ostrom, E., R. Parks, and G. Whitaker. 1974. "Do We Really Want to Consolidate Urban Police Forces? A Reappraisal of Some Old Assertions." *Public Administration Review* 33(5): 423–32.

Ostrom, V. 1980. "Artisanship and Artifact." *Public Administration Review* 40: 309–17.

Ostrom, V., C. Tiebout, and R. Warren. 1961. "The Organization of Government in Metropolitan Areas: A Theoretical Inquiry." *American Political Science Review* 55: 831–42.

Pickett, S. T. A., W. R. Burch Jr., S. E. Dalton, T. W. Foresman, J. M. Grove, and R. Rowntree. 1997. "A Conceptual Framework for the Study of Human Ecosystems in Urban Areas." *Urban Ecosystems* 1: 185–99.

Pickett, S. T. A., I. C. Burke, V. C. Dale, J. R. Gosz, R. G. Lee, S. W. Pacala, and M. Shachak. 1994. "Integrated Models of Forested Regions." In *Integrated Regional Models: Interactions between Humans and Their Environment*, edited by P. Groffman and G. Likens, 120–41. New York: Chapman and Hall.

Pickett, S. T. A., M. L. Cadenasso, and J. M. Grove. 2008. "Beyond Urban Legends: An Emerging Framework of Urban Ecology, as Illustrated by the Baltimore Ecosystem Study." *BioScience* 58(2): 139–50.

Plott, C. 1986. "Rational Choice in Experimental Markets." *Journal of Business* 59: 301–27.

Riker, W. 1980. "Implications from the Disequilibrium of Majority Rule for the Study of Institutions." *American Political Science Review* 74: 432–51.

Robbins, P., and J. Sharp. 2003. "Producing and Consuming Chemicals: The Moral Economy of the American Lawn." *Economic Geography* 79: 425–39.

Roy Chowdhury, R., K. Larson, M. Grove, C. Polsky, E. Cook, J. Onsted, and L. Ogden. 2011. "A Multiscalar Approach to Theorizing Socio-Ecological Dynamics of Urban Residential Landscapes." *Cities and the Environment* 4(1): 6.

Sanesi, G., C. Gallis, and H. D. Kasperidus. 2011. "Urban Forests and Their Ecosystem Services in Relation to Human Health." In *Forests, Trees, and Human Health*, edited by K. Nilsson et al., 23–40. Dordrecht, the Netherlands: Springer.

Schotter, A. 1981. *The Economic Theory of Social Institutions*. New York: Cambridge University Press.

Shepsle, K. 1975. "Congressional Committee Assignments: An Optimization Model with Institutional Constraints." *Public Choice* 22: 55–78.

———. 1979. "Institutional Arrangements and Equilibrium in Multidimensional Voting Models." *American Journal of Political Science* 23: 27–59.

———. 1989. "Studying Institutions: Some Lessons from the Rational Choice Approach." *Journal of Theoretical Politics* 1: 131–47.

Shepsle, K., and B. Weingast. 1984. "When Do Rules of Procedure Matter?" *Journal of Politics* 46: 206–21.

———. 1987. "The Institutional Foundations of Committee Power." *American Political Science Review* 81: 85–104.

Tidball, K. G., M. Krasny, E. Svendsen, L. Campbell, and K. Helphand. 2010. "Stewardship, Learning, and Memory in Disaster Resilience." *Environmental Education Research* 16(5–6): 591–609.

Tucker, C. 2009. "Exploring Forest Governance: Insights, Challenges, and Lessons Learned." Paper prepared for the Workshop on the Workshop (WOW4) conference, Indiana University, Bloomington, June 3–5, 2009.

Ullmann-Margalit, E. 1977. *The Emergence of Norms*. New York: Oxford University Press.

USDA-FS (United States Department of Agriculture Forest Service). 2009. "STEW-MAP: The Stewardship Mapping and Assessment Project." USDA-

FS Northern Research Station web page: http://www.nrs.fs.fed.us/nyc/focus/stewardship_mapping/.

Van Wassenaer, P., and A. Kenney. 2010. "Sustainable Urban Forest Management: Planning Using Criteria and Indicators." Urban Natural Resources Institute Webcast Resources. http://www.unri.org/webcasts/archive/%20january-2010/.

Wake, M. H. 2008. "Integrative Biology: Science for the 21st Century." *BioScience* 58(4): 349–53.

Williamson, O. 1985. *The Economic Institutions of Capitalism*. New York: Free Press.

Wolf, K. 2004. "Economics and Public Value of Urban Forests." *Urban Agriculture Magazine* 13: 31–33.

———. 2005. "Business District Streetscapes, Trees, and Consumer Response." *Journal of Forestry* 103: 396–400.

Wolf, K., and L. Kruger. 2010. "Urban Forestry Research Needs: A Participatory Assessment Process." *Journal of Forestry* 108: 39–44.

Wu, J. 2008. "Toward a Landscape Ecology of Cities: Beyond Buildings, Trees, and Urban Forests." In *Ecology, Planning, and Management of Urban Forests: International Perspectives*, edited by M. Carreiro, et al., 10–28. New York: Springer.

Ye, W. 1997. "Discussion of Several Problems of Urban Forest Planning and Construction (Continued)." *Guang-dong Forest* 2: 29–30.

Young, R. F., and S. A. Wolf. 2006. "Goal Attainment in Urban Ecology Research: A Bibliometric Review 1975–2004." *Urban Ecosystems* 9: 179–93.

Zhang, Y., B. Zheng, B. Allen, N. Letson, and J. Sibley. 2009. "Tree Ordinances as Public Policy and Participation Tools: Development in Alabama." *Arboriculture & Urban Forestry* 35(3): 166–72.

Zipperer, W., S. Sissinni, R. Pouyat, and T. Foresman. 1997. "Urban Tree Cover: An Ecological Perspective." *Urban Ecosystems* 1: 229–46.

PART III

Development and Nested Governance

8

Levels, Scales, Linkages, and Other "Multiples" Affecting Natural Resources

Amy R. Poteete

Socio-ecological systems involve several types of "multiples." Natural systems consist of numerous components, which interact in a variety of biological, chemical, social, and physical processes. Multiple human actors and organizations within various fields of action take decisions and actions at multiple scales that interact with biophysical resources and processes. Actions are in turn channeled through and influenced by institutions at many levels, including many organizations that are themselves designed as multi-level institutions. Scholars and practitioners characterize socio-ecological systems as complex largely because of the multiplicity of factors, actors, interactions, and processes within them. Failure to recognize important components and processes limits understanding of these systems and is an important source of uncertainty about the responses to management practices and policies. The first goal of analysis is often simply to identify the key elements of the system and the relationships among them. These goals are advanced by taking a broad perspective, at least as a point of departure.

Perhaps inevitably, despite agreement on the need to analyze various "multiples" affecting natural resources, there is no consensus as to how best to do so. This chapter considers two concepts that are widely used in research on socio-ecological systems: "multi-level institutions" and "multi-scale linkages." Neither concept represents a full theoretical framework. Neither is linked exclusively to a single framework. Nonetheless, these terms represent alternative frames for analysis, where a frame refers to a particular conceptualization of something that has multiple dimensions and can be viewed from several different perspectives (Chong and Druckman 2007). The choice of frame influences the types of "multiples" that are seen and given priority as well as how relationships among those "multiples" are understood. Does either conceptualization of the "multiples" in socio-ecological systems have an advantage in terms of either breadth of perspective or analytical leverage?

To answer this question, the chapter first discusses the elements that come into focus in the analysis of "multi-level institutions" and "multi-scale linkages." Second, recognizing that both concepts are decomposable, I then consider the implications of a shift in the frame of analysis from institutions to linkages and from scales to levels in terms of both inclusiveness and analytical leverage. The breadth of perspective increases with a shift from institutions to linkages, but a lack of conceptual clarity limits the analytical value of conceptualizing the multiples associated with socio-ecological systems in terms of either multiple levels or multiple scales. "Multi-dimensional linkages" combines elements of these concepts and goes beyond them to achieve a more comprehensive overview of the multiples inherent in socio-ecological systems, thereby decreasing the risk of overlooking important interactions. In conclusion, I argue in favor of "multi-dimensional linkages" as an initial frame of analysis in order to gain a broader perspective and reduce the likelihood that important interactions will be excluded. This broader perspective should be combined with further conceptual development to draw out distinctions among the variety of dimensions affecting socio-ecological systems.

Two Common Frames

The relationships among the multiple actors, social and natural conditions, and processes associated with natural resource systems are often analyzed in terms of "multi-level institutions" or "multi-scale linkages." To some extent, the choice of terminology reflects differences in disciplinary background and the separate development of research traditions with overlapping theoretical and substantive concerns (Armitage 2008). Research on the commons blurs disciplinary boundaries and many analysts use both terms, sometimes treating them as synonymous. Even if "multi-level institutions" and "multi-scale linkages" refer to related phenomena, they are not truly interchangeable terms. Each directs attention to somewhat different factors, processes, and relationships.

Multi-Level Institutions

Multi-level institutions are a central concern in policy-oriented research on decentralization, special-purpose organizations, urban politics, federalism, the European Union, and other international organizations. The analysis of multi-level institutions tends to focus on institutional design and the consequences of particular institutional arrangements for policy. This framing directs attention to the agency of policy elites, institutional arrangements, and alternative policy goals.

There are several strands of institutionalism that define institutions in somewhat different ways (Hall and Taylor 1996; Immergut 1998). North (1990) argued forcefully that institutions or rules should be distinguished from organizations as collective actors to enable analysis of interactions between the two. Many scholars, especially those working in the rational choice tradition, agree (e.g., Ostrom 2005). This distinction, however, can be difficult to apply since organizations involve durable sets of rules as well as actors. Thus, many policy analysts and scholars consider organizations to be institutions (Pierson 2004).[1] Despite broad agreement that informal institutions play an important role, studies of multi-level institutions typically examine formal institutions, especially formal jurisdictions.

Multi-level institutions refer to two types of institutional arrangements: (1) those based on territorial, usually multi-purpose jurisdictions and (2) those based on functional areas, usually with overlapping territories (Hooghe and Marks 2003). The territorial model of multi-level institutions involves a hierarchy of nested jurisdictions. Within a given territorially defined level in an organizational hierarchy, multiple jurisdictions exist but do not overlap (e.g., many municipalities or provinces). Moving within the hierarchy, each lower-level jurisdiction fits neatly within a single jurisdiction at the next territorial level (e.g., each municipality or province falls within a single country). In essence, in a territorial model of multi-level institutions, movement between levels means movement between jurisdictions with smaller or larger territorial extent. Even if interactions across tiers of multi-purpose government receive more attention, the territorial model of multi-level institutions could be applied to other multi-purpose organizations with nested territorially based levels (e.g., large non-governmental organizations with local chapters, political parties, religious organizations).

In the functional model of multi-level institutions, movement across levels has a territorial dimension but cannot be reduced to changes in territorial extent. Jurisdictions are defined in terms of a specific task or field of action, such as the management of schools, the provision of public transportation, or the management of a river basin. The jurisdictions do have a defined territory, but are non-exclusive in terms of spatial extent and membership. For example, functional organizations such as school boards, public transportation networks, and river basin management committees have overlapping territories and membership. Functionally defined organizations include government agencies, voluntary organizations such as a neighborhood watch committee, and government-sponsored organizations such as non-governmental user group committees and public-private stakeholder forums. Even if their functions are distinct, functionally defined jurisdictions coexist with each other and with multi-purpose jurisdictions. In the functional model of multi-level institutions, interactions across levels refer to interactions across jurisdictions that overlap partially in terms of territory, membership, or function.

Multiple levels of institutions can promote learning, adaptation, and coordination (Eaton and Connerley 2010; Hooghe and Marks 2003). Multi-level institutions may enhance accountability by more clearly defining relations between specific institutions and groups of stakeholders. Issues that might be overlooked in a multi-purpose organization (or a higher level of government) can receive more attention in an agency with a narrower agenda (or a more local level of government). Community-based organizations composed of stakeholders in a particular forest, for example, may focus more on issues of forest management than larger-scale and multi-purpose governments, whether municipal or national. Functionally defined organizations might be better positioned to address externalities than either territorial or multi-purpose organizations. Nesting local or specialized institutions within more encompassing organizations can help balance attentiveness to localized concerns or conditions with the management of externalities and inequalities.

Multi-level institutions involve trade-offs. Common problems include (1) poor alignment of institutional boundaries with community or functional boundaries, (2) coordination problems associated with institutional complexity, and (3) blurred lines of accountability. "Community" is a multi-dimensional concept (Agrawal and Gibson 1999). In the context of multi-level institutions, it may refer to the people residing within the jurisdiction of a territorially defined general-purpose government, a community of interest as recognized by a functionally defined organization, a self-defined community of interest, or a self-defined community based on identification (e.g., shared past, common culture, similar structural position). To some extent, institutions define community by recognizing particular bases of identification (Skelcher 2005; Ribot, Chhatre, and Lankina 2008). However they are defined, institutional and community boundaries frequently do not coincide with the boundaries of natural systems such as forests, watersheds, or the global climate. Analysts often blame policy failures on poorly aligned institutions and argue that multi-level institutional designs based on functional boundaries could facilitate the management of these systems.

Improved alignment between institutions and policy functions implies a proliferation of institutions, which in turn gives rise to coordination problems. There are two types of coordination problems across institutions. First, coordination problems arise from the need for agreement across institutions. As the number of institutions that act as veto points increases, so does the difficulty of reaching agreement (Tsebelis 1995). Particularly for natural resource systems that cross international boundaries, it is common for multiple institutions with veto authority to participate in policy making. In such situations, the risk of a joint decision trap is very real (Scharpf 1988). A joint decision trap refers to the production of systematically suboptimal outcomes that can occur when two levels of government exist and policy decisions require agreement at both levels. Such situations arise when an improvement for the group as a whole involves costs for some participants because those who stand to lose from the change can block it. Second, coordination problems arise when institutions at various levels fail to *acknowledge* each other, so that actions taken within the context of one institution competes with actions and decisions taken within the context of other institutions. Such situations may reflect a problem of institutional design, resulting in a lack of "nesting" (Ostrom 1990, 2005). Alternatively, inattention or blind spots may produce poor coordination. Organizations concerned with watersheds or agriculture, for example, may not pay attention to the initiatives of organizations concerned with climate change or conservation, and yet decisions within these different fields of action interact. In yet other situations, overt competition exists between organizations, as when state bureaus compete for resources (Moe 1990; Poteete 2009) or traditional authorities challenge agents of the modern state (Lund 2006). These organizations are very much aware of each other. They do not acknowledge each other in the sense that they deny one another's authority; each claims that its own authority has priority over that of its rivals.

Multi-level institutions also present challenges for accountability. Accountability requires a clearly defined constituency, clear criteria for assessing accountability to that constituency, and mechanisms for enforcing accountability (Grant and Keohane 2005; compare Ackerman 2004). Institutional membership or constituencies can be defined in different ways, and the choice of criteria for membership or representation has implications for accountability (Ribot, Chhatre, and Lankina 2008). By definition, functionally defined institutions such as user groups will not be accountable to those who have no recognized standing, including people who may be affected by their decisions and actions (Manor 2004). Multi-level institutions also undermine accountability by making it more difficult to discern who is responsible for what (Papadopoulus 2003). Who should be held responsible for outcomes that reflect the decisions and actions of two or more organizations or the interactions of several policies? Mechanisms for accountability include audits, provisions for consultation, and elections. Many of these mechanisms are, on their own, relatively blunt tools. Even in combination, they cannot fully compensate for the lack of transparency associated with the involvement of many institutions. Relations of dependency, uneven access to information, and sporadic attention to public affairs further limit their effectiveness. When any level in a multi-level system lacks effective mechanisms of accountability, accountability is weakened within the system as a whole (Bardhan 2002).

Policy analysts recognize these challenges and typically respond by proposing strategies for improving institutional design (e.g., Ackerman 2004; Haas 2004). Framing analysis in terms of multi-level institutions thus directs attention to the interaction of institutions with social, economic, and ecological conditions. The institutions are understood as products of human agency. Institutions may be sticky, but are subject to change. This conceptualization treats social, economic, and ecological conditions as background conditions that influence and are influenced by the development and operation of institutions. Despite this recognition of interaction between the various factors and processes, most research on multi-level institutions trains attention on human action over relatively short periods of time.[2]

Multi-Scale Linkages

Multi-scale linkages feature prominently in both ecological research and analyses of socio-ecological processes. This concept directs attention to relationships and processes that cross seemingly distinct spheres of activity or organization. The central concerns include the multi-directional influence of organization and activity at different scales, the social production of scales, power relations within and across scales, how agency interacts with structural dynamics, and, more generally, sources of systemic reproduction and dynamism.

There is considerable debate around the conceptualization of scale. Especially in policy circles and interdisciplinary work, scale is often a synonym for "level" defined in terms of spatial extent.[3] When used in this manner, interactions across scales refer to interactions that span the local, regional, national, and international or global. The conflation of scale with spatial extent or size, however, has been sharply critiqued (Gibson, Ostrom, and Ahn 2000; Neumann 2009). Geographers and the natural sciences understand scale in terms of the grain or resolution of observation. Gibson, Ostrom, and Ahn (2000, 218), for example, define scale as "the spatial, temporal, quantitative, or analytical dimensions used to measure and study any phenomenon." "Level" refers to the units on the scale. Even when referring to a single dimension (e.g., distance or temperature), there may be a choice of scales (e.g., miles v. kilometers and Celsius v. Fahrenheit). Cash et al. (2006) identify a number of scales that are relevant for socio-ecological systems, including spatial, temporal, jurisdictional, management, and knowledge. When scale is understood as the dimension used in observations, movement along a single scale—perhaps from an ecologically defined patch to a landscape on a spatial scale—involves a change in levels, not a change in scale. By implication, local-national or local-global interactions do not involve multiple scales but multiple levels on a single scale. Cross-scale interactions play out in multiple dimensions of analysis, such as spatial, jurisdictional, and temporal.

Many political ecologists and geographers go further, insisting that scale is a product of social and ecological processes (Neumann 2009). Given the existence of multiple relevant scales, social actors must choose which scale or scales are relevant in a given situation. From this perspective, scaling refers to the socio-ecological processes that influence the choice of a particular scale (or set of scales) and rescaling refers to changes in the resolution or dimension of observation and analysis. Lebel, Garden, and Imamura (2005), for example, discuss how the Thai government rescaled water development as an international regional issue rather than an issue of local development.

Multiple scales are linked in several respects. First, many processes are scale dependent in the sense that the relationships observed at one scale may not hold at other scales of analysis (Gibson, Ostrom, and Ahn 2000; Ostrom and Nagendra 2006; Rudel 2008). Cross-national studies suggested that population growth contributed to deforestation, for example, but that pattern does not hold up in comparisons of localities or regions within countries. Likewise, observations over a few years might link changes in resource conditions to patterns of resource extraction while missing the influence of long-term changes in biophysical conditions or climate. Patterns of human behavior, the mobilization of knowledge, and responses to institutional arrangements, for example, may be scale-dependent (Cash et al. 2006). Consequently, the choice of scale influences what is seen in analysis. Second, interactions between processes at different scales are pervasive if unpredictable.[4] Policy processes that unfold within a jurisdictional scale interact with ecological and socio-economic processes within a spatial scale. All processes also play out on a temporal scale. Even when processes have independent drivers, they coexist and often interact. Interactions across scales alter processes within scales. These unavoidable multi-scale linkages are important sources of dynamism. Third, while the social production of scale may generate a self-reinforcing dynamic that contributes to stability, there are often powerful incentives to push for rescaling and it occurs regularly. In the Thai example mentioned above, for example, rescaling water development as a regional issue had several benefits for the government; it deflected the opposition of domestic environmentalists, appealed to Thais who would benefit from less expensive imported water, and shifted the costs of water development projects to neighboring countries (Lebel, Garden, and Imamura 2005).

Linkages across multiple scales are sources of complexity, resilience, and dynamism. Because they are sources of complexity and dynamism, multi-scale linkages represent obstacles to understanding and reduce predictability. As such, multi-scale linkages make policy making more challenging. The cognitive challenge of discerning cause-effect relations varies, but can be substantial (Poteete and Welch 2004; Wilson 2002). Cash et al. (2006) highlight three further challenges: mismatch across scales, ignorance of multi-scale linkages, and the plurality of scales. A mismatch of scales occurs when scales affected by human action (e.g., ecological, economic) do not correspond with scales that guide human action (e.g., jurisdictional, temporal, management). Some policy makers respond to complexity by attempting either to limit interactions across scales or, through the social construction of scale, impose a monolithic scale. Such strategies often fail miserably (e.g., Scott 1998). When policy making (or scientific activity) is organized around sectors (or disciplines), ignorance of interactions across sectors becomes more likely. Ignorance also arises from the cognitive challenge of grappling with complex systems. A dominant policy paradigm creates additional blind spots by ignoring the inherent plurality of scales.

The challenges identified by Cash et al. (2006) parallel the concerns about the poor alignment of institutional boundaries with functional tasks and poor coordination across multi-level institutions. Where the multi-level institutions framing then turns to questions of accountability, research conceptualized in terms of multi-scale linkages asks questions about power relations. Power—the ability to get others to do what they might not do otherwise—may be derived from diverse sources: political or administrative position, material wealth, structural position, and control over information and procedures, among others (Poteete and Ribot 2011).[5] Power dynamics motivate and influence the social construction of scale (Lebel, Garden, and Imamura 2005; Neumann 2009) as well as efforts to create cross-scale linkages and the ability to sustain those linkages (Adger, Brown, and Tompkins 2006). Rescaling issues alters what is seen and what is overlooked. Establishing new linkages across scales defines new audiences or constituencies. These changes generate shifts in power dynamics as they reshape alliances, reveal new options, and alter the flow of resources. Both rescaling and connecting scales require some initial power. Powerful actors have access to a variety of resources through which they can influence the social construction—or reconstruction—of scale. They also have greater ability to identify and establish potentially beneficial cross-scale linkages (Adger, Brown, and Tompkins 2006).

The multi-scale linkage framing directs attention to interactions among a variety of distinct yet linked processes over some period of time. The approach adopts a fairly macro perspective. Recognition of the social construction of scale and power relations highlights the agency of collectivities such as interest groups, industries, or agencies. Analyses vary considerably in the emphasis given to social versus economic versus ecological processes, but they always consider interactions across at least two distinct sets of processes.

What Happens When We Change Frames?

Multi-scale linkages and multi-level institutions train attention on partially overlapping sets of concerns. These overlaps are most prominent in policy-oriented analyses of multi-scale linkages, which often recommend multi-level institutions as a strategy for managing these linkages. And yet, these concepts differ in important respects. To draw out how these differences influence analysis, this section decomposes these concepts and considers the implications of (1) an emphasis on institutions or linkages and (2) the organization of observations and analysis around *scales* versus *levels*.

What Happens with the Shift from Institutions to Linkages?

Framing analysis with reference to *institutions* directs attention to formal institutions, actors, and relations of authority. The emphasis is on institutional structure and institutional design. This approach offers valuable insight into the sorts of institutional layering characteristic of socio-ecological systems. Since institutional arrangements interact with socio-economic and ecological processes, it is also important to consider other factors. Framing analysis in terms of *linkages* offers a broader perspective. It encompasses various types of relationships, including but not limited to those involving institutions.

Institutional analysis understands institutions as both products of intentional action and constraints on choice.[6] Thus, analysis involves identification of the various actors involved in institutional design or with an interest in attempting to influence institutional design. Two sets of actors are central: those directly involved in institutional design and those affected by a particular set of institutional arrangements. Collective actors and policy elites—organizations such as government agencies and bureaus, NGOs, interest groups, and international organizations—feature prominently in institutional design. Groups affected by institutions are generally conceptualized in terms of social categories such as gender, ethnicity, caste, class, and livelihood strategy (e.g., farmers, timber producers). The prominence of agency encourages a focus on either comparative statics (e.g., before and after an institutional change) or periods of institutional design.

Institutional analysis links actors and institutions through interests that influence participation in institutional design, incentives created by institutions, and relations of authority among actors and institutions. Relations of authority take diverse forms. Debates center on the trade-offs of alternative relations of authority such as nesting institutions, hierarchy or its absence, and exclusive versus overlapping jurisdictions. For better or for worse, non-exclusive jurisdictions with no clear hierarchy exist in many situations. Research on multi-level institutions directs attention to the possibilities these sorts of arrangements present for both forum- or venue-shopping, in which actors direct conflicts and claims to the institutions expected to yield the most favorable outcomes (Baumgartner and Jones 1991; Berry 1993), and shopping forums, in which authorities associated with different institutions compete to address the concerns of disputants or claimants (Lund 2006; von Benda Beckmann 1981).

Linkages refer to relationships, connections, and interactions. Analysis concerned with *linkages* considers relationships among institutions and organizations, but may also include relationships between other types of factors (e.g., actors, structures) and various processes. The boundary on the types of relationships under consideration depends on whether and how "linkages" is combined with another concept. Institutional linkages, for example, narrow attention to relationships among institutions. Multi-scale linkages include a greater variety of relationships that affect socio-ecological systems. The next section addresses the relative merits of framing analysis in terms of scales.

Intentional efforts to establish linkages have gained attention as sources of dynamism and shifts in power relations (Adger, Brown, and Tompkins 2006). But agency is not the only source of linkages. Some processes are inherently linked. Biological and physical processes within an ecosystem, for example, cannot be fully separated. Nor is it possible to isolate social, economic, and political processes. Other processes that are generally independent may intersect in some situations. When such processes do intersect, the linkage may alter one or more of the processes.[7]

The greatest overlap with the concerns of institutional analysis occurs in research on intentionally created institutional linkages. Even here, however, reframing analysis in terms of linkages rather than institutions implies a broader understanding of power relations and may encourage greater attention to the unfolding of processes over a longer period of time. Institutional analysis encourages an equation of power relations with relations of authority, defined by institutions, especially formal institutions.[8] In refocusing on linkages rather than institutions, non-institutional sources of power may become visible. Similarly, because institutional design occurs in an episodic manner, institutional analysis encourages a focus on relatively narrow periods of time. Linkages—even institutional linkages—develop and operate over time. Although a study of the establishment of new linkages might focus on a shorter period, the linkage framing encourages attention to longer periods of time.

A shift from institutions to linkages broadens the frame of analysis. As such, it reduces the likelihood that important aspects of socio-ecological systems will be overlooked. Much depends, however, on the type of linkages under consideration.

Multiple Levels or Multiple Scales?

What happens when analysis is framed in terms of multiple scales rather than multiple levels? Is one framing more encompassing than the other? Does either offer an edge in terms of analytic leverage? Are there complementarities between these concepts? Responses to these questions depend in part on how each concept is defined, given that both concepts have multiple meanings. However they are defined, neither concept emerges as clearly superior.

Depending on how "scale" and "level" are conceptualized, multi-scale linkages may subsume multi-level institutions, multi-level may subsume multiple scales, or the concepts may refer to very similar phenomena. Multiple scales subsume multiple levels if each scale involves multiple levels, and analysis is concerned with movement and linkages across levels as well as across scales. When institutions, defined as territorial jurisdictions, represent just one of several scales, specific institutions might be placed at different levels in terms of the jurisdictional hierarchy. Multi-level institutions organized along functional lines might be associated with alternative scales.

The literature on multi-level institutions explicitly encompasses institutions defined based on territory or function, those that are organized hierarchically and those that have overlapping authority. It might be appropriate to equate territory with level and function with scale, but the institutional patchwork cannot be reduced to matters of level and scale. Even if the scholarship on multi-level institutions distinguishes among levels related to territory, function, and scope of jurisdiction, it obscures the differences between relationships across different scales and those involving organizations with varying scope. Nor does it fully capture concerns with interactions across different fields of action—say climate change mitigation and the development of non-timber forest products (NTFP) as a poverty alleviation strategy, or environmental policy and electoral considerations.

The conceptualization of scale as a dimension of observation or analysis is clear enough when thinking of the choice between metric and English scales of spatial measurement or interactions between spatial and temporal scales. The concept is not always very clear, however, when applied in social scientific and interdisciplinary research. Confusion arises in part from a lack of conceptual consensus. Despite repeated critiques (Gibson, Ostrom, and Ahn 2000; Neumann 2009), the conflation of level and scale remains widespread, as can be seen in a quick review of titles and abstracts of recent articles in interdisciplinary journals. The equation of "scale" with "extent" follows every-day use and is likely to persist, especially in interdisciplinary outlets, even as more precise conceptualizations gain wider adoption in some disciplines and interdisciplinary research traditions.

Even in research traditions that conceptualize scale as a dimension of observation or analysis, there is considerable variation in the precision with which the concept is applied. Use of the same terms (e.g., local, global) to refer to levels on different scales (e.g., spatial, jurisdictional) creates confusion. Likewise, reference to changes in levels on a single scale as "rescaling" obscures the distinction between levels and scales. In some studies, all linkages are conceptualized as involving multiple scales. Indeed, definition of scale as "the spatial, temporal, quantitative, or analytical dimensions used to measure and study any phenomenon" (Gibson, Ostrom, and Ahn 2000, 218) invites application of the concept to a wide variety of phenomena. Many scholars bemoan the problem of conceptual stretching: If every linkage is a multiple scale linkage, the concept ceases to distinguish among different types of phenomena and becomes less valuable analytically. Some have gone so far as to advocate the total avoidance of "scale" as an analytical concept, but most accept that the term is too firmly entrenched to uproot.[9] The same criticisms apply to the conceptualization of "level."

The ambiguities in conceptualization of multiple levels and multiple scales limit their analytical value. Neither framing offers a clear analytical advantage. Nor does either fully subsume the other.

Let's Recognize Multi-Dimensional Linkages

At a minimum, the lack of conceptual consensus underlines yet again the importance of defining terms clearly for any particular analysis. Framing analysis in terms of linkages encourages a broader perspective, but what kinds of linkages should be examined to understand socio-ecological systems? Both multiple scales and multiple levels are important, but neither concept captures all important linkages. The limitation of these two common frames indicates the need for a more radical conceptual redevelopment. I argue for the recognition of multi-dimensional linkages, combined with the development of a more extensive conceptual menu to distinguish among the various dimensions that characterize and influence socio-ecological systems.

Definitions establish conceptual boundaries. Precise definitions increase analytical value by distinguishing clearly between phenomena that are and are not covered by a concept. Stretching concepts reduces their analytical value by reducing the set of phenomena that fall outside the conceptual boundary (Sartori 1991). Concept stretching may seem to be inherent in any effort to broaden the frame of analysis, as advocated in this chapter. It is not. The frame of analysis should be broad enough to include the essential features of phenomenon of interest—socio-ecological systems, in this case. But breadth of perspective does not preclude the development of precise concepts to distinguish among those features. Indeed, broadening the frame of analysis to recognize multiple dimensions can contribute to conceptual refinement.

Recognition of multi-dimensional linkages acknowledges the importance of interactions between levels and scales, but also that levels and scales are not the only important features of these relationships. The next step is to develop concepts to distinguish among other important dimensions of these linkages. Lebel, Garden, and Imamura (2005) take a step in this direction by distinguishing three dimensions of spatial relationships: scale, position, and place. They argue persuasively that important spatial dynamics related to position (e.g., upstream versus downstream, side of a river or boundary) or place (e.g., particular localities) cannot be reduced to matters of scale. Indeed, characterization of these interactions as cross-scale linkages would be misleading.

The previous section suggests that scale is often conceptualized in a manner that conflates the resolution of observation with the choice of metric of dimension of observation. Arguably, discontent over concept stretching reflects differences in the weight given to two aspects of its underlying meaning: the *resolution* of observation and the *framing* of observation. Distinguishing between resolution of observation and choice of metric for observation would increase analytical leverage. Conceptualization of scale in terms of resolution corresponds with long-established practices in a variety of fields, including those like cartography and photography that are at least superficially familiar to scholars regardless of their own disciplinary background. While people do choose scales for measurement or observation, conceptualizing these sorts of choices as rescaling depends on a less intuitive understanding of scale. As such, it is less accessible to an interdisciplinary audience. Conceptualizing the choice of metric as the choice of frame and distinguishing it from the choice of scale as resolution may encourage cross-fertilization with the well-established interdisciplinary literature on framing and framing effects (Chong and Druckman 2007). After all, the explanatory role attributed to the choice of metric for observation hinges on its framing effects.[10] As discussed above, for example, the rescaling of water development projects in Thailand prevented the mobilization of political mobilization by framing the issue in a manner that obscured environmental costs.

A further distinction might be made between both scale and frame of observation and the field and scope of action. These distinctions are inspired by functionally defined multi-level institutions. Where the term "function" suggests something innate and immutable, "field of action" alludes to social definition of these functions. Socially constructed fields of action vary in scope, where scope refers to how narrowly or broadly a field of action is defined (e.g., management of invasive species versus agriculture, forestry or water resources versus the environment). At first glance, issues of framing would seem to subsume fields of action. In fact, the two concepts refer to distinct if related dimensions. The difference comes to the fore when we consider linkages between different fields of action (e.g., range and wildlife management) that occur even in the absence of any effort to link them through reframing. Strategies for range management, such as the erection of disease control fences or the promotion of capital-intensive ranching, reduce both the land available for wildlife and the possibilities for wildlife migration. The promotion of wildlife, especially efforts to protect predators and mega-fauna, increases the risk of predation and other forms of wildlife damage (e.g., trampled fences or buildings) and reduces the prospects for livestock production. These interactions occur even if nobody draws attention to them, perhaps by reframing these management strategies in terms of land use or rural development. The array of recognized fields of action can be expected to influence possibilities for reframing. This possibility, however, can only be explored if fields of action and framing effects are recognized as distinct dimensions. The possible distinctions presented in this chapter are far from exhaustive. Indeed, reflecting my background as a social scientist, they focus on social linkages.

Concepts matter. They frame analysis, influencing both the breadth of perspective and the interpretation of what is seen. Complex dynamic systems such as socio-ecological systems present an analytical challenge precisely because they involve many elements, interaction effects, and non-linear processes. A broad perspective, at least as a point of departure, decreases the risk of overlooking important elements and interactions (Armitage 2008). This chapter has evaluated how two concepts widely adopted in interdisciplinary research concerned with the "multiples" characteristic of socio-ecological systems—multi-level institutions and multiple scale linkages—influence the types of "multiples" included in the analysis. Each term has advantages, but also important limitations. I have argued that framing the analysis of socio-ecological systems in terms of multi-dimensional linkages offers a broader perspective and is less likely to overlook important elements, relationships, or processes. A broader framing will be most effective if combined with conceptual refinements to distinguish among the various dimensions of linkage that characterize socio-ecological systems.

Acknowledgments

Thanks to Esther Mwangi and Andrew Wardell for inviting me to participate in the workshop on "Multi-Level Institutions for the Governance of Forests" at the 2011 IASC meeting in Hyderabad, India, to workshop participants for lively discussions that have enriched this contribution, and to two anonymous reviewers who pushed me to sharpen my arguments. I bear full responsibility for all remaining limitations in the chapter.

Notes

This chapter was originally published in *International Journal of the Commons* 6(2) (August 2012): 134–50.

1. This perspective is associated with historical institutionalism. For sociological (Hall and Taylor 1995) or organizational institutionalism (Immergut 1998), institutions encompass systems of symbols and moral codes as well as rules and organizations. Sociological or organizational institutionalism focuses more on dynamics within organizations and does not use the multi-level institution framing.
2. The coexistence of processes with variable time horizons has important implications for institutional analysis, as discussed by Pierson (2004, esp. chap. 3) and Wilson (2002).
3. Young (2002, 296), for example, operationalizes "the concept of level of social organization as a means of describing scale delimited in spatial terms." He has since moved away from this conceptualization of scale (e.g., Cash et al. 2006).
4. See Cash et al. (2006) for a graphical depiction of several climate-related processes that operate on different spatial and temporal scales.
5. Accountability is a type of power relation. Accountability implies that one actor *should* act on behalf of another, but might not; assessments of accountability evaluate the extent to which such action can be ensured. Power relations do not rule out action on behalf of others but emphasize the prevalence of competing interests and related struggles.

6. Many but not all scholars who recognize limitations in the knowledge, cognitive capacities, and foresight of actors assume that they act intentionally. The concern here is not with assumptions about rationality but the emphasis given to agency.

7. Pierson (2004) discusses some examples.

8. As noted before, although the importance of informal institutions is generally recognized in theory, many applications focus on formal institutions.

9. See review of this debate in Neumann (2009).

10. Framing theory characterizes this sort of rescaling as a change in the "frame of communication": a deliberate effort at persuasion by emphasizing some aspects of a situation or choice and downplaying others (Chong and Druckman 2007, 106ff.).

References

Ackerman, J. 2004. "Co-Governance for Accountability: Beyond 'Exit' and 'Voice.'" *World Development* 32(3): 447–63.

Adger, W., K. Brown, and E. Tompkins. 2006. "The Political Economy of Cross-Scale Networks in Resource Co-Management." *Ecology and Society* 10(2): 9.

Agrawal, A., and C. C. Gibson. 1999. "Enchantment and Disenchantment: The Role of Community in Natural Resource Conservation." *World Development* 27(4): 629–49.

Armitage, D. 2008. "Governance and the Commons in a Multi-Level World." *International Journal of the Commons* 2(1): 7–32.

Bardhan, P. 2002. "Decentralization of Governance and Development." *Journal of Economic Perspectives* 16(4): 185–205.

Baumgartner, F. R., and B. D. Jones. 1991. "Agenda Dynamics and Policy Subsystems." *Journal of Politics* 53(4): 1044–74.

Berry, S. 1993. *No Condition is Permanent: The Social Dynamics of Agrarian Change in Sub-Saharan Africa*. Madison: University of Wisconsin Press.

Cash, D. W., W. Neil Adger, F. Berkes, P. Garden, L. Lebel, P. Olsson, L. Pritchard, and O. Young. 2006. "Scale and Cross-Scale Dynamics: Governance and Information in a Multi-Level World." *Ecology and Society* 11(2): 8.

Chong, D., and J. N. Druckman. 2007. "Framing Effects." *Annual Review of Political Science* 10: 103–26.

Eaton, K., and E. Connerley. 2010. "Democracy, Development, and Security as Objectives of Decentralization." In *Making Decentralization Work: Democracy, Development, and Security*, edited by E. Connerley, K. Eaton, and P. Smoke, 1–24. Boulder, CO: Lynne Rienner.

Gibson, C. C., E. Ostrom, and T. K. Ahn. 2000. "The Concept of Scale and the Human Dimensions of Global Change: A Survey." *Ecological Economics* 32(2): 217–39.

Grant, R. W., and R. O. Keohane. 2005. "Accountability and Abuses of Power in World Politics." *American Political Science Review* 99(1): 29–43.

Haas, P. M. 2004. "Addressing the Global Governance Deficit." *Global Environmental Politics* 4(1): 1–15.

Hall, P. A., and R. C. R. Taylor. 1996. "Political Science and the Three New Institutionalisms." *Political Studies* 44(5): 936–57.

Hooghe, L., and G. Marks. 2003. "Unraveling the Central State, but How? Types of Multi-Level Governance." *American Political Science Review* 97(2): 233–43.

Immergut, E. M. 1998. "The Theoretical Core of the New Institutionalism." *Politics and Society* 26(1): 5–34.

Lebel, L., P. Garden, and M. Imamura. 2005. "The Politics of Scale, Position, and Place in the Governance of Water Resources in the Mekong Region." *Ecology and Society* 10(2): 18.

Lund, Christian. 2006. "Twilight Institutions: Public Authority and Local Politics in Africa." *Development and Change* 37(4): 685–705.

Manor, J. 2004. "User Committees: A Potentially Damaging Second Wave of Decentralisation." *European Journal of Development Research* 16(1): 192–213.

Moe, T. M. 1990. "The Politics of Structural Choice: Toward a Theory of Public Bureaucracy." In *Organization Theory: From Chester Barnard to the Present and Beyond*, edited by O. E. Williamson, 116–53. New York: Oxford University Press.

Neumann, R. P. 2009. "Political Ecology: Theorizing Scale." *Progress in Human Geography* 33(3): 398–406.

North, D. 1990. *Institutions, Institutional Change and Economic Performance.* New York: Cambridge University Press.

Ostrom, E. 1990. *Governing the Commons: The Evolution of Institutions for Collective Action.* New York: Cambridge University Press.

———. 2005. *Understanding Institutional Diversity*. Princeton, NJ: Princeton University Press.

Ostrom, E., and H. Nagendra. 2006. "Insights on Linking Forests, Trees, and People from the Air, on the Ground, and in the Laboratory." *Proceedings of the National Academy of Sciences* 103(51): 19224–31.

Papadopoulus, Y. 2003. "Cooperative Forms of Governance: Problems of Democratic Accountability in Complex Environments." *European Journal of Political Research* 42(4): 473–501.

Pierson, P. 2004. *Politics in Time: History, Institutions, and Social Analysis.* Princeton, NJ: Princeton University Press.

Poteete, A. R. 2009. "Defining Political Community and Rights to Natural Resources in Botswana." *Development and Change* 40(2): 281–305.

Poteete, A. R., and J. C. Ribot. 2011. "Repertoires of Domination: Decentralization as Process in Botswana and Senegal." *World Development* 39(3): 439–49.

Poteete, A. R., and D. Welch. 2004. "Institutional Design in the Face of Complexity: Developing Rules for Managing Forest Resources." *Human Ecology* 32(3): 279–311.

Ribot, J. C., A. Chhatre, and T. Lankina. 2008. "Introduction: Institutional Choice and Recognition in the Formation and Consolidation of Local Democracy." *Conservation and Society* 6(1): 1–11.

Rudel, T. K. 2008. "Meta-Analyses of Case Studies: A Method for Studying Regional and Global Environmental Change." *Global Environmental Change* 18(1): 18–25.

Sartori, G. 1991. "Comparing and Miscomparing." *Journal of Theoretical Politics* 3(3): 243–57.

Scharpf, F. 1988. "The Joint-Decision Trap: Lessons from German Federalism and European Integration." *Public Administration* 66(3): 239–78.

Scott, J. C. 1998. *Seeing Like a State: Why Certain Schemes to Improve the Human Condition Have Failed.* New Haven, CT: Yale University Press.

Skelcher, C. 2005. "Jurisdictional Integrity, Polycentrism, and the Design of Democratic Governance." *Governance* 18(1): 89–110.

Tsebelis, G. 1995. "Decision-Making in Political Systems: Veto Players in Presidentialism, Parliamentarism, Multicameralism, and Multipartyism." *British Journal of Political Science* 25: 289–326.

von Benda-Beckmann, K. 1981. "Forum Shopping and Shopping Forums: Dispute Processing in a Minangkabu Village in West Sumatra." *Journal of Legal Pluralism* 19: 117–59.

Wilson, J. 2002. "Scientific Uncertainty, Complex Systems, and the Design of Common-Pool Institutions." In *The Drama of the Commons*, edited by E. Ostrom, T. Dietz, N. Dolsak, P. C. Stern, S. Stonich, and E. U. Weber, 327–59. Washington, DC: National Academies Press.

Young, O. R. 2002. "Institutional Interplay: The Environmental Consequences of Cross-Scale Interactions." In *The Drama of the Commons*, edited by E. Ostrom, T. Dietz, N. Dolsak, P. C. Stern, S. Stonich, and E. U. Weber, 263–91. Washington, DC: National Academies Press.

9

Selections from Aid, Incentives, and Sustainability: An Institutional Analysis of Development Cooperation

Elinor Ostrom, Clark Gibson, Sujai Shivakumar, and Krister Andersson

Chapter 1—The Problems of Aid, Incentives, and Sustainability

Recent studies of development assistance programs conclude that despite tremendous efforts and good intentions, aid has produced generally disappointing results. Sida [Swedish International Development Cooperation Agency], along with other bilateral and multilateral aid agencies, has observed that the lack of proper incentives generated by aid itself may be an important factor undermining its sustainability. As commissioned by Sida's UTV [Department for Evaluation and Internal Audit], this report explores how the incentives that arise in the system of development assistance affect the goal of sustainable development.

This report highlights four major contexts where perverse incentives operate. First, perverse incentives are found in many day-to-day situations facing citizens in all countries of the world. Second, the policy processes in recipient countries frequently do not lead public officials to search out better ways of improving institutional arrangements facing their citizens in their everyday economic, social, and political lives. Third, the international development assistance system itself is a complex tangle of relationships. Aid sustainability hinges critically on how this system, and the incentives created with it, interacts with the operational and policy-making contexts in the recipient country. Finally, incentives exist within most donor agencies themselves, as well as between these agencies and contractors and other donor country organizations. Few incentives may exist here to vigorously pursue strategies of individual and organizational learning about how to achieve sustainable learning development initiatives.

This chapter sets out basic definitions and concepts used throughout this report. *Institutions* are defined as formal and informal rules that are generally followed by individuals. Such rules structure incentives in human exchange, whether political, social, or economic. *Incentives* refer to the rewards and punishments perceived by individuals to be related to their actions and those of others. *Development and development cooperation* involve improving the material conditions of individuals, often through processes of deliberate intervention. By *sustainability*, we mean the longevity of development cooperation's effects, rather than particular projects or activities themselves. Finally, *ownership* of a development assistance project or program is identified with four dimensions: enunciating demand, making a tangible contribution, obtaining benefits, and sharing responsibility for long-term continuation or noncontinuation of a project.

Perverse Incentives and Sustainability of Development Assistance

Prompted by the generally disappointing performance of so many development projects, multiple studies of development assistance programs have been undertaken during the past decade (see, e.g., Adam and O'Connell 1999; Tsikata 1998; Lancaster 1999a, 1999b; Mosley 1991; Martens et al. 2002; van de Walle and Johnston 1996; World Bank 1996a, 1996b; Birdsall and Londono 1997). Despite notable achievements—several of which are the result of Swedish aid efforts—few development programs or projects have been evaluated as achieving long-term sustainable results (Edgren 1995; White 1992, 1998, 1999; Elgstrom 1992; Catterson and Lindahl 1999). These findings led members of the Department for Evaluation and Internal Audit (UTV) of the Swedish International Development Cooperation Agency (Sida) to posit that one of the key factors behind these repeated findings "is likely to be the perverse incentives generated by aid itself" (Sida 1999, 1). Further, they concluded:

> If perverse incentives are a problem of significant importance for achieving sustainable projects, it is imperative to weaken these incentives and

> enhance the "proper" incentives in order to promote the effectiveness of aid. This requires that knowledge about the problem is taken into consideration in Sida's design and implementation of activities. (Sida 1999, 1)

The conclusion that perverse incentives adversely affect the capabilities of recipient countries to utilize donor aid to achieve sustainable improvements in the life prospects of their citizens, led UTV to issue a call for proposals to examine the incentives in development assistance. [. . .] Given our own extensive studies of institutions and incentives, we were pleased when the Workshop in Political Theory and Policy Analysis at Indiana University was awarded the contract to undertake this study in the spring of 2000. In light of the research we have subsequently conducted for this study, we agree with UTV's assessment that perverse incentives are at the heart of the difficulty in achieving sustainable development assistance programs.

Perverse incentives are a source of difficulties in *all* countries of the world. They are responsible for gross inefficiencies and maldistribution of resources. Perverse incentives motivate some to engage in violence and even warfare against others. This much is evident. Yet, the identification of perverse incentives—as a key factor associated with unsustainable international assistance by itself, does not make it easy to find solutions to these difficult problems.

Why is it so difficult to design international aid programs that avoid perverse incentives and are sustainable over time? Why are perverse incentives more pervasive in recipient countries than in donor countries? We address these central questions in this report. To do so, we must first grasp the processes at work in recipient countries as well as the processes at work in the development assistance processes. The difficulties in finding sustainable solutions to problems in development are due in part because these processes operate in a complex and interrelated manner. To recommend how to overcome the problems of unsustainable development assistance, one must first identify where and why the perverse incentives exist. We consequently identify four major types of settings where perverse incentives operate.

Four Contexts for Perverse Incentives in Development Assistance

First, perverse incentives are found in many day-to-day situations facing citizens in *all* countries in the world. In donor countries, many potentially negative incentives have been changed by designing institutions that alter incentives so as to structure situations of daily life leading to mutually productive, rather than mutually unproductive, outcomes. In recipient countries, citizens continue to face incentives that make it difficult to invest in economic activities, to provide public goods, to improve common-pool resources, and generally to arrive at mutually productive day-to-day arrangements. [. . .]

Second, the policy processes in recipient countries frequently do not lead public officials to search out better ways of improving the institutional arrangements facing their citizens in everyday economic, social, and political life. Perverse incentives unfortunately exist at the policy level as well as in the day-to-day operational level. [. . .]

Third, the international development assistance system itself is a complex system of relationships that might enhance the likelihood of overcoming perverse incentives at an operational or policy level in recipient countries. Unfortunately, few self-correcting mechanisms are to be found when one examines aid processes at a systemic level. As Deborah Brautigam (2000, l) stresses: "Large amounts of aid delivered over long periods, create incentives for governments and donors that have the potential to undermine good governance and the quality of state institutions." [. . .]

Fourth, few incentives exist within most international development agencies, and between these agencies and the contractors they employ, to vigorously pursue strategies of individual and organization learning about how to achieve sustainable development initiatives. [. . .]

We illustrate the theoretical arguments made in this report with examples drawn from the literature on development assistance processes, with knowledge acquired by extensive interviews of Sida staff members, contractors, recipient government officials, and beneficiaries. [. . .]

One cannot understand the lack of sustainability of development assistance without understanding the base problems that are an excessive burden on the energies, creativity, and productivity of the people living in developing countries. Without such an understanding, it is tragically possible to undermine progress that may be underway in fostering more effective institutions within a recipient country. In this report, we use a particular approach—institutional analysis—to examine the basic problems that are at the core of why economic and political "development" has not been achieved in a large number of countries in the world. We then use the same approach to examine the incentives in the overall development assistance process and within development assistance agencies and their relationships with contractors.

Before we turn to our more general analysis though, we will lay out our meaning of some of the key terms used throughout this entire report. We do so since these terms—including "institutions," "incentives," "development," and "sustainability"—are defined in so many different ways. We define and use these terms carefully to better communicate with our readers. We define these four core terms in [the second] section of this chapter.

In [the third] section of this chapter, we discuss the relationship of development cooperation to achieving more effective solutions to collective-action problems. When development assistance was initiated in the 1950s, the presumption was that the problem was "missing money." It was thought that less-developed countries were poor and lacked physical infrastructure. If developed countries would transfer funds and build roads, schools, health centers, and other infrastructure, this should enable poor countries to develop more rapidly than they would on their own. In more recent times, scholars and donors recognize that "missing institutions" are more at the core of the problems of development than missing money.

Another concept that has emerged in recent times as practitioners and scholars have tried to understand the lack of sustainability of international assistance is that of "ownership." In [the fourth] section of this chapter, we discuss this concept in some depth. It is both an important aspect of the current Swedish policy related to development assistance as well as a concept that is generally accepted as being of considerable importance in the achievement of better and more sustainable outcomes.

Concepts Linking Institutions and Sustainability

Before we dig deeply into the linkage between institutions, incentives, and the sustainability of development assistance, let us devote a few pages to the definitions of four key terms: institutions, incentives, development, and sustainability. All of these terms are used in multiple ways by different authors. We want to clarify for the reader how we use these terms before we proceed further.

Institutions

Much of this report describes how institutions alter the incentives of individuals interacting in situations whose actions affect the productivity and sustainability of efforts in development cooperation. Like many other key terms defined in this and the next section, many authors use different definitions of institutions.

Douglass North has made us all aware of the importance of separating the concept of organizations from that of institutions. Organizations can be thought of as "groups of individuals bound by some common purpose to achieve objectives" (North 1990, 5). Organizations are thus the teams of individuals engaged in collective action to produce jointly valued outcomes. Simple organizations can be analyzed as an individual action situation. Complex organizations are simultaneous and sequentially linked action situations. Action situations—as we discuss further in chapter 2—are the many structured interactions where individuals must make decisions about actions that affect them and others.

Central to many definitions of institutions is the notion of humanly designed constraints. By constraining behavior, institutions increase the predictability of human interactions and thus make possible some activities that would not otherwise be possible. Think for a minute about a modern highway system without rules of the road that are accepted and enforced. The potential chaos would be so great that few would venture to use such a system. Thus, the key aspect of all institutions are shared rules about what actions individuals must take, must not take, or are permitted to take in particular settings (Crawford and Ostrom 1995).

Rules are predictably enforced by agents responsible to external authorities or to those directly involved (or both) for monitoring conduct and for imposing sanctions. These prescriptions are the rules of the game that coordinate human interaction, they "structure incentives in human exchange, whether political, social, or economic" (North 1990, 3). We focus primarily on the rules-in-use in particular settings—that is, the rules as they are understood, generally followed by participants, and enforced—rather than focusing only on formal rules written in legislation, contracts, or court decisions that may not be known to participants and affect their incentives and behavior.

Norms are shared and internalized understandings by those involved about the "do's and don'ts" involved in particular types of situations. In contrast to rules that are generally enforced, norms are usually not enforced in a regular way by designated agents. Individuals involved in situations with participants who do not follow group norms may gossip about each other and refuse to engage in reciprocity with those who break norms. When rules are accepted as norms in a community, someone who breaks a rule faces a high likelihood of receiving both formal sanctions as well as various forms of disapproval extended to them by others in the group.

Strategies are the plans for action that individuals make within a structure of incentives produced by rules, physical goods, and attributes of a community; the consequent expectations that an individual has of the likely behavior of others; and the perceptions of likely benefits or costs they may receive or pay in light of actions and outcomes.

Incentives

The dictionary definition of an incentive is "that which incites or encourages; a motive; a stimulus" (*MacMillan's Modern Dictionary*). Thus, the concept implies both an external stimulus and an internal motivation. In institutional analysis, one uses the term to refer to rewards and punishments that are perceived by individuals to be related to their actions and those of others. The payments people receive or costs they have to pay, the respect they earn from others, the acquisition of new skills or knowledge are all external stimuli that may induce more of some kinds of behavior and less of other kinds. Donors use a variety of external stimuli in their effort to change behavior of officials and beneficiaries in recipient countries.

Perceived rewards and punishments can motivate individuals to take actions that are genuinely productive for all involved. The positive incentives within a well-structured, competitive market for private goods where private rights are well enforced, for example, lead most participants to invest in activities that help themselves while generating benefits for others. Incentives are considered perverse when they lead individuals to avoid engaging in mutually productive outcomes or to take actions that are generally harmful for others.

Many of the incentives involved in international assistance programs involve adding funds to government budgets so as to encourage more spending and activities in those domains that a donor perceives to be important. Additional training, supplemental technical assistance, overseas travel opportunities are all incentives used in aid processes. Major questions raised by an institutional analysis of these processes relate to whether apparent short-term changes are real, whether they are congruent with a donor's goals, whether positive changes in behavior occur, and whether they are sustainable.

Development and Development Cooperation

Individuals and groups working in the development field engage in heated discussions over the meaning of foundational concepts such as "development" and "development cooperation." As discussed above, we generally view *development as a process* where individuals, through the design and use of institutions at many scales, help to solve more collective-action problems more effectively. Given that this is a report written for Sida, it is important to explore how the terms are being used in the Swedish context. We have paid special attention to how these terms are used in Sida documents and by Sida staff since these uses are most likely to influence their incentives and outcomes.

The concept of *development* itself is quite elastic. Although generally used to refer to the betterment of material conditions for individuals, development has been applied to other areas such as politics, culture, and religion. We will stick in this report with the concept of development as applying to the improvement of the material conditions for individuals; this occurs through improving the institutions they use to solve encountered problems of collective action.

In the case of Swedish development cooperation, Sweden's Parliament has set out six goals:

- economic growth;
- economic and social equality;
- economic and political independence;
- democratic development;
- care for the environment; and
- equality between women and men (Sida 1997b, 9–10; hereafter referred to as *Sida at Work*).

Achieving these six goals is expected to produce the "overall goal" of Swedish development cooperation: *poverty reduction*. In this report, we assume that these seven goals provide the general definition of development that Sida follows. Development cooperation, in turn, refers to those actions taken by donors and recipients intended to further these seven goals.[1]

We also subscribe to these seven goals. Thus, we view our task in this report as sharing our best work with colleagues at Sida devoted to achieving the most important goals of the new millennium. This is an enormous task.

Sustainability

Since we have been asked to examine how the incentives derived from participation in development assistance processes affect sustainability, another key concept that we use in this report is *sustainability*. Arriving at a single definition for sustainability, however, is challenging. In a recent effort to examine the concept and measurement of sustainability, Bell and Morse (1999) argue that the concept has been used in such a variety of contexts and with so many meanings that the concept ranges from being an empty slogan to a loaded normative term used primarily for political purposes.

Not only does the economics literature boast a variety of definitions,[2] but, during the course of this consultancy, we also found that Sida documents and staff members employ different meanings of the term. For example, in *Sida at Work*, we read that development cooperation projects should be "socially, economically and environmentally *sustainable*, i.e., lead to results which live on after the support has been discontinued" (*Sida at Work*, 51; original emphasis). This definition emphasizes that sustainability is related to the continuation of a project's results. In the "Analysis Guide" to *Sida at Work*, the questions a staff member should ask about a project include: "Is there policy and legislation in place which is judged to be able to guarantee the continuation of *the project* when Swedish support has been phased out?" "Is it realistic to count on management and institutional capacity and financial resources being available to run *the project* without development assistance?" and "Is the cooperation partner willing and prepared to take on responsibility/ownership of *the activity* in the long run?" (emphasis added). Thus, three (out of five) questions, recommended as a way of determining sustainability, underscore the continued existence of a project or activity per se, not the results of a project.[3] In *Sida vid Sida*, on the other hand, Sida's mission is stated as contributing to "endurable and sustainable effects" (see also Sida Director General Tham's preface to the 1989 Sida Annual Report).

The understanding of Sida staff, both in Sweden and in the field, reflected these multiple definitions of the concept of sustainability. Some thought that Sida's goal of sustainability referred to activities begun by projects, others to projects per se, and still others understood sustainability to mean the enduring results of a project. Several staff members listed all three as important. For this report, we refer to the goals laid out by the Swedish Parliament regarding development: clearly these seven goals refer to the endurance of results and not to projects or post-project activities alone. Thus, we understand sustainability to refer to the longevity of development cooperation's effects, rather than particular projects or activities.

Approaching sustainability in this manner frees one from a sense that every project should be continued indefinitely. This view of sustainability—which we share with many colleagues at Sida—is that projects, programs, and other modalities are only the means in the effort to achieve the long-term goals of development assistance. Because of their contribution to poverty reduction and the other goals, some projects should continue for a long time and thus be sustainable at the project level. Others may have made their contribution to development goals in their early years and continuing the project as such is not necessarily the optimal investment to achieve the broader goals.

Development, Development Cooperation, and Collective-Action Problems

How do the incentives facing Sida staff, recipient country officials, and others involved in development assistance affect a recipient country's potential for economic growth, economic and social equality, economic and political independence, democratic development, care for the environment, gender equality, and poverty reduction? Achieving broad goals such as these is a never-ending challenge for all donors and recipients of aid. It is especially so for recipient countries who were the objects of past colonial domination. Many of these countries had productive, indigenous institutions destroyed or suppressed by the colonial experience and further weakened by the authoritarian or centralized systems of rule that often replaced colonial rule.

Progress toward achieving the goals of development involves the provision of many kinds of public goods that are available to all individuals within a society, whether or not they contribute to their provision. To stimulate economic growth, for example, one must invest in physical, human, and social capital, including the creation of effective property-rights systems and ways of adjudicating disputes at relatively low costs. Once economic growth is stimulated, more substantial opportunities may become available to *all* who live in a regime regardless of their prior contributions. In particular, growth provides a better opportunity to address distributional inequities. While not all societies have taken full advantage of using growth to reduce inequities, without growth it is extremely difficult to reduce poverty significantly.

Working for economic and social equality and environmental improvement requires finding peaceful means of productively and equitably combining the efforts (and often the unevenly distributed social and economic assets) of individuals. The currently most powerful individuals in recipient countries—the autocratic leaders in particular—nearly always have the most to lose from changes leading to democratic development. They may forcibly resist such efforts. Achieving economic and political independence and democratic development requires substantial time and energy to be invested by a large number of individuals. Reducing poverty requires investing resources and hard work to create opportunities for the less advantaged.

Missing Money?

In the immediate post-colonial period, many researchers studying development, as well as public officials trying to improve economic performance, thought the core problem to be a lack of sufficient monetary resources needed to build necessary physical infrastructure and to enhance investment in local economies (see Rostow 1960; Prebisch 1970; Huntington and Weiner 1987). In other words, the problem was identified as "missing money." The proposed solution was a simple and short-term one—send money. If this had actually been the core problem and the right solution, the billions of dollars that donor countries have allocated to developing countries over the last four decades should have gone a long way toward solving the problem of underdevelopment (for an extensive review, see van de Walle and Johnston 1996). Many individual infrastructure, health, and educational projects have had notable successes (for examples, see Bosc and Hanak-Freud 1995; Maipose, Somolekae, and Johnston 1997). Sending money has, however, not substantially reduced the relative poverty levels of most recipient countries (Krueger, Michalopoulos, and Ruttan 1989; Blomstrom and Lundahl 1993). In fact, the problem of poverty in many African and Asian countries is in many ways more severe today, at the beginning of the twenty-first century, than it was half a century ago (Boone 1996). Even in countries with growth, the plight of the poorest has worsened. "A small elite got richer and richer, but the mass of the people remained as poor as ever" (Elgstrom 1992, 46).

Missing Institutions?

After decades of trying to understand the problems of development, it is now widely accepted that the core problem is "missing institutions" or "perverse institutions" instead of "missing money" (see, e.g., World Bank 1998; North 1990, 1994; Burnside and Dollar 1997). Rather than emphasizing the lack of material or human resources, an increasing number of analysts now point to the ways in which the incentives facing people within their own country as well as those generated by development assistance lead to a general lack of productivity (Bates 1998; Catterson and Lindahl 1999; Killick, Gunatilaka, and Mar 1998). Their work indicates that no matter how well-intentioned those providing assistance are, or how many resources are transferred, development will occur only if political and economic institutions generate incentives that facilitate individuals' achievement of development goals.

As discussed above, institutions are the rules used by individuals in a wide diversity of repeated situations that they confront in life. The rules that individuals adopt, along with other contextual factors discussed in chapter 2, directly affect their incentives and consequently the likelihood that they will achieve higher levels of productivity in the many collective-action situations faced in everyday life. Thus, institutions help or hinder the efforts of individuals to be optimally productive in the activities they undertake with others.

Collective-Action Situations at the Core of Development

The most important situations affecting development are what we call collective-action situations. A *collective-action situation*, as we use the term in this report, occurs whenever the input of several individuals is required to achieve a desirable joint outcome. Almost all productive relationships involve some form of collective action. For example, while one person can produce agricultural products from a single, small agricultural plot, the amount of agricultural product per inputs is greatly enhanced by creating diverse forms of teamwork through family, community, or corporate arrangements to increase the size of the enterprise. Similar benefits of increasing the number of participants who bring different skills and resources occur in almost all manufacturing or service activities.

Collective-action situations, given this broad definition, pervade both the public and private sectors of all countries. Collective-action *situations* become collective-action *problems* when actors in the situation choose actions that produce outcomes that are evaluated to be less desirable than others available to them. The classic example of a collective-action problem in the public sector is the provision of a public good such as a national highway network or the reduction of environmental harms (such as smog at a local level or global warming at a global level) (Olson 1965). Analysts tend to focus on collective-action problems in the public sector. Yet, as Miller (1992) has clearly demonstrated, simply creating a public bureaucracy to tackle the provision of public goods or the protection of natural resources does not automatically solve the initial collective-action problem and may even stimulate still further problems.

The core questions facing the members of any team effort in the public or private sector are who should contribute what, when, and where? Who will coordinate their efforts? How will joint returns be distributed? Unless participants share clear and efficiency-enhancing rules and norms, some may shirk (free-ride) on the efforts of others or try to deflect joint returns primarily to themselves. Once participants hold back on their contributions to joint efforts or allocate considerable time to gaining more than their share of benefits, the level of productive outcomes achieved by their joint efforts starts to deteriorate. Unfortunately, such dynamic processes lead toward lower and lower levels of returns for all involved, and the perverse incentives tend to be self-reinforcing.

In the 1960s and 1970s, the theoretical presumption was that citizens themselves could not solve most collective-action problems that involved public goods or common-pool resources, and that a centralized government was necessary to impose solutions from the center (Olson 1965; V. Ostrom 1999). Now, in light of considerable theoretical and empirical research, most institutional analysts recognize that individuals are capable of crafting solutions to their own diverse problems of collective action. Yet, this requires a rich set of general and special institutional arrangements at local, regional, and national levels in both the private as well as public spheres of life (McGinnis 1999a, 1999b; V. Ostrom, Feeny, and Picht 1993; Scott 1998; de Soto 2000). The institutional arrangements that may facilitate the effective provision of national defense are likely to differ from those that facilitate the protection of natural resources, the construction and maintenance of effective physical infrastructure, the provision of education, the stimulation of technological innovation, and the creation of more equal economic and political powers in diverse arenas.

Ownership in Development

The essential quandary of development has been how to provide assistance that is successful and sustainable in terms of achieving the types of goals identified by the Swedish Parliament (listed above) or similar goals specified by almost all major donor organizations. In the first several decades of extensive development assistance, the presumption was that donors should take the lead in designing and implementing programs and projects (Morss 1984). By the early 1990s, however, it was realized that the heavy donor voice in the planning of development assistance deprived recipients of "ownership" over the programs and projects designed for their benefit (van de Walle and Johnston 1996; OECD/DAC 1992; Johnson and Wasty 1993; Brunetti and Weder 1994; Wilson and Whitmore 1995). Without such ownership, critics argued, recipients are unlikely to make the kind of commitments needed to ensure the realization of the intended long-term results of donor assistance. Thus, without institutional development to increase the ownership capabilities of the beneficiaries, development aid is thought to be unsustainable and empirical studies have demonstrated this relationship.[4]

For example, in their review of the sustainability of twelve development projects supported by Sida in Tanzania, Catterson and Lindahl (1999) repeatedly refer to problems of ownership involved in the projects that were not evaluated as sustainable. One example is the Folk Development Colleges (FDCs) that had been viewed as a problematic project early in its life and was finally phased out in 1996. The program was supported for twenty-one years and an estimated investment of SEK120 million made in these training schools. In trying to understand why support was maintained for more than two decades, Catterson and Lindahl (1999, 77) reflect that "there was a strong sense of Swedish *ownership* of the Programme, both influencing the pattern of support and the phase out problems. . . . The lack of Tanzanian ownership was reflected in the role of Linkoping University, which, according to the 1996 evaluation, *approached the TANDEM project as missionaries to advocate a purist approach to adult education as seen from a Swedish perspective*" (original emphasis; see also Rogers, Chadwick, and Oglesby 1997).

In response to the growing awareness of the importance of ownership, Sida, as a leader among donor organizations, has formally adopted the idea of recipient ownership of development assistance and placed it at the center of its expressed philosophy of donor assistance. According to *Sida at Work*, a project's owner is "the party which requests support and which is responsible for the planning and implementation of the project, by having, for example, the organization and staff for the task. The project owner finances part, often a large part, of the costs of the project" (1997b, 15). In turn, Sida vests its partner in development cooperation with full rights to use the resources provided within the framework laid down in the project agreement. Sida understands that this "complete ownership" requires that political bodies, as well as target groups, support and participate in the decision-making process. Through these ideas and procedures, Sida hopes to have the recipient "own" its development processes (1997b, 17). Further, in the same document, Sida stresses the importance of clear and mutually understood definitions of responsibilities among stakeholders.

Terminological Confusion

Ownership has thus become an important and fashionable concept within Sida and among most development assistance agencies in the world today. The leaders of recipient countries are also using the term in their efforts to examine critically the post-independence experience and learn how to do things differently.[5] The theoretical conception of what ownership means is not entirely clear, however, from reading official documents or from talking with donor or recipient country officials. Moreover, it becomes even murkier when confronted with the reality of development ownership in the field. As Brautigam (2000, 32) notes, the question of what "ownership" means in development assistance is not clearly answered either in the scholarly literature or by donor agencies.

Consider the relatively simple case of technical assistance: the core actors involved in this would be Sida-Stockholm, the Sida field office, the consultant, the recipient government ministries, and the target group. It is easy to imagine several of these actors "requesting support," and each bearing different types of "responsibility." Each is also likely to have a different interpretation of the distribution of ownership assignments, and the prerogatives and responsibilities that go along with them. This lack of common understanding of the concept of ownership and the resulting lack of clear responsibility for long-term results appears to lie at the heart of the incentive problem in development.[6]

Sida recognizes that the concept of ownership in development cooperation is often complex. Owners of development cooperation can vary "between different levels and areas, from government policy to different aspects of a project," as well as with different types of aid; ownership "can also lie with different groups of people" (Sida 1997b, 18). Sida also promotes the idea of "popular ownership," which seems to mean that target groups might be allowed some role in the design or implementation of assistance (1997b, 18). Finally, Sida's staff is encouraged to develop a sense of ownership as "close as possible to the target group and other interested parties" (1997b, 18).

Tension exists among these different aspects of Sida's view of ownership. For example, the closer the ownership is to the target group for many projects—particularly, large-scale infrastructure investments—the less likely it is that this group will have the finances to underwrite "a large part" of a project. While the target group may be organized for some purposes, it may not always have the staff or organization to implement many types of development projects and their concomitant accounting procedures. Also, because development cooperation requires approval by the recipient government, these governments will always have a share of the ownership, regardless of the level of the target group. Further, it is not clear what "popular ownership" means. Indeed, the fundamentals of the definition of ownership in *Sida at Work* appear to exclude popular ownership. "Popular ownership" in the Sida context appears far closer to "participation" than ownership per se. Finally, since Sida is the source of the aid, it must retain a great deal of control over the distribution of these resources—hence, the advice that Sida staff "has the task of finding a practical, feasible balance between promoting ownership and exercising control" (1997b, 18).

Ownership and Collective Action

Can we, in resolving this problem of multiple definitions, refer to a clear meaning of ownership in the context of development assistance? In economics, ownership generally refers to the rights that individuals possess in relationship to one another with regard to an asset. Full ownership pertains to a bundle of rights in regard to an asset (Schlager and Ostrom 1992). These include the rights of access and use, the rights to make management decisions, the rights to determine who else (if anyone) can become a joint owner, and the right to give up or transfer all of these rights (called the right to alienation).

A clear understanding of ownership and its consequence for aid sustainability must take into account collective-action problems in development. As we have seen, collective-action problems can occur when individuals receive benefits that are not tied directly to what they contribute to a combined effort. Individuals may hold back on their contribution for a variety of reasons, leading to a deterioration of the productive outcomes of their joint efforts. An individual's reluctance to contribute may stem from the fact that he or she does not perceive a collective activity to be legitimate. An individual may also feel that his or her contribution will have very little impact on the outcome. Such perceptions can be strengthened, especially if the individual was not consulted before beginning a project. Noncontribution to the joint effort, in such circumstances, may seem fair. Yet, because the individual hesitates to exercise ownership, the project is likely to fail.

Four Dimensions of Ownership

In our effort to understand collective-action problems as a reflection of inadequate realization of a sense of ownership in a joint project, we have identified four dimensions of ownership: (l) enunciating demand, (2) making a tangible contribution, (3) obtaining benefits, and (4) sharing responsibility for long-term continuation or noncontinuation of a project. Sometimes one or another of these aspects is stressed in official documents. It is important to clarify these components analytically.

Ownership can be viewed as incorporating the following processes:

1. Participation in *provision* by articulating what asset, project, or program is needed and deciding how resources should be mobilized to provide for this need.
2. Participation in *production* by making tangible contributions. Time, effort, and other resources contributed to production are a costly signal that beneficiaries expect to derive benefits from a project.
3. Participation in *consumption* of the benefits if the project is successful and in a share of responsibility if the project fails.
4. Participation in decisions related to the *alienation* of the rights to a project (the decision to continue or not continue a project once it has been initiated).

When one is dealing with a strictly private asset, these decisions can be made by a single individual, family, or firm. In regard to the type of project involved in development assistance, however, all of the above processes are collective in nature and are, further, shared by local beneficiaries, an implementing agency or agencies, national government officials, and the officials of a donor country. The relative mix of contributions by multiple parties varies.

In the early years of development assistance, local beneficiaries were expected to participate in the consumption of benefits but not much more. The recent focus on ownership stresses their role in the other three aspects of this concept.

In some development projects, ownership is enhanced by having beneficiaries more actively engage in both provision and production processes. By making investment in these processes, beneficiaries are not simply consumers of someone else's largesse. They have had to articulate their own preferences and allocate their own resources. Projects that require beneficiary participation in provision and production activities usually involve considerably more time and effort by the staff of an implementing agency. If a donor is willing to pay the full costs of a project, it is easier and faster for the implementing agency to design the project and arrange all aspects of production. Once the implementing agency has gone to the effort of designing and producing the project, however, it becomes more of an owner than the beneficiary (Catterson and Lindahl 1999).

In regard to a private good, the key attribute of ownership stressed in the analytical literature is the right to alienate (or give up) all rights to a good (Alchian and Demsetz 1972; but see Larson and Bromley 1990, who challenge this narrow view of ownership). At first glance, any of the actors could be seen as having a potential veto over continuation of any project. The donor country could withdraw funding, government officials cancel permits, and local people stop participating. (Note that the consultants and other implementing agencies that formally enter at the production stage—but may also play an unofficial role at the provision stage—have less control over alienation, since other actors could always be selected to implement a given provision decision.) This is where Sida's overriding goal of sustainability becomes crucial. Projects may be sustainable if local (or government) participants can continue it even after Sida funding ends. At a deeper level, each project should enhance a society's capacity to sustain progress on the goals of economic growth, equity, and so forth. Since any particular aid project will have a limited duration, the expected situation at the end of the project should be a focus of its design in the first place.

Any one project should be terminated whenever its continuation detracts from the realization of any of the basic goals of a development assistance program. Does it foster an attitude of dependence? Does it further the career goals of staff members of a recipient or donor government (or of a contractor) rather than enhance local capacity? Deciding when and how to terminate projects turns out to be a critical issue, one that is highlighted by an emphasis on ownership and sustainability.

Complex institutional arrangements, tailored to the exigencies of particular situations, are required to increase the voice and role of the eventual beneficiaries in all aspects of ownership. It is relatively easy for the agency responsible for most of the funding to be heavily involved in the provision and alienation processes—while helping to choose the implementing agency that engages in production. If the eventual beneficiaries are not involved at all in provision, production, or alienation decisions, it is less likely that effective benefits will be generated for them to consume.

To be effective and sustainable, a donor's intervention has to help solve underlying collective-action problems—not just provide another project and the temporary infusion of funds and jobs associated with a project. This response, in turn, has to incorporate the local knowledge about the needs, preferences, and problems of target beneficiaries that only they themselves possess. Access to this localized knowledge requires active beneficiary ownership—meaning a role in all four aspects of ownership—rather than just the consumption of whatever is produced. As such, *ownership is a necessary, though not sufficient, condition for aid sustainability.* Consequently, we will focus on the issue of ownership throughout this report as involving major incentives related to development.

[. . .]

Chapter 4—Incentives across Situations: The International Development Cooperation Octangle

Action situations, in any modern complex society, are rarely isolated from one another. Instead, the outcomes of any one situation provide input into other situations. In this way, situations link within a *system.* Sometimes the system is contained entirely within one organization and is represented in a simplified form by an organization chart. In regard to international development assistance, the set of linked situations crosses many organizational and national boundaries.

Some action situations function more effectively when linked within a system (Simon [1947] 1965, 1972). Further, the effectiveness of a given system depends on the way its action situations are linked together. An effectively structured federal governance system, for example, links national, regional, and local units so that each can undertake those activities for which it is most efficient. In this way, each provides goods and services complementary to those provided by other levels of government (V. Ostrom 1997). Conditioned competition among these units can lead toward substantially greater efficiency. Information flows can lead to greater accountability than could be achieved in the absence of an overall system.[7]

Development cooperation can similarly be thought of as a system or network of linked action situations. The conventional way of thinking about these linkages is as a "chain of aid delivery," which we will discuss in [the first] section. This stresses the primacy of the donor as a principal who must work through a series of hierarchically organized agents to reach the final beneficiary (see Figure 9.1). In an era when most donors are stressing the importance of ownership, however, this top-down way of thinking about a chain of relationships is a particularly inappropriate representation. In fact, the only two-way relationships in the chain of aid are those between an individual donor and other donors. Even the recipient government is viewed here as being no more than an agent of a donor government. While this may be, in fact, how some view the process of development cooperation, we think it is more valuable to think about a set of nested situations that may take on any of a variety of productive or unproductive relationships.

In our effort to understand the complexities of development cooperation, we have developed a schema that we call the International Development Cooperation Octangle—or "the Octangle," for short. [The second] section derives the Octangle from its component parts. In essence, we scale up our analysis so as to look at linked action situations rather than isolated situations. Each set of relationships among the relevant actors is outlined, and the entire interlinked set of relationships (the Octangle) arrays all relevant actors in their dynamic contexts. In contrast to the metaphor of the chain, which brings to mind linear linkages from one actor to the next, the Octangle reveals a multifaceted set of relationships among the actors in development cooperation.

Taken together, the relationships within and across countries, agencies, and their citizens are a tangle of relationships among a donor, a recipient, and the other six types of organizations involved. For example, whereas the donor pays for the services of a contractor, the nominal principal is the recipient government. Meanwhile, the consultant, typically, has more information about ground realities than do officials of the donor or of the recipient agencies—or of the citizens of either country. The result of this tangle of relationships is that many individuals are responsible for ensuring the effectiveness and sustainability of aid, but no one is really held accountable.

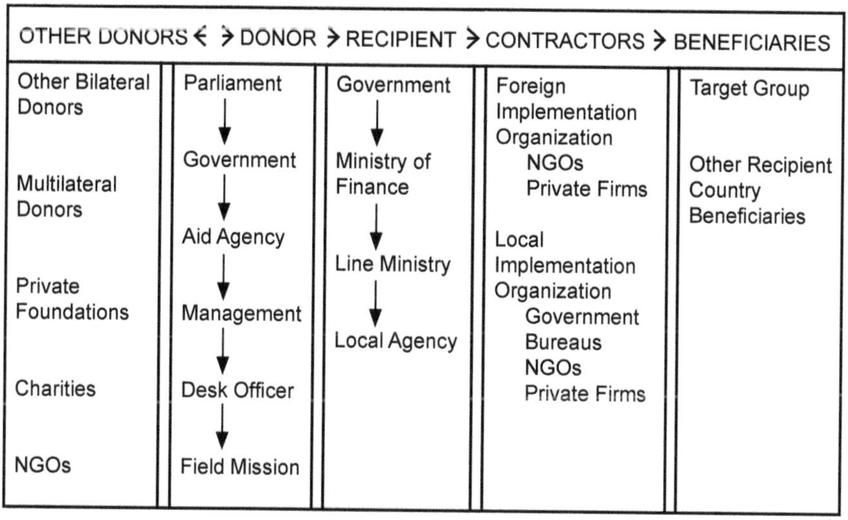

Figure 9.1. The chain of aid delivery.

The Chain of Aid Delivery

The bilateral aid delivery process is often interpreted in analogy to a linear chain that links a donor government to a recipient country beneficiary via various concatenated intermediary organizations. These intermediaries include (an assortment of) recipient government ministries and agencies, nongovernmental organizations, other donors, and private implementation contractors. As schematized in Figure 9.1, it clearly shows that international development cooperation involves a very large number of actors.[8] In this representation, the internal workings of the donor government and agency appear remote from the problems beneficiaries face in the recipient country. By conceiving of development cooperation in this way, donors may infer (incorrectly) that the incentive structures of their internal aid-disbursing operations are far-distanced, and thus insulated and largely unrelated to problems of aid sustainability on the recipient side.

Figure 9.1 portrays how aid funds and responsibilities are transmitted, left to right, from the donor to the beneficiary through intermediary organizations. It highlights, mainly, the principal-agent relationships involved in development cooperation. While many of the links in aid do involve a principal-agent structure, other types of relationships—including Samaritan's Dilemmas, along with the whole host of other collective-action problems identified in chapter 3—are also often involved. The chain of aid, thus, does not reveal fully the varied institutional contexts within which each of these multiple actors in development cooperation link, in practice, to each other.

To understand how incentives enhance or detract from aid sustainability, we first need to identify the major types of actors involved in the aid system. Eight types of actors (many of whom are themselves composed of multiple actors) repeatedly have a strategic role to play in a series of linked action situations. The eight major actors are:

1. the donor government;
2. the recipient government;
3. other donors;
4. the donor's international development agency (IDA);
5. sectoral ministries and agencies within the recipient government;
6. third-party implementing organizations, including nongovernmental organizations (NGOs) and private consultants and contractors;
7. organized interest groups and civil society organizations within the donor and recipient countries; and finally
8. the target beneficiaries.

Second, we need to see how these actors in their situations are connected to each other, as within a system. Beyond the internal structure of any one of the situations involved in development assistance, each situation is complexly interlinked to others. The nature of this complex linkage affects the incentives of those involved and the sustainability of the programs they design or implement. Our Octangle captures a simplified picture of the configuration of linked individual situations.

The sustainability of aid depends on how incentives structure interactions between or among the key corporate and individual actors involved in development cooperation. These structures may result from a conscious effort to design and impose rules governing donor-recipient relations, or from an evolutionary process designed by no one in particular. They may involve asymmetries in power or asymmetries in information, pose moral hazard problems, or yield the Samaritan's Dilemma. (Chapter 2 provides a discussion of these basic problematic situations.)

The International Development Cooperation Octangle

The International Development Cooperation Octangle—by which we intend to convey the tangle of interrelationships among the eight major

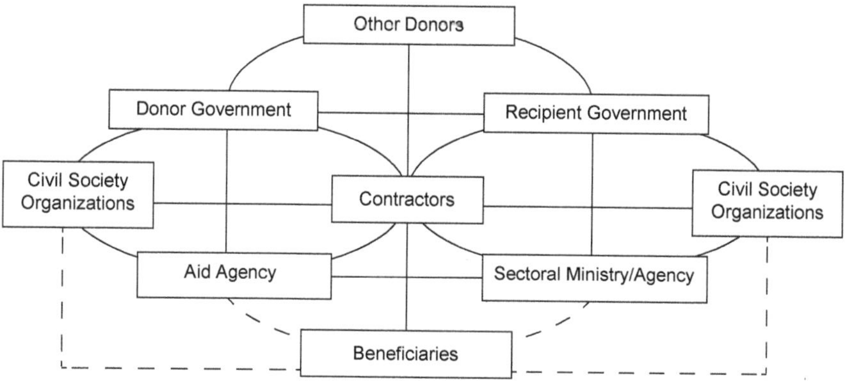

Figure 9.2. The international development cooperation octangle.

types of actors—provides an alternative conceptual scheme to that of the Chain of Delivery image.

The Full Octangle

Figure 9.2 brings together the full set of linkages among all eight types of actors involved in the system of international development assistance. The reason for exploring the full set of relationships among the major actors involved in international assistance is to examine whether "the system" as a whole creates positive incentives that counteract some of the negative incentives that exist in many of the individual action arenas examined in chapters 2 and 3. We are responding to the call of many scholars to examine the linkages *among* the major actors in development aid and not just *within* any one agency (see Tendler 1975 for example). As van Ufford (1988, 13) expressed the need:

> It is vital to study the nature of the interorganizational linkages between the different levels. In what ways do the agencies influence each other? How autonomous are they, how much do they depend on the others? How is the policy process changed, adapted or even blocked as funds flow from one level to the next?

While the potential for counteracting negative incentives does exist, it appears that instead of reducing the severity of problems, many of the problems of collective action are accentuated within the larger system of the Octangle.

One relationship is obvious when one examines the Octangle closely. Contractors lie at the center of this schematic representation since they conceivably interact with all the other types of actors. Civil society organizations (in both donor and recipient) are arrayed on the "sidelines," but they can have important impact[s] in some situations. These organizations can, potentially, reinforce beneficiary interests or be pushed effectively aside and have little role. When conducting an analysis, one may be able to examine only one or two linkages from any node in this "Octangle" in relative isolation from others. In fact, most actors in development cooperation, surveying the world from where they stand, do not see the full Octangle. Yet, in practice, the actions of all actors (and their component parts) influence each other over time. Each type of actor may thus be able to play a major role in determining whether the results of aid are sustainable over time.

[. . .]

Chapter 5—Focusing on a Part of the Octangle: An Institutional Analysis of Donor-Recipient Negotiations

Development assistance processes involve multiple interlinked action situations as discussed in chapter 4. A key dyad within the Octangle is the negotiation arena involving a donor and a recipient government. Both actors in this dyad must reach a basic agreement for a development assistance program of any kind to exist within a recipient country.

To illustrate how the IAD [Institutional Analysis and Development] framework could be used to analyze the multiplicity of dyads, triads, and the many-party situations involved within the Octangle, we conduct an initial institutional analysis of the negotiation arena between a donor and a recipient government. We provide a sketch of how an analyst would approach a more extended examination of this action situation. The questions used in this chapter illustrate the types of questions an institutional analyst uses to conduct an analysis.

The specific context and strategies of each donor-recipient negotiation differ, depending on many factors. Three tentative lessons, gleaned from the analysis of this hypothetical, generalized situation, are relevant for a bilateral donor such as Sida. These lessons are presented as "tentative" since they are hypotheses derived from this application of our theoretical framework and analysis.

1. Adopting a policy, such as Sida has already done, that foreign aid will largely be allocated to programs or projects where the recipient government is committed or "owns" the proposed activity is generally more sustainable than when the recipient does not have real ownership.
2. The best outcomes are potentially achievable when a long-term commitment to a recipient country is made, as Sida does when it makes a country-frame agreement. If recipient governments are *not* committed to serious institutional and economic reform, long-term commitments involve substantial investments that produce few desirable results. This could lead to the least efficient and sustainable investment of all.
3. When facing recipient governments whose leaders are not benefited by institutional reforms and effective economic policies, donors are faced with a choice between helping a few citizens with short-term gains versus pulling out and waiting for more auspicious opportunities. Pulling out may be the only way to help those citizens in the long run, especially if donors can form alliances with other donors not to support countries resisting reform.

Currently, Sida is experimenting with making long-term commitments to a *region*, rather than to a particular country in the region. This may greatly help to get incentives oriented toward producing more sustainable development assistance. While making a long-term commitment to a set of countries, Sida is able to pull out of one country that does not take reform efforts seriously.

A Further Application of the IAD Framework

Within the large set of dyads and triads contained within the International Cooperation Assistance Octangle, is the important initial negotiation situation between a donor and a recipient government.[9] We select this situation to illustrate an application of the IAD framework, since if an agreement is not reached here, the other nodes of the Octangle are not reached at all. We examine a generalized structure rather than a specific negotiation process so as to gain a broader insight than is possible when looking only at one case. We ask how various possible characteristics of an action situation and of the actors involved affect the incentives involved and the likely interactions between the actors as these may affect the sustainability of projects or programs agreed upon in this situation.

We begin by looking at the underlying contextual variables in order to understand the type of material goods and services that might eventually flow from an agreement, the broad national and international rules affecting a specific negotiation process, and the nature of the political community in each country as well as the broad international situation at a particular point in time. With that contextual background, we then try to understand the structure of the negotiations arena between a particular donor and a particular recipient government. The following questions provide an initial general guide to an institutional analysis of donor-recipient project negotiation relationships. (See appendix A for an illustrative set of questions for an institutional analyst interested in understanding a common-pool resource situation.). Obviously, a deeper analysis would require still further questions many of which would be formulated in response to the first set of answers. The general structure of relationships can, however, be assessed by asking the following kinds of questions:

1. *Which actors are involved in this particular negotiation process? Who is directly or indirectly involved in this negotiation?*

   A. Are there representatives from two countries—one a donor country and one a recipient country, or is one or more actors from a multilateral donor?
   B. Is there more than one bilateral donor providing development assistance to the recipient?
   C. If so, have the bilateral donors developed mechanisms to avoid being played off against one another—so that they can be considered a coalition rather than single players?
   D. Are these governments starting a new relationship or continuing a long-established one?

2. *What are the positions of the officials representing the recipient government and donor government within their own countries and in regard to each other?*

   A. How are the recipient government leaders chosen in their home country? In open democratic elections or by authoritarian means?
   B. How recently have the recipient government leaders assumed office? How close was the contest for national office (if there was a contest)?

C. How dependent are the recipient government leaders on entrenched interests who receive benefits from the status quo?
D. Have recipient government leaders been selected for their reform policies?
E. How are donor government leaders chosen?
F. Do donor government leaders represent a new coalition or one that has been in power for some time?
G. How secure are donor government leaders if they pursue strong development assistance programs? (e.g., how committed is the donor country population to development assistance?)
H. How dependent are donor government leaders on domestic coalitions that benefit from some kinds of development assistance (e.g., tied trade) but not others?
I. Can these officials make final decisions for their respective governments or do they have to submit proposed negotiated settlements to others in their government?

3. What are some of the key actions (sets of strategies) that donors and recipients can take in the planning and negotiations stage of the process?

The specific actions will always have to do with the issues that are involved in a particular case. To illustrate the method, however, let us outline a stylized version of some of the types of strategies that donor and recipient governments have taken in the past. The actual array of potential strategies is much larger than the strategies outlined here and will depend in a particular instance on many contextual variables. For example, bilateral donors could form a coalition and provide untied funding to support a portion of a broad development plan proposed by a recipient government (see Kanbur and Sandler 1999). We focus, however, on well-known strategies to illustrate how the broad method helps to identify general relationships.

In negotiating either a development program or a particular project, the *recipient government* needs to decide which of the following general strategies to pursue:

A. Say yes to any development program or project proposed by the donor without investment in planning and a commitment to follow through. (Get the project!)
B. Say yes to all programs and projects with strong commitment to follow through on those proposed and supported by own ministries and little commitment otherwise.

C. Say no to proposed reforms, programs, or projects not consistent with own development policies and plans of recipient government, say yes to those that are consistent.

For the *donor government*, it must decide which of the following strategies to pursue:

A. Make annual project-by-project decisions.
   (1) Support proposals designed primarily by own IDA and contractors or by other donor agencies and IFI's [International Financial Institutions].
   (2) Support proposals designed primarily by recipient government participants.
B. Make long-term commitments to support reforms, programs, and projects for three to five years.
   (1) Support proposals designed primarily by own IDA and contractors or by other donor agencies and IFI's.
   (2) Support proposals designed primarily by recipient government participants.

4. How are these actions linked to potential outcomes?

There are always many specific outcomes related to the type of agreements reached that can result from this kind of negotiation process. Each outcome can be evaluated using any of the criteria discussed above. First, we want to examine whether an agreement is likely or not, whether the agreement will be for a short-term project, or whether the agreement will span a long time horizon in which both the donor and the recipient government can gain substantial information about performance and be able to adapt the assistance to local needs and capabilities. Then we will ask which of these outcomes is more likely to be sustainable over the long term.

One way of showing this linkage is illustrated in Figure 9.3. In regard to the immediate outcome of achieving an agreement or not, given the specified strategies, we would expect a negotiation process structured in this manner to achieve agreements in two-thirds of the possible combined strategies. Of those eight potential outcomes, half are likely to be of short-term duration and half are likely to be of long-term duration.

A donor may be in the situation of facing a recipient government who cannot do anything other than select Strategy A given that it does not have a skilled bureaucracy to design and follow through on programs

	Recipient Country Strategies		
Donor Country Strategies	A. Say yes to all, but no involvement or commitment	B. Say yes to all; Commit to own	C. Say no to proposals outside own policies; Say yes and commit to own
A. Short-Term			
A1: Fund Own or Other Donor-Designed Proposals	1–1 Short-Term Agreement	1–2 Short-Term Agreement	1–3 No Agreement
A2: Fund Recipient-Designed Proposals	2–1 Nothing Proposed	2–2 Short-Term Agreement	2–3 Short-Term Agreement
B. Long-Term			
B1: Fund Own or Other Donor-Designed Proposals	3–1 Long-Term Agreement	3–2 Long-Term Agreement	3–3 No Agreement
B2: Fund Recipient-Designed Proposals	4–1 Nothing Proposed	4–2 Long-Term Agreement	4–3 Long-Term Agreement

Figure 9.3. Action-outcome linkages for simplified donor-recipient negotiation situations.

and projects. The recipient government may be eager or even desperate to receive foreign assistance and will agree to any proposal. No matter what strategy the donor adopts, if the recipient government chooses Strategy A, either there is no agreement and no foreign assistance, or the projects that are funded are unlikely to be sustainable, given the lack of commitment by the recipient government. If the donor is highly motivated to provide assistance to this particular country, the donor will find itself in a Samaritan's Dilemma.

A recipient government, on the other hand, may design some programs or projects on its own and have a real commitment to them, but still agree to any proposal made by the owner (Strategy B). In this case, an agreement is likely, but if the donor funds only proposals that it has confidence in because of its own efforts in their design, the ensuing activities are not likely to be sustainable. If the donor adopts either a short-term or long-term strategy to fund projects where the recipient country shows real ownership, then agreement is likely and those funded under a long-term commitment by the donor are more likely to be sustainable due to the increased knowledge that the donor has about the recipient and the increased confidence that the recipient has that risks that may need to be taken as a result of a foreign assistance may be compensated for over the long run.

From the evidence offered by Sida (1996a, 1996b, 1996c, 1997a), World Bank (1997, 1998), and others (Brautigam 2000; van de Walle and Johnston 1996), projects designed primarily by a donor country's own IDA and its own consultants (or by other external IFI's who have defined a major reform program) are less likely to be sustainable than projects where the recipient government has a greater voice in the design and has a real commitment to long-term sustainability. In other words, when the recipient country is the "real" owner of a program or project, in the sense that they have had an active voice in the design of the project and have made a commitment to the activities involved in the project, the probabilities of sustainability are presumed to be much higher than if the donor country is the effective owner of the program or project. Projects that are undertaken with a longer time horizon are likely to be more sustainable—in the sense defined in chapter 1—than those undertaken with a short time horizon.

If the recipient government adopts Strategy C and is actually willing to say no to some programs and projects as being outside its own plans, a stalemate is likely to follow if the donor is committed to its own proposals. The tougher stand of the recipient, however, leads to a chance of receiving foreign aid for programs and projects that fit well into its overall development program. Thus, when a donor faces a somewhat tougher recipient country and makes a long-term commitment to support proposals that fit into a recipient country's policies, there is a higher probability of achieving sustainable projects. And, if the recipient government has adopted reform policies leading to less corruption, a more open public realm, an independent and well-paid public service, and supportive of effective market institutions, projects may not only be sustainable, but also generate substantial benefits that have a widespread impact (Dollar and Easterly 1999).

Thus, as shown by the cells [4–2 and 4–3] in Figure 9.3, two out of the twelve possible outcomes are more likely to be sustainable than the other outcomes. And, if Outcome 4–3 is reached in a recipient country that has adopted major political and economic reforms, the result may be highly beneficial for all. Unfortunately, there are many reasons why donors and recipients do not choose the strategies leading to Outcome 4–3 and that recipients do not adopt serious political and economic reforms. Many of these relate to the costs and benefits involved, so we will continue our analysis of the working parts of this type of an action situation.

5. What are the costs and benefits assigned to actions and outcomes?

In simple situations, it may be possible to find a way of assigning costs and benefits to all actions and outcomes using a single metric, such as a monetary unit, and derive a clear-cut overall assessment of the net-benefits present in all action-outcome combinations. For this analysis, we can only illustrate the types of benefits and costs that may be involved for different kinds of participants in this bargaining situation. One of the key problems in assigning benefits to outcomes of development assistances is the problem of fungibility of foreign aid (Cassen 1994; Feyzioglu, Swaroop, and Zhu 1998). A donor country may have as a high priority supporting education or health projects and be willing to invest substantially in such projects either designed by itself or designed by the recipient government. The donor country hopes that its investment will be added to the investment in health or education that the recipient country already plans to make. The recipient country, however, may have other priorities.

In some cases, the recipient government may actually reduce its own level of government spending after a grant or loan than it had spent previously.[10] Of course, the donor country may support a reduction in a government budget that reduces deficits as part of an overall reform package. Even if the amount of aid provided is translated into an equivalent increase in the recipient government's budget, a further question is whether the aid results in higher spending in the sector supported. Governments receiving foreign aid to support education, for example, may actually reduce the amount of funds they spend for education and allocate extra funds to another sector (Pack and Pack 1993). Since foreign aid is frequently fungible, it can crowd out domestic sources of funds—a phenomena that is often observed in regard to the allocations made to a particular sector by a national government. Thus, regardless of whether the total government budget increases, decreases, or is unaltered after donor funding, there is usually some level of crowding-out taking place.

Given the difficulty of assessing the overall benefits of programs or projects, let us instead assume that any of the projects funded would bring at least substantial short-term benefits to the recipient country. If any of these projects were sustained, we would further assume that they would generate more benefits than costs and thus be evaluated as both sustainable and efficient in the long term. This allows us in this illustrative example to proceed with an initial analysis of the costs of diverse strategies to the participants. Since the costs are proximate to those involved and the benefits are diffusely spread across many others and in the future, the costs to participants may be the more relevant factor that affects strategic choice in this type of bargaining situation.

If the government of the recipient country is a relatively entrenched authoritarian regime that owes its continuity in office to its distribution of benefits to key supporters, the costs of the three strategies vary rather substantially. Strategy A is the lowest cost strategy. No investment has to be made in establishing a strong, independent, public service capable of making coherent long-term policies and designing and implementing good projects. So long as donor countries are willing to lend funds, the recipient can get by with promises of commitments, without any real commitments to any externally or internally imposed reforms (see Pedersen 1996, 1998). If the government is relatively corrupt, then the benefits from diverting funds either directly from the project or through the fungibility of the national budget allow the government to siphon funds that are made available to top government officials and to enter issue-attractive contracts favored by supporters.

This strategy has been adopted so often over the past forty years that many stories are told about countries that make promises during negotiations but do not carry them out during the implementation phase. These stories illustrate what is meant by the term *moral hazard*. The "dance" between the donors and a recipient was well captured in a 1995 story in *The Economist*:

> Over the past few years Kenya has performed a curious mating ritual with its aid donors. The steps are: one, Kenya wins its yearly pledges of foreign aid. Two, the government begins to misbehave, backtracking on economic reform and behaving in an authoritarian manner. Three, a new meeting of donor countries looms with exasperated foreign governments preparing their sharp rebukes. Four, Kenya pulls a placatory rabbit out of

> the hat. Five, the donors are mollified and the aid is pledged. The whole dance then starts again. (August 19, 1995)

The "dance" continues until the present—only now with a slightly different tune. In 1997, the IMF [International Monetary Fund] did stop paying out a large loan it had approved in 1996. With a bad drought in both aid funds and weather, President Daniel Arap Moi has been quite desperate about this situation and is now willing to promise to meet the toughest set of conditions ever imposed by the IMF. This set of promises did open up the flow of $18 million during the summer of 2000 to help relieve the drastic effects of the recent drought (see *The Economist*, August 5, 2000). Several of the senior Sida staff members interviewed in March of 2000 recounted similar stories of prolonged "dances" in the relations between Sweden and countries such as Nicaragua, Tanzania, and Zambia.

For a corrupt government, Strategy C is very costly, as it involves at least some level of political and economic reform. Such reforms may lead to the end of the regime itself and are rarely adopted by entrenched authoritarian regimes. Strategy B may be less costly than C, but even this strategy involves some reform efforts in order to come up with programs and plans that a donor would be willing to fund and to commit oneself to follow-through when funding is completed. Most corrupt governments do not have the capacity or desire to make such a commitment. Consequently, a donor can expect that authoritarian regimes are most likely to adopt Strategy A and at most Strategy B. Trying to impose conditions that would move the recipient country closer to institutional and policy reform is unlikely to work. The World Bank, reflecting on its own experience, reports that "policy reforms rarely succeed unless the government is genuinely convinced that the reforms have to be implemented and considers the reform program its own" (World Bank 1997, 37).

In the last decade, however, more developed countries have initiated serious institutional and policy reforms with the help of bilateral and multilateral donors. Governments who must rely on a broad constituency, rather than a narrow clientele base, are also more likely to resist large government deficits, avoid overdependence on loans, and invest more heavily in elementary and secondary education (Bueno de Mesquita and Root 2000). Countries with newly elected reform governments are more likely to be committed to reform than even democratically elected governments who have been in power ten or fifteen years (Dollar and Svensson 1998). Thus, such governments are more likely to adopt Strategy C. When Strategy C is actually adopted, a donor that makes long-term commitments to provide aid and develops some mutually agreed-upon conditional loans may help achieve Outcome 4.3. Such loans enable the reform government to make a public commitment to its reforms and send a signal to private investors that it is now safer to invest in the recipient country.

For the donor country, expending funds to design projects themselves is more costly than relying on design prepared by recipient governments. Thus, assuming equally attractive benefits, a donor would always prefer the second option under either short-term or long-term strategies. Consultants often prepare project designs for recipient governments and it is difficult for a donor to know whether the design represents a genuine interest by the recipient government or a project that a consultant thinks the donor will find attractive. We discuss this puzzle further in chapter 8.

6. What is the information that is available to each participant about the situation?

A major problem facing both donor and recipient governments is determining which strategy the other will adopt and then choosing their own best response to that choice. Both participants have a considerable amount of private information about the level of benefits and costs of diverse actions and outcomes, but in general there is more information about the donor's costs and benefits than about the recipient's. The asymmetry of information is largely a function of the fact that in most donor countries a free press exists, and considerable information exists about public opinion and government policy regarding aid.

What the recipient country has a hard time knowing, however, is the strength of the donor government's determination to withdraw further funding if the recipient country does not keep its commitments. As the story in *The Economist* quoted above illustrates, many donor countries have found it difficult to withhold funds from a recipient country that does not keep its promises to perform in certain ways. Once funds have been committed in a donor government's budget, there are potential risks to the donor country's future aid budget of withholding funds to a recipient. Funds that are not spent during one budgetary period are sometimes viewed by legislative bodies as "surplus" to be retrieved from an ineffective agency (see Wildavsky 1984). Once a donor has been forgiving in the past, however, it has a hard time convincing a recipient country that it will be tough in the future (see the discussion of the Samaritan's Dilemma in chapter 3).

The donor country, on the other hand, has a hard time knowing whether a recipient has chosen Strategy A or Strategy B. A donor country that thinks a recipient has chosen Strategy A should withdraw entirely from the situation. With Strategy B, there is at least a little hope. A clever recipient government that wants to choose Strategy A, however, only needs to hire a consultant who has good knowledge of the donor and wants to implement a funded project. The government asks the consultant to devise a credible proposal likely to attract the donor's interest (and offers to pay the consultant only if the project is funded!). Thus, the simple presentation of plans and proposals by the recipient does not provide credible proof of the real commitment of the recipient and does not help the donor sort out between Strategy A and Strategy B. (If one wanted to analyze this situation closely, one would need to add one more strategy to Figure 9.3 where a consultant's plans were put forward without a strong commitment to follow-up.) Thus, determining when a government *really* has a sense of ownership for reforms, programs, or projects turns out in practice to be extremely difficult. And, given the high volume of demands on the officials in a donor country's IDA, actually determining what strategy the recipient government is likely to choose may not be feasible in many donor-recipient bargaining situations.

7. What is the level of control that participants have over the choice of strategy?

For the donor, one needs to ask whether ambassadors or heads of development cooperation agencies in the field are authorized to make independent decisions or whether they must carry out policies designed by the Foreign Ministry, Ministry of Finance, or the cabinet. For the recipient, one needs to ask what decision rules recipient government officials must use before coming to a decision about choice of strategy.

In the initial negotiations over an aid agreement, one can think of the direct participants in the negotiation process as agents of their own country's government. Where the level of control that these agents possess can be very important is when there are disagreements about whether one or the other government has lived up to its "agreements." This can happen, for example, when a recipient government has agreed to conditions attached to a foreign assistance grant and the ambassador for the donor country thinks that the recipient government is not keeping its agreement. An important aspect of the ongoing action situation is how much freedom has the ambassador—who has more direct information about the ongoing strategies of the recipient—been given to cancel future payments due to nonperformance of the recipient government. If the ambassador has little control over continuing payments, a recipient government uninterested in keeping reform commitments may find itself in a setting with more freedom to adopt Strategy A while professing to have adopted Strategy B or even Strategy C. This problem is exacerbated due to the severe information constraints and asymmetries that frequently characterize this situation.

Initial Theoretical Lessons Regarding the Donor-Recipient Negotiations Process

As one can see from the above, analyzing the structure of interactions between a donor and a recipient government (ignoring for the moment the discussion on embedding of bilateral negotiations in the context of many other donors interacting with the same recipient) involves bringing together a diverse set of analytical elements. These elements include those related to the context including the nature of the physical world being acted upon, the kind of rules that are involved, and the broad sense of community involved within the donor and recipient countries and between them. Further elements have to do with the structure of particular types of situations such as the types of actors, the positions involved, the actions or strategies that can be adopted, the outcomes that are likely, the control, the relevant information, and the payoffs. Perceived incentives are the result of how all of these elements combine to create a particular structure. And, to make analysis more difficult, the result of changes in any one element frequently depends on the particular values of the other elements.

The specifics of each donor-recipient bargaining situation will differ, depending on a large number of factors having to do with political relationships and dependencies in each country, the history of the interaction, and the subsequent principal-agent relations with those who implement funded programs or projects. But three broad hypotheses can be gleaned from the analysis of this generalized situation. And, the posited relations are based on the empirical evidence presented by many scholars linking effective ownership and a longer-term perspective to an increased likelihood of sustainability (see discussion of sustainability and ownership in chapter 1, as well as in the concluding chapter). Assuming that these hypotheses are correct, we can reach three broad tentative lessons that are relevant for a bilateral donor such as Sida.

Tentative Lesson One: Adopting a policy, such as Sida has already done, that foreign aid will largely be allocated to programs or projects where the recipient government is committed or "owns" the proposed activity is generally more sustainable (two out of twelve possible outcomes with at least some probability of sustainability) than when the recipient does not have real ownership.

Tentative Lesson Two: The best outcomes are potentially achievable when a long-term commitment to a recipient country is made, as Sida does when it makes a country-frame agreement. If recipient governments are not committed to serious institutional and economic reform and accept aid without a firm commitment to sustain, however, long-term commitments can involve substantial investments that produce few desirable results. This could lead to the least efficient and sustainable project of all.

Tentative Lesson Three: When facing recipient governments whose leaders are not themselves benefited by institutional reforms and effective economic policies (due to their reliance for continuance in office on supporters who are advantaged by the status quo), donors are faced with a choice between helping a few citizens with short-term gains versus pulling out and waiting for a more auspicious opportunity. Pulling out may be the only way to help those citizens in the long run, especially if donors can form alliances with other donors to hold firm, but may make it more difficult to obtain large aid budgets in the future as such actions bring public attention to the strategic actions of authoritarian and corrupt recipient regimes.

Currently, Sida is contemplating making long-term commitments to a *region*, rather than to a particular country in the region. This may greatly help to get incentives oriented toward producing more sustainable development assistance. While making a long-term commitment, Sida is able to pull out of a country that does not take reform efforts seriously.

In all cases, however, considerable knowledge about the history and current political context of a regime is needed to apply these tentative lessons wisely in settings where information is scarce about the strategies adopted by a recipient government. Before international aid has the possibility of achieving beneficial outcomes for the citizens of the recipient country (and, if successful, for the citizens of the donor country), further analysis is needed of the role of special interests, of principal-agent relationships between both countries and with implementing organizations, and of their relationships with the citizens being served. All of the actors involved in the international assistance octangle described in chapter 4 are likely to have a greater or lesser impact on the sustainability, efficiency, and growth-enhancing capabilities of foreign aid. And, all of these actors are involved in potentially difficult, collective-action problems and principal-agent relationships that were earlier discussed.

These tentative lessons help to summarize the specific findings for many studies, but each should be viewed as a theoretical hypothesis for which some initial empirical support exists. Further testing of these hypotheses will be important as a foundation for future policies.

If one is interested in changing the structure of the relationships in a particular arena, one needs to look to other arenas as possible sources of incentives for the actors in a particular arena as well as examining the underlying physical and material conditions, cultural views, and the rules-in-use affecting the constraints and opportunities within a particular arena. The action situation will differ, for example, if participants come from similar cultures and thus can easily understand each other as contrasted to a situation where they come from diverse cultures and do not know how to read subtle cues about each other's intentions. Trying to develop a sustainable program of building major infrastructures within a country involves a different set of problems than increasing the level of people-centered services (E. Ostrom, Schroeder, and Wynne 1993). And, constitutional rules in each country—as well as public policies adopted by each country regarding giving and receiving foreign aid—affect the specific actions that each participant can or cannot take in a particular bargaining situation.

[. . .]

Chapter 11—Lessons and Recommendations

[Editors' note: This chapter draws excerpts from only two of the eight sections in which the authors state their recommendations.]

This study has examined how incentives structured in the system of development assistance affect sustainable outcomes. In chapters 1 through 4, we explored how all collective human endeavors are plagued by incentive problems related to motivation and information. We then investigated how institutions shape the choices of individuals and the organizations within which they work, and how these institutions can lead to better—or worse—outcomes. In the sphere of foreign aid, these organizations are arranged in a complex set of relationships that we called the International Development Cooperation Octangle. In chapters 5 through 9, we employed these theoretical insights to analyze the incentive structures of Sida's aid modalities, the organization of Sida-Stockholm, development assistance contractors, and specific Sida-funded projects in India and Zambia. We found many institutions—some inherent in development assistance and some specific to the structure of Sida that foster incentives that both promote and undermine Sida's goal of sustainable development. In this chapter, we explore some options that may help Sida mitigate some of the perverse incentives found in the system of aid.

This chapter contains suggestions about how to improve development assistance. It is, first of all, important not to lose sight of how well Sida already accomplishes many of its tasks. Throughout our work in Stockholm, India, and Zambia, the Workshop team was consistently impressed with the caliber and motivation of Sida staff. Indeed, these skills and commitments allow Sida to overcome some of the perverse incentives that the system of development cooperation generates for its participants. Time after time, we encountered Sida staff members who had worked far beyond the normal demands of their jobs in order to ensure better outcomes for the Swedish development assistance program. Indeed, Sida's courage to request this consultancy is testimony to its commitment to better the plight of the needy in developing countries. Such dedication increases the chances for sustainable development, but is not sufficient to achieve it.

In the rest of this chapter, we indicate how things might be done better, building on what Sida seeks to accomplish with its staff and resources. [. . .]

Ownership and Sustainability

Sida, as an innovative donor, has rejected the idea of development assistance as a short-term infusion of funds from the wealthier to the poorer nations. This approach to development was based on early theories in development, which sought to use aid monies to facilitate major investments in the infrastructure of poorer countries. This was seen as a way to build capacity, allowing poorer nations to take off economically. Later theories in development emphasized the complementary need to improve governance and strengthen democratic procedures. These approaches have also not worked in many cases given that underlying and introduced incentives systems were, again, not properly taken into account. As a result, development assistance has often not produced sustainable results (chapter 1).[11]

Sida voices a strong concern for the sustainability of development cooperation. It considers that long-term positive change is a better return on investment than more temporary results. Sida seeks to improve the outcomes related to its efforts in development cooperation by giving ownership of aid to recipients. Managers at Sida insist that projects belong to the recipient agency, and characterize Sida's role as that of a concerned partner, advisor, and financier. Fostering ownership is thought to promote sustainable outcomes.

The recent stress by Sida and other donors on ownership is an implicit recognition of the problems that development cooperation generates for provision, production, consumption, and alienation (chapter 1). If recipient agencies (and targeted beneficiaries) are included in these activities, perverse incentives may be ameliorated. Allowing the recipients to participate in the provision process may help align the incentives of donor and recipients as well as make better use of local knowledge and institutions. Participation in the production process may help prevent recipients from free riding on the aid. Participation in the consumption of benefits and costs may motivate greater concern for appropriate outcomes. Finally, participation in the alienation of aid may generate information likely to reduce the probabilities of continuing unsuccessful projects or programs. Thus, including recipients in true ownership can help solve some of the severe incentive effects related to information and motivational problems in development cooperation discussed in this report. As we have repeatedly stressed, however, this is not a sufficient condition to ensure sustainability.

Our theoretical findings demonstrate that applying the concept of ownership and sustainability to actual development cooperation relationships is, in practice, quite difficult. Our analysis shows that motivational and information problems in aid are very deeply embedded. As challenging as these problems are in the context of individuals with full ownership rights in an arena of well-enforced institutions, they pale in comparison with the multi-actor, multi-level, multi-owner characteristics of development assistance. Our representation of the system of aid—the Octangle—demonstrates how every dyad and triad in aid is subject to these motivational and information problems. And our analysis of different aid modalities and characteristics demonstrates that no type of development cooperation is free from powerful perverse incentives.

Furthermore, the difference between a *recipient* and a *beneficiary* of development cooperation highlights the difficulty of parceling ownership. In some cases, recipients of aid are the targeted beneficiaries; in other cases, the beneficiaries have little or no voice. The official owner is the national government that may in fact have little knowledge about or interest in the problems facing the targeted beneficiaries. The responsibility and accountability that an owner has, in the conventional meaning of the word, is transformed to nearly unrecognizable forms by the system of development assistance. When the owner is not one of the beneficiaries, endowing a distant government's agent with ownership may do little to change the perverse incentives of the beneficiaries or anyone else involved in traditional development assistance. Nor does it affect the flow and accuracy of information from beneficiaries to the official owner.

[. . .]

Despite Sida's important efforts to change the orientation of its development assistance, it remains in many important ways a de facto owner of development assistance. Sida remains the primary actor in decisions related to the terms of its funding and often has a large input into the design of the project. It is also clear that beneficiaries rarely exercise much ownership in most cases, especially when project implementers and project beneficiaries are different groups (which is the usual situation).

The everyday usage of the term "ownership" conveys an individual or organization with clearly defined responsibilities who receives the benefits and pays the costs resulting from its exercise of these responsibilities. Within development cooperation processes, responsibilities and accountability are unclear. Who "owns" the project when things go wrong? The large number of actors within development cooperation allows each actor with partial ownership to deny full ownership, and therefore accountability. The entire Octangle may be filled with actors pointing to each other as the source of problems.

Given aid's complexity regarding relationships and incentives, it is understandable that Sida staff and documents should offer various views of ownership and sustainability. As mentioned in chapter 1, Sida staff, recipient government personnel, and private sector consultants expressed different views of what the concepts of ownership and sustainability mean in practice. Defining these core concepts clearly is far from an academic exercise: in fact, our team would argue that it is an essential first step for any IDA that seeks to be more effective in its development efforts.[12]

Recommendations

We suggest that Sida revisit its concept of ownership. The common meaning of ownership does not translate automatically to the realities of development assistance. While the term has been fashionable within aid circles, it has rarely led to changes in the incentives facing actors in development assistance situations.

We argue that Sida needs to allow sufficient opportunities for the "owner(s)" to contribute to the design, implementation, and mid-course corrections of the project/program. A final step is to allow the owner full participation in the final evaluation of a project/program. We set out four criteria for beneficiary ownership. Beneficiary owners need to (1) enunciate a *demand* for aid, (2) allocate at least some of their own *assets* to the project or program so that they have a real stake in the way their own and other actors' assets are used, (3) obtain benefits, and (4) have clear-cut responsibilities and be able to participate in decisions regarding continuance or noncontinuance of a project.

[. . .]

Genuine devolution of ownership may mean less control for Sida and its agent/contractor. While less control is not without its attendant risks, we argue that it is necessary to achieve more sustainable results.

Less control, however, does not mean less Sida involvement in ongoing activities in partner countries. In fact, we find that Sida staff can play a crucial facilitative role to ensure that ownership of activities is anchored primarily with beneficiaries, and not taken over by consultants or individuals within recipient organizations. The incentive structures that emerge in each Sida-supported undertaking are greatly influenced by Sida's interventions, or lack thereof. In general, we think Sida staff in the field are overstretched in their work to gather and evaluate information about their projects and programs. Devolving ownership may involve allocating greater resources to project monitoring.

We further recommend that Sida focus on the concepts of responsibility and accountability as they relate to ownership. Sida staff should articulate which specific responsibilities they seek to devolve to which actors, and how such actors can be held accountable for their actions. Such an exercise should include an examination of the institutional context and the incentive it generates, as well as the incentives produced by different aid modalities.

As ownership is thought to affect sustainability, we also suggest that Sida revisit its idea of sustainability in development cooperation. As discussed in this report, this term's imprecision and application to diverse outcomes has left it without much meaning. Sida should make clear, in each project or program of development cooperation, precisely what is intended to be sustainable, how its development assistance helps produce sustainability, what time frame is being used, and how sustainability will be measured. Thus, project-planning documents should clearly identify the intended owners and include an analysis of the anticipated impact that this designation of ownership will have on sustainability. Such documents should also detail how meaningful ownership will be vested and what evidence will be gathered to ascertain success in these goals. In designing its projects/programs, Sida officers must also keep in mind that the greater the number of owners, the smaller the stakes will likely be for any particular owner to ensure success.

These recommendations are not easy palliatives. To implement them effectively will be, in fact, very, very challenging. The findings from our team suggest that development agencies have little time for developing, requiring, collecting, and evaluating such evidence. This task is also challenging since Sida finances projects and programs and thus always remains a de facto owner; Sida may find itself in a Samaritan's Dilemma. Further, Sida must operate within the political logics of its own and a recipient country, which may not be amenable to the aim of promoting sustainable development. Even so, steps can still be taken to improve a sense of ownership among recipients and beneficiaries.

[. . .]

Putting Beneficiaries First

Effective and sustainable development assistance must center on beneficiaries and the problems they face with respect to their collective-action problems. Evaluations of projects and programs with a focus on beneficiary incentives can help a concerned donor to address how individuals in the action situation relate to each other and how they might overcome their problems and dilemmas through institutional change. This process requires that beneficiaries—rather than recipients—take ownership of their developmental prospects in all four senses of that term (i.e., provision, production, consumption, and alienation). The tools developed in this report can help. They allow the analysis of the institutional change that will be required to allow beneficiaries to overcome their collective-action problems and realize their own developmental potential. Supporting research on indigenous institutions, norms, and local knowledge systems also provides essential understanding for helping to build contemporary institutions on the healthy roots of earlier normative systems used to solve collective-action problems. This requires, as well, that donors rethink their own role. Sida's mission statement—*creating the requisite conditions for development*—points in the right direction.

Recommendations

Development assistance should focus on the intended beneficiaries and the problems they face. To be sustainable, aid should address how beneficiaries relate to each other in dealing with diverse collective-action problems. Without this deeper analysis and programs focused on institutional change to facilitate the long-term improvement in the lives of beneficiaries, aid is likely to provide only short-term benefits.

As part of the design phase of any project or program, we suggest that questions like the following be asked:

- What underlying collective-action problem(s) do beneficiaries face?
  - Is it a public good problem/free-rider problem/tragedy of the commons problem? (For example, the Indian power case is at root a free-rider problem.)
  - What are the basic incentive problems facing beneficiaries at an operational level? Motivational? Missing information? Asymmetric information? Other?
  - What are the developmental implications of this collective-action failure?
  - What rules or norms have been used in this cultural tradition in the past that may be the source of modern rules that resonate with beneficiaries as fair and can be understood easily?
  - What incentives have precluded beneficiaries from resolving their own collective-action problem at a collective-choice level in the absence of aid? How would they be affected by a proposed aid project or program?
  - Are needed institutions missing or weak, or are perverse institutions in place?
  - Would a modification in rules affecting this underlying problem be threatening to the power elite of this country?

- In what ways have previous aid interventions altered similar collective-action problems?
  - Did aid abet or exacerbate power or information asymmetries or adverse selection?
  - What ownership attributes do the targeted beneficiaries possess?
  - Have aid interventions affected the capacity of the beneficiary group to address the collective-action failure?
  - Have they exacerbated existing perverse incentive structures (as is the situation in the Indian power case)?

- What are the implications for sustainability?
  - How have the underlying collective-action problems been addressed by the aid intervention?
  - In what ways are such issues included in the feedback loops of the Octangle?
  - Given the roles of the contractor and the recipient, are the prospects for an appropriate solution to the underlying collective-action problem enhanced or reduced?

  [. . .]

Notes

This chapter was originally published in *Aid, Incentives, and Sustainability: An Institutional Analysis of Development Cooperation—Main Report*, Sida Studies in Evaluation #02/01 (Stockholm, Sweden: Swedish International Development Cooperation Agency [Sida]). It encompasses selections taken from chapters 1, 4, 5, and 11 (pp. 1–251), for which we have inserted "[. . .]" to designate our removal of text from the original versions of these chapters. The complete report can be found online via Sida's website (http://www.sida.se).

1. Since the focus of this report is on the developing countries of Africa, Asia, and Latin America, we do not include the four different goals of Swedish development cooperation for Eastern and Central Europe.

2. See, for example, Salmi (1996), who identifies nine major contexts within which the concept of sustainability is invoked, including allocative efficiency, intergenerational equity, resource substitutability, externalities, and property rights. In dealing with its Agenda 21, the United Nations has developed 132 Sustainability Indicators (S.I.s) measuring driving forces, states of the world, and responses. See discussion of the UN and other efforts to develop systematic S.I.s by Bell and Morse (1999), who present an in-depth treatment of the concept of sustainability and the grave problems of its measurement.

3. Catterson and Lindahl also define sustainability by project: Sustainability is "the capacity of an aid support project, institution, or programme to continue to function post-aid" (1999, 25).

4. For a discussion of the importance of institutional development and *project* sustainability, see Cernea (1987), who evaluated twenty-five World Bank projects that had originally been judged to be successful at the time of project completion and to have good prospects for long-term sustainability. Only twelve of the twenty-five projects actually achieved long-term sustainability. At the design

stage, all of the sustainable projects involved very specific efforts to enhance the institutional capacities of beneficiaries (Cernea 1987, 3).

5. The president of South Africa, Thabo Mbeki, and other African leaders have developed the Millennium African Renaissance Programme in which they call for all African leaders to "take ownership and responsibility for the sustainable economic development of the continent" (reported in *The Economist*, February 24, 2001, p. 17).

6. This is illustrated in chapters 8, 9, and 10 of this report.

7. Of course, it is also possible to link units of government in a federal system so that these benefits are not achieved, and the overall result is less than could be achieved by either a fully centralized or a fully decentralized system of governance.

8. Figure 9.1 can be drawn from the descriptions of the project cycle and of processes in development cooperation presented in *Sida at Work*.

9. Concrete institutional analyses of other relationships inherent in development cooperation are taken up in the case studies and analysis found in chapters 9 and 10. These include project-specific analyses.

10. Studies of how much impact foreign aid has had on recipient government budgets have come up with varied responses as one would expect, but studies of a large number of countries have most frequently shown that development financing does not translate uniformly into an increase in funding. Feyzioglu, Swaroop, and Zhu (1998), for example, found that $1 in concessional loans led to 63 cents in additional government spending for the 38 countries in their sample. Cashel-Cordo and Craig (1990) found no effect of bilateral loans on government spending in their study of 46 countries. Studies of individual countries have not found as much fungibility. Pack and Pack (1990), for example, found that $1 in aid to Indonesia led to $1.50 in additional spending. Thus, one cannot make any firm estimation of how much fungibility there may be in a particular setting, but has to be wary that the amount of foreign aid spent does not automatically translate into added government spending.

11. Recent studies have found, however, that development assistance allocated to countries that have themselves invested in institutions that enhance economic performance is much more likely to have sustainable results (see Rodrik 1999 and studies cited in chapter 1).

12. While there could exist a Sida document in which ownership is clearly defined in a development assistance context, we found none in the documents we reviewed.

References

Adam, Christopher S., and Stephen A. O'Connell. 1999. "Aid, Taxation and Development in Sub-Saharan Africa." *Economics and Politics* 11(3): 225–53.

Alchian, Armen A., and Harold Demsetz. 1972. "Production, Information Costs, and Economic Organization." *American Economic Review* 62(5): 777–95.

Bates, Robert. 1998. "Institutions as Investments." In *The Political Dimensions of Economic Growth*, edited by S. Borner and M. Paldham. New York: Macmillan.

Bell, Simon, and Stephen Morse. 1999. *Sustainability Indicators: Measuring the Immeasurable*. London: Earthscan.

Birdsall, Nancy, and Juan Lius Londono. 1997. "Asset Inequality Matters: An Assessment of the World Bank's Approach to Poverty Reduction." *American Economic Review* 82(2): 32–37.

Blomstrom, Magnus, and Mats Lundahl, eds. 1993. *Economic Crisis in Africa: Perspectives on Policy Responses*. New York: Routledge.

Boone, Peter. 1996. "Politics and the Effectiveness of Foreign Aid." *European Economic Review* 40: 289–329.

Bosc, Pierre-Marie, and Ellen Hanak-Freud. 1995. *Agricultural Research and Innovation in Tropical Africa*. Paris: Centre de Cooperation Internationale en Recherche Agronomique Pour le Developpement.

Brautigam, Deborah. 2000. *Aid Dependence and Governance*. Stockholm: Almqvist & Wiksell International.

Brunetti, Aymo, and Beatrice Weder. 1994. "Political Credibility and Economic Growth in Less Developed Countries." *Constitutional Political Economy* 5(1): 23–43.

Bueno de Mesquita, Bruce, and Hilton L. Root, eds. 2000. *Governing for Prosperity*. New Haven, CT: Yale University Press.

Burnside, Craig, and David Dollar. 1997. "Aid Spurs Growth—In a Sound Policy Environment." *Finance & Development* (December): 4–7.

Cashel-Cordo, Peter, and Steven Craig. 1990. "The Public Sector Impact of International Resource Transfers." *Journal of Development Economics* 32(1): 17–42.

Cassen, Robert. 1994. *Does Aid Work?* Oxford, UK: Clarendon.

Catterson, Julie, and Claes Lindahl. 1999. *The Sustainability Enigma: Aid Dependency and the Phasing Out of Projects: The Case of Swedish Aid to Tanzania*. Stockholm: Almqvist and Wiksell International.

Cernea, Michael. 1987. "Farmer Organization and Institution Building for Sustainable Development." *Regional Development Dialog* 8(2): 1–24.

Crawford, Sue E. S., and Elinor Ostrom. 1995. "A Grammar of Institutions." *American Political Science Review* 89(3): 582–600.

de Soto, Hernando. 2000. *The Mystery of Capital: Why Capitalism Triumphs in the West and Fails Everywhere Else*. New York: Basic Books.

Dollar, David, and William Easterly. 1999. "The Search for the Key: Aid, Investment and Policies in Africa." Policy Research Working Paper 2070. Washington, DC: World Bank.

Dollar, David, and Jakob Svensson. 1998. "What Explains the Success or Failure of Structural Adjustment Programs?" Policy Research Working Paper 1938. Washington, DC: World Bank Development Research Group.

The Economist. 2000. "The Kenya-Fund Dance." August 5.

Edgren, Gus. 1995. "Indo-Swedish Development Cooperation: Objective, Issues and Achievements." In *Sharing Challenges, The Indo-Swedish Development Cooperation Programme*. Stockholm: Ministry for Foreign Affairs.

Elgstrom, Ole. 1992. *Foreign Aid Negotiations*. Aldershot, England: Avebury.

Feyzioglu, Tarhan, Vinaya Swaroop, and Min Zhu. 1998. "A Panel Data Analysis of the Fungibility of Foreign Aid." *World Bank Economic Review* 12(1): 29–58.

Huntington, Samuel P., and Myron Weiner, eds. 1987. *Understanding Political Development*. Boston, MA: Little, Brown.

Johnson, John H., and Sulaiman S. Wasty. 1993. "Borrower Ownership of Adjustment Programs and the Political Economy of Reform." Discussion Paper no. 199. Washington, DC: World Bank.

Kanbur, Ravi, and Todd Sandler. 1999. "The Future of Development Assistance: Common Pools and International Public Goods." Policy Essay no. 25. Washington, DC: Overseas Development Council.

Killick, Tony, Ramana Gunatilaka, and Ana Mar. 1998. *Aid and the Political Economy of Policy Change*. London and New York: Routledge Press.

Krueger, Anne O., Constantine Michalopoulos, and Vernon Ruttan, eds. 1989. *Aid and Development*. Baltimore, MD: Johns Hopkins University Press.

Lancaster, Carol. 1999a. *Aid to Africa*. Chicago, IL: University of Chicago Press.

———. 1999b. "Aid Effectiveness in Africa: The Unfinished Agenda." *Journal of African Economies* 8(4): 487–503.

Larson, B. A., and Daniel W. Bromley. 1990. "Property Rights, Externalities, and Resource Degradation: Locating the Tragedy." *Journal of Development Economics* 33(2) (October): 235–62.

Maipose, Gervase, Gloria Somolekae, and Timothy Johnston. 1997. "Effective Aid Management: The Case of Botswana." In *Foreign Aid in Africa: Learning from Country Experiences*, edited by Jerker Carlsson, Gloria Somolekae, and Nicolas van de Walle, 16–35. Uppsala: Nordic Africa Institute.

Martens, Bertin, with Uwe Mummert, Peter Murrell, and Paul Seabright. 2002. *The Institutional Economics of Foreign Aid*. New York: Cambridge University Press.

McGinnis, Michael D., ed. 1999a. *Polycentric Governance and Development: Readings from the Workshop in Political Theory and Policy Analysis*. Ann Arbor: University of Michigan Press.

———, ed. 1999b. *Polycentricity and Local Public Economies: Readings from the Workshop in Political Theory and Policy Analysis*. Ann Arbor: University of Michigan Press.

Miller, Gary. 1992. *Managerial Dilemmas: The Political Economy of Hierarchy*. New York: Cambridge University Press.

Morss, Elliott R. 1984. "Institutional Destruction Resulting from Donor and Project Proliferation in Sub-Saharan African Countries." *World Development* 12(4): 465–70.

Mosley, Paul. 1991. *Aid and Power: The World Bank and Policy-Based Lending.* 2 vols. London: Routledge.

North, Douglass C. 1990. *Institutions, Institutional Change, and Economic Performance.* New York: Cambridge University Press.

———. 1994. "Economic Performance through Time." *American Economic Review* 84: 359–68.

OECD/DAC (Organisation for Economic Co-operation and Development/Development Assistance Committee). 1992. *Principles for Affective Aid.* Paris: OECD.

Olson, Mancur. 1965. *The Logic of Collective Action.* Cambridge, MA: Harvard University Press.

Ostrom, Elinor, Larry Schroeder, and Susan Wynne. 1993. *Institutional Incentives and Sustainable Development: Infrastructure Policies in Perspective.* Boulder, CO: Westview Press.

Ostrom, Vincent. 1997. *The Meaning of Democracy and the Vulnerability of Democracies: A Response to Tocqueville's Challenge.* Ann Arbor: University of Michigan Press.

———. 1999. "Cryptoimperialism, Predatory States, and Self-Governance." In *Polycentric Governance and Development: Readings from the Workshop in Political Theory and Policy Analysis*, edited by Michael McGinnis, 166–85. Ann Arbor: University of Michigan Press.

Ostrom, Vincent, David Feeny, and Hartmut Picht, eds. 1993. *Rethinking Institutional Analysis and Development.* San Francisco, CA: ICS Press.

Pack, Howard, and Janet Rothenberg Pack. 1990. "Is Foreign Aid Fungible? The Case of Indonesia." *Economic Journal* 100(399): 188–94.

———. 1993. "Foreign Aid and the Question of Fungibility." *Review of Economics and Statistics* 75(2): 258–65.

Pedersen, Karl R. 1996. "Aid, Investment and Incentives." *Scandinavian Journal of Economics* 98(3): 423–38.

———. 1998. "Incentives and Aid Dependence." EGDI Working Paper 1998:1. Stockholm: Ministry for Foreign Affairs.

Prebisch, Raul. 1970. *Change and Development: Latin America's Great Task.* Washington, DC: Inter-American Development Bank.

Rodrik, Dani. 1999. "The New Global Economy and Developing Countries: Making Openness Work." ODC Policy Essay 24. Washington, DC: ODC.

Rogers, A., A. Chadwick, and K. Oglesby. 1997. *TANDEM Project with the Folk Development Colleges in Tanzania 1990 to 1996.* Stockholm: Sida Evaluation 97/22.

Rostow, Walt W. 1960. *The Stages of Economic Growth: A Non-Communist Manifesto.* London: Cambridge University Press.

Salmi, Jyrki. 1996. "Economics of Sustainability: Neo-Classical Viewpoint." Unpublished manuscript, Department of Economics, University of Helsinki.

Schlager, Edella, and Elinor Ostrom. 1992. "Property-Rights Regimes and Natural Resources: A Conceptual Analysis." *Land Economics* 68(3): 249–62.

Scott, James C. 1998. *Seeing Like a State: How Certain Schemes to Improve the Human Condition Have Failed.* New Haven, CT: Yale University Press.

Sida. 1996a. *Aid Dependency: Causes, Symptoms, and Remedies: Project 2015.* Stockholm: Sida.

———. 1996b. *Bistand pa Kredit.* Stockholm: Sida.

———. 1996c. *Landstrategi Indien.* Stockholm: Sida

———. 1997a. *Development Cooperation in the 21st Century.* Stockholm: Sida.

——— 1997b. *Sida at Work: Sida's Methods for Development Cooperation.* Stockholm: Sida.

———. 1999. "Terms of Reference for a Study of How Aid, Incentives and Sustainability are Related." Stockholm: Sida.

Simon, Herbert A. [1947] 1965. *Administrative Behavior: A Study of Decision-Making Processes in Administrative Organization.* New York: Free Press.

———. 1972. "Theories of Bounded Rationality." In *Decision and Organization: A Volume in Honor of Jacob Marschak*, edited by C. B. McGuire and Roy Radner, 161–76. Amsterdam: North Holland.

Tendler, Judith. 1975. *Inside Foreign Aid.* Baltimore, MD: John Hopkins University Press.

Tsikata, Tsidi M. 1998. "Aid Effectiveness: A Survey of the Recent Empirical Literature." IMF Paper on Policy Analysis and Assessment. New York: IMF, Policy Development and Review Department.

van de Walle, Nicolas, and Timothy A. Johnston. 1996. *Improving Aid to Africa.* Washington, DC: Overseas Development Council.

van Ufford, Philip Q. 1988. "Development Bureaucracies in between Intentions and Outcomes." In *The Hidden Crisis in Development: Development Bureaucracies*, edited by Philip Q. van Ufford, Dirk Kruijt, and Theodore Downing, 9–38. Tokyo: United Nations University Press.

White, Howard. 1992. "The Macro-Economic Impact of Development Aid: A Critical Survey." *Journal of Development Studies* 21(2): 163–240.

———, ed. 1998. *Aid and Macroeconomic Performance.* London: Macmillan Press.

———. 1999. *Dollars, Dialogue and Development: An Evaluation of Swedish Programme Aid.* Stockholm: Sida.

Wildavsky, Aaron B. 1984. *The Politics of the Budgetary Process.* 4th ed. Boston, MA: Little, Brown.

Wilson, M. G., and Elizabeth Whitmore. 1995. "Accompanying the Process: Principles for International Development Practice." *Canadian Journal of Development Studies* (special issue): 61–77.

World Bank. 1996a. *Poverty Reduction and the World Bank: Progress and Challenges in the 1990s.* Washington, DC: World Bank.

———. 1996b. *Serving a Changing World: Report of the Task Force on Multilateral Development Banks.* (The Wapenhans Report). Washington, DC: World Bank.

———. 1997. "Annual Review of Development Effectiveness." Report 17196. Washington, DC: World Bank, Operations Evaluation Department.

———. 1998. *Assessing Aid: What Works, What Doesn't and Why*. Written by David Dollar and Lant Pritchett. Oxford, UK: Oxford University Press.

10

Nested Governance for Effective REDD+: Institutional and Political Arguments

PRAKASH KASHWAN AND ROBERT HOLAHAN

The international environmental policy community is debating proposals for Reducing Emissions from Deforestation and Forest Degradation, and Enhancement of Forest Carbon Stocks in Developing Countries (REDD+). Though REDD+ means different things to different countries, organizations, and individuals (Angelsen et al. 2009, 2; for an extensive review, see Seymour 2013), the kernel of REDD+ relates to its international scope and market-based or market-like arrangements for financing forest protection and conservation.

According to UN-REDD, REDD is a mechanism to create incentives for developing countries to protect, better manage, and wisely use their forest resources. To this end, REDD entails creating a financial value for the carbon stored in trees. Once this carbon is assessed and quantified, the final phase of REDD involves *developed* countries paying *developing* countries carbon offsets for their standing forests.[1] The "plus" in REDD+ refers to the inclusion within REDD the role of conservation, sustainable management of forests, and enhancement of forest carbon stocks in reducing emissions.

Though the international demand for forest-based carbon sequestration is the main driver of REDD+, forest protection strategies must be designed to be effective on the ground. This cross-scale nature of REDD+ explains why scholars and policy makers increasingly favor nested governance arrangements over either fully centralized or fully decentralized regimes. Nevertheless, a review of key articles and reports on nested REDD+ shows that a majority of the literature on nested REDD+ focuses on ex post monitoring, reporting, and verification (MRV) of carbon emissions. Such a focus on MRVs detracts attention from the substantive agenda of REDD+: engendering effective forest protection, conservation, and reforestation on the ground. The MRV-focused literature on nested REDD+ does not also address the need for developing an institutional architecture and policy reforms needed to foster forest conservation in the developing countries (Angelsen et al. 2008; Larson et al. 2013).

We build on the work of the scholars who conceive nested REDD+ as a means for multitier forest governance (Forsyth 2009; Herold and Skutsch 2011). Nevertheless, we show that many proposals about nested REDD+ architecture are based on inadequate, and at times, incorrect interpretations of the principles of nestedness developed by the scholars of common property and polycentric decentralized governance (Ostrom 1990; Marshall 2008; Agrawal and Angelsen 2009; Hayes and Persha 2010). We first clarify the conceptual roots of nestedness. We then develop an approach to nested REDD+ that enables the development of a "middle tier of institutions and governance enabling conditions" necessary for successful implementation of REDD+ (Seymour 2013, 17).

The success in controlling deforestation or avoiding forest degradation depends crucially on how REDD+ finances are used and whether the actors involved in resource harvesting and management on the ground are credibly committed to producing positive environmental outcomes. Achieving this requires careful institutional design that will help align incentives at both the national and subnational levels. In addition, to address the political-economic drivers of deforestation, REDD+ proponents must systematically address the political dimensions, that is, the questions of legitimacy of and accountability in REDD+.

Nested REDD+ architecture must be based on cross-scale linkages that are independent of the government hierarchy. In the absence of such independent structures, national governments rely on fines, fences, and guns as the primary tools of enforcement, which will jeopardize the legitimacy of REDD+ interventions among forest users (Petkova, Larson, and Pacheco 2010; Colfer 2011; Larson et al. 2013). Such adverse outcomes are far less likely if REDD+ arrangements recognize and empower both government and nongovernment actors working across scales, each working as a check against the potential failures of others. In particular, we argue for strengthening intercommunity forestry associations and forest rights movements and allowing such civil society groups an increased space during the implementation of REDD+.

In the following section, we offer a concise, yet up-to-date, summary of previous proposals for nested REDD+. In the second section, we outline a more comprehensive and theoretically informed proposal for nested REDD+ architecture. We also discuss the political dimensions that affect the success of nested REDD+. The third section provides new insights derived from the literature on international forestry regarding monitoring and enforcement in REDD+. The fourth section discusses the political dimensions of nested REDD+ by specifying cross-scale linkages between forest user groups, intercommunity forestry associations, and forest rights movements. The chapter concludes by discussing potential limitations to our approach and by proposing policy recommendations for a transition to nested REDD+.

Nestedness in REDD+: Current Proposals

The Evolution of the Idea of REDD+

REDD+ is modeled on payment for environmental services (PES) programs, which link sellers and buyers via voluntary, conditional agreements over "a well-defined environmental service—or a land use presumed to produce that service" (Wunder 2007, 48). REDD+ is conceived as a mechanism for industrialized countries to provide "performance-based financial incentives to developing countries to alter their forest-based emissions trajectories compared to an agreed baseline" (Seymour 2013, 2). Angelsen and McNeill (2012, 46) argue that for the success of PES-type REDD+ programs, national governments must introduce policy reforms to recognize the property rights of local forest users. National-level policy reforms, however, are frequently blocked by powerful actors and agencies that stand to lose under the reforms (Thompson, Baruah, and Carr 2011; Angelsen and McNeill 2012). Such formidable opposition has forced international policy makers to focus on incentivizing national governments in the hope that national governments will carry out needed reforms (Thompson, Baruah, and Carr 2011).

As negotiations over the development of a formal policy continue, however, NGOs, donors, and private corporations are already implementing REDD+ pilot projects at the local or subnational level (Angelsen and McNeill 2012). The pragmatic goals of enlisting the support of national-level governments and of ensuring the continued operation of the ongoing projects have shaped the nested REDD+ proposals currently on the table (Seymour 2013). We summarize these proposals in the following section.

Existing Proposals for Nested REDD+

REDD+ proponents typically argue for one of two forms of nested REDD+ architecture: (1) a "hybrid" approach, which provides for simultaneous financing of local projects and the development of a national-level institutional architecture (Sunderlin and Sills 2012), and (2) an MRV-focused multilevel approach designed to cope with the uncertainties surrounding binding international agreement about REDD+ (Pedroni et al. 2009).

Responding to the question of "What is the right scale for REDD?," Angelsen et al. (2008, 1) highlight the flexibility of a hybrid (nested) approach that combines features of direct, international support to projects operating at a subnational level with additional direct support to national-level governments. Under such a hybrid nested approach, countries that "initiate [REDD projects] at the subnational level would be able to scale up to a national approach as they increase their capacities and improve their governance" (2008, 3). Seen in this vein, the role of a nested approach is to "attract private capital (and to) . . . incentivize early activities *while countries are still getting ready*" (2008, 217; emphasis added). Similarly, the report of the sixteenth session of the Conference of the Parties (Cancun) held toward the end of 2010 encouraged developing countries to develop, "*in the interim*," subnational forest reference emission levels, and subnational monitoring and reporting systems (UNFCCC 2011, 12–13; emphasis added). By implication, once a national REDD+ architecture is in place, a nested approach is no longer necessary.

The second main approach to nested REDD+ focuses on developing "integrated accounting system[s] for emissions and emission reductions resulting from national and subnational REDD efforts" (Pedroni et al. 2009, 209). This MRV-focused vision has been influential among a number of international private agencies such as Forest Trends, Climate Focus, and, the Nature Conservancy (Chagas et al. 2011). The most important influence of this work is reflected in the Jurisdictional and Nested REDD+ (JNR) Initiative of Verified Carbon Standards (VCS), which is considered one of the world's leading voluntary greenhouse gas programs. The JNR focuses almost exclusively on accounting of carbon emission reductions under a number of alternative policy scenarios.[2] While the JNR "nests" different types of emission reductions into a comprehensive emission inventory, it says nothing about the institutional arrangements needed for fostering forest protection outcomes, or about questions of benefit sharing, transparency, and accountability.

To summarize, for the proponents of a hybrid approach, nested REDD+ is conceptualized mainly as an intermediary step toward the development of a national-level REDD+ architecture. Even if national governments do not have the required institutions in place, a hybrid nested REDD+ architecture would allow subnational interventions to begin immediately if a worthy project is ready (Pedroni et al. 2009; Herold and Skutsch 2011). On the other hand, the architects of the MRV-focused approaches, such as the JNR, have sought to create a system that allows for proper accounting of MRVs under all plausible REDD+ scenarios.

Both the hybrid and MRV-focused approaches to nested REDD+ architecture overlook on-the-ground considerations. For example, both leave open the question of who will be responsible for protecting and conserving forests ex ante. This is a surprising omission because one of the main goals of REDD+ is the protection of existing forest stocks. We believe this omission is a consequence of how proponents of hybrid and MRV approaches conceptualize the problem of institutional supply—who supplies domestic institutions and why?

Institutional Supply

Some prominent observers of REDD+ have argued that international agencies should not interfere in how national governments implement REDD+ domestically (Wunder 2010). Because there are inherent efficiency gains from operating at multiple levels, the argument goes, national governments will have incentives to endogenously create nested systems within their countries. The operational principles of pilot REDD+ projects developed by the UN-REDD and the Forest Carbon Partnership Facility of the World Bank similarly focus on national-level governments as the primary locus of REDD+ implementation (Thompson, Baruah, and Carr 2011). However, REDD+ proposals aimed at incentivizing *national governments* are at risk of repeating the mistakes of the past international efforts to control tropical deforestation. Those interventions failed precisely because national governments failed to develop robust and accountable institutions of forest governance (Kaimowitz 2000).

Previous studies have shown that national governments and public officials often lack the motivation to devolve substantive rights and promote transparent forest governance in practice (Agrawal and Ostrom 2001; Ribot, Agrawal, and Larson 2006). Significant donor support for forestry decentralization programs of the 1990s is a case in point. While developing country governments enacted attractive decentralization policies, they retained ownership of the majority of forests, which put severe limits on the benefit that forest-dependent people earned from forestry decentralization (RRI 2012; see also Ribot, Agrawal, and Larson 2006; Tacconi 2007).

Past studies have also shown that a sudden deluge of funds, without first putting in place appropriate institutional arrangements across different levels, creates adverse incentives, which may lead to significant governance problems (Auer 2007). The concern that REDD+ will prompt governments to recentralize forest governance (Sandbrook et al. 2010) has, to some extent, been validated. For example, forestry agencies in India have proposed to bring the former Swidden fields under carbon forestry plantations (UNDP 2009), even though indigenous *Adivasi* people's rights to those lands have been recognized in a recent statute (Kashwan 2011). The governments of Indonesia and Malaysia argued for the recognition of large-scale commercial palm oil plantations, which often cause grave ecological damage to peat swamp forests, as "forests" eligible for REDD+ finance.[3]

These events, combined with a neglect of tenure reforms by national governments (Larson et al. 2013), lend credence to the fears that governments are "anxious to gain more political and economic control over their nation's forests via the REDD mechanism" (Skutsch and McCall 2010, 401). However, developing country governments are not alone in pushing through carbon enclosures. Carbon Conservation, a private carbon forestry company, announced deployment of former Aceh rebels to provide military-type security cover for the Ulu Masen Project in Aceh Province.[4] Forest-dependent groups in Tanzania turned hostile to REDD+ projects after international environmental NGOs ignored persistent but peaceful local protests against exclusionary REDD+ program design (Beymer-Farris and Bassett 2012).

Evidence available through various studies suggests that left to their devices, national governments are unlikely to invest in forest tenure reforms and carefully designed benefit-sharing mechanisms. Instead, the allocation of rights, responsibilities, and rewards for local forest protection must be secured through *binding* international agreements (Larson 2011). Governments and nongovernment organizations interested in participating in REDD+ must be required to meet such conditions, first and foremost, because they are critical to the effectiveness of forest protection efforts, and therefore, to the core mandate of REDD+. Because such conditions also meet the normative criteria of equity and social justice, they will further contribute to the legitimacy and sustainability of REDD+ interventions on the ground.

In the following section, we discuss the key features of nested enterprises proposed by Ostrom (1990) and Marshall (2008) that the proponents of hybrid and MRV focused approaches have largely overlooked. Then, we build on the literature about common property and forestry decentralization to show how the nested architecture we propose helps synergize inputs from public, civic, and market institutions (Hayes and Persha 2010; Ostrom 2010; Agrawal, Nepstad, and Chhatre 2011).

Nested REDD+: A Theoretically Informed Proposal

An international agreement that promises significant new investments in forest protection and conservation, if not structured carefully, may instead inadvertently harm subnational and local efforts of forest protection (Sandbrook et al. 2010; Cronkleton, Bray, and Medina 2011; Larson et al. 2013). Attempting to avoid this pitfall, some REDD+ scholars have misinterpreted the principle of nested enterprises. For instance, Forsyth (2009, 116; emphasis added) compares nested enterprises to a Russian doll such that "each local set of rules and incentives fits within *the rules and objectives set at larger scales*." Such a top-down understanding of nestedness, however, is a misreading of the concept of nested enterprises, especially if it is read along with Ostrom's other design principles.

Instead of simply fitting *within* the scope of larger-scale policies, Ostrom (1990) argues that effective policy frameworks allow users on the ground to operate, on most occasions, *without* higher-level interference. Marshall (2008, 77) conceptualizes nested arrangements as inclusive systems that aid autonomous functioning of smaller, more exclusive units operating within broadly agreed principles. A nested system is one in which key governance functions, like monitoring and enforcement of resource use, are organized into multiple, reinforcing, layers of governance (Ostrom 1990).

Such a perspective on nestedness allows for multiple types of rules to coexist in a quilt patch of local and external interventions and control. Following the principles of subsidiarity (Marshall 2008), we recognize that participation in REDD+ entails forest users giving up a certain amount of autonomy so that local decisions related to harvesting of nonforest produce does not run afoul of REDD+'s forest conservation goals (cf. Bray 2013). At the same time, the nested REDD+ architecture we propose values locally effective rules related to routine monitoring of forest protection activities, intracommunity conflict resolution, and about election of leaders who represent forest users in negotiations with outsiders (Agrawal and Angelsen 2009). We also show below that participation of forest users in REDD+ activities is necessary, but may prove insufficient if they do not have the support of government agencies who own most of the forests in the developing countries. The roles and responsibilities of key actors in the nested REDD+ architecture we propose are outlined in Table 10.1.

Forest Users

Forests are subject to multiple overlapping and contested claims, such that it is ill-advised to propose rigid criteria to determine which groups or communities should be recognized as key REDD+ stakeholders. Still, there is a broad consensus that people who live in and around forest areas and are dependent on forests for subsistence, who we refer to as "forest users," are the most important local stakeholders in REDD+ (Angelsen et al. 2009; Thompson, Baruah, and Carr 2011; Larson et al. 2013; Sunderlin et al. 2013). Estimates of the number of "people living in tropical forest areas" range between 600 million (Wollenberg et al. 2008) and 1.3 billion people (Chao 2012).

Our argument about the recognition of forest users' rights differs from that of the scholars who draw on human rights and indigenous rights frameworks to demand for secured rights for forest peoples (Sikor et al. 2010). The rights proponents tend to emphasize the role of international conventions about indigenous and human rights in the context of REDD+ (Lyster 2011). We recognize the need for drawing on such diverse approaches for the effective advocacy of the rights of forest users (see Sikor and Stahl 2011). Nevertheless, our arguments in favor of recognizing user rights are related to the key tenets of institutional analysis.

First, user rights must be attached to nontrivial economic gains. Because REDD+ changes the economic relationship between a user group and its forest, unless the new management practices provide a greater economic return to user groups than status quo practices, it is unlikely that recognizing existing property rights will alone be sufficient to induce collective action. As we discuss in the next section, compensating forest users for their role in routine forest monitoring and carefully designed carbon auditing will ensure that REDD+ is beneficial to them.

Second, user rights are of little use if they are not backed by an institutional framework intended to facilitate both the local and cross-scale collective action needed for effective forest protection (Agrawal and

Table 10.1. Roles and responsibilities in a nested REDD+ architecture

REDD+ activity	*Key actor/s*	*Primary level of action*
Forest protection, conservation, and routine monitoring	Forest user groups	Village/village clusters
Organization/mobilization of forest user groups	Intercommunity forestry associations (FAs)/forest rights movements	District/Province/ National
Domestic benefit sharing	Provincial governments acting through elected local governments/FAs	Province
Accountability and safeguards	FAs/forest rights movements/ nongovernment organizations (NGOs)	Province/National
Accounting of carbon emission reductions	Subnational agencies with support of forestry associations and forest users	Subnational/ Local
Auditing changes in carbon stock	Conducted jointly by third-party monitoring agencies and environmental NGOs; with the assistance of forest user groups	National/Province
Policy reforms	Federal and provincial governments	National/Province
International carbon finance and regulation	UNFCCC/national governments	International/ National

Angelsen 2009; Hayes and Persha 2010). Because national governments own more than 86 percent of the world forests (Agrawal, Nepstad, and Chhatre 2011), nested REDD+ architecture must incorporate mechanisms for holding the state to account. Such mechanisms of cross-scale linkages are extremely important to address the criticism that user groups are often exclusive and lack accountability (Ribot, Chhatre, and Lankina

2008). The long time horizon of many REDD+ plans will allow project proponents to address these concerns by linking user groups to elected local governments.

The linkages between forest users and local governments are important for ensuring both democratic accountability and the continuity of REDD+ activities through the institutions of elected local governments (Mwangi and Wardell 2012). At the same time, the small-scale operations of a large number of forest-dependent groups and local governments beg a number of obvious questions: how will these smaller units deliberate with one another and aggregate their forest emissions? Equally important, how will they become part of the cross-sectoral partnerships that seem essential for operationalizing nested REDD+ arrangements (see Forsyth 2009, 119)?

Intercommunity Forestry Associations/Federations

Forest user groups and local government bodies are most effective when they are part of cross-sector partnerships. Such partnerships often work through intercommunity forestry associations (FAs), forestry federations, or forest rights movements that are already active in many countries in Asia (Ojha 2009), Africa (Igoe and Croucher 2007; Asare, Kyei, and Mason 2013), and Latin America (Cronkleton, Bray, and Medina 2011; Hajek et al. 2011; Bray 2013; García-López 2013).

The FAs are often instrumental in supporting forest protection efforts beyond the confines of villages, act as nodal agencies for mobilizing forest users for deliberations over REDD+ projects, provide monitoring of forest protection efforts, help resolve intercommunity conflicts, and act as a bridge between actors working across scales. With appropriate assistance from governments and NGOs, the FAs have successfully helped aggregate the activities and efforts of smaller community groups, and have helped strengthen the voices of forest users in the political arena (Cronkleton, Bray, and Medina 2011). Such an expanded role for intercommunity FAs takes them closer to Ostrom's (1990) proposal of nested enterprises.

Government Forestry Agencies

Commons scholars have shown that forest users must have the backing of public forest agencies and other higher-level institutional arrangements to deal with incursions beyond their capacity (Agrawal 2001; Hayes and Persha 2010; Kashwan 2011). Under the nested REDD+ architecture, higher-level public officials and agencies with superior enforcement capacities are mandated to work with locally organized groups to monitor and act decisively against any instances of unauthorized harvesting by powerful outside actors. The interactions between forestry associations and government agencies create networks in which forest users can petition for help when needed.

Furthermore, higher-level government authorities can also monitor against community failures or any collective violation of norms of forest management agreed to in the context of REDD+. However, such powers will have to be supplemented by appropriate procedural rights vested in forest user groups so that they are not punished unfairly.

Provincial and National-Level Governments

As shown in Table 10.1, in the nested framework we propose, national and provincial governments are in charge of policy reforms and for creating the MRV systems that have been the core focus of previous scholarship on nested REDD+ (Pedroni et al. 2009; Chagas et al. 2011). In addition, a direct engagement with intercommunity associations and social movements will help government leaders respond effectively to the interests and concerns of key local actors.

The nested architecture we propose should preferably be ratified by national parliaments, thereby allowing national democratic institutions, including the judiciary, to step in, if necessary (for linkages between international agreements and domestic judicial institutions, see Benvenisti 2008). Nevertheless, leaving the implementation of subnational REDD+ governance mechanisms entirely to the discretion of central governments will create perverse incentives for governments vested in maintaining continued control of forests (Sandbrook et al. 2010; Angelsen and McNeill 2012). Mitigating these concerns requires that the international community play an active role in instituting domestic checks and balances to hold national-level governments to account.

UNFCCC and Other International Agencies

The discussion above shows that REDD+ governance cannot be effective if it remains a soft and nonbinding instrument (Larson 2011). Scholars have argued that UNFCCC interventions need to go beyond proposing social and environmental "safeguards" to actively promote tenure reforms and institutions for local participation (Chhatre et al. 2012). Under the framework we propose, UNFCCC and other intergovernmental bodies require that governments interested in participating in REDD+ put in place transparent benefit-sharing mechanisms and concrete checks and balances during the implementation of REDD+ programs. We argue that the international agencies supporting REDD+ interventions should also incentivize developing country governments to formally engage with subnational governments and nongovernment actors involved in activities related to forest use and management. Equally important, international agencies and transnational NGOs must be encouraged to engage with national-level and regional forest rights movements that are often in a position to provide countervailing power of mass mobilization of forest users, an argument we further develop in the fourth section.

As discussed in this section, the broadly defined roles and responsibilities of various actors in a REDD+ architecture should be laid out up-front, but should also be flexible enough to allow adaptation to specific local circumstances. In the remainder, we discuss institutional and political considerations that will arise during REDD+ design and implementation.

Monitoring Forests and Forest Carbon Stocks in Nested REDD

When forest users have direct stakes in a forest (e.g., rights to undertake regulated and limited harvesting of nontimber forest produce), and they receive a significant share of the carbon forestry proceeds, they are more likely to contribute to forest protection under inclusive REDD+ architecture. However, as we indicated above, rights to benefit from forest protection are necessary but insufficient unless robust arrangements for monitoring and enforcement are put in place (Gibson, Williams, and Ostrom 2005; Coleman 2009).

Our review of the literature on nested REDD+ reveals that the term "monitoring" is most frequently equated to carbon auditing. However, monitoring is defined more broadly in the common-pool resource literature. Groups of users who benefit from a common-pool resource, such as pastures or forests, take turns at patrolling the resource boundaries to monitor rule conformance by their fellow community members and the nonmembers trying to harvest illegally (Ostrom 1990). However, monitoring is invariably paired with sanctioning. Forest users have incentives to follow the rules agreed upon collectively only if those violating the rules are appropriately sanctioned (Ostrom 1990; Gibson, Williams, and Ostrom 2005; Coleman 2009).

Even though local groups are competent in routine monitoring of forest use, it does not necessarily mean that locally organized groups are able to fend off incursions by powerful external actors (Hayes and Persha 2010; Kashwan 2011). In other words, while the routine monitoring of actual forest use is most efficiently handled at a local level, the support of higher-level authorities is likely to be critical not only in confronting particular cases of violations by external actors, but also in maintaining the credibility and viability of local forest protection initiatives. The implication is that the effectiveness of local monitoring is inseparable from a constructive deployment of the authority of government agencies to ward off illegitimate activities of outsiders capable of overwhelming forest users.

As different from the monitoring of routine forest protection activities, accounting and auditing of carbon emission reductions are most efficiently organized at a national level (Pedroni et al. 2009). In a fully developed system of international REDD+ finance, carbon auditing and accounting has to be conducted at the national level. Still, placing monitoring and auditing functions *exclusively* in the hands of external monitors will increase transaction costs. These considerations have led the UNFCCC to stipulate that carbon auditing and accounting should be conducted through "an appropriate combination of remote sensing and ground-based forest carbon inventory" (Herold and Skutsch 2011, 2).

The choice of methods and means of carbon accounting and auditing is also related to questions of accountability in REDD+. Recent reports suggest that government agencies that control forest lands have used remote sensing analyses to exaggerate the extent of forest cover, for instance, by including commercial plantations as forests (Nagendra 2007; cf. Downton 1995). Therefore, including nonstate actors in the process of accounting for and auditing carbon emission reductions will also institute checks against the misuse of powers by governments and government agencies.

Skutsch and Ba (2010) offer an excellent illustration of a multilevel approach to carbon accounting through a project that developed participatory geographical information systems. Community members with four to seven years of education were trained in user-friendly and IPCC-compliant carbon stock measurements through real-time monitoring and data recording (Skutsch and Ba 2010; see also Skutsch et al. 2009). Similarly, the PES programs in Cameroon (Sonwa and Minang 2009) and Mexico (Cacho,

Marshall, and Milne 2005) that ensured effective local participation reduced transaction costs and yielded better returns to participating farmers. While these projects have been facilitated by research institutes and donor agencies, in many cases intercommunity associations are capable of handling such interventions in the long run (see fourth section below).

Under the nested REDD+ architecture we propose, forest users are the main party vested with the task of routine monitoring of forest protection efforts on the ground. Local forest users are usually in a better position to observe activities within the forests than are central bureaucrats or external auditors. Greater attention to the development of carbon accounting systems based on user monitoring and accounting activities will go a long way in facilitating these efforts (Skutsch et al. 2009).

Forest users can also be enlisted to assist in auditing of forest conditions and assessment of carbon stock, thereby achieving carbon auditing at low costs. To avoid potential conflicts of interest among forest users, however, the task of carbon auditing must be separated from the task of monitoring. To that end, the integrity of the auditing process can be ensured by involving forest users from other localities in the region. Moreover, finer carbon sequestration measurements need to be conducted at randomly selected sample sites as part of third-party validation processes. Such a combination of local and external monitoring and auditing stands to offer synergistic conservation, development, and governance benefits.

The Political Dimension Cross-Scale Linkages in Nested REDD+

Recent reviews of multilevel governance point to the challenges associated with the two prominent ways of "bridging the distance between the higher and the local level, viz., decentralisation and participation" (Mwangi and Wardell 2013, 85). Both of these solutions frequently fall prey to the entrenched power asymmetries between government agencies and forest users (Ribot, Agrawal, and Larson 2006), and power differences among forest users. The onus of restoring a balance of power often falls on national and transnational NGOs. Notwithstanding the important contributions these outside actors make under supportive policy environments, previous studies have shown that priorities of these outside actors may not match those of forest users, which in turn poses a challenge for the legitimacy of external interventions (Colfer 2011; Thompson, Baruah, and Carr 2011; Beymer-Farris and Bassett 2012).

Addressing the challenges outlined above requires that nested architecture is geared to strengthen countervailing powers as a check against powerful government agencies. The relations of accountability will be strengthened through active engagement between intercommunity forestry associations/federations and national and transnational NGOs. The intercommunity forestry associations play an active role in facilitating policy and programmatic linkages while forest rights movements help build political pressure against erring government agencies and governments.

Cross-Scale Linkage through Subnational Governments and Intercommunity Associations

In line with the dual institutional-political focus of the nested architecture we propose, we argue that the success of REDD+ requires government agencies and REDD+ proponents working closely with intercommunity forestry associations and local governments. The success of intercommunity associations, documented by scholars cited in the second section above, shows that important synergistic effects can be achieved by creating a policy space for intercommunity forestry associations already active on the ground. However, most discussions of cross-scale linkages tend to be theoretical and conceptual; rarely do they specify how such linkages are achieved in practice. Here we discuss specific examples of such cross-scale organizations that policy makers in developing countries are working with for implementing multitier forest governance mechanisms.

A well-documented example of nested organizations in Asia is the national-level Federation of Community Forestry Users, Nepal (FECOFUN), which represents more than 11,200 Community Forest User Groups.[5] User groups are organized into district-level federations, which elect their representatives to the national-level FECOFUN general assembly. While the district federations work very closely with the government district forest officers, the national body of FECOFUN functions autonomously. Such autonomy enables FECOFUN to negotiate with, rather than being subordinate to, national government agencies (Ojha 2009). FECOFUN has been acting as the mediating agency between the community forestry user groups and a variety of international development agencies, such as the Forest Stewardship Council and Forest Carbon Trust Fund. The success of FECOFUN has prompted the Forest Carbon Trust Fund to help establish a watershed-level REDD-Network, which led to reduced transaction costs for REDD+ implementation in the pilot sites (Khatri et al. 2013).

Ghana's Community Resource Management Areas (CREMAs) combines the strength of locally grounded rules of resource management with institutional arrangements that facilitate the accountability of elected local governments (cf. Ribot, Chhatre, and Lankina 2008). The CREMAs are backed by the power and authority of the district assembly constituted under the local government statute (Asare, Kyei, and Mason 2013). Most importantly, at various stages of the policy process, the CREMAs facilitate participation of forest user groups, traditional authorities, wildlife management authorities, district assemblies, and the Minister for Lands and Natural Resources at national level. Asare, Kyei, and Mason (2013) show that CREMAs are best placed to channel REDD+ related cross-scale linkages. Similarly, a number of scholars have documented the success of Mexico's intercommunity forestry associations. These associations have helped secure for community forestry groups financial support for local forestry projects, greater participation in policy making, stronger rights, and, political representation in the policy-making processes (Klooster and Masera 2000; Bray 2013; Garcia-Lopez 2013).

Despite the multiple policy and programmatic benefits that have accrued to the members of intercommunity forestry associations, they are not a panacea, as evident from the challenges that forestry associations have encountered in different settings (for related discussions, see Wollenberg et al. 2006; Cronkleton, Bray, and Medina 2011). Instead, we use the example of forestry associations to make a larger point about the importance of engaging civic associations and other membership-based organizations. Such engagements will help forest users make cross-scale linkages without necessarily having to climb through the rigid hierarchies of government bureaucracies. The recognition of existing federations and the establishment of legal frameworks that *allow* forestry associations or federations to form in new places are likely to foster robust cross-scale linkages and improve accountability.

Forest Rights Movements in REDD+

The problem of "recentralization" of forest governance can be mitigated partly through international regulations; for instance, by making the payment of REDD+ benefits contingent on national governments undertaking meaningful forest governance reforms (Sikor et al. 2010; Larson 2011). Nevertheless, in addition to binding national governments to transparent and fair benefit-sharing mechanisms agreed upon internationally, governments must also be held accountable through domestic mobilization of the affected populations.

The need for strengthening domestic mobilization is apparent from the failure of international indigenous rights movements to force governments to develop transparent REDD+ benefit-sharing mechanisms (Schroeder 2010; Sikor and Stahl 2011). Such failures have been attributed, in part, to indigenous rights advocates' reliance on a "timeless vision of indigeneity," and romantic notions of indigenous people's commitment to environmental conservation (Fabricant 2013). In the process, the questions of central concern to indigenous and other forest-dependent people, such as economic development and forest-dependent livelihoods, tend to be relegated to the sidelines of indigenous rights advocacy. While it is important to attend to questions of justice and rights at national and international levels (Colfer 2011; Sikor and Stahl 2011), without simultaneously engaging questions of livelihood and economic development, transnational indigenous movements cannot claim to represent the voices of indigenous peoples at large (Brysk 2000; Mustalahti et al. 2012).

Forest users often face a Catch-22 situation (Hayes and Persha 2010, 548): forest users and their associations desire autonomy, but they also need the support and backing of government agencies to successfully deal with external threats. Local users cannot afford to antagonize government agencies, which may explain why indigenous peasants in some places have opted to engage with REDD+ programs despite an awareness of the potential risks involved (Osborne 2011). Therefore, national and international forest rights movements must also be willing to engage with government agencies. Such engagement is likely to prompt government agencies into action, while also helping alleviate fears of retribution against forestry associations and forest rights movements that question local authorities.

Greater collaboration between national and transnational forest rights movements will also lend strength to transnational advocacy on behalf of forest users. Stronger linkages between transnational and national movements, and the intercommunity forestry associations, wherever they exist, will compel government delegations, say, at the UNFCCC, to listen to the demands of transnational forest rights movements. Failing that international indigenous rights groups can work with their developing country partners to call for domestic protests, and in some cases, for punishing the ruling party at the ballot box (see Fox 2007). Such linkages will also lend strength to the decidedly less powerful and less resourceful smaller forest rights movements and intercommunity associations while keeping national and international groups informed about local efforts (Wollenberg et al. 2006; Larson et al. 2013).

In the concluding section, we summarize the key arguments, discuss some of the challenges remaining, and point to a research agenda that might contribute to the development of innovative institutional solutions in the short to medium term.

Discussion and Conclusion

Considering the long history of state control (and exploitation) of forests, the innovative designing of REDD+ architecture remains a major challenge. Building on recent contributions and concerns of REDD+ literature (Hayes and Persha 2010; Thompson, Baruah, and Carr 2011; Larson et al. 2013; Sunderlin et al. 2013), we have argued for developing operational linkages across subnational, national, and international agencies. In parallel to Poteete's (2012) work, we have also argued for focusing separately on institutional and political dimensions of REDD+ governance. To this end, we employed the concept of nested enterprises proposed by Elinor Ostrom (1990), and supplemented it with a discussion of the political dimensions of cross-scale linkages, that is, accountability and legitimacy.

The fundamental goal of REDD+ is to create appropriate incentives for state and nonstate actors in positions to contribute to forest conservation outcomes. We include nonstate actors among the key REDD+ actors because decades of international environmental conservation efforts have shown that governments alone cannot ensure conservation even if they were genuinely committed to it (Ostrom 2010). Moreover, given the proper incentives, while governments can institutionalize well-designed policy instruments, good policies do not necessarily translate to the desired results on the ground. Therefore, REDD+ proponents cannot leave the task of ensuring effective forest conservation to the discretion of national-level governments. REDD+ must be designed to *systematically and formally* link national policy reforms with the organization and execution of subnational (regional and local) forest conservation efforts led by forest users.

The early proponents of nested REDD+ argued that successful conservation actions at subnational level would go unrewarded because of the failures elsewhere in a country (Pedroni et al. 2009). Such problems are likely to be exacerbated if national architecture subsumes the interim nested REDD+ measures proposed currently. The interim nature of nested REDD+ arrangements also creates perverse incentives for public agencies to bide time without investing in building subnational capacities. Therefore, we argue that a nested REDD+ should be conceived as an enduring institutional arrangement, not a short-term precursor to nationalization. Mandating domestically created, enduring nested REDD+ architecture will offer additional leverage to nonstate actors pushing for forest policy reforms within a country.

By citing examples from ongoing policy debates and relevant empirical material, we showed how national, regional, and local initiatives could be formally interlinked, allowing for institutional and political synergies in REDD+ governance. We argued that subnational actors should have a more prominent, formally recognized role, even in the face of reluctance or opposition by national governments (see Sandbrook et al. 2010; Larson 2011). Even so, instead of proposing a blueprint for the nested REDD+ architecture, we have proposed broader principles for facilitating the effective participation of subnational actors and agencies. In addition, we demonstrated the potential gains to be had from tapping into institutional and political energies of intercommunity forestry associations and forest rights movements representing actively mobilized forest user groups.

Notwithstanding that the approach for nested REDD+ we outline in this chapter builds on empirical research and theories of common-pool resource management, there are limitations to our approach. The specifics of cross-scale linkages will have to be worked through deliberations between forest users, government agencies, and nongovernment groups in each specific national context (Forsyth 2009; Sikor et al. 2010). Adopting such a deliberative approach is likely to increase the up-front transaction costs (Forsyth 2009). However, these transaction costs will contribute to significant savings over the costs of organizing public consultations, forest monitoring, and forest carbon auditing. More important, as Hajek et al. (2011, 201) argue, REDD+ planners need to "encourage innovation and flexibility, and facilitate research into the governance and transnational systemic nature of the emerging value chain." Investments in building cross-scale linkages will also contribute significantly to the success of broader forest governance reforms, which in turn will help sustain the gains anticipated under REDD+.

In effect, a carefully designed and enforced nested REDD+ architecture offers the best option for dealing with an inherent policy paradox that emerges from debates over REDD+: A national architecture, while necessary for avoiding leakages and facilitating economies of scale in REDD+ transactions, also creates the possibility that national governments will behave in a predatory fashion (Sandbrook et al. 2010; Larson et al. 2013). The nested REDD+ architecture we propose fosters systemic interdependencies aimed at facilitating two types of accountability relations: downward (to the forest users) and upward (to the international supporters of REDD+ project). National and subnational governments play a number of important roles: coordinating domestic policy and programs, establishing national-level MRVs, and overseeing equitable benefit-sharing arrangements that are also transparent.

Nevertheless, because of the past history of repeated policy failures and a lack of accountability on the part of governments and government agencies, we argue for stronger and binding accountability mechanisms. In addition to the international mechanisms for safeguards compliance, we have shown that REDD+ proponents would benefit from engaging with intercommunity associations and forest rights movements that are often the main sources of endogenous demands for compliance and accountability.

Such a conceptualization of nested REDD+ architecture as a hybrid institutional and political medium offers a concrete policy approach for achieving the secondary goal of utilizing REDD+ as an opportunity for democratization of forest governance (Sikor et al. 2010; Larson 2011). Importantly, the nested REDD+ architecture we propose will ensure that the goal of democratizing forest governance is not left solely to the discretion of national governments. In particular, we argue that enduring nested governance will motivate key actors active at different levels to take ownership of the process, ensure REDD+'s legitimacy, and will help maintain political pressure against potential recentralization of forest governance by national governments.

Acknowledgments

We would like to thank Kerry Krutilla, Shanna Dietz, Elinor Ostrom, Edward Webb, Achim Schlüter, and the reviewers for their helpful comments on earlier drafts. Earlier versions of this chapter were presented at the fifth biennial conference of the Indian Society for Ecological Economics at Ahmedabad, India, in January 2009 and the 13th Biennial Conference of the International Association for the Study of the Commons (IASC) at Hyderabad, India, in January 2011, where it was presented as part of the IFRI-CIFOR panel on REDD+. Usual disclaimers apply.

Notes

This chapter was originally published in the *International Journal of the Commons* 8(2) (August 2014): 554–75.

1. http://www.un-redd.org/FAQs/tabid/586/Default.aspx. Emphasis in original.
2. http://www.v-c-s.org/JNRI.
3. http://www.thejakartapost.com/news/2010/02/16/palm-estate-forest-says-ministry.html.
4. http://www.abc.net.au/site-archive/rural/news/content/200804/s2214030.htm.
5. http://fecofun.org.np/index.php.

References

Agrawal, Arun. 2001. "Common Property Institutions and Sustainable Governance of Resources." *World Development* 29(10): 1649–72.

Agrawal, Arun, and Arild Angelsen. 2009. "Using Community Forest Management to Achieve REDD+ Goals." In *Realising REDD+: National Strategy and Policy Options*, edited by Arild Angelsen, M. Brockhaus, M. Kanninen, E. Sills, W. D. Sunderlin, and S. Wertz-Kanounnikoff, 201–12. Bogor, Indonesia: Center for International Forestry Research (CIFOR).

Agrawal, Arun, Daniel Nepstad, and Ashwini Chhatre. 2011. "Reducing Emissions from Deforestation and Forest Degradation." *Annual Review of Environment and Resources* 36(1): 373–96.

Agrawal, Arun, and Elinor Ostrom. 2001. "Collective Action, Property Rights, and Decentralization in Resource Use in India and Nepal." *Politics and Society* 29(4): 485–514.

Angelsen, Arild, M. Brockhaus, M. Kanninen, E. Sills, W. D. Sunderlin, and S. Wertz-Kanounnikoff. 2009. *Realising REDD+: National Strategy and Policy Options*. Bogor, Indonesia: Center for International Forestry Research (CIFOR).

Angelsen, Arild, and Desmond McNeill. 2012. "The Evolution of REDD+." In *Analysing REDD+: Challenges and Choices*, edited by Arild Angelsen, M. Brockhaus, W. D. Sunderlin, and L. V. Verchot, 31–50. Bogor, Indonesia: Center for International Forestry Research (CIFOR).

Angelsen, Arild, Charlotte Streck, Leo Peskett, Jessica Brown, and Cecilia Luttrell. 2008. "What is the Right Scale for REDD?" In *Moving Ahead with REDD: Issues, Options and Implications*, edited by Arild Angelsen, M. Brockhaus, M. Kanninen, E. Sills, W. Sunderlin, and S. Wertz-Kanounnikoff, 31–40. Bogor, Indonesia: Center for International Forestry Research (CIFOR).

Asare, Rebecca A., Andrew Kyei, and John J. Mason. 2013. "The Community Resource Management Area Mechanism: A Strategy to Manage African Forest Resources for REDD+." *Philosophical Transactions of the Royal Society B: Biological Sciences* 368: 1–9.

Auer, Matthew. 2007. "More Aid, Better Institutions, or Both?" *Sustainability Science* 2: 179–87.

Benvenisti, Eyal. 2008. "Reclaiming Democracy: The Strategic Uses of Foreign and International Law by National Courts." *American Journal of International Law* 102(2): 241–74.

Beymer-Farris, Betsy A., and Thomas J. Bassett. 2012. "The REDD Menace: Resurgent Protectionism in Tanzania's Mangrove Forests." *Global Environmental Change* 22(2): 332–41.

Bray, David Barton. 2013. "When the State Supplies the Commons: Origins, Changes, and Design of Mexico's Common Property Regime." *Journal of Latin American Geography* 12: 33–55.

Brysk, Alison. 2000. "Democratizing Civil Society in Latin America." *Journal of Democracy* 11: 151–65.

Cacho, O. J., G. R. Marshall, and M. Milne. 2005. "Transaction and Abatement Costs of Carbon-Sink Projects in Developing Countries." *Environment and Development Economics* 10(5): 597–614.

Chagas, Thiago, Charlotte Streck, Robert O'Sullivan, Jacob Olander, and Joerg Seifert-Granzin. 2011. *Nested Approaches to REDD+: An Overview of Issues and Options*. Washington, DC: Forest Trends and Climate Focus.

Chao, Sophie. 2012. *Forest Peoples: Numbers across the World*. Moreton-in-Marsh, UK: Forest Peoples Programme.

Chhatre, Ashwini, Shikha Lakhanpal, Anne M. Larson, Fred Nelson, Hemant Ojha, and Jagdeesh Rao. 2012. "Social Safeguards and Co-Benefits in REDD+: A Review of the Adjacent Possible." *Current Opinion in Environmental Sustainability* 4: 654–60.

Coleman, Eric. 2009. "Institutional Factors Affecting Biophysical Outcomes in Forest Management." *Journal of Policy Analysis and Management* 28(1): 122–46.

Colfer, Carol J. Pierce. 2011. "Marginalized Forest Peoples' Perceptions of the Legitimacy of Governance: An Exploration." *World Development* 39(12): 2147–64.

Cronkleton, Peter, David Barton Bray, and Gabriel Medina. 2011. "Community Forest Management and the Emergence of Multi-Scale Governance Institutions: Lessons for REDD+ Development from Mexico, Brazil and Bolivia." *Forests* 2(2): 451–73.

Downton, Mary W. 1995. "Measuring Tropical Deforestation: Development of the Methods." *Environmental Conservation* 22: 229–40.

García-López, Gustavo A. 2013. "Scaling Up from the Grassroots and the Top Down: The Impacts of Multi-Level Governance on Community Forestry in Durango, Mexico." *International Journal of the Commons* 7(2): 406–32.

Gibson, Clark C., John T. Williams, and Elinor Ostrom. 2005. "Local Enforcement and Better Forests." *World Development* 33: 273–84.

Fabricant, Nicole. 2013. "Good Living for Whom? Bolivia's Climate Justice Movement and the Limitations of Indigenous Cosmovisions." *Latin American and Caribbean Ethnic Studies* 8: 159–78.

Forsyth, T. 2009. "Multilevel, Multiactor Governance in REDD." In *Realising REDD+: National Strategy and Policy Options*, edited by Arild Angelsen, M. Brockhaus, M. Kanninen, E. Sills, W. Sunderlin, and S. Wertz-Kanounnikoff, 113–22. Bogor, Indonesia: Center for International Forestry Research (CIFOR).

Fox, Jonathan. 2007. *Accountability Politics: Power and Voice in Rural Mexico*. Oxford Studies in Democratization. New York: Oxford University Press.

Hajek, Frank, Marc J. Ventresca, Joel Scriven, and Augusto Castro. 2011. "Regime-Building for REDD+: Evidence from a Cluster of Local Initiatives in Southeastern Peru." *Environmental Science & Policy* 14(2): 201–15.

Hayes, Tanya, and Lauren Persha. 2010. "Nesting Local Forestry Initiatives: Revisiting Community Forest Management in a REDD+ World." *Forest Policy and Economics* 12(8): 545–53.

Herold, Martin, and Margaret Skutsch. 2011. "Monitoring, Reporting and Verification for National REDD+ Programmes: Two Proposals." *Environmental Research Letters* 6(1): 1–10.

Igoe, Jim, and Beth Croucher. 2007. "Conservation, Commerce, and Communities: The Story of Community-Based Wildlife Management Areas in Tanzania's Northern Tourist Circuit." *Conservation and Society* 5: 534.

Kaimowitz, D. 2000. "Forestry Assistance and Tropical Deforestation: Why the Public Doesn't Get What It Pays For." *International Forestry Review* 2: 225–31.

Kashwan, Prakash. 2011. *Democracy in the Woods: The Politics of Institutional Change in India's Forest Areas*. PhD diss., Indiana University.

Khatri, D. B., N. S. Paudel, R. Bista, and K. Bhandari. 2013. "REDD+ Financing: What Can We Learn from the Piloting of Forest Carbon Trust Fund in Nepal?" In *Secondary REDD+ Financing: What Can We Learn from the Piloting of Forest Carbon Trust Fund in Nepal?* Kathmandu: ForestAction Nepal.

Klooster, Daniel, and Omar Masera. 2000. "Community Forest Management in Mexico: Carbon Mitigation and Biodiversity Conservation through Rural Development." *Global Environmental Change* 10: 259–72.

Larson, Anne M. 2011. "Forest Tenure Reform in the Age of Climate Change: Lessons for REDD+." *Global Environmental Change* 21(2): 540–49.

Larson, Anne M., Maria Brockhaus, William Sunderlin, Amy Duchelle, Andrea Babon, Therese Dokken, Thu Thuy Pham, I. A. P. Resosudarmo, Galia Selaya, Abdon Awono, and Thu-Ba Huynh. 2013. "Land Tenure and REDD+: The Good, the Bad and the Ugly." *Global Environmental Change* 23: 678–89.

Lyster, Rosemary. 2011. "REDD+, Transparency, Participation and Resource Rights: The Role of Law." *Environmental Science & Policy* 14(2): 118–26.

Marshall, Graham. 2008. "Nesting, Subsidiarity, and Community-Based Environmental Governance beyond the Local Scale." *International Journal of the Commons* 2(1): 75–97.
Mustalahti, I., A. Bolin, E. Boyd, and J. Paavola. 2012. "Can REDD+ Reconcile Local Priorities and Needs with Global Mitigation Benefits? Lessons from Angai Forest, Tanzania." *Ecology and Society* 17(1): 16.
Mwangi, Esther, and Andrew Wardell. 2012. "Multi-Level Governance of Forest Resources (Editorial to the Special Feature)." *International Journal of the Commons* 6(2): 79–103.
Nagendra, Harini. 2007. "Thomas K. Rudel, Tropical Forests—Regional Paths of Destruction and Regeneration in the Late Twentieth Century." *Landscape Ecology* 22(7): 1109–11.
Ojha, H. 2009. "Civic Engagement and Deliberative Governance: The Case of Community Forest Users' Federation, Nepal." *Studies in Nepali History and Society* 14(2): 303–34.
Osborne, Tracey Muttoo. 2011. "Carbon Forestry and Agrarian Change: Access and Land Control in a Mexican Rainforest." *The Journal of Peasant Studies* 38: 859–83.
Ostrom, Elinor. 1990. *Governing the Commons: The Evolution of Institutions for Collective Action*. New York: Cambridge University Press.
———. 2010. "Polycentric Systems for Coping with Collective Action and Global Environmental Change." *Global Environmental Change* 20(4): 550–57.
Pedroni, Lucio, Michael Dutschke, Charlotte Streck, and Manuel Estrada Porrua. 2009. "Creating Incentives for Avoiding Further Deforestation: The Nested Approach." *Climate Policy* 9(2): 207–20.
Petkova, Elena, Anne Larson, and Pablo Pacheco. 2010. "Forest Governance, Decentralization and REDD+ in Latin America." *Forests* 1: 250–54.
Poteete, Amy R. 2012. "Levels, Scales, Linkages, and Other 'Multiples' Affecting Natural Resources." *International Journal of the Commons* 6(2): 134–50.
Ribot, Jesse C., Arun Agrawal, and Anne M. Larson. 2006. "Recentralizing While Decentralizing: How National Governments Reappropriate Forest Resources." *World Development* 34(11): 1864–86.
Ribot, J. C., A. Chhatre, and T. Lankina. 2008. "Institutional Choice and Recognition in the Formation and Consolidation of Local Democracy." *Conservation & Society* 6: 1–11.
RRI (Rights and Resources Initiative). 2012. *What Rights? A Comparative Analysis of Developing Countries' National Legislation on Community and Indigenous Peoples' Forest Tenure Rights*. Washington, DC: RRI.
Sandbrook, C., F. Nelson, W. M. Adams, and A. Agrawal. 2010. "Carbon, Forests and the REDD Paradox." *Oryx* 44(3): 330–34.
Schroeder, Heike. 2010. "Agency in International Climate Negotiations: The Case of Indigenous Peoples and Avoided Deforestation." *International Environmental Agreements: Politics, Law and Economics* 10: 317–32.

Seymour, F. 2013. "REDD Reckoning: A Review of Research on a Rapidly Moving Target." In *Plant Sciences Reviews 2012*, edited by David Hemming, 147–60. Boston, MA: Cabi.

Sikor, Thomas, and Johannes Stahl. 2011. *Forests and People: Property, Governance, and Human Rights*. New York: Routledge.

Sikor, Thomas, Johannes Stahl, Thomas Enters, Jesse C. Ribot, Neera Singh, William Sunderlin, and Lini Wollenberg. 2010. "REDD-plus, Forest People's Rights and Nested Climate Governance." *Global Environmental Change* 20(3): 423–25.

Skutsch, Margaret M., and Libasse Ba. 2010. "Crediting Carbon in Dry Forests: The Potential for Community Forest Management in West Africa." *Forest Policy and Economics* 12(4): 264–70.

Skutsch, Margaret M., Michael K. McCall, Bhaskar Karky, E. Zahabu, and Graciela Peters-Guarin. 2009. *Case Studies on Measuring and Assessing Forest Degradation: Community Measurement of Carbon Stock Change for REDD.* Forest Resources Assessment Working Paper 156. Rome: Food and Agriculture Organization of the United Nations (FAO).

Skutsch, Margaret M., and Michael K. McCall. 2010. "Reassessing REDD: Governance, Markets and the Hype Cycle." *Climatic Change* 100(3): 395–402.

Sonwa, Denis, and Peter Minang. 2009. "REDD+ Realities in Cameroon." In *Realising REDD+: National Strategy and Policy Options*, edited by Arild Angelsen, M. Brockhaus, M. Kanninen, E. Sills, W. D. Sunderlin, and S. Wertz-Kanounnikoff, 36–37. Bogor, Indonesia: Center for International Forestry Research (CIFOR).

Sunderlin, William, Anne Larson, Amy Duchelle, Ida Aju Pradnja Resosudarmo, Thu Ba Huynh, Abdon Awono, and Therese Dokken. 2013. "How Are REDD+ Proponents Addressing Tenure Problems? Evidence from Brazil, Cameroon, Tanzania, Indonesia, and Vietnam." *World Development* 55: 37–52.

Sunderlin, William, and Erin O. Sills. 2012. "REDD+ Projects as a Hybrid of Old and New Forest Conservation Approaches." In *Analysing REDD+: Challenges and Choices*, edited by Arild Angelsen, M. Brockhaus, W. D. Sunderlin, and L. V. Verchot, 31–50. Bogor, Indonesia: Center for International Forestry Research (CIFOR).

Tacconi, Luca. 2007. "Decentralization, Forests and Livelihoods: Theory and Narrative." *Global Environmental Change* 17(3–4): 338–48.

Thompson, Mary C., Manali Baruah, and Edward R. Carr. 2011. "Seeing REDD+ as a Project of Environmental Governance." *Environmental Science and Policy* 14: 100–10.

UNDP. 2009. *India: SLEM/CPP—Sustainable Land Management in Shifting Cultivation Areas of Nagaland for Ecological and Livelihood Security*. New York: United Nations Development Programme.

UNFCCC. 2011. "Decision 1/CP.16. The Cancun Agreements: Outcome of the Work of the Ad Hoc Working Group on Long-Term Cooperative Action

under the Convention." Edited by Conference of Parties. Cancun: United Nations Framework Convention on Climate Change.
Wollenberg, E., M. Colchester, G. Mbugua, and T. Griffiths. 2006. "Linking Social Movements: How International Networks Can Better Support Community Action about Forests." *International Forestry Review* 8(2): 265–72.
Wollenberg, Eva, Ramses Iwan, Godwin Limberg, and Moira Moeliono. 2008. "Locating Social Choice in Forest Co-Management and Local Governance: The Politics of Public Decision Making and Interests." In *Public and Private in Natural Resource Governance: A False Dichotomy*, edited by Sikor Thomas, 27–44. New York: Earthscan.
Wunder, Sven. 2007. "The Efficiency of Payments for Environmental Services in Tropical Conservation." *Conservation Biology* 21(1): 48–58.
———. 2010. "Forest Decentralization for REDD? A Response to Sandbrook et al." *Oryx* 44(03): 335–37.

PART IV

Integrating Multiple Actors, Interests, and Perspectives

11

Analysing Decentralised Natural Resource Governance: Proposition for a "Politicised" Institutional Analysis and Development Framework

Floriane Clement

Natural resource policies in developing countries have often failed to deliver on promises. In Africa, Asia, and Latin America, decentralised forest management policies, which have replaced previously criticised top-down approaches, have rarely transferred significant financial and authority power to local governments (Ribot 2003; Ribot, Agrawal, and Larson 2006; Xu and Ribot 2004) and have mostly remained biased against rural communities (Larson and Ribot 2007). In the irrigation water sector, the institutional reforms transferring water management from bureaucracies to water user associations have also showed significant shortcomings. Whereas large-scale public irrigation systems managed by local government agencies had not delivered on expectations of increased performance and cost efficiency (Lam 1998), the decentralisation of water management has had mixed results across the world regarding irrigation performance, equity, and impacts on agricultural productivity and farm income (Garces-Restrepo, Vermillion, and Muñoz 2007; Meinzen-Dick 2007).

A major challenge that is currently faced by policymakers and researchers is to avoid the fallacy of devising new panaceas or blueprint approaches (Meinzen-Dick 2007; Ostrom, Janssen, and Anderies 2007). Instead, we need to reform or draft new institutions that are geographically and contextually grounded. Localised analyses of policy failures—and successes—are determinant to guide such an endeavour, particularly insofar as they contribute to identify the factors and unveil the processes contributing to the gaps between policy intentions and outcomes. However, whereas decentralisation reforms have revived the relevance of conducting local analyses of commons management, studies examining the failures of decentralisation policies have underlined the role of factors located outside communities in policy outcomes (Andersson and Ostrom 2008; Andersson, Gibson, and Lehoucq 2006; Ribot, Agrawal, and Larson 2006). Analyses of decentralised natural resource policies need to go beyond the understanding of how the decisions of local communities[1] are affected by centrally designed policies. Exploring the gaps between rhetoric and actual outcomes requires considering the multiple governance tiers through which the meaning and implementation of policies are negotiated and transformed, from the policy design stage until the arena where final resource users make decisions.

Identifying the roots for policy discrepancies thus necessitates a multi-level approach that can link the decisions of actors across institutional levels. In a recent article published in this journal, Andersson and Ostrom (2008) proposed to apply theories of polycentricity to analyse the multi-level dynamics of decentralised natural resource governance. Animated by a similar concern to improve studies linking national policies with the decisions of local natural resource users, I posit a methodological development of the Institutional Analysis and Development (IAD) framework, one of the most commonly used frameworks for the study of the commons (Kiser and Ostrom 1982; Ostrom 1999; Ostrom, Gardner, and Walker 1994). The IAD framework precisely offers a multi-level structure, linking the operational level where actors make decisions on natural resource management (NRM) to the collective-choice and constitutional levels, where actors decide on the rules for decision making. Yet most commons literature has been restricted to the study of collective action among local communities without expanding the framework to higher government and institutional levels. This limitation is rooted in a number of caveats, which are discussed in the following sections. Nevertheless, the framework still holds great promises for the analysis of decentralised NRM, because it offers a robust analytical frame that facilitates comparative studies. The development I propose in this chapter aims at "politicising" the framework, that is, adding to its ability to analyse natural resource policy processes, including the assessment of policy impacts and policy change, across multiple governance levels. It is hoped that the modifications to the framework will support more accurate analyses of the success and failure of decentralised natural resource policies, guide the design of sound policy recommendations, and ultimately contribute to improved policies.

A Common Ground for Commons Studies?

With the theme "Governing shared resources: connecting local experience to global challenges," the 2008 biannual conference of the International Association for the Study of the Commons (IASC) clearly emphasised multi-scalar governance as a core issue. However, among the 488 papers presented, only 108 addressed multiple governance levels.[2] Despite recent attempts to locate commons in a multi-level world,[3] most common property and collective-action literature has had a limited focus on how local communities organise to manage natural resources—with often little or superficial consideration of the social and political context in which they operate. This body of knowledge has advanced our understanding of the conditions of success and failure of collective action to manage land, water, forest, or fisheries within various combinations of rules, biophysical conditions, and cultural and social attributes (e.g., Acheson 2006; Cardenas, Stranlund, and Willis 2000; National Research Council 2002; Gibson, McKean, and Ostrom 2000; Lam 1998; Leach, Mearns, and Scoones 1999; Ostrom 1990; Sproule-Jones 1999). Yet most commons scholars have little acknowledged how the historical context and politico-economic structure affect local rules-in-use and local people's decisions on NRM. Other bodies of knowledge have paid more attention to the linkages between local outcomes and the decisions of stakeholders located at higher governance levels. Notably, the environmental entitlements scholarship developed by Leach, Mearns, and Scoones' (1999) studies on the decentralisation of NRM and political ecology—political ecology can be defined as "empirical, research-based explorations to explain linkages in the condition and change of social/environmental systems,[4] with explicit consideration of relations of power" (Robbins 2004, 12)—have emphasised the role of the macro politico-economic context and micro power distribution at multiple governance levels. However, these approaches (labelled thereafter "power-centred approaches") have in turn been criticised for their overlook of how biophysical characteristics might affect society-environment interaction and policy outcomes (Vayda and Walters 1999). Furthermore, some scholars (e.g., Schubert 2005; Torras 2005) have deplored the methodological eclecticism characterising political ecology and the lack of a robust theoretical framework in this field, which has someway reinforced a particular weakness of this body of literature: its difficulty at proposing policy recommendations in a structured and comprehensive form to decision makers (weakness that has been acknowledged by Robbins 2004; Walker 2006).

The objective of this chapter is to enrich the IAD framework with concepts and theories borrowed from these bodies of knowledge in order to make it more suitable to the analysis of decentralised natural resource policies at multiple governance and government levels. The discussion extends recent essays aiming at conciliating institutions with discourses and context in the field of NRM (Armitage 2008; McCay 2002; Schmidt 2010). The aim is not to propose a supra-theory neatly covering theoretical divergences but to develop a pertinent frame to guide enquiry and policy analysis, which can grasp the complexity of the reality, while at the same time allow general lessons to be drawn. The next sections discuss how the proposed developments can advance our understanding of natural resource governance at multiple levels, first theoretically, then with an illustration of the application of the framework to the study of state afforestation policies in Northern Vietnam. How such an approach supports the design of well-grounded policy recommendations is finally debated.

Sketching a Common Theoretical Ground

The IAD Framework

The IAD framework is one of the most distinguished and tested frameworks in the field of policy sciences (Carlsson 2000; Gibson et al. 2005; Imperial 1999; Rudd 2004). It has notably been used as a basis for developing a theory of common-pool resource management and has been supported in this field by a strong record of empirical research and theoretical development (e.g., Lam 1998; Ostrom, Gardner, and Walker 1994; Thomson 1992; Thomson and Schoonmaker Freudenberger 1997).[5]

The focal level of analysis (Figure 11.1) consists of an action arena, composed of actors located within action situations and affected by a set of external variables. Actors' interaction within action situations leads to outcomes, which feed back into the external variables and the action arena.

The external variables are the biophysical conditions (i.e., the physical state of the environment where actors evolve), the attributes of the community, and the rules-in-use. How the biophysical conditions affect the action arena depends on several aspects, particularly on the subtractability and exclusion of the resources. Other attributes of the resources might greatly affect their use, for example, their size, abundance, uncertainty (Wilson 2002), resilience, or vulnerability (Ostrom 2007). The nature of the resources[6] considered is an essential factor for the design of

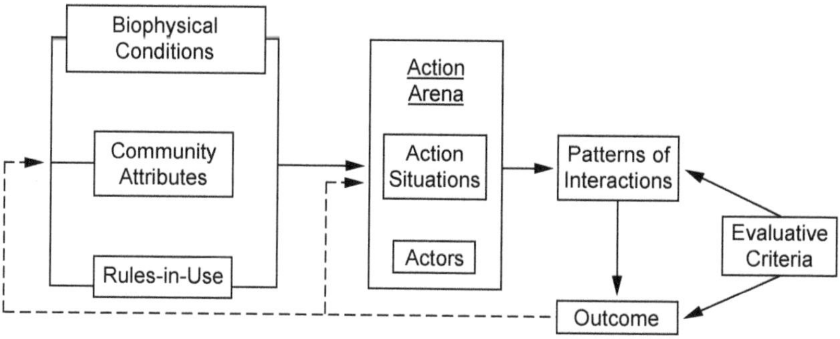

Figure 11.1. The focal level of analysis of the IAD framework.

Source: Adapted from Ostrom, Gardner, and Walker (1994, 37).

appropriate institutional arrangements defining resource access and use (Ostrom, Gardner, and Walker 1994). The attributes of the community that have proved to matter for NRM include the shared values—or "culture" of the community (Cleaver 2000; Klooster 2000; Mosse 1997), level of common understanding or trust within the community, its size (Agrawal and Goyal 2001; Olson 1965), and heterogeneity (Hong and Page 2004). Lastly, the rules-in-use are defined as the "shared understandings that refer to enforced prescriptions about what actions (or states of the world) are required, prohibited, or permitted" (Ostrom 1999, 50). They refer to both formal and informal prescriptions, for example, legal documents issued by central governments, informal rules allowing lower governance tiers to interpret these documents with relative freedom, and collective rules orally shared within a community.

The three variables of the IAD framework represent nature, society, and the rules that govern nature-society interaction. On the one hand, the broadness of these three categories makes the framework compatible with a wide range of theories and sufficiently flexible to adapt to multiple biophysical, social, and cultural contexts. On the other hand, the framework has gained popularity for "its aptness for micro-scale analysis and operational clarity" (Auer 2006, 216). Its decomposability allows the analyst to study a complex phenomenon by breaking it down into several components and handling it as imbrications of systems within larger systems (Ostrom 2005). The long-term refinement of the framework has led to define pertinent categories for the analysis of human decisions in collective actions and of institutional performance under a wide variety of settings. For instance, the action situation is decomposable into the types of actions that actors are allowed to make, which actors can participate, what information and control do they have over influencing the outcomes, and what are the costs and benefits assigned to actions and resulting outcomes. Similarly, the rules-in-use can be decomposed into seven categories (position rules, boundary rules, choice rules, aggregation rules, information rules, payoff rules, and scope rules), defined according to that element of the action situation they affect (Figure 11.2). The framework thus offers a solid theoretical frame to guide the analysis of complex social phenomena.

Among other assets, the framework takes into account the co-action of the external variables and the action arena. For instance, the suitability of a set of rules-in-use for an action arena depends on the ecosystem considered (biophysical conditions) and the characteristics of the community that manages the ecosystem (Ostrom 2005, 247–54). The IAD framework is thus sensitive to local conditions and does not make any claim on the universal superiority of a type or set of rules-in-use (e.g., decentralisation) over another. Lastly, a key feature is its multi-layered structure, which extends from the operational level, where decisions directly affect resource access and use, to the collective-choice level, where the rules that govern resource access and use are designed, to the constitutional level, where decisions affect the rules that govern how decisions are taken at the collective-choice level (Figure 11.3).

It facilitates the analysis of the linkages between local resource users' decisions and policy change. Yet the application of the framework to the study of NRM has often been restricted to the study of operational rules designed by the communities managing natural resources with little consideration of policy decisions taken at higher governance and government levels[7] (exceptions include Agrawal and Ostrom 2001; Ghate 2003; Gibson et al. 2005; Lam 1998; Sproule-Jones 1999). I discuss in the following subsections several major limitations of the framework regarding its use for policy analysis across government levels and consider how the framework could benefit from other bodies of knowledge.

Power and Institutions

The IAD framework links the decisions of actors located at multiple governance levels through the nested set of operational, collective-choice, and constitutional rules (Figure 11.3). However, a major limitation to its application across governance and government levels is an inadequate consideration of the role of power and interests in the crafting of institutions

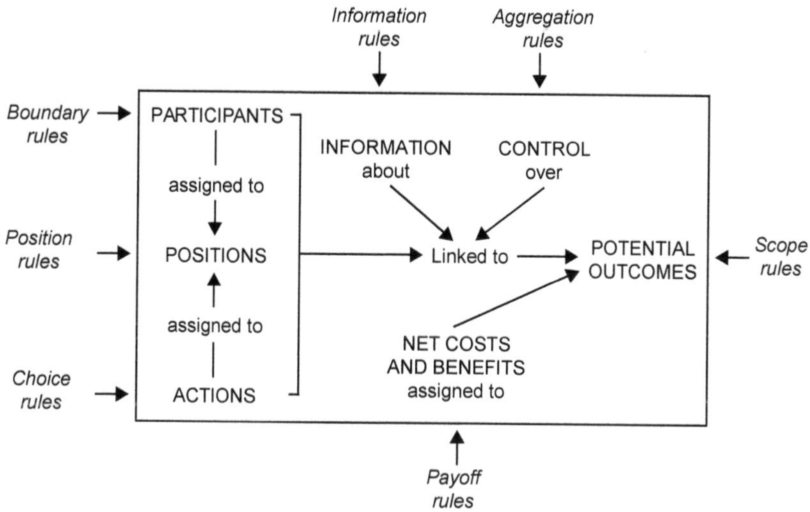

Figure 11.2. The internal structure of the action situation related to rules in the IAD framework.

Source: Ostrom (2005, 189).

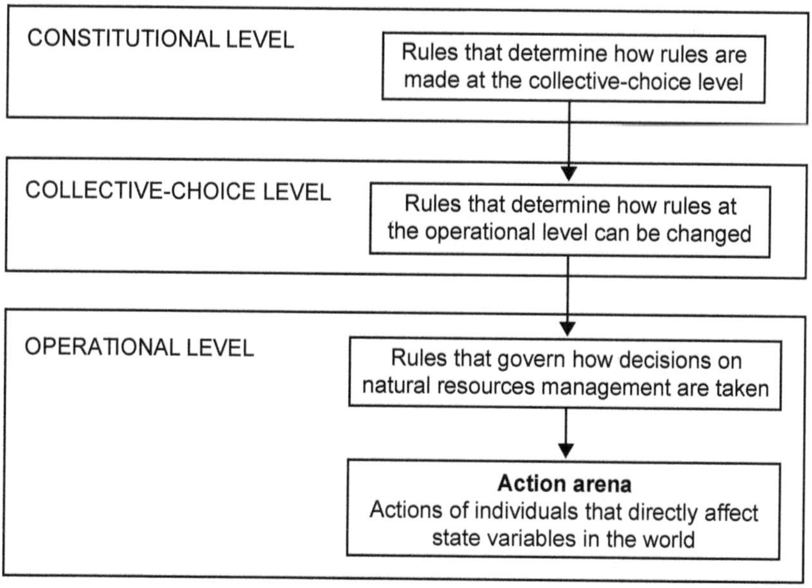

Figure 11.3. The three levels of analysis in the IAD framework.

Source: Based on Ostrom (1999, 60).

(Agrawal and Ostrom 2001; Sikor 2006). Institutions do not only emerge from rational individual decisions led by a set of incentives. They are also significantly shaped by power distribution at the collective-choice and at the constitutional levels (Ribot 2006). By institutions, I refer in this chapter to Ostrom's definition (2005, 3): "the prescriptions that humans use to organize all forms of repetitive and structured interactions including those within families, neighborhoods, markets, firms, sports leagues, churches, private associations, and governments at all scales." It includes all kinds of formal and informal prescriptions stemming from, for example, legal documents issued by central governments, implicit norms governing policy implementation, or collective rules-in-use orally shared within a community. The definition of power used in this chapter goes beyond the capacity of an agent to influence a target (French and Raven 1959). It encompasses the third dimension of power introduced by Lukes (2005): power manifests itself just by being, it shapes values,[8] norms, and preferences by its mere existence. It is close to the form of power imagined by Foucault (1975), who argues that power is not the instrument of a dominant State, but rather is situated in the daily enforcement of social and political practices. It is this "third view" of power that I am most interested in to capture in the revised framework, the micro forms of power that are made, transformed, or sustained by institutions. In this sense, institutions and power are closely interrelated. On the one hand, institutions directly affect power distribution and practices. For Searle, it is actually a major purpose of institutional design: "the essential role of human institutions and the purpose of having institutions is not to constrain people as such, but, rather, to create new sorts of power relationships" (Searle 2005, 10). On the other hand, power distribution within the group of actors who act at the collective-choice and constitutional levels directly impacts on the design of institutions and rules implementation at lower governance levels.

A group of scholars who have specifically evaluated the success of decentralisation policies in the field of NRM have drawn on new institutionalism in the way they have addressed institutional design and looked at the role of institutions in outcomes and in the behaviour of policymakers (e.g., Andersson, Gibson, and Lehoucq 2006). However, they have demarcated themselves from institutional analysts by placing power—rather than institutions—at the core of their analysis. They have namely explored actors' attitudes and behaviour within formal and informal micro-structures and practices of power, power networks, and distribution (e.g., Dressler, Kull, and Meredith 2006; Larson 2003; Ribot 2003; Shackleton et al. 2002; Wardell and Lund 2006). An important lesson is that the devolution of legal rights is not sufficient per se to achieve democratic decentralisation (Ribot 2003; Ribot, Agrawal, and Larson 2006). In particular, local structural and relational mechanisms of access are critical for communities to actually derive benefits from these rights (Ribot and Peluso 2003). Their perspective has offered an insightful focus on the gap between legal rules and actual practices and the power mechanisms that come into play. Political ecologists have also paid considerable attention to power across government levels, being primarily concerned with the power that one party exerts to control the environment of another party (Bryant and Bailey 1997). Noticeably, together with entitlement scholars, they have stressed local power struggles over natural resources within communities and between communities and state actors (e.g., Leach, Mearns, and Scoones 1999; Nygren 2000; Post and Snel 2003; Springate-Baginski and Blaikie 2007b).

It is worth noticing that a major divide between institutional analysis and power-centred approaches actually lies in the definition of the term "institution." In the latter, the meaning of "institution" has often been restricted to formal organisations[9] or pieces of legislation (cf. in Batterbury 2006; Ribot, Agrawal, and Larson 2006) whereas the term "institutional arrangements" refers to the legal rules-in-use. Some scholars (Leach, Mearns, and Scoones 1999; Nunan 2006) have argued that "indirect" approaches, for example, "empowerment, creating networks of structures for lake management, ensuring accountability, devolving rule-making powers, establishing poverty-focused access rights, managing conflict" (Nunan 2006, 1317), are preferable to changing institutions. According to the definition of institution used by Ostrom (2005) and adopted in this chapter, these "indirect" approaches are actually changing institutions, either at the collective-choice level (e.g., changing the boundary rule defining who has access to natural resources by establishing poverty-focused access rights) or at the constitutional level (e.g., devolving rule-making power). Similarly, many scholars from the decentralisation literature have emphasised the importance of accountability and representation over the role of institutions to reach efficient and equitable political outcomes (Agrawal and Ribot 2000; Larson 2003; Ribot, Agrawal, and Larson 2006). In the IAD framework, accountability stands as a core evaluation criterion of institutional performance, which directly results from institutional design.

To sum up, the nature and performance of institutions have been recognised as critical factors in policy outcomes by both commons and power-centred bodies of scholarships (given the broad definition of institution presently adopted). But an important distinction lies in the means used to reach this conclusion. Although commons scholars have focused their efforts on identifying and developing principles for institutional design (cf. Baland and Platteau 1996; McKean 2000; Ostrom 1990; Snidal 1995), power-centred analysts have stressed power struggles and inequities as both a determinant and a result of institutional performance. Despite a fundamentally different perspective, the two approaches are necessary and can be used in a complementary manner. On the one hand, it is important to better understand which rules and criteria matter for institutions to be efficient, equitable, and acceptable. On the other hand, this understanding will be naïve and incomplete if the analyst ignores power relations and ordering. Rules and criteria for institutional performance need to take into account what are the interests of the actors participating to institutional design and how institutional design in turn affects power distribution.

Contextualising Decisions

To analyse power mechanisms and practices, one has to understand the macro and micro political and economic structures that shape power distribution and in which institutions have emerged, sustained, and collapsed. It has arisen indeed as another common criticism of the IAD framework and of commons literature in general: actors' decisions have often been presented as independent of the larger historical and social context in which actors operate (Agrawal 2001; Edwards and Steins 1999; Klooster 2000). As early as in the 1980s, several scholars have blamed the focus of commons studies on local rules and their overlook of the underlying socioeconomic historical change and distant political forces (Bryant and Bailey 1997; Muldavin 1996)—their reaction leading to the development of political ecology (Blaikie 1985; Blaikie and Brookfield 1987). Proponents of the "power-centred approaches" to the study of NRM have advanced commons theory by showing that the design and sound implementation of adequate rules at the local level is significantly constrained by decisions made at higher governance levels and by the structure of the economy. Political ecology has built on political economy to link environmental change and the decisions of local resource users with existing political, economic, and social inequities (Blaikie 1985; Blaikie and Brookfield 1987; Bryant and Bailey 1997; Muldavin 2000). Largely inspired by neo-Marxist theories, early political ecology studies have denounced capitalist economies as responsible for the appropriation of communal capital away from locals, leading to land degradation and community disempowerment, issues that cannot be resolved by rule crafting within the community (Muldavin 1996). In their analysis of the factors affecting the decisions of local civil servants, studies of the decentralisation of NRM have also evidenced the central role of the politico-economic context in institutional performance (Andersson, Gibson, and Lehoucq 2006; Larson 2003).

Contextualising not only entails enlarging to higher governance levels but also entails situating actors' decisions in history. Many studies have illustrated the relevance of historical analysis to explain the outcomes of policy change (Armitage 2004; Batterbury 2006; Edmunds and Wollenberg 2001). It is necessary to understand why power has been shaped in a certain manner (Mosse 1997) and whose power and which institutions are seen as legitimate. For instance, Springate-Baginski and Blaikie (2007a) argue that relating the power wielded by the forest administration in India to historical heritage was central to understand the strong reluctance of civil servants to actually devolve responsibilities to local people over forest management. A historical approach is all the more crucial in the field of natural resource governance because a dynamic and long-term perspective is generally needed to evaluate and explain environmental change. Since NRM policies have been often based on accounts of environmental change,[10] it is critical to assess whether these accounts are grounded on sound arguments. One of the commonly evidenced misconceptions of policymakers is the assumption that environmental change has been linear over time (Fairhead and Leach 1996). Such a claim might lead to a misinterpretation of the drivers of environmental change and to ill-defined policies (Forsyth 2003).

Collective-action literature would therefore benefit from a greater attention to the historical and social context in which natural resource users make decisions to enlarge explanations of environmental change (Johnson 2004; Mosse 1997). Though recognised by many commons scholars (Agrawal 2001; Campbell et al. 2001; McCay 2002; Ostrom et al. 1999), such resolutions have been little applied in practice. Formalising the role of the macro politico-economic structure into the IAD framework might support a wider consideration of context in future commons studies.

Social Construction

Collective-action literature has usually posited nature as an objectively measurable variable, which can be characterised unambiguously by the analyst and that affects the decisions of all actors in a similar way. In the IAD framework, the subcomponents of the actor distinguish the information and the perception actors have of the action situation (Ostrom 2005, 104). Thus, the framework acknowledges that (1) there is not a unique and indisputable way of describing the world and (2) actors' decisions depend on their perception of the world rather than on the actual characteristics of the social and ecological system they evolve in. However, because it does not consider how actors' beliefs emerge, change, or sustain, it has not encouraged critical examinations and discussions of actors' multiple social constructions of the social and physical reality.

Constructivists' and post-empiricists' approaches offer useful methodological tools for such a task. Discourse analysis is particularly pertinent for the analysis of environmental policy-process (Hajer 2005). Discourse is defined in this chapter as "a specific ensemble of ideas, concepts, and categorizations that is produced, reproduced, and transformed in a particular set of practices and through which meaning is given to physical and social realities" (Hajer 1995, 60). By dictating how social and physical phenomena should be conceptualised, discourses shape beliefs, norms, and values. Under this perspective, they form both an important factor of and tool for policy change. Hajer (1995) argues that whether or not environmental problems call for institutional change depends largely on the way they are framed and defined in discourses. For instance, global environmental discourses have created and exacerbated a lowland–upland polarity, blaming upland people for lowland problems, for example, regarding the relationship between deforestation and flooding, erosion and river sedimentation (Blaikie and Muldavin 2004). These discourses have considerably reduced the legitimacy of upland people to decide how to manage forest and land and have resulted in policy decisions rendering illegal certain land-use practices of upland communities (e.g., shifting cultivation). The consideration of discourses helps to understand why particular policy options have gained predominance over others and thus allows a critical analysis of the terms of the debates related to NRM policies.

Discourse analysis is also particularly pertinent in the representation of power proposed by Foucault: power is expressed by the multiple micro-practices of a myriad of actors distributed among the society (Foucault 1975, 1976). In this perspective, discourses are both an expression and instrument of power and knowledge, which continuously transform the society. Particularly, the categorisations of the world that discourses convey apply a specific structure of knowledge and power on society (Foucault 1980), prescribing what is right and wrong, normal and abnormal, legal and criminal. This has notably been illustrated in the study of land and forest policies that have stressed the significant discursive power that administration holds by controlling the production of official knowledge through land and forest mapping and classification (Sowerwine 2004; Springate-Baginski and Blaikie 2007a).

The role of discourses and narratives in policy change has particularly been investigated by political ecologists. They have provided fresh insights on the ways in which environmental knowledge and concepts of environmental change emerge and are interpreted, and more broadly, on how nature is socially constructed (Escobar 1996; Fairhead and Leach 1996; Peet and Watts 1996; Simitzis et al. 1996). They have particularly investigated how environmental claims are rooted in the political and economic systems that produce and sustain them. This post-structuralist line of enquiry has been furthered by studies on the relationships between science and politics (Forsyth 2003; Stott and Sullivan 2000). These studies have called for an examination of the politics of environmental knowledge. Many widespread—and often taken-for-granted—scientific explanations of environmental change are actually grounded on little sound science but have become popular because they meet particular policy agendas, reinforce the power of influential stakeholders, or are "good stories" (Walker 2006). Some of these explanations have become accepted "environmental orthodoxies" that guide policies on the basis of oversimplified, inaccurate, and sometimes false accounts of human-environment relations (cf. Forsyth 2003). As evidenced further in this chapter, identifying the discursive mechanisms contingent to policy design is of particular importance for scholars engaged in policy debates and striving for policy change.

To summarise the discussion, the IAD analytical frame offers a strong and well-tested foundation for the analysis of decentralised natural resource governance by its identification of the key factors that affect actors' decisions at different governance levels. What is more, it offers a solid basis for multi-level studies by relating the decisions of actors across governance levels. However, the framework has been little applied insofar to the study of environmental policy processes across government levels because of a number of weaknesses. First, it lacks locating the unit of analysis in its historical, social, and discursive context. Of particular relevance to trace the design and implementation of natural resource policies is the influence of the political and economic context on institutional change. As a result, it does not help the analyst to explain why some of the identified variables are more important in some contexts than in others.

Secondly, the framework does not offer the adequate tools to explore how some variables have come into being, sustained, or evolved over time. The framework does not adequately capture how power distribution at each governance level and between different levels affects rule crafting and the transformation of rules into actual practices. Neither does it consider how beliefs, norms, and values emerge.

Enriching the IAD Framework

Components of the Framework

On the basis of these theoretical considerations, two exogenous variables were added to the original IAD framework (Figure 11.4; added variables appear in dot-filled boxes): the politico-economic context and discourses. These variables impact both the action situation—notably in the way they position actors—and the actors, as they shape values, norms, and preferences.

The examination of the role of the politico-economic context and discourses is meant to bring the analyst to explicitly consider power and values within the action arena. The politico-economic context is to be examined under a dynamic perspective to understand how power has been distributed among actors who take decisions and how political and economic interests have driven actors' decisions within a particular set of rules-in-use. In a next step, the examination of rules can inform the analyst on how the current set of rules-in-use affects power distribution and whether and how institutional change can lead to more-equitable outcomes. Discourses are linked to the rules-in-use not only because discourses affect institutions but also because the emergence and persistence of discourses depend on the institutional and politico-economic context (Hajer 1995). Discourses confer power to institutions by reinforcing or undermining their credibility. In return, institutions influence discourses as the latter depend on the institutional practices in which they are embedded (Hajer 1995; Schmidt 2010).

The consideration of discourses stresses the social construction of the biophysical and social reality and gives a greater emphasis to the role of beliefs in the internal valuation mechanism that actors use to make decisions. However, contrary to the advocacy coalition framework proposed by Sabatier et al. (Sabatier and Jenkins-Smith 1999; Sabatier and Weible 2007), beliefs are not considered as an external variable but are internalised

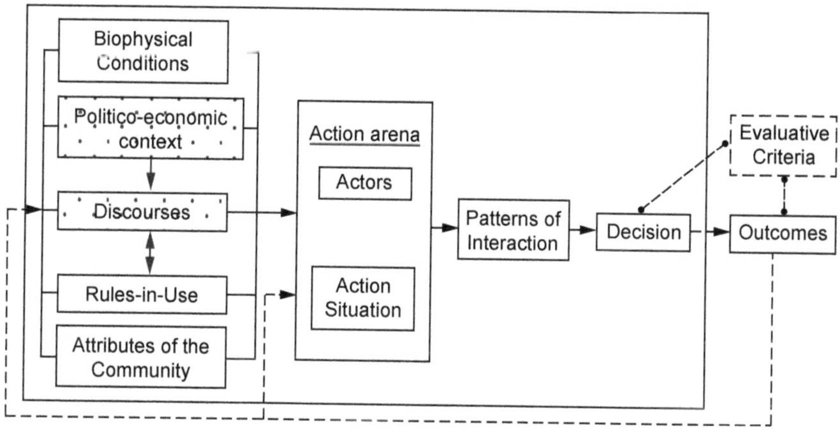

Figure 11.4. Detail of the extended framework.

within the holon "actors." In this perspective, discourses rather than beliefs are posited as drivers for policy change (as proposed by Fischer 2003; Hajer 1995). Adopting a social constructionist approach also encourages the analyst to adopt a critical view on information and knowledge—this issue is further elaborated in the section on policy recommendations.

Coherence of the Approach

Some might argue that combining these perspectives in a single conceptual framework will result in an internally contradictory and messy approach, with a limited explanatory capacity. Other scholars have argued that there was a too strong divide between commons theory and historical and contextual approaches to reconcile them (Johnson 2004). I defend that it is possible to reconcile these theoretical strands through a coherent ontological approach, based on critical realism. One has also to consider that a framework is not to be considered as a supra-theory but to be used as a way of structuring analysis through the definition and categorisation of key variables and their relationships. It is distinct from a theory or model in the sense that it aims at identifying the general elements that one needs to consider but does not make any presumption on which elements are relevant to which context (Ostrom 2005, 28). A key feature of the IAD framework, which has supported its present selection as the foundational framework for analysis, is indeed its compatibility with other schools of thoughts and theories (Ostrom 2005, 28). This adaptability is favoured by the general character of the variables and components of the framework. It has to be used as a menu of questions to be asked when conducting the analysis. The addition of two variables puts forward new questions, namely "why have these institutions emerged?" and "why have beliefs been shaped in a certain way?"

Critical Realism

Critical realism is an ontological approach, developed in the 1970s by two philosophers of science, Bhaskar (1975) and Harré (1972). It does not reject the existence of a "real" world but acknowledges that our understanding of the structures of the society and of the biophysical world is partial and depends on social and political framings that influence research approaches. Critical realism maintains that all environmental problems are perceived differently according to cultural beliefs, the claim of belonging to a social group, or political reasons. Critical realism thus provides a coherent and solid ontological basis for applying the extended framework since it encourages relying on both realist and constructivist approaches, using biophysical data to assess environmental change while at the same time critically evaluating how the latter is socially constructed through discursive analysis.

Human and Environmental Agency

A very much debated topic in the commons literature is the model of the actors chosen for the analysis. Theories of individual choice compatible with the IAD framework have primarily stemmed from neoclassical economics and rational choice theory (Ostrom 1999): according to the information they receive on external conditions, individuals make calculations to select choices that will maximise their self-interest. Limits inherent to the maximisation behaviour have been increasingly recognised by mainstream institutional economists (a review of these criticisms is proposed in van den Bergh, Ferrer-i-Carbonell, and Munda 2000). Already long ago, North argued that neoclassical economic theory fails to account for "behaviour in which calculated self-interest is not the motivating factor" (North 1981, 11) and proposed a theory of institutions that combines a theory of the costs of transacting with a theory of human behaviour (North 1990). In her analysis of the actor's mental model, Ostrom (2005) proposed to integrate beliefs and values in the IAD framework by adding a positive or negative delta parameter to the payoffs related to a particular action. These parameters represent the perceived costs and rewards of obeying or breaking rules related to the sociocultural context, originating from internal sources (e.g., guilt, shame, or pride) or external sources (costs to establish a reputation) (Ostrom 2005, 146). This perspective is close from that of the post-empiricists who posit ideas, norms, and values do not only affect actors' behaviour but also shape their interests (Fischer 2003). Nevertheless, it lacks the contextualisation of ideas and values within the historical and socio-ecological structure in which actors are embedded. The extended framework recognises the simultaneous role of structure, agency, and discourses in policy analysis (a similar approach has been adopted by Forsyth 2003; Keeley and Scoones 2003). Actors' intentionality is recognised, but their decisions are influenced by the structural and cultural systems in which they evolve. Structure, agency, and discourses are considered to be interdependent but are theoretically examined separately to bring greater explanatory power—this is another distinctive feature of critical realism (Greener 2005).

Not only human beings but also nature is considered to actively participate in policy outcomes. The IAD framework acknowledges the role of environmental agency by considering how nature affects actors' decisions through the perception they have of the biophysical conditions. Furthermore, the characteristics of the resource considered (e.g., abundance, size, subtractability, and excludability) directly affect institutional performance, independently of the interpretation actors make of their environment (Acheson 2006; Wilson 2002). This aspect, extensively studied in commons theory, has been omitted in most analyses of the power-centred literature. Yet many failures of natural resource policies have been rooted in their inadequacy with the local characteristics of the ecosystem considered (Adger et al. 2001).

Application of the Framework to the Study of Afforestation Policies in Northern Vietnam

This section illustrates the relevance of using the extended version of the framework by applying it to the analysis of a state-led afforestation programme, called the Five Million Hectare Reforestation Programme, in the northern mountain region (NMR) of Vietnam (Figure 11.5). Data collection has involved semi-structured interviews with farmers in three villages (80 respondents), local authorities and provincial authorities (30 respondents) in four provinces, and central policymakers including donors, NGOs, researchers, civil servants, and consultants (36 respondents).

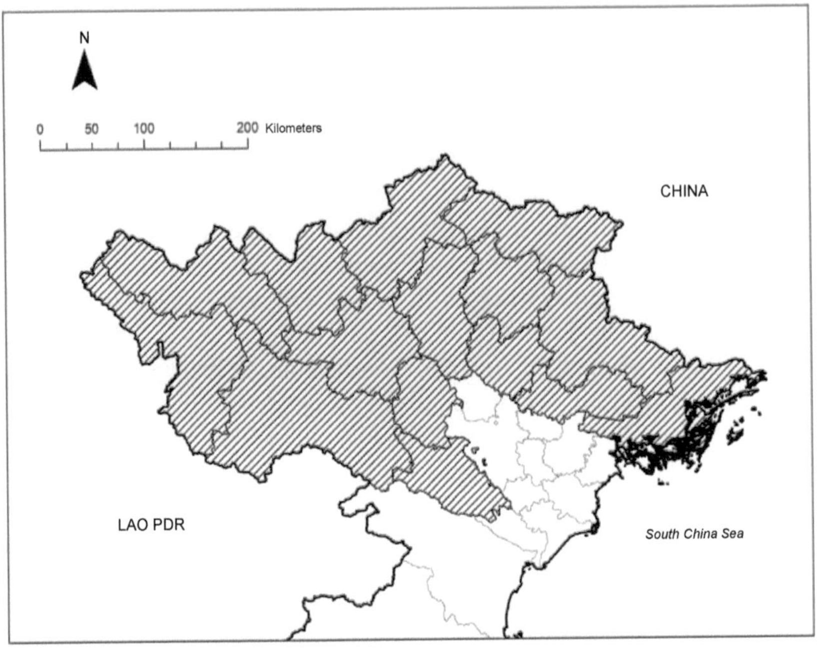

Figure 11.5. Administrative map of the northern mountain region of Vietnam.

Context: Forest, Land, and People in Northern Vietnam

The protection and management of forest has received particular attention in Vietnam since the 1990s. Rules regulating the access and use of forest and land have been defined and revised in more than one hundred laws and regulations for the past two decades. A particular driver for this political effervescence was an acute concern among policymakers regarding forest loss and the existence of widespread areas of bare land in the uplands. National statistics reported alarming rates of deforestation, with a drop from 43 percent of forest cover as the reference[11] figure in 1943 to figures varying from 17 percent in the late 1980s (De Koninck 1999), 25 percent in 1985 (World Bank 1995), and 28 percent (World Bank 1995) or 20 percent (Vo Quy 1996) in 1993. In 2007, statistics reported a forested area of approximately 12.7 million hectares (M ha), that is, 38.5 percent of the territory (Forest Protection Department 2008). The government has been particularly preoccupied with land degradation and low agricultural productivity in the upland regions (which area constitutes 75 percent of the total territory). Land and forest policies have aimed at protecting existing forest, "covering and re-greening" bare land by establishing new tree plantations, and using the land through "rational" (meaning fixed) cultivation. Major state initiatives have included forest and land classification, the devolution of forest- and land-use rights to households and communities, and tree planting through large-scale afforestation programmes.

Of major importance in recent institutional changes is the classification of forest and forestry land.[12] Forestry land is one of the six land categories defined by the Land Law (National Assembly of Vietnam 1993) and designates either land with an existing forest cover or with no forest cover but planned for afforestation (National Assembly of Vietnam 1991). Three categories were defined in the 1991 Forest Protection and Development Law according to their intended uses: (1) special-use forest/forestry land with an intended use for nature conservation (biodiversity preservation) and landscape protection (including historical and cultural heritage); (2) protection forest/forestry land with an intended use for protecting water resources and soil; and (3) production forest/forestry land with an intended use for commercial activities: exploitation of timber or non-timber forest products. Forest and land classification determines the categories of recipients for forest- and land-use rights as well as their rights and responsibilities. Special-use and protection forest and forestry land are managed by the state—but the management of protection forestry land can also be contracted to individuals and households. Production forest is to be allocated to individuals, households, and communities. Productive activities on protection forestry land are strongly restricted and have to follow strict procedures defined by the state. On production forestry land, households have choice over tree species selection and harvesting when trees are established with their own funds. They are also entitled to agricultural activities up to 20 percent of the allocated area.

Long-term land-use rights have been officially allocated to households and individuals since 1994 in order to halt shifting cultivation and improve agricultural productivity. It was also a response to the huge financial crisis that was facing the forestry sector in the mid-1980s. The state forestry enterprises (SFEs), the logging companies[13] established by the socialist state in the 1960s, were running at a loss because of a reduction in state financial support and a shortage of forest resources to exploit (Tan 2006). As the country was initiating a shift from a centrally planned to a market-based economy under the "Đổi Mới" political and economic reforms, it was believed that a greater involvement of households in forestry activities would invigorate the sector. Today, the current formal contribution of the forestry sector in Vietnam represents only 1 percent of the gross domestic product (GDP) (MARD 2005). Although not important for the economy, forestry is intended to be so by the Government of Vietnam to meet the increasing domestic and international demand for timber (De Jong, Sam, and Hung 2006). Among a total territory of 33.1 M ha, around 19.0 M ha (i.e., 57.4 percent of the land area) have been designated as forestry land. In the NMR, forestry land and forest cover represent, respectively, 72.4 percent (Forest Protection Department 2007) and 42.7 percent of the total land area (Forest Protection Department 2008).

The first major state afforestation initiative, Programme 327, also called the "Greening the Barren Hills Programme," was launched in 1992. It was replaced in 1998 by Programme 661, also known as "the Five Million Hectare Reforestation Programme" (5MHRP). Although it also includes social and economic targets, the primary stated objectives of the 5MHRP are environmental: "to increase the forest cover to 43% of the national territory, protect the environment, decrease the severity of natural disasters, increase water availability, . . . , protect biodiversity" (Prime Minister of the Government of Vietnam 1998). The programme has encompassed the decentralisation of responsibilities regarding land planning and classification to provinces and the allocation of substantial funding,[14] channeled through SFEs, for a set of 1,800 projects to be formulated by provincial authorities until 2010 (Tran Duc Vien, Quang, and Thanh 2005). Its implementation has also been tightly linked with the allocation of land-use rights, which is presented as a critical condition for the 5MHRP to realise its objectives (Tan 2006)—the rationale being that long-term land-use rights will provide the institutional incentives for households to protect and plant forest (Sikor 2001).

According to recent forest statistics, forest cover in Vietnam has dramatically increased during the past decade, rising from 30.2 percent in 2000 (FAO 2003, 133) to 38.5 percent in 2007[15] (Forest Protection Department 2008). Yet several studies have questioned the actual contribution of state-led afforestation programmes to environmental protection and livelihoods (Thuan 2005; Muller, Epprecht, and Sunderlin 2006; Ohlsson et al. 2005; Sunderlin and Huynh 2005). Whereas economic growth in the lowland areas has been impressive, poverty and vulnerability still prevail in the mountainous areas targeted by state forest policies (Minot et al. 2006; Zingerli 2003). What is more, the actual contribution of the new tree plantations to the environment is questionable (ADB et al. 2007). Afforestation projects have almost exclusively focused on the establishment of mono-tree plantations of exotic species (pine, eucalyptus, and

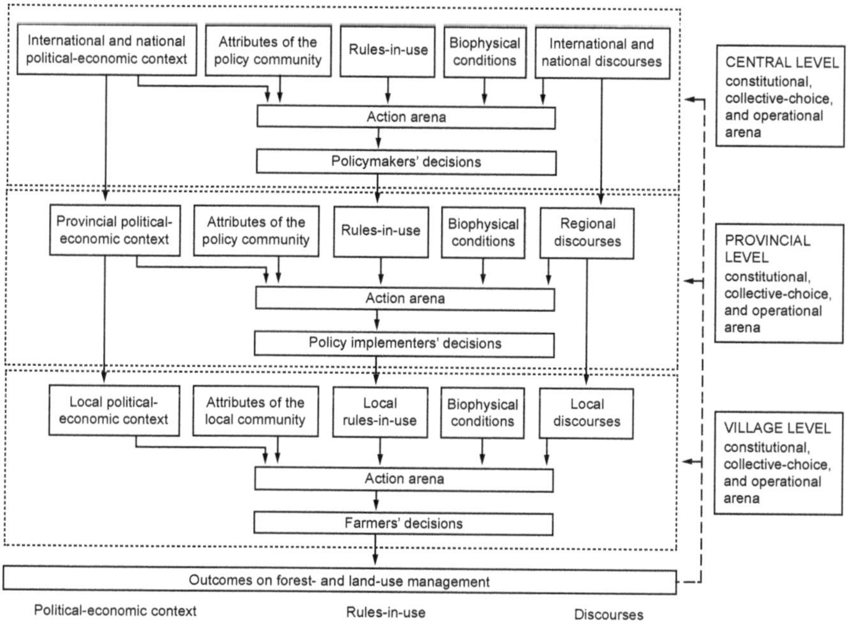

Figure 11.6. Overview of the overall framework adopted for the study of forest policies in Vietnam.

acacias) (De Jong, Sam, and Hung 2006) and the quality of forest has been reported to be as a whole very poor (Prime Minister of the Government of Vietnam 2007). Therefore, whereas forest cover has increased, the actual benefits of the programme on poverty reduction and environmental protection are dubious.

In order to assess whether observed afforestation in Vietnam has been indeed a success story, policy achievements were evaluated against the official objectives of the programme, with a particular concern to investigate whether objectives had been attained for the stated reasons and whether their attainment had contributed to improved livelihoods and environmental conditions. The extended framework (Figure 11.6) was used to understand the roots of the gap between stated policy intentions and outcomes (for the series of corresponding papers at, respectively, local, regional, and provincial level, see Clement and Amezaga 2008, 2009; Clement et al. 2009).

Analysing the Gaps between Policy Intentions and Outcomes

Figure 11.7 offers an overview of the major roots for policy failures located across institutional and administrative levels.[16] The framework was shown to be a powerful tool to highlight the factors that have contributed to widen or reduce the gap between policy intentions and outcomes and link them across multiple levels. The following discussion emphasises the contributions of the additions made to the IAD framework, that is, the role of the politico-economic context, discourses and beliefs on policy outcomes, and particularly variable interdependence and cross-scale linkages, which have been little discussed in the literature on natural resource governance (Acheson 2006; Berkes 2002). Because of space limitation, only a few variables are discussed in this section but readers can refer to Clement and Amezaga (2009) for a more detailed analysis.

One of the strong claims of the programme is its commitment to develop "social forestry," that is, household-based forestry activities, and give a key role to households in forest management and protection. Yet there was a consensus among the provincial officials interviewed to acknowledge that the 5MHRP has not succeeded in involving households in the forestry sector. According to the VHLSS estimates, the average share of forestry in household income reached only 4.5 percent in the NMR and 0.8 percent at the national level in 2006. This is related to the marketing and biophysical conditions (e.g., little accessibility) prevalent in the northern region but also to the fact that the 5MHRP has actually provided few economic incentives to make forestry an attractive option for farmers (Figure 11.7, Pf1). The central government has allocated investment funds exclusively to special-use and protection forestry land,[17] where the establishment and exploitation of tree plantations have to follow strict state planning schemes. The establishment of production forest has only been subsidised through a loan scheme, the Development Support Fund, but loans are de facto difficult to access for most farmers and their interest rate is too high to be attractive. Besides its failure to provide adequate support to smallholder forestry, the programme has induced a bias in land classification. Because the central budget has been directed to special-use and protection forest, provinces have extended the area of protection forestry land with the aim to attract more funding and support the financially fragile SFEs. This bias has severe implications for livelihood and food security as it has resulted in a significant diminution of the area of land available for productive activities. In 2005, the area of protection forestry land reached over 9 M ha (out of 19 M ha of forestry land), far beyond

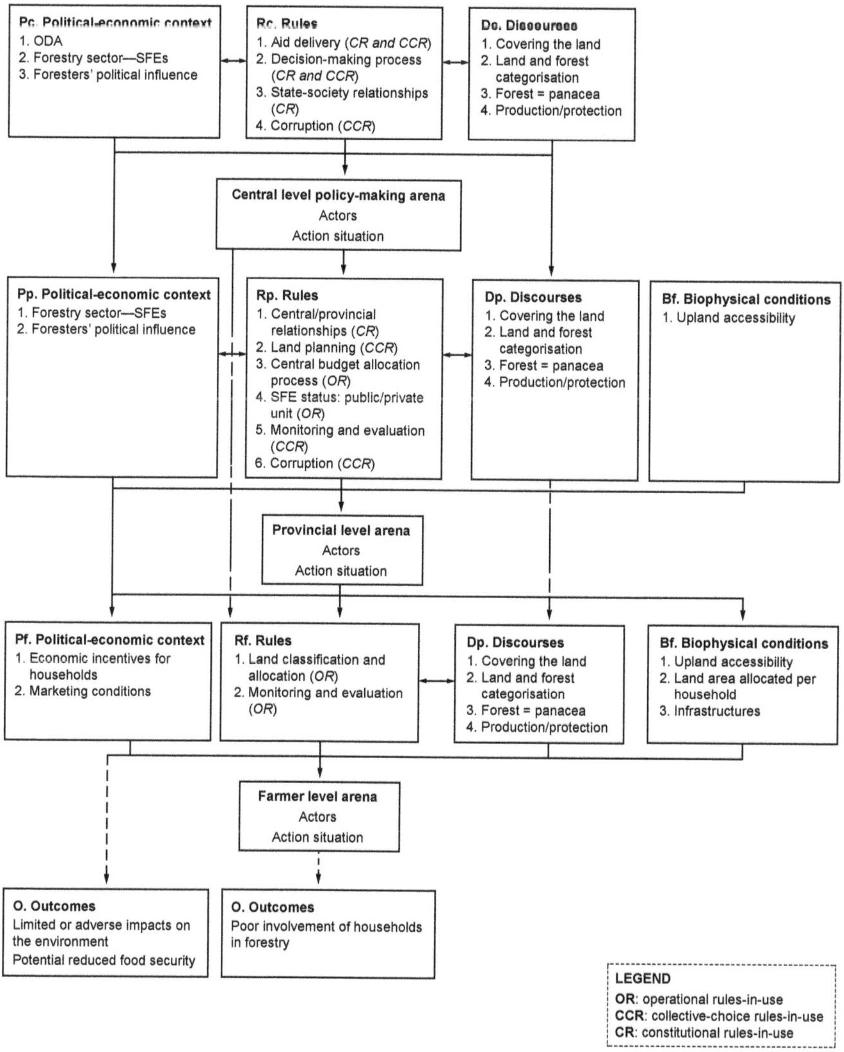

Figure 11.7. Extended IAD framework outlining the prominent drivers for the decisions of actors regarding the 5MHRP and afforestation at the village, province, and national levels.

the 6 M ha that had been initially planned by the central government in the National Forestry Development Strategy 2001–2010. Constitutional rules have facilitated this bias to some extent by granting relative freedom to provincial authorities to transform central policies into provincial guidelines (Rp1). Whereas decentralisation has been mostly limited to the allocation of funds and delegation of administrative tasks (Dupar and Badenoch 2002; Zingerli 2003), central authorities have in practice a limited ability to impose their will upon lower governance levels (Fforde 1997 in McCarty 2002). Noteworthily, the land policy area cumulates the largest number of reported "fence-breaking"[18] incidents in the daily newspapers between 1990 and 2000 (Malesky 2004).

The constitutional and collective-choice rules-in-use have thus largely contributed to create a gap between policy intentions and outcomes. At this stage, a "standard" institutional analysis would primarily focus on the design of new rules and the conditions for these new rules to lead to improved outcomes. By examining the cross-scale interaction of the political-economic context and discourses with institutions, the extended framework advances the analysis by drawing the attention to the drivers behind the formulation of these rules and to the processes that have legitimised and sustained institutions.

The central government of Vietnam was already aware of the tendency of provincial authorities to overclassify land under the protection category during Programme 327. It is thus suspected that conserving the same set of rules for the 5MHRP budget allocation resulted from a deliberate will to support indirectly SFEs at a time where the latter had to become financially autonomous private units (Pc1 and Pp1). The critical financial situation of SFEs and the strong political influence of foresters at the central and provincial levels were key elements of the political-economic context impacting institutional design. Besides, blurred discourses on the distinction and role of production, protection, and special-use categories (Figure 11.7, Dc4 and Dp4) have contributed to legitimise unclear classification criteria for the categorisation of land and forest (Figure 11.7, Rp2). Scholars have highlighted the role of policy implementation in outcomes (O'Toole 2000) and in particular of the lack of human, financial, or other resources in the failure of natural resource policies (Larson 2002; Repetto 1988). In the present case study, the extended framework rather points toward the motives, beliefs, and values of policymakers that have driven the design of particular rules for policy implementation. The importance of these factors has also been evidenced earlier in decentralisation studies (Agrawal and Ostrom 2001; Ribot, Agrawal, and Larson 2006).

The framework also clearly highlighted how the co-action of power, discourses, and institutions has led to observed policy outcomes. Forest management has gathered in Vietnam a wide range of actors with multiple interests. These actors, central and provincial governments, international donor organisations, non-governmental organisations (NGOs), have supported afforestation for various, and often conflicting, reasons. The consensual style of decision making (Figure 11.7, Rc2) prevalent in the policy arena in Vietnam has supported a specific discursive form called black-boxing.[19] Black-boxing has offered the advantage of neatly accommodating divergent interests under a broad rallying point: increasing forest cover. To legitimise this overall encompassing goal, afforestation has been depicted in public discourses as a panacea (Figure 11.7, Dc3 and Dp3). Increasing forest cover has become a goal per se under the rationale that all forests are a universal remedy for the environment, poverty reduction, economic development, and so on.

Panacea discourses have had several tangible impacts. First, black-boxing has masked the complexity and diversity of forest ecological systems and services. The disparities of afforestation impacts related to different tree species or climatic conditions (cf. Calder 1999, 2005) have been ignored by policymakers and little attention has been paid on the ground to the actual appropriateness and benefits of tree plantations in respect to local conditions. Secondly, the "panacea narrative" has helped the central and provincial governments to pursue some of their vested interests driven by the current political and economic context (Figure 11.7, Pc1&2 and Pp1&2). The argument that "production forest" can also be "protection forest"—because any type of forest is said to be always beneficial for the environment—has justified the establishment of fast-growing exotic species on protection forestry land for feeding the pulp and paper industry. The environmental benefits of the newly established "protection forest" are questionable. Scientific findings have warned against the negative impact of eucalyptus and pine tree plantations on stream flow and soil quality (Jackson et al. 2005) and their uncertain or limited effect on flood prevention and soil erosion (Bruijnzeel et al. 2005; Calder 1999, 2005). Lastly, panacea discourses have also strengthened institutions and power distribution at the constitutional level. The communist regime has used propaganda as a major tool for establishing its action around unifying goals that help to conserve and strengthen its legitimacy (Figure 11.7, Rc3). Afforestation has been erected in public discourses (e.g., in the mass media or on panels stretching along the roads) as a national effort in which every citizen should be involved. Campaign-style afforestation programmes have provided an opportunity for the party-state to show its effectiveness in acting for the collective good of the nation by demonstrating with increasing figures of forest cover that it has successfully addressed what is presented in public discourses as one of the "most important" environmental threats faced by the country. "Successes" of forest cover increase are regularly reported in the newspapers (e.g., cf. Vietnam News Agency 2006)—but there is never any mention of whether increased forest cover has resulted or is likely to result in environmental, social, or economic benefits.

Discussion and Conclusion

Implications for Policy Recommendations

One of the core presumptions of institutional analysis is that we can modify actors' behaviour by changing the rules-in-use and thereby the incentives and constraints actors face. The use of the extended framework reveals that this is not sufficient. One does not only need to change the rules-in-use but also the prevailing discourses that legitimate the rules. The examination of discourses permits on the one hand to analyse how problems have been framed in the policy-making arena and on the other hand to understand why current policies have emerged as rational solutions to these problems and relate policy change with discursive shifts. The last point is particularly relevant when designing policy recommendations, as these might not be considered if they run counter to dominant narratives. Narrative analysis provides a useful entry point in this respect by guiding the policy analyst in the design of metanarratives (cf. Roe 1991, 1994). Deliberative processes engaging stakeholders and researchers are also a promising avenue to facilitate democratic policy learning (Fischer 2003).

What is more, the extended framework enables to (1) examine whether actors might be willing or not to design new rules if supplied with new information (e.g., in this case study, why policymakers were not willing to change the criteria for budget allocation for the 5MHRP), (2) determine the most appropriate times for policy change, and (3) identify which actors or groups of actors have interest to support our arguments, which is also particularly important to select the appropriate path of dissemination of research results (Crewe and Young 2002).

The analysis of the role of power, context, and discourses in the birth and life of institutions is thus critical both to design and to communicate effectively policy recommendations. Institutional analysis enables to take a step forward compared to power-centred approaches as, besides the study of power distribution, it guides the identification and understanding of the rules-in-use that enable actors to gain, legitimize, and exercise power. One can also act on discourses, norms, and values by modifying the rules for discursive exchanges. What is more, the focus on rules design—rather than power or discourses—facilitates the development of policy recommendations intelligible to policymakers. Guiding the current research along an institutional perspective aims at overcoming one of the recognised shortcomings of political ecology, that is, its limitations to formulate well-grounded, clear, and applicable policy recommendations and communicate them in an effective manner (Neumann 2005).

Conclusion

Designing sound natural resource policies requires both to tailor governance systems to the diversity and complexity of social and ecological settings (Ostrom, Janssen, and Anderies 2007) and to ensure that institutions can guarantee equitable access to and benefits from natural resources. Scholars and policymakers striving toward this goal need to examine simultaneously these two objectives because of their tight interdependence: natural resource policies are "hybrids," to use Latour's term (1993), that is, composites of nature, society, and discourses. To facilitate such an endeavour, I posit a methodological development of the Institutional Analysis and Development (IAD) framework that "politicises" the framework by integrating concepts from political ecology, decentralisation studies, and discourse analysis. The enrichment of this well-tested framework for commons management aims at analysing policy processes across government and governance levels and at investigating the gaps between policy intentions and actual outcomes.

The framework was applied to the study of the 5 Million Hectare Reforestation Programme (5MHRP), a nationwide afforestation programme in Vietnam. The analysis revealed why policy outcomes, which seem relatively successful when measured in terms of forest cover increase, have actually contributed little to environmental protection and livelihood improvement. The extended framework was essential to (1) identify the incentives and discourses that have favoured certain policy choices. For instance, "panacea discourses" on universal forest benefits have legitimised a campaign-style approach that has paid little attention to the local ecological and socioeconomic conditions that support them; (2) locate these incentives and discourses within the politico-economic context in which rules have emerged, sustained, or collapsed: in the case study of Vietnam, the diverging interests of multiple actors under a consensual style of decision making have supported panacea discourses in order to accommodate these multiple objectives; and (3) understand how and why particular rules meet the interests of influential actors and reinforce or threaten current power distribution. It was illustrated by examining how the lack of clarity of the land classification criteria have eased an overclassification into the protection category, thereby facilitating the channelling of central funds to state forest enterprises.

Locating institutions within the discursive and politico-economic context allows the institutional analyst to design policy recommendations that are not naive and adopt a strategy to disseminate them effectively. For instance, it might be of little impact to propose to adapt the reforestation programme to the local ecological and economic conditions as the current form of blanket campaign is supported by the strong conjunction of panacea discourses, the conflicting politico-economic interests of policymakers and institutions. Instead, it might be more effective to challenge prevailing discourses by introducing counter narratives (Roe 1994), for example, on the intricacy and variability of forest benefits.

Although the main objective of extending the IAD framework was to make it better suited to the analysis of multi-level policy processes, it can also be applied to understand policy change at a single policy-making level. On the one hand, it draws the attention of institutional analysts to the role of power distribution and discourses at multiple levels in institutional design and performance. On the other hand, it offers a robust theoretical frame oriented toward the design of practical policy recommendations to scholars whose work is rooted in political ecology and other power-centred approaches. Generally, the revisions made to the framework aim at helping the analyst to move from "how-questions" (e.g., how national public policies impact the decisions of natural resource users) to "why-questions" (e.g., why policies have led to observed impacts). The final goal is to provide a strong analytical foundation for the design of policy recommendations.

Acknowledgments

This chapter emerged from my doctoral research, conducted at Newcastle University in 2004–2008, in collaboration with the French Institut de Recherche pour le Développement (IRD), the International Water Management Institute (IWMI), and the Vietnamese Soil and Fertilisers Research Institute within the MSEC programme. My sincere thanks to my PhD supervisors Dr. Jaime M. Amezaga, Prof. Ian R. Calder, and Dr. Andy R. G. Large at Newcastle University and to Dr. Didier Orange (IRD) for their guidance and support during the time this framework was developed and tested. The development of this framework greatly benefited from discussions with Professor Elinor Ostrom and with the participants of the PhD School "The Challenge of Self-Governance in Complex, Globalizing Economies: Responding to Walter Eucken's Challenge" at the Institute of Forestry Economics of the Albert Ludwigs University, April 17–26, 2007 and of the 12th Biennial International Association for the Study of the Commons (IASC) conference, held in Cheltenham, July 14–18, 2008. My PhD study was conducted thanks to the financial support of IRD, IWMI, and the French Ministry of Foreign Affairs through an international science fellowship; of the British Council through an Entente Cordiale scholarship; and of the French Foundation Marcel Bleustein-Blanchet through a "Bourse pour la Vocation" grant.

Notes

This chapter was originally published in *Policy Sciences* 43 (2010): 129–56. Reprinted with the permission of Springer Science+Business Media. Figure 11.1 reprinted with the permission of the University of Michigan Press. Figure 11.2 reprinted with the permission of Princeton University Press.

1. Local community is understood in this chapter as a local unit of actors using or making decisions over natural resources. It is not necessarily a homogeneous group with similar interests and objectives.

2. A search was made on the terms "international," "national," or "regional" in the abstracts. The selected papers were then reviewed individually to check whether they spanned over several governance levels.

3. It was the focus of a special issue of the *International Journal of the Commons*, 2008, vol. 2, no. 1.

4. A recent development of political ecology has also focused on the politics behind the production of environmental knowledge (Forsyth 2003).

5. For more references on this topic, see Ostrom (2005, 9).

6. The nature of resources (e.g., common-pool resources) is inherent to the resources and should not be confused with the type of property regime (e.g., common-property regime) that defines the access and use of the resources.

7. Readers will note that the institutional levels of the IAD framework do not necessarily correspond to administrative levels. For instance, local communities can operate at the collective-choice or at the constitutional levels when crafting their own rules or deciding on rule-crafting modalities.

8. Values are understood in this chapter as the personal or societal standards of a person or society that define what is valuable in life.

9. For example, in their analysis of the decentralisation of resource management in six countries, Ribot, Agrawal, and Larson (2006) refer to "local institutions" as "local authorities."

10. For instance, in several Asian countries, settlement programmes targeting ethnic minority groups in mountainous areas have been justified by accounts of forest loss.

11. This figure is contestable according to Mellac (2000), who asserts that there is no valid reference to estimate forest cover in Vietnam before the 1960s.

12. The term "forest land" has been generally used in English. I prefer, however, "forestry land," which literally corresponds to the Vietnamese term "đất lâm nghiệp." The term "forest land" may be confusing as it suggests that the designated land has an existing forest cover.

13. SFEs range from small exploitations managing forest plantations to large exploitation and production units including wood processing companies.

14. The 5MHRP features as one of the most costly national programmes for the government. The state investment for 2006–2010 was around 310 million USD (National Assembly of Vietnam 2004).

15. Figures on forest-cover area are controversial though—some observers refute claims of substantial afforestation in Vietnam (Sunderlin and Huynh 2005).

16. As appears on the right-hand side of Figure 11.6, administrative levels are located at multiple institutional levels.

17. The state investment funds that concern production forest are only for the establishment of "forest with rare and precious tree species with a production cycle of 30 years or more" (Prime Minister of Government of Vietnam 1999).

18. Fence-breaking is used here to describe acts of autonomy (Malesky 2004). Examples include the creation of illegal land markets, trade violations (Malesky 2004), or the modification of central policies for land allocation when transferred into provincial guidelines (Sikor 2004).

19. Black-boxing is the process of considering only the input and output of a complex phenomenon and thus conceiving its internal nature as immutable and unquestionable (cf. Latour 1987).

References

Acheson, J. M. 2006. "Institutional Failure in Resource Management." *Annual Review of Anthropology* 35: 117–34.

ADB (Asian Development Bank), AECI (Agencia Espanola de Cooperacion Internacional), AusAID (Australian Agency for International Development), Royal Embassy of Belgium, CIDA (Canadian International Development Agency), Embassy of Denmark, et al. 2007. *Vietnam Development Report*

2007. *Aiming High. Joint Donor Report to the Vietnam Consultative Group Meeting*. Hanoi: Joint Donor report to the Vietnam Consultative Group Meeting, Hanoi, December 14–15, 2006.

Adger, W. N., T. A. Benjaminsen, K. Brown, and H. Svarstad. 2001. "A Political Ecology of Environmental Discourses." *Development & Change* 32(4): 681–715.

Agrawal, A. 2001. "Common Property Institutions and Sustainable Governance of Resources." *World Development* 29(10): 1649–72.

Agrawal, A., and S. Goyal. 2001. "Group Size and Collective Action." *Comparative Political Studies* 34(1): 63–93.

Agrawal, A., and E. Ostrom. 2001. "Collective Action, Property Rights, and Devolution of Forest and Protected Area Management." In *Collective Action, Property Rights and Devolution of Natural Resource Management: Exchange of Knowledge and Implications for Policy*, edited by R. S. Meinzen-Dick, A. Knox, and M. Di Gregorio, 73–109. Feldafing, Germany: Zentralstelle fur Ernaehrung und Landwirtschaft (ZEL), Food and Agriculture Development Centre (DSE).

Agrawal, A., and J. C. Ribot. 2000. *Analyzing Decentralization: A Framework with South Asian and West African Environmental Cases*. Washington, DC: World Resources Institute.

Andersson, K. P., C. C. Gibson, and F. Lehoucq. 2006. "Municipal Politics and Forest Governance: Comparative Analysis of Decentralization in Bolivia and Guatemala." *World Development* 34(3): 576–95.

Andersson, K., and E. Ostrom. 2008. "Analyzing Decentralized Resource Regimes from a Polycentric Perspective." *Policy Sciences* 41(1): 71–93.

Armitage, D. 2004. "Nature-Society Dynamics, Policy Narratives, and Ecosystem Management: Integrating Perspectives on Upland Change and Complexity in Central Sulawesi, Indonesia." *Ecosystems* 7: 717–28.

———. 2008. "Governance and the Commons in a Multi-Level World." *International Journal of the Commons* 2: 7–32.

Auer, M. 2006. "Contexts, Multiple Methods, and Values in the Study of Common-Pool Resources." *Journal of Policy Analysis and Management* 25(1): 215–27.

Baland, J.-M., and J.-P. Platteau. 1996. *Halting Degradation of Natural Resources: Is There a Role for Rural Communities?* Oxford: Clarendon Press for FAO.

Batterbury, S. 2006. "Rescaling Governance and the Impacts of Political and Environmental Decentralization: An Introduction." *World Development* 34(11): 1851–63.

Berkes, F. 2002. "Cross-Scale Institutional Linkages." In *The Drama of the Commons*, National Research Council, Committee on the Human Dimensions of Global Change, edited by E. Ostrom, T. Dietz, N. Dolšak, P. C. Stern, S. Stovich, and E. U. Weber, 293–321. Washington, DC: National Academies Press.

Bhaskar, R. 1975. *A Realist Theory of Science*. Sussex: Harvester Press.

Blaikie, P. M. 1985. *The Political Economy of Soil Erosion in Developing Countries*. London: Longman.

Blaikie, P. M., and H. C. Brookfield, eds. 1987. *Land Degradation and Society*. London: Methuen.

Blaikie, P. M., and J. S. S. Muldavin. 2004. "Upstream, Downstream, China, India: The Politics of Environment in the Himalayan Region." *Annals of the Association of American Geographers* 94(3): 520–48.

Bruijnzeel, L. A., M. Bonell, D. A. Gilmour, and D. Lamb. 2005. "Forests, Water and People in the Humid Tropics: An Emerging View." In *Forests, Water and People in the Humid Tropics*, edited by L. A. Bruijnzeel and M. Bonell, 906–25. Cambridge: Cambridge University Press.

Bryant, R. L., and S. Bailey, eds. 1997. *Third World Political Ecology*. London: Routledge.

Calder, I. R. 1999. *The Blue Revolution*. London: Earthscan.

———. 2005. *Blue Revolution*. 2nd ed. London: Earthscan.

Campbell, B., A. Mandondo, N. Nemarundwe, B. Sithole, W. De Jong, M. Luckert, et al. 2001. "Challenges to Proponents of Common Property Resource Systems: Despairing Voices from the Social Forests of Zimbabwe." *World Development* 29(4): 589–600.

Cardenas, J. C., J. Stranlund, and C. Willis. 2000. "Local Environmental Control and Institutional Crowding-Out." *World Development* 28(10): 1719–33.

Carlsson, L. 2000. "Policy Networks as Collective Action." *Policy Studies Journal* 28(3): 502–20.

Cleaver, F. 2000. "Moral Ecological Rationality, Institutions and the Management of Common Property Resources." *Development & Change* 31(2): 361–83.

Clement, F., and J. M. Amezaga. 2008. "Linking Reforestation Policies with Land Use Change in Northern Vietnam: Why Local Factors Matter." *Geoforum* 39(1): 265–77.

———. 2009. "Afforestation and Forestry Land Allocation in Northern Vietnam: Analysing the Gap between Policy Intentions and Outcomes." *Land Use Policy* 26(2): 458–70.

Clement, F., D. Orange, M. Williams, C. Mulley, and M. Epprecht. 2009. "Drivers of Afforestation in Northern Vietnam: Assessing Local Variations Using Geographically Weighted Regression." *Applied Geography* 29(4): 561–76.

Crewe, E., and J. Young. 2002. "Bridging Research and Policy: Context, Evidence and Links." Working Paper 173. London: Overseas Development Institute.

De Jong, W., D. D. Sam, and T. V. Hung. 2006. *Forest Rehabilitation in Vietnam: Histories, Realities and Future*. Bogor, Jakarta: CIFOR.

De Koninck, R. 1999. *Deforestation in Viet Nam*. Ottawa: IDRC.

Dressler, W., C. A. Kull, and T. C. Meredith. 2006. "The Politics of Decentralizing National Parks Management in the Philippines." *Political Geography* 25(7): 789–816.

Dupar, M., and N. Badenoch. 2002. *Environment, Livelihoods and Local Institutions: Decentralization in Mainland Southeast Asia*. Washington, DC: World Resources Institute.

Edmunds, D., and E. Wollenberg. 2001. "Historical Perspectives on Forest Policy Change in Asia." *Environmental History* 6(2): 190–212.

Edwards, V. M., and N. A. Steins. 1999. "A Framework for Analysing Contextual Factors in Common Pool Resource Research." *Journal of Environmental Policy & Planning* 1(3): 205–21.

Escobar, A. 1996. "Constructing Nature: Elements for a Poststructural Political Ecology." In *Liberation Ecologies: Environment, Development and Social Movements*, edited by R. Peet and M. Watts, 46–67. London: Routledge.

Fairhead, J., and M. Leach. 1996. *Misreading the African Landscape: Society and Ecology in a Forest-Savanna Mosaic*. New York: Cambridge University Press.

FAO (Food and Agriculture Organization of the United Nations). 2003. *State of the World's Forests*. Rome: FAO.

Fforde, A. 1997. *Vietnam Economic Commentary and Analysis*. Vol. 9. Canberra: Aduki Pty.

Fischer, F. 2003. *Reframing Public Policy: Discursive Politics and Deliberative Practices*. Oxford: Oxford University Press.

Forest Protection Department. 2007. *Số liệu diễn biến rừng hàng năm*. (Figures on the evolution of forest by year). http://www.kiemlam.org.vn/Desktop.aspx/News/So-lieu-dien-bien-rung-hang-nam/Nam_2007/.

———. 2008. *Số liệu diễn biến rừng hàng năm*. (Figures on the evolution of forest by year). http://www.kiemlam.org.vn/Desktop.aspx/News/So-lieu-dien-bien-rung-hang-nam/Nam_2008/.

Forsyth, T. 2003. *Critical Political Ecology: The Politics of Environmental Science*. New York: Routledge.

Foucault, M. 1975. *Surveiller et Punir: Naissance de la Prison*. Paris: Gallimard.

———. 1976. *Histoire de la Sexualité, vol. 1: La volonté de savoir*. Vol. 1. Paris: Gallimard.

———. 1980. *Power/Knowledge: Selected Interviews and Other Writings, 1972–1977*. London: Harvester Wheatsheaf.

French, J. R. P., and B. H. Raven. 1959. "The Bases of Social Power." In *Studies in Social Power*, edited by D. Cartwright, 150–67. Ann Arbor, MI: Institute for Social Research.

Garces-Restrepo, C., D. Vermillion, and G. Muñoz. 2007. *Irrigation Management Transfer: Worldwide Efforts and Results*. Rome: FAO.

Ghate, R. 2003. "Global Gains at Local Costs: Imposing Protected Areas: Evidence from Central India." *International Journal of Sustainable Development and World Ecology* 10(4): 377–89.

Gibson, C. C., K. Andersson, E. Ostrom, and S. Shivakumar, eds. 2005. *The Samaritan's Dilemma: The Political Economy of Development Aid*. New York: Oxford University Press.

Gibson, C. C., M. A. McKean, and E. Ostrom, eds. 2000. *People and Forests: Communities, Institutions, and Governance*. Cambridge, MA: MIT Press.

Greener, I. 2005. "The Potential of Path Dependence in Political Studies." *Politics* 25(1): 62–72.

Hajer, M. J. 1995. *The Politics of Environmental Discourse: Ecological Modernization and the Policy Process*. Oxford: Oxford University Press.

———. 2005. "A Decade of Discourse Analysis of Environmental Politics: Achievements, Challenges, Perspectives." *Journal of Environmental Policy and Planning* 7(3): 175–84.

Harré, R. 1972. *The Philosophies of Science*. Oxford: Oxford University Press.

Hong, L., and S. E. Page. 2004. "Groups of Diverse Problem Solvers Can Outperform Groups of High-Ability Problem Solvers." *Proceedings of the National Academy of Sciences in the United States of America* 101(46): 16385–89.

Imperial, M. T. 1999. "Institutional Analysis and Ecosystem-Based Management: The Institutional Analysis and Development Framework." *Environmental Management* 24(4): 449–65.

Jackson, R. B., E. G. Jobbagy, R. Avissar, S. B. Roy, D. J. Barrett, C. W. Cook, et al. 2005. "Trading Water for Carbon with Biological Carbon Sequestration." *Science* 310(5756): 1944–47.

Johnson, C. 2004. "Uncommon Ground: The 'Poverty of History' in Common Property Discourse." *Development & Change* 35(3): 407–33.

Keeley, J., and I. Scoones. 2003. *Understanding Environmental Policy Processes: Cases from Africa*. London: Earthscan.

Kiser, L., and E. Ostrom. 1982. "The Three Worlds of Action: A Metatheoretical Synthesis of Institutional Approaches." In *Strategies of Political Inquiry*, edited by Elinor Ostrom, 179–222. Beverly Hills, CA: Sage.

Klooster, D. 2000. "Institutional Choice, Community, and Struggle: A Case Study of Forest Co-Management in Mexico." *World Development* 28(1): 1–20.

Lam, W. F. 1998. *Governing Irrigation Systems in Nepal: Institutions, Infrastructure, and Collective Action*. Oakland, CA: ICS Press.

Larson, A. M. 2002. "Natural Resources and Decentralization in Nicaragua: Are Local Governments Up to the Job?" *World Development* 30(1): 17–31.

———. 2003. "Decentralisation and Forest Management in Latin America: Towards a Working Model." *Public Administration and Development* 23(3): 211–26.

Larson, A. M., and J. C. Ribot. 2007. "The Poverty of Forestry Policy: Double Standards on an Uneven Playing Field." *Sustainability Science* 2(2): 189–204.

Latour, B. 1987. *Science in Action: How to Follow Scientists and Engineers through Society*. Milton Keynes: Open University Press.

———. 1993. *Nous n'avons Jamais été Modernes*. Paris: Poche.

Leach, M., R. Mearns, and I. Scoones. 1999. "Environmental Entitlements: Dynamics and Institutions in Community-Based Natural Resources Management." *World Development* 27(2): 225–47.

Lukes, S. 2005. *Power: A Radical View*. 2nd ed. Basingstoke, England: Palgrave Macmillan.

Malesky, E. 2004. "Leveled Mountains and Broken Fences: Measuring and Analyzing De Facto Decentralization in Vietnam." *European Journal of South East Asian Studies* 3(2): 307–37.

MARD (Ministry of Agriculture and Rural Development). 2005. *Draft National Forestry Strategy 2006–2020*. Hanoi: MARD.

McCarty, A. 2002. *The Policy Making Process in Vietnam*. Hanoi: Mekong Economics.

McCay, B. J. 2002. "Emergence of Institutions for the Commons: Contexts, Situations, and Events." In *The Drama of the Commons*, National Research Council, Committee on the Human Dimensions of Global Change, edited by E. Ostrom, T. Dietz, N. Dolšak, P. C. Stern, S. Stovich, and E. U. Weber, 361–402. Washington, DC: National Academies Press.

McKean, M. A. 2000. "Common Property." In *People and Forests: Communities, Institutions, and Governance*, edited by C. C. Gibson, M. A. McKean, and E. Ostrom, 27–55. Cambridge, MA: MIT Press.

Meinzen-Dick, R. 2007. "Beyond Panaceas in Water Institutions." *Proceedings of the National Academy of Sciences in the United States of America* 104: 15200–205.

Mellac, G. M. 2000. *Des Forêts Sans Partage. Dynamique de l'espace et utilisation des ressources dans un district de montagne au Nord Viet Nam*. PhD diss., Université Michel de Montaigne—Bordeaux III, France.

Minot, N., M. Epprecht, T. T. T. Anh, and L. Q. Trung. 2006. *Income Diversification and Poverty in the Northern Uplands of Vietnam*. Washington, DC: International Food Policy Research Institute (IFPRI).

Mosse, D. 1997. "The Symbolic Making of a Common Property Resource: History, Ecology and Locality in a Tank-Irrigated Landscape in South India." *Development and Change* 28(3): 467–504.

Muldavin, J. 2000. "The Paradoxes of Environmental Policy and Resource Management in Reform-Era China." *Economic Geography* 76(3): 244–71.

Muldavin, J. S. S. 1996. "The Political Ecology of Agrarian Reform in China: The Case of Helongjiang Province." In *Liberation Ecologies: Environment, Development and Social Movements*, edited by R. Peet and M. Watts, 227–59. London: Routledge.

Muller, D., M. Epprecht, and W. D. Sunderlin. 2006. *Where are the Poor and Where are the Trees?: Targeting of Poverty Reduction and Forest Conservation in Vietnam*. Bogor, Jakarta: CIFOR.

National Assembly of Vietnam. 1991. *Law on Forest Protection and Development* (Vol. 58-LCT/HĐNN8). Hanoi: National Political Publishing House.

———. 1993. *Land Law*. Hanoi: National Political Publishing House.

———. 2004. *Law on Forest Protection and Development*. Hanoi: National Political Publishing House.

National Research Council. 2002. *The Drama of the Commons*. Committee on the Human Dimensions of Global Change. Elinor Ostrom, Thomas Dietz, Nives Dolšak, Paul Stern, Susan Stonich, and Elke Weber, eds. Washington, DC: National Academies Press.

Neumann, R. P. 2005. *Making Political Ecology*. London: Oxford University Press.

North, D. C. 1981. *Structure and Change in Economic History*. New York: Norton.

———. 1990. *Institutions, Institutional Change and Economic Performance*. New York: Cambridge University Press.

Nunan, F. 2006. "Empowerment and Institutions: Managing Fisheries in Uganda." *World Development* 34(7): 1316–32.

Nygren, A. 2000. "Development Discourses and Peasant–Forest Relations: Natural Resource Utilization as Social Process." *Development & Change* 31(1): 11–24.

O'Toole, L. J., Jr. 2000. "Research on Policy Implementation: Assessment and Prospects." *Journal of Public Administration Research and Theory* 10(2): 263–88.

Ohlsson, B., M. Sandewall, R. K. Sandewall, and N. H. Phon. 2005. "Government Plans and Farmers Intentions: A Study on Forest Land Use Planning in Vietnam." *Ambio* 34(3): 248–55.

Olson, M. 1965. *The Logic of Collective Action: Public Goods and the Theory of Groups*. Cambridge, MA: Harvard University Press.

Ostrom, E. 1990. *Governing the Commons: The Evolution of Institutions for Collective Action*. New York: Cambridge University Press.

———. 1999. "Institutional Rational Choice: An Assessment of the Institutional Analysis and Development Framework." In *Theories of the Policy Process*, edited by P. A. Sabatier, 35–71. Boulder, CO: Westview Press.

———. 2005. *Understanding Institutional Diversity*. Princeton, NJ: Princeton University Press.

———. 2007. "A Diagnostic Approach for Going beyond Panaceas." *Proceedings of the National Academy of Sciences in the United States of America* 104: 15181–87.

Ostrom, E., J. Burger, C. B. Field, R. B. Norgaard, and D. Policansky. 1999. "Revisiting the Commons: Local Lessons, Global Challenges." *Science* 284(5412): 278–82.

Ostrom, E., R. Gardner, and J. Walker. 1994. *Rules, Games, and Common-Pool Resources*. Ann Arbor: University of Michigan Press.

Ostrom, E., M. A. Janssen, and J. M. Anderies. 2007. "Going beyond Panaceas." *Proceedings of the National Academy of Sciences in the United States of America* 104(39): 15176–78.

Peet, R., and M. Watts. 1996. "Liberation Ecologies: Development, Sustainability, and Environment in an Age of Market Triumphalism." In *Liberation Ecologies: Environment, Development and Social Movements*, edited by R. Peet and M. Watts, 1–45. London: Routledge.

Post, J., and M. Snel. 2003. "The Impact of Decentralised Forest Management on Charcoal Production Practices in Eastern Senegal." *Geoforum* 34(1): 85–98.
Prime Minister of the Government of Vietnam. 1998. *On Objectives, Tasks, Policy and Organisation for the Implementation of the 5 Million Hectares Afforestation National Programme. Decision 661/QD-TTg*. Hanoi: National Political Publishing House.
———. 1999. *Circular on Management of State Funds for the National Five Million Hectares Reforestation Programme.* Vol. Decision No. 28/199/TT-BTC. Hanoi: National Political Publishing House.
———. 2007. *On the Approval of the Forestry Development Strategy for the Period 2006–2020.* Vol. Decision No. 18/2007/QD-TTg. Hanoi: Official Gazette.
Repetto, R. 1988. *The Forest for the Trees? Government Policies and the Misuse of Forest Resources*. Washington, DC: World Resources Institute.
Ribot, J. C. 2003. "Democratic Decentralization of Natural Resources: Institutional Choice and Discretionary Power Transfers in Sub-Saharan Africa." *Public Administration and Development* 23(1): 53–65.
———. 2006. "Editorial. Choose Democracy: Environmentalists' Socio-Political Responsibility." *Global Environmental Change* 16: 115–19.
Ribot, J. C., A. Agrawal, and A. M. Larson. 2006. "Recentralizing While Decentralizing: How National Governments Reappropriate Forest Resources." *World Development* 34(11): 1864–86.
Ribot, J. C., and N. L. Peluso. 2003. "A Theory of Access." *Rural Sociology* 68(2): 153–81.
Robbins, P. 2004. *Political Ecology: A Critical Introduction*. Oxford: Blackwell.
Roe, E. 1991. "Development Narratives, or Making the Best of Blueprint Development." *World Development* 19(4): 287–300.
———. 1994. *Narrative Policy Analysis, Theory and Practice*. Durham, NC: Duke University Press.
Rudd, M. A. 2004. "An Institutional Framework for Designing and Monitoring Ecosystem-Based Fisheries Management Policy Experiments." *Ecological Economics* 48(1): 109–24.
Sabatier, P. A., and H. C. Jenkins-Smith. 1999. "The Advocacy Coalition Framework: An Assessment." In *Theories of the Policy Process*, edited by P. A. Sabatier, 117–66. Boulder, CO: Westview Press.
Sabatier, P. A., and C. M. Weible. 2007. "The Advocacy Coalition Framework: Innovations and Clarifications." In *Theories of the Policy Process*, 2nd ed., edited by P. A. Sabatier, 189–220. Boulder, CO: Westview Press.
Schmidt, V. A. 2010. "Give Peace a Chance: Reconciling Four (Not Three) 'New Institutionalisms.'" In *Ideas and Politics in Social Science Research*, edited by D. Béland and R. H. Cox. New York: Oxford University Press.
Schubert, J. 2005. *Political Ecology in Development Research: An Introductory Overview and Annotated Bibliography*. Bern: NCCR North–South.

Searle, J. R. 2005. "What is an Institution?" *Journal of Institutional Economics* 1(1): 1–22.

Shackleton, S., B. Campbell, E. Wollenberg, and D. Edmunds. 2002. "Devolution and Community-Based Natural Resource Management: Creating Space for Local People to Participate and Benefit?" *ODI Natural Resource Perspectives* 76: 1–6.

Sikor, T. 2001. "The Allocation of Forestry Land in Vietnam: Did it Cause the Expansion of Forests in the Northwest?" *Forest Policy and Economics* 2(1): 1–11.

———. 2004. "Local Government in the Exercise of State Power: The Politics of Land Allocation in Black Thai Villages." In *Beyond Hanoi: Local Government in Vietnam*, edited by B. J. T. Kerkvliet and D. Marr, 171–200. Copenhagen and Singapore: Institute for Southeast Asian Studies (ISEAS) Publications and NIAS Press.

———. 2006. "Analyzing Community-Based Forestry: Local, Political and Agrarian Perspectives." *Forest Policy and Economics* 8: 339–49.

Simitzis, J., K. Karagiannis, L. Zoumpoulakis, and A. Escobar. 1996. "Construction Nature: Elements for a Post-Structuralist Political Ecology." *Futures* 28(4): 325–43.

Snidal, D. 1995. "The Politics of Scope: Endogenous Actors, Heterogeneity and Institutions." In *Local Commons and Global Interdependence: Heterogeneity and Cooperation in Two Domains*, edited by R. O. Keohane and E. Ostrom, 47–70. London: Sage.

Sowerwine, J. 2004. "Territorialisation and the Politics of Highland Landscapes in Vietnam: Negotiating Property Relations in Policy, Meaning and Practice." *Conservation and Society* 2(1): 97–136.

Springate-Baginski, O., and P. Blaikie. 2007a. "Introduction: Setting Up Key Policy Issues in Participatory Forest Management." In *Forests, People and Power: The Political Ecology of Reform in South Asia*, edited by O. Springate-Baginski and P. Blaikie, 1–24. London: Earthscan.

———, eds. 2007b. *Forests, People and Power. The Political Ecology of Reform in South Asia*. London: Earthscan.

Sproule-Jones, M. 1999. "Restoring the Great Lakes: Institutional Analysis and Design." *Coastal Management* 27(4): 291–316.

Stott, P., and S. Sullivan, eds. 2000. *Political Ecology: Science, Myth and Power*. London: Arnold.

Sunderlin, W. D., and T. B. Huynh. 2005. *Poverty Alleviation and Forests in Vietnam*. Bogor, Jakarta: CIFOR.

Tan, N. Q. 2006. "Trends in Forest Ownership, Forest Resources Tenure and Institutional Arrangements: Are They Contributing to Better Forest Management and Poverty Reduction? Case Study from Vietnam." In *Understanding Forest Tenure in South and Southeast Asia—Forestry Policy and Institutions Working Paper No. 14*, vol. 14, 355–407. Rome: FAO.

Thomson, J. T. 1992. *A Framework for Analyzing Institutional Incentives in Community Forestry*. Rome: FAO.

Thomson, J. T., and K. Schoonmaker Freudenberger. 1997. *Crafting Institutional Arrangements for Community Forestry*. Rome: FAO.

Thuan, D. D. 2005. *Forestry, Poverty Reduction and Rural Livelihoods in Vietnam*. Hanoi: Labour and Social Affair Publishing House.

Torras, M. 2005. "Ecological Inequality in Assessing Well-Being: Some Applications." *Policy Sciences* 38(4): 205–24.

Tran Duc Vien, Nguyen Vinh Quang, and Mai Van Thanh. 2005. *Decentralization of Forest Management and Impacts on Livelihoods of Ethnic Minority Groups in Vietnam's Uplands: A Study on Decentralization Process in Forest Management in Northern and North Central Uplands of Vietnam*. Hanoi: Agricultural Publishing House.

van den Bergh, J. C. J. M., A. Ferrer-i-Carbonell, and G. Munda. 2000. "Alternative Models of Individual Behaviour and Implications for Environmental Policy." *Ecological Economics* 32(1): 43–61.

Vayda, A. P., and B. B. Walters. 1999. "Against Political Ecology." *Human Ecology* 27(1): 167–79.

Vietnam News Agency. 2006. "Forest Coverage Reaches over 60 Percent in Four Provinces." July 18—4:34 p.m.

Vo Quy. 1996. "The Environmental Challenges of Vietnam's Development, Draft Report." Regional seminar on environmental education, March 19–22, 1996, pp. 4–20. Hanoi: Center for Natural Resources and Environmental Studies, University of Hanoi.

Walker, P. 2006. "Political Ecology: Where is the Policy?" *Progress in Human Geography* 30(3): 382–95.

Wardell, A. D., and C. Lund. 2006. "Governing Access to Forests in Northern Ghana: Micro-Politics and the Rent of Non-Enforcement." *World Development* 34(11): 1887–906.

Wilson, J. 2002. "Scientific Uncertainty, Complex Systems, and the Design of Common-Pool Institutions." In *The Drama of the Commons*, National Research Council, Committee on the Human Dimensions of Global Change, edited by E. Ostrom, T. Dietz, N. Dolšak, P. C. Stern, S. Stovich, and E. U. Weber, 327–59. Washington, DC: National Academies Press.

World Bank. 1995. "Viet Nam: Environmental Programme and Policy Priorities for a Socialist Economy in Transition. Volume I. Executive Summary and Main Report." Washington, DC: World Bank, Agriculture and Environment Operations Division.

Xu, J., and J. C. Ribot. 2004. "Decentralisation and Accountability in Forest Management: A Case from Yunnan, Southwest China." *European Journal of Development Research* 16(1): 153–73.

Zingerli, C. 2003. "Vietnam's Mountain Problematique: Debating Development, Policy and Politics in Mountain Areas." PhD diss., East Anglia, Norwich.

12

Building Negotiated Agreement: The Emergence of Community-Based Tourism in Floreana (Galápagos Islands)

Esteban Ruiz-Ballesteros and Eduardo S. Brondizio

Community-based tourism (CBT) refers to local involvement in the planning, development, and management of tourism. It assumes that this local participation has positive effects on both socioeconomic development and conservation. These outcomes, however, are subject to extensive academic debate (Hiwasaki 2006; Kruger 2005; Li 2006; Okazaki 2008; Roberts and Tribe 2008; Ruiz-Ballesteros 2011; Ruiz-Ballesteros and Hernández-Ramírez 2010; Stem et al. 2003; Stronza 2010; Tao and Wall 2009; Theodori 2005; Tosun and Timothy 2003; Wunder 2000). CBT is a polysemic term representing various forms of tourism operating in different contexts; thus, scholars and practitioners agree that there is no mechanical correspondence between CBT and economic development and conservation. On the other hand, CBT has offered a framework strongly supported by international organizations and NGOs (WTO 2006; World Wide Fund for Nature 2001), governments, international development agencies, and indigenous peoples. It has also become a strategy for implementing tourism and sustainable management particularly within and around protected and indigenous areas.

The goal of this chapter is to discuss and analyze the emergence of CBT as part of multilevel processes of institutional crafting. We examine the design of a CBT proposal involving the island community of Floreana, located within the Galápagos National Park (GNP) in Ecuador. In particular, we discuss the process of rule-crafting within and between levels of governance guiding tourism development. We examine the role of different stakeholders, their worldviews and priorities regarding intended outcomes, and how these differences influence the crafting and change of different types of rules, that is, boundary, position, scope, and choice rules (Ostrom 1990), required for the transition toward CBT. Our approach integrates ethnographic fieldwork and discourse analysis with the Institutional Analysis and Development (IAD) framework (Ostrom 1990, 2011).

Theoretical and Methodological Framework

Tourism is a type of activity that draws upon (sometimes not exclusively) the various resources available in a socio-ecological system. Frequently, its development entails a new, specific, and complementary use of pre-existing resources or even the emergence of new resources. The goods and services used through tourism activities are of a highly heterogeneous nature encompassing biophysical and cultural elements in their tangible and intangible dimensions (e.g., wildlife, landscape, forest, sea, cultural practices, architecture, arts, public infrastructure, and so forth). Moreover, tourism-related resources are subject to different types of property regimes: open access, communal, public, and private, while combining different types of goods (i.e., private, public, or toll), depending on the scale at which one considers them. Although tourism involves a complex and comprehensive use of resources within a socio-ecological system, it cannot be conceptualized in itself as a good nor as a common-pool resource (CPR), but instead as a rationale for using them. There is a growing literature proposing the analysis of tourism from the perspective of common-pool resources (Briassoulis 2002; Healy 2006; Holden 2005; Moore and Rodger 2010; Stronza 2010), as the nature of the most important goods and services used in tourism makes this perspective relevant.

Community-based tourism in protected areas entails a particular way of using resources at the local level. These goods and services are subject to different levels of exclusion and subtraction and overlapping types of property regimes in their production or consumption (McGinnis 2011a; Ostrom 1990). It seems worthwhile, albeit challenging, to analyze this type of tourism from a CPR's perspective for the following reasons: (1) following the criteria of subtractability and high costs of exclusion, most of the main resources used in community-based tourism activities have the character of common-pool resources (e.g., landscape, forest, sea, cultural practices); (2) tourism management entails community-based normative institutions; and (3) the emergence and/or expansion of community-based tourism, as it involves new forms of use of multiple resources, adds institutional and economic complexity to CPR management (Stronza 2010). Thus, analyzing community-based tourism through the lens of CPRs may help us to capture the complexity of tourist activities within a socio-ecological system more comprehensively than other perspectives.

A good deal of literature indicates the centrality of local governance systems in regulating the use and management of CPRs (Acheson 2006; Ostrom 1990, 2005). Initiatives to change tourism activities from business-as-usual to CBT usually aim at improving the participation of local communities in the process. As with other CPR governance initiatives, however, tourism involves local and regional actors, state agencies, NGOs, and a variety of private interests, thus requiring consideration of multiple levels of collective action and governance (see Berkes 2002; Brondizio, Ostrom, and Young 2009; Taylor and Cheng 2012). Consequently, transforming tourism initiatives into community-based projects is not a single-actor endeavor. Only coordinated action across levels allows for substantial transformation in tourism practices.

The Galápagos Islands have a long and controversial history of tourism management, often serving as an example of the negative social and environmental impacts of conventional tourism. Efforts to develop a new model of tourism management, strongly shaped by a particular community, offer a quasi-experimental case of rule-crafting aimed at developing a participatory, multilevel governance system. As in all inhabited protected areas, there is a fine line between the worldview and politics of conservation and economic development aimed at improving the well-being of local communities (West, Igoe, and Brockington 2006). Tourism, CBT in particular, is often assumed to offer a potential path toward balancing these goals, notwithstanding the complex challenges involved in the process. It also poses a challenge to analytical strategies aimed at understanding the process and outcomes of tourism development.

Through a case study approach (Poteete, Janssen, and Ostrom 2010; Yin 2009) linking the local (Floreana Island) and regional (Galápagos archipelago) levels, we seek to identify key elements associated with the process of transformation from business-as-usual to CBT in the region. Through this case study, we discuss the crafting of a new tourism governance system as a process resulting from the dynamics of collective action within and across local and regional levels. We use the IAD framework (Ostrom 2011) to analyze such action at the regional and local levels, as well as the linkages between them. The strength of this framework lies in its holistic approach to the analysis of collective action; that is, its consideration that individuals and groups operate within a nexus of biophysical, political, cultural, and economic factors defined by various sets of rules and constraints (Ostrom, Gardner, and Walker 1994). In combination with extensive ethnographic fieldwork and discourse analysis, the IAD framework helps us to define relationships between participants, context (within and across levels), existing and proposed rules associated with changes in tourism, and the alignment (or lack thereof) of different types of rules (Ostrom, Gardner, and Walker 1994).

We find these analytical tools particularly useful to examine changes in various categories of rules and the social processes involved in crafting them as social groups compete and cooperate to transform a multifaceted activity such as tourism. Organizing these social dynamics as "action situations" provides us with analytical resources "that can be utilized to describe, analyze, predict, and explain behavior within institutional arrangements" (Ostrom 2011, 11). Within these action situations, we attend to participants as endowed with resources, perceptions, knowledge, alliances, and worldviews that are central to understanding differences in intended outcomes and the formulation of rules to achieve them. Following Ostrom (2011), we recognize that IAD also has limitations as an analytical tool. Nonetheless, it provides a comprehensive and flexible structure that allows us to represent the system in its multilevel complexity and to delineate different categories of rules involved in the crafting of new institutions.

IAD and its subsidiary theoretical stance on bounded rationality (Poteete, Janssen, and Ostrom 2010) offer a systematic analytical framework to examine institutional crafting as a process. Following other scholars (Acheson 2011; Sick 2008; Taylor and Cheng 2012; Wagner and Talakai 2007), we maintain that such analyses must be grounded in solid ethnographic evidence. Through ethnography, we can approach the "attributes of the community" as set out in the IAD framework, focusing on such central issues as trust, reciprocity, common understanding, and worldviews and their effects on the collective-action process (McGinnis 2011a). An anthropological approach based on the analysis of discourses and practices brings to the fore participants' perceptions as they play out within particular contexts and social situations (Natcher, Davis, and Hickey 2005; Neves-Graça 2004). Thus, ethnographic work is essential to understanding the negotiations, power relations, and worldviews of participants. This complementarity of approaches allows for a fine-grained examination of action situations within and across the levels (Berkes 2002; Ostrom 1990) involved in the transformation of tourism governance, both in Galápagos and elsewhere.

Our analysis is based on seven months of ethnographic research in Galápagos and the island of Floreana carried out by three investigators from 2009 to 2011. The research team dedicated significant time to participant observation in meetings and deliberations pertaining to the development and consolidation of a CBT model for Floreana. At the level of Floreana, the team carried out comprehensive ethnographic research including sociodemographic, institutional, and economic assessments at household and community-levels, as well as in-depth interviews regarding local perspectives about quality of life, tourism, development, and environment. At a regional level, interviews and participant observation focused on the organizational structure and narratives of NGOs and the management office of the GNP. Our inquiries sought to elicit their views on implementing a new model of tourism throughout the archipelago and in Floreana in particular. It also afforded a systematic analysis of institutional crafting as shaped by social and power dynamics and the worldview of participants within and across levels of negotiations. With our ethnographic work across these levels, we also hope to establish a foundation from which to follow the process into the future.

Study Context: Galápagos and Floreana

Few places in the world have the significance of Galápagos as natural space. The islands' geoenvironmental conditions and their late settlement by humans have transformed them in a "paradise" of endemic flora and fauna and a laboratory for the study of biological evolution. With its declaration as a national park (1959) and a World Heritage Site (1979), the Galápagos acquired a privileged position within nature tourism on a global scale. Since then, the natural, scientific, and touristic significance of these islands have constituted an inextricable whole (Grenier 2007).

The evolution of this socio-ecological system is marked by two main factors. One is the increase in the permanent human population from only 4,000 inhabitants in 1974 to 25,124 in 2010 (INEC 2011) due to marked in-migration. The other is the increasing presence of introduced (non-native) species; despite eradication campaigns and the fact that 97 percent of the territory is under strict environmental protection, this has resulted in a notable alteration of the islands' ecology (Gardener, Atkinson, and Rentería 2010; Watson et al. 2010). The factors driving these changes include state subsidies, abandonment of agriculture, institutional and political instability, and weak governance and leadership, but above all tourism (Gonzalez et al. 2008). The tourist development of the Galápagos seems unstoppable, despite attempts to control it. The number of visitors increased from 11,795 in 1979 to 185,028 in 2011 (GNP 2012). This reflects an unprecedented "opening up" of an archipelago that was practically isolated from the exterior until the 1970s (Grenier 2007).

Galápagos exemplifies the dilemmas of managing tourism in CPR contexts. Despite multiple laws and regulations designed to control it (e.g., defining site visits, caps on the number of visitors), tourism continues to grow at a marked pace. The first modality of cruise ship tourism controlled by large corporations has been complemented by a second modality of "daily tours" using small boats, which centers on the populated areas and encourages, as CBT does, increased local involvement in the benefits from the tourism. Nevertheless, this second type of tourism is becoming increasingly problematic because of the inherent difficulty of controlling and regulating it. Therefore, even though this modality assumes that benefits will flow to local populations, it also carries potential negative environmental (and social) impacts. Moreover, it implies moving a step closer to the abandonment of other activities, especially agriculture and ranching, which are highly relevant for the socio-ecological sustainability of the archipelago (Andrada, Cantero, and Ruiz-Ballesteros 2010).

Each island in the Galápagos exhibits different conditions and dynamics with respect to the development of tourism. These island-level particularities must be taken into account when examining tourism in the park as a whole (Andrada, Cantero, and Ruiz-Ballesteros 2010). The delayed incorporation of Floreana Island into the principal tourist flows of GNP and its relative isolation until recent years resulted in low population levels, and a focus on a quasi-subsistence economy to locals are very attached. This economy has been slowly modified as a result of two parallel processes: on one hand, the increasing presence of the State as an agent of administration and conservation; and on the other, the development of tourism.

With a land area of 173 km^2, Floreana has the smallest population in the Galápagos archipelago (just 164 inhabitants in 2011). Ninety-eight percent of the island's territory is theoretically segregated from any human activity or settlement as part of the GNP, and the rest is divided between the village settlement on the coast (39 hectares) and agricultural land in the central part of the island (271 hectares) (see Figure 12.1). The main property regime on the island is public, extended over the entire area of the GNP and the urban infrastructure; housing and the agricul-

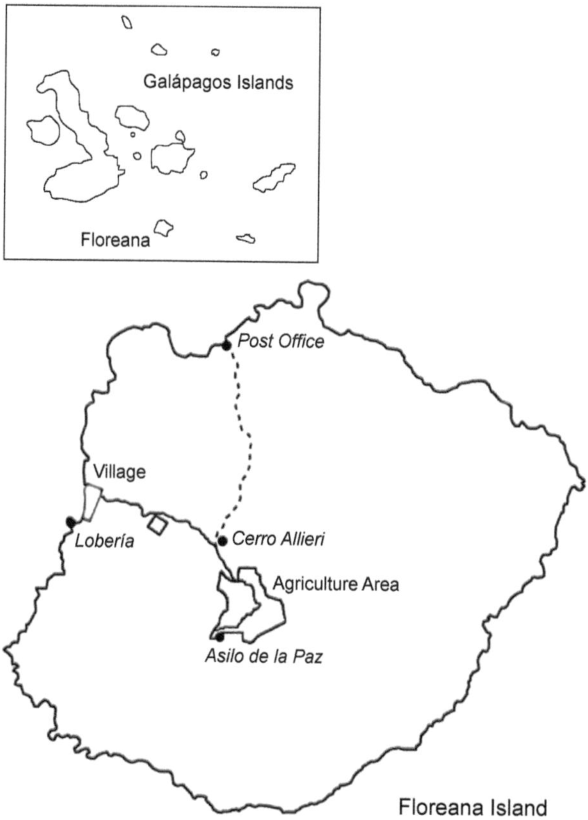

Figure 12.1. Galápagos and Floreana.

tural zones are under private property. The island was officially occupied in 1832, but afterwards it suffered several periods of abandonment. Since the 1930s, the island has remained populated, but half of the families that live there today arrived less than thirty years ago. The island receives cruise ships on its uninhabited northwest coast (Post Office), and consequently this modality of tourism provides no benefit to the local population.

Since 2008, the development of the "daily tour" form of tourism has drastically changed the impact of tourism on the island. In 2011, there were an estimated 23,000 visitors. These tourists come from the island of Santa Cruz and stay only an average of five hours in Floreana. They visit the higher elevation points of the island, where there are remains of the first human occupation of the archipelago (Asilo de la Paz) and eat lunch in one of the town's restaurants. Our data reveal that the cost of the trip is approximately $70 per person of which only 15 percent stays in Floreana while the rest goes to the tour operators and the boats' owners from Santa Cruz. An average of 64 tourists visit the island daily, but during the high season, this number is much greater and surpasses the local population. While limited in number, these visits have had an impact on the island unknown only four years ago. Floreana's residents provide transportation and food services to tourists. The few that stay overnight (according to our data, less than 20 percent) represent the atypical island visitor but have nonetheless had some impact on the local economy.

To understand how the island's economy operates, we took as a reference its 31 households. Our data show that in 2011, 27 of these households (91 percent) produced food for home consumption, dedicating only 26.1 percent of their production for sale (INEC 2009). In addition, 15 households (almost 50 percent) received income from tourism, 19 (63.1 percent) from employment in government or NGOs, and 11 in construction projects. This can be described as a diversified economic system combining market-based employment and a logic of self-consumption. This balance substantially influences the socio-ecological reality of the island, as well as its perspectives for the future. Although based in a regime of private property, agro-livestock activities are highly marked by norms of reciprocity and mutual help, particularly through collective work and owners' willingness to share land (free of charge) with non-owners. It could be expected that tourism development would hasten the abandonment of these quasi-subsistence farming and livestock activities, as has occurred in other islands in the Galápagos. For now, however, the trend in Floreana has been in the opposite direction. New land under cultivation, the sale of land, and the creation of a local farmers' association underscore this trend.

Floreana's inhabitants are fully cognizant of what has taken place in other islands with the development of commercial fishing first, and tourism later: the rapid disappearance of norms of reciprocity and community solidarity, an increase in population, and an irreversible process in which tourism imposes itself on the rhythm of life. All of this makes Floreanos zealous in defending their way of life. This does not, however, imply that they are uninterested in improving their consumptive capacity, and above all their connectivity to the rest of the archipelago and the continent. As a result, tourism is the object of collective reflection in Floreana, as confirmed during our extended fieldwork.

Toward a New Tourism: A CPR Governance System in Floreana

For the organizations working on conservation in the Galápagos, Floreana offers the final opportunity to develop a model of sustainable tourism. In 2010, the GNP, NGOs, and regional and national authorities reflected on the suitability of modifying the tourist model in the Galápagos. A number of meetings, seminars, and encounters took place, leading to the establishment of a model of ecotourism for the archipelago. Regional and national tourism entrepreneurs, who until now were isolated from Floreana in their dealings, have come to understand that the island represents the future of the tourism business in the archipelago.

At the beginning of our fieldwork in 2009, we were able to confirm local uneasiness regarding the development of tourism on the island. In 2010, given the possibility that the GNP would offer new quotas for daily small boat tours, some Floreana businessmen declared to the Park's directors the de facto impossibility of locals to access these quotas. Upon our return to the island in 2011, we noticed a significant transformation in the tourism infrastructure such as new infrastructure in the docking area, arts and crafts shops, and new lodging all denoting increased local participation in tourism. A rumor circulated that a regional entrepreneur was going to build a new hotel. One of the neighbors of the intended hotel site said, "A hotel like that with multiple floors means another car, another boat, and more water consumption." Speaking more explicitly to the change of lifestyle that such a project could imply for the island, she lamented, "We will have to close the door upon leaving [our houses], something that we are not used to here."

Without a doubt, the local community desires tourist development to improve their consumption capacity and quality of life, but there are at least three factors that hinder this goal: (1) their inability to access and to secure, much less control, the flow of tourist benefits; (2) the evidence of foreign investment in Floreana with potential to further limit opportunities for local control and development of local tourism; and (3) the evident danger that some forms of tourism would negatively impact local values and a lifestyle cherished by residents, one of tranquility, security, and social cohesion. For these reasons, locals petitioned for protection from external investors and proposed a model of CBT for which the community would become the main agent. The model recognized community members as operators of daily tours and consequently the main managers of tourist flows.

In this way, Floreana is configured as a place where there is a confluence of two levels of decision making (regional and local) in a joint initiative to transform tourism on the island into a community-based model. CBT is expected to satisfy the ecotourism requirements of the GNP and, at the same time, the local protection and control of tourism that Floreanos explicitly demanded through their community assembly, the main local decision-making institution. This goal implies a new model of CPR management with tourism use that, as we will see, requires the crafting of new institutions.

This process may be simple in appearance, but as we dig deeper into its dynamics and consequences it becomes far more complex. It requires a transformation of the system of governance of CPRs around tourist activities, which will only be possible if there is collective action at the local and regional levels. The ethnographic registry of the events is very rich, showing the different dimensions of the process, the variety of meanings they acquire, and above all their intricate and nonlineal nature. From this perspective, the institutional approach synthesized in the IAD framework (Ostrom 1990, 2011) has been useful in helping us understand the whole process, and two of its central analytical concepts—rules and action situations—have served as tools to organize our data.

A transformation in the governance system of a set of resources (e.g., landscape, species, history, culture) implies a change in the basic rules that regulate the appropriation and use of these CPRs. In designing a new form of tourism, Floreanos seek to confront an impinging "appropriation problem," in other words, a situation where outside resource users would benefit disproportionately from the use of local CPRs. This is likely to occur in the absence of collective-action mechanisms regulating the distribution and long-term outcomes of tourism. There are rules-in-use that need to change at the regional and local levels. Following the IAD framework, we can identify rules that regulate different aspects of the appropriation of resources. The process that is sought in Floreana implies a transformation in the rules-in-use that regulate CPRs toward a set of intended rules at regional and local levels (see Table 12.1). The analysis of this rule-crafting process allows us to characterize the development of CBT in Floreana.

This intended transformation of the appropriation and use rules of local CPRs would clearly have a spatial effect in the flows of tourists to the island, reducing their size while at the same time opening new sites for visits. The objective is to reduce tourist visits by one-third (from 23,000 to 8,000), and open de facto three sites (see Figure 12.1). Among these are Lobería and Cerro Allieri, which are currently not used because of

Table 12.1. Rules transformation

	Rules-in-use	*Intended rules—regional level*	*Intended rules—local level*
Boundary Rules	Tourist activities in GNP are subject to quotas that can only be acquired by individuals or corporations. The local Floreana population is de facto excluded from the new quotas.	Community access (as a collective) to tourist quotas: local community becomes a tourist actor. Limits on private use of tourist CPRs.	All the members of the community would have rights to participate in the community tourism organization.
Position Rules	No consideration for local community participation in tourist activities.	Creation of a local (community) tourism organization.	Creation of a governing board in the community tourism organization. Integration of nontourism stakeholders into the community tourism organization.
Scope Rules	Delimitation of sites that can be visited and the types of tourist activities within the GNP.	Opening of new sites in Floreana and exclusive concession to the community organization for their use. Provide quotas of regulated activities (daily tours, scuba diving tours) to the community. Reduction of the number of tourists that visit the island.	Criteria of reciprocity, equity, and inclusiveness of locals in their participation in tourist activities. Combination of private and community tourist activities.
Choice Rules	The quotas and regulations for tourist activities within the GNP in Floreana are decided at the regional level.	Drafting of new legislation that allows for some degree of exclusivity for community-led tourist activities in Floreana.	Development of regulations and system of community-led tourist activities by the local assembly.

the short length of the daily tours, and Post Office, which is located on the northwest coast. While it is one of the emblematic places to visit in the whole archipelago, Post Office is currently reserved exclusively for cruise ship tourism. In this way, Asilo de la Paz would not be the only place visited by land, and there would be an attractive site enabling tourists to remain for several days. This in turn would generate local demand for food and lodging services, guides, and other activities such as sailing, scuba diving, and snorkeling.

This first approximation of rule changes toward the development of CBT represented a point of departure for a series of interactions within and between local and regional levels, to which we turn our attention subsequently. To organize our data in a way that is intelligible and comparable between levels, we have used the conceptual unit called action situation (AS) (Ostrom 2011), conceived of as a context of interaction, negotiation, and creativity and composed of a complex web of multiple and recursive relations. The potential components of these action situations are open to adaptation to specific case studies. In our analysis, we delimit two different AS, corresponding to each of the two main levels in which the process of developing CBT takes place: the regional and the local. Within these AS, we pay attention to seven fundamental components each having their respective internal dynamics: (1) the CPRs subject to use in tourist activities; (2) the actors that participate in collective-action situations; (3) perceptions, knowledge, and worldviews that actors use to direct their actions toward the CPRs; (4) forms and contexts of the actions; (5) governance tools (e.g., regulations, management plans, assessment mechanisms) that they use in their actions; (6) intended rule-crafting; and (7) the expected outcomes. In this way, the AS helps organize ethnographic data and determine the tensions, contradictions, limitations, and catalysts of collective action both within each level of analysis as well as between them (see Figure 12.2). We must bear in mind that the AS in our study is focused on generating a new governance framework for the use and appropriation of CPRs.

The Archipelago as an Action Situation

At the regional level, we find eight main actors grouped in two camps according to our interpretation of their worldviews. The first set is comprised of the Environment Ministry, the GNP, and a group of NGOs (especially the World Wildlife Fund and the Charles Darwin Foundation) that

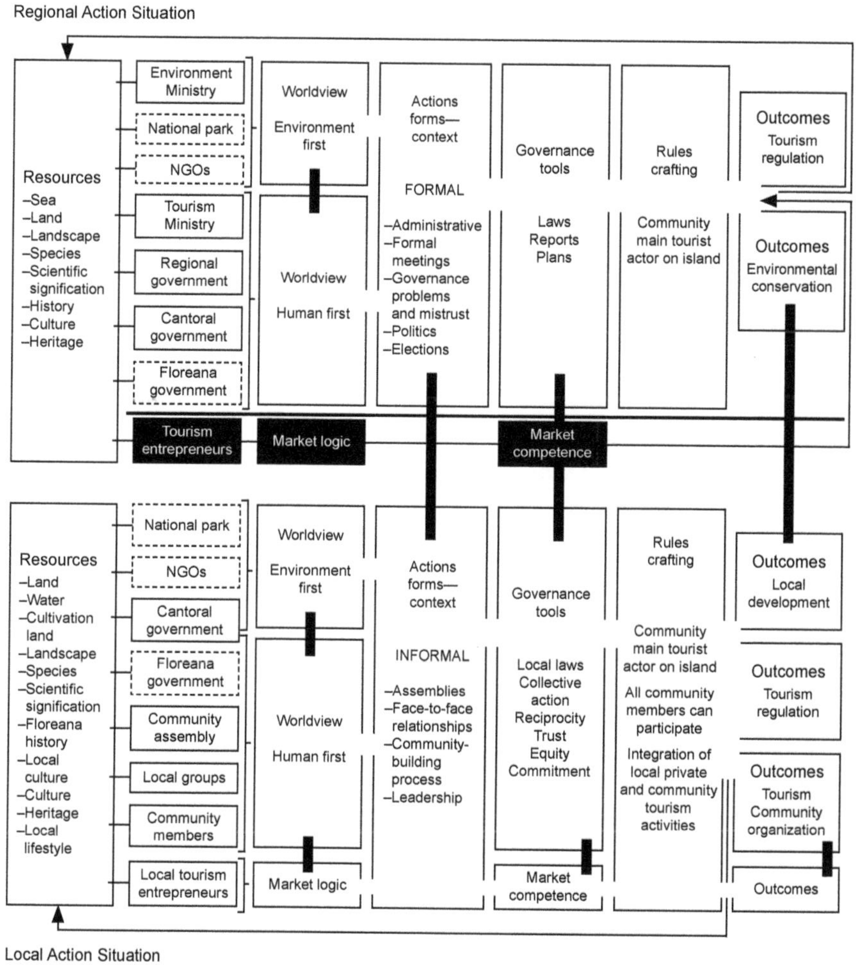

Each action situation (AS) (regional and local) is composed of seven elements that are represented in columns formed by boxes, from left to right: (1) the main CPRs subject to use in tourist activities, (2) the actors that participate in collective-action situations (in dashed boxes the protagonists of the process), (3) worldviews (perceptions, knowledge) that the actors use to direct their actions toward CPRs, (4) forms and contexts of actions, (5) the governance tools that actors use in their actions (e.g., regulations, management plan, assessment mechanisms), (6) the rule-crafting intended, and (7) the expected outcomes (separated in boxes). Boxes are articulated from left to right, so that the actors are linked to resources and, in turn, are grouped around worldviews, continuing the different elements of the process toward outcomes. Although this is not a linear process, it acquires this appearance for illustrative/graphic purposes. At the end of each AS, arrows link outcomes and resources indicating that the outcomes end up affecting the use and management of resources. At the regional AS, the actor "tourism entrepreneurs" (dark box at the bottom) is formally outside the AS and appears separate from the set by a line. However, an arrow connected to outcomes contemplates its de facto influence on the process. In the case of the local AS, the local tourism entrepreneurs are entirely integrated to the process. Through the lines, we show the main tensions of the process, both within each AS (e.g., between worldviews) and also between the components of the two AS (e.g., between forms and contexts of the actions, the governance tools, and even the outcomes within or between levels).

Figure 12.2. Regional and local action situations.

habitually work with the GNP in financing different activities and providing technical support for the park's conservation policies. This set shares a similar worldview from which the archipelago is understood as an integrated whole subject to environmental protection. While the human population is increasingly taken into account as an active agent in the socio-ecological system, there is still a lingering perception of them as the environmental problem. For this set of actors, the tourist model in the Galápagos, despite being the financial base for conservation, follows a problematic course that endangers the socio-ecological system. From this position, an improvement in the quality of life of the population from the archipelago serves as a means for environmental conservation, but not an end in itself. We call this worldview "environment first."

A second set of actors at this level is composed of the Tourism Ministry, the council of the Galápagos government, regional authorities, and the local government of Floreana. This group shares a vision of Galápagos based on local populations and the perspective of socioeconomic development, which we call "humans first." Despite its increasing adoption of an environmental sensibility, these actors hold that the improvement in the conditions of local inhabitants is an end in itself, and that tourism is the means to achieve it.

Over the course of our research, we participated in multiple meetings and gatherings of these two groups of actors to discuss the issue of Floreana and its future. On several occasions, these have been supported by the GNP and on others by the Tourism Ministry, which has sought to put special emphasis on the possibilities and benefits of CBT as it has been developed in state-level policy. From a communicative point of view, all of these meetings have been marked by an administrative, highly formal tone. Notwithstanding this bureaucratic veneer, in many cases the political and electoral interests that motivate these actors became evident. In general, the framework and the forms of action in this AS are highly marked by the problems of interinstitutional governance and mistrust in the archipelago. Nonetheless, the strong leadership of the GNP and some NGOs are evident at all times in this process of collective action.

Notably absent in the group of participants at this level are regional tourism entrepreneurs, who are formally excluded from meetings discussing the transformation of appropriation and use of CPRs in Floreana. These entrepreneurs would see a reduction in their present and future business opportunities on the island if the proposed set of rules for CBT is implemented as outlined above. Their worldview is quite distinct from the two other groups described here; for them, the islands are seen through the logic of the market enabling them to secure benefits through the development of tourism. Their forms of governance (market-based competition) and desired outcomes distinguish them from the rest of the actors in this AS. Their lack of formal participation does not, however, mean that they are unable to act upon the process, even if indirectly or implicitly. This is very evident for Floreana locals, who do not hesitate in expressing, as one informant stated, that "what some people are afraid of is that if we organize and begin to function collectively, we are an example, if not a threat, to the other ways of doing tourism here."

At the level of this AS, governance over the CPRs is based mainly on formal rules. The tools that the various actors propose for effecting an eventual transformation in the rules that govern the island's CPR include legislation and legal sanctions, new projects, and management plans aimed at setting the scope of CBT in Floreana within the regional context of the GNP. The intended rules shown in Table 12.1 seek in general terms to make the community the central actor of tourism on the island, to limit the presence of external private initiatives, and to open new visiting spaces within the park's territory in Floreana. The main expected outcomes would be a new set of regulations guiding tourism and environmental conservation.

The Island of Floreana as Action Situation

At the local level, CPRs are defined in more specific terms and new actors appear: the canton government, the community assembly, local groups (e.g., kinship, the agriculture association), the general population, and local tourism entrepreneurs. The GNP and NGOs also participate at this level. Thus, we have three actors repeated at both levels (GNP, NGOs, and local government); they are the protagonists of the process. The worldview that we labeled "environment first" is constrained at the local level and reveals itself as tangential, in spite of the presence of the GNP and conservation NGOs. The hegemonic worldview at the local level is what we call "humans first." The market vision is explicitly present given that local tourism entrepreneurs have a central role in the process. At this level, then, we find an arguably more complex landscape of different worldviews.

It is also important to take into account that in this AS, the forms and contexts of communication to generate collective action assume a very different nature from the administrative, highly formal, and technical tone of the regional AS. The assemblies and face-to-face relationships in the community are the main arenas of interaction in which the leadership of the elected local government's president is crucial. The forms and contexts of collective action are therefore mainly informal, something unusual for the GNP and NGO officials who nevertheless also have a protagonist role at the local level. Officials exert a significant level of control over strategic resources necessary for the process of implementing CBT in Floreana. They firmly support the development of a solid CBT as they think that this strategy could help to regulate and control tourist flows. In this local action situation, formal governance (local regulations for instance) also has a marked presence, but it is mediated by community norms regarding reciprocity, trust, equity, and commitment.

The local action situation intends to promote rule crafting (see Table 12.1) with the explicit objective of opening tourist activities to the local population (boundary and scope rules) and the development of a community organization to govern the use of the tourism-related CPRs (choice rules). In this sense, the process to generate rules at this level can be considered more complex than that found at the regional level. Their implementation at the regional level does require the acquiescence of higher levels of state administration that authorize this exceptionality for Floreana; it also needs to avoid the pressure coming from the business sector (boundary rules), but at the local level it requires the development of an entirely new community tourism organization (position rules) and consistent commitment from families and individuals.

Floreanos are quite clear in private (interviews) and public statements (assemblies) that they do not want the current tourism model, but they differ in their preferred alternatives and the means to procure them. This internal heterogeneity, even in such a small locality, cannot be ignored, as it underscores the level of trust necessary to implement a CBT program. In the face of external actors GNP and NGOs, such as in meetings and general gatherings, the community presents itself as much more cohesive than what it later shows in internal meetings. The CBT initiative, proposed originally by some local entrepreneurs, invites mistrust among those who think the process is nothing more but a stratagem of some to advance their personal interests. While they are also members of the community, local entrepreneurs have their own worldview based on governance tools guided by competition rather than equity or reciprocity. They also have their own intended outcomes (e.g., an increase in economic benefits from tourism) that only partially coincide with the outcomes expected at the local level, such as tourism regulation, maintenance of tranquility and safety, local development, and the establishment of a community organization for tourism-related activities.

To the majority of the community, tourism is understood as a means to an end, as stated publicly by one of its members:

> [Tourism is] an engine that needs to strengthen fishing, agriculture, craftsmanship. Everything rotates around the motor. But tourism should not change our lives so that we buy everything in Santa Cruz. We need to take into account that not all of us will be in tourism; fishing and agriculture are necessary. We need to strengthen those other sectors besides tourism.

Local tourism entrepreneurs move in an ambivalent position in which they strongly support community control of tourist activities, while at the same time they are afraid that community control may endanger their private activities. Consequently, their basic objective is to clearly untangle the collective and private parts of tourist activities, and it is here that mistrust emerges. Overcoming this constraint is key to the process at the local level and where we have found the main tensions and contradictions.

The local government, with the leadership of its president (a member of a family dedicated to tourism), seeks the integration of the entire community and to promote development beyond tourism. In November 2011, a document was drafted to form a "Pre-association for development and tourism in Floreana" as the nucleus of the future local tourism organization. In preparatory meetings, it was decided that the pre-association should include a representative from each of the island's families, regardless of their direct link to the tourism business. The document attempted to synthesize all the sensibilities of community members and in doing so, it sought consensus. First, it included a general proposal (developed in a previous workshop) for a CBT organization pursuing the following goals: articulation of private and community interests, community management of tourist flows, and direct community control in some strategic activities (e.g., transport) combined with substantial opportunities for private sector initiatives (e.g., lodging, restaurants). Secondly, the document posited a definition of tourist development not as a strategy in itself but as a means toward more general development for the community. This included the promotion of agricultural development (of much interest to a significant part of the population) and directing resources generated in tourist activities to finance other aspects of community life (e.g., professional training, education). Finally, there were commitments by the community for a more eco-friendly management of their lifestyle on the island. This was an explicit effort to address urban, energy, and resource issues to conform to the objectives of sustainability as expected in the national park. In this way, the predicted costs and benefits of the process were defined. With all of this, what was intended was to gain a consistent degree of commitment within the community, as well as to pressure higher levels of government to prevent the arrival of external investors in the tourism sector, a common objective of the local population.

The document was presented and discussed collectively and explained to different individuals and groups informally by the members of the local government; the objective was to gain the signatures from all the families in the community. We participated in the entire process and witnessed the concerns and doubts of some, as well as the strong support of others. In this way, we were able to consistently evaluate the advantages and disadvantages of CBT as perceived by Floreana's population. The document was not signed by a majority of community members as intended because some people maintained doubts about the real beneficiaries of an initiative of this type. Local people not involved in tourist activities consider that the CBT initiative could benefit mostly local tourism entrepreneurs, increasing their income instead of ensuring community access to this activity. This fact creates tension around the potential effect of the CBT: would it sustain community cohesion or increase internal differentiation? Obviously, that will depend on the way that CBT is organized, but in any case, it reflects a lack of trust within the local community. As a counterpoint, however, all the members of the local government, which represents the different local interests, did sign it.

From that time, the process of developing CBT in Floreana has continued to advance despite the challenges. In 2012, evaluation reports required to open new spaces for tourism in the GNP have been drafted, several workshops were organized to set ecological guidelines in the construction and use of resources, and a consultant was hired to design the community tourism organization. In addition, the GNP has continued to consistently support the process, and state agencies seem willing to grant exclusivity to the community organization in the management of tourism-related activities on the island. Within the community, however, there still persist doubts and mistrust, which give the local AS a more complex and uncertain dynamic than what could be supposed from the outside and without an ethnographic consideration of the process.

Within-Level and Cross-Level Challenges for CBT Development

In Floreana, and probably in most protected areas where CBT projects are proposed, it is necessary to consider the multilevel nature of the process of transforming the use and appropriation of CPRs by tourist activities, since these are subject to different regimes of property use and control. In addition, in this case both levels of action (regional and local) maintain a particular configuration where, despite a hierarchical relationship, there is a significant level of mutual dependence: both levels are needed to achieve their objectives. The development of CBT would be impossible from the regional or local levels operating independently. This multilevel alignment is not surprising given that the process (CBT development) emerged as a proposal from different sectors, at both levels, which are dissatisfied with the current tourism model. The intended rules themselves (see Table 12.1) do not reveal incompatibilities between levels but rather complementarity and overlap. On the other hand, the multilevel institutional framework, which is being configured around CBT in Floreana, seems a priori to be compatible with the design principles that characterize robust institutions for CPR management (Cox, Arnold, and Villamayor Tomás 2010; Ostrom 1990). In particular, the process has aimed at defining boundaries clearly, to develop congruence between appropriation and provisioning rules and local conditions, to recognize the rights of participants and affected parts to self-organize and craft rules, and to propose a system organized as a nested enterprise. It is not clear, however, how monitoring, sanctions, and mechanisms for conflict resolution will be developed and implemented. Is this then a process that, despite seeking a marked change in the use of CPRs, will be unproblematic? Dividing collective action into different signifying components and articulating them into two action situations at distinct levels helped us to better understand the process of development of the CBT in Floreana, including highlighting tensions and contradictions within and between levels.

The process of developing CBT in Floreana points to three discussion points that could be common to other cases. The first is the importance of local participation and the role of higher-level actors in excluding other actors from the process. While the exclusion of regional and national entrepreneurs could represent a roadblock for the process, the full inclusion of Floreana's entrepreneurs, in spite of local tensions, is helping to legitimize the process of implementing a new model of tourism. The second is the importance of considering worldviews and the intended outcomes in the internal dynamics of each action situation as well as the articulation between them. Finally, our analysis highlights the importance of coherence in crafting rules (at different levels and for different types of rules) defining control and regulation of CBT development and of tourism operations. The analysis of the case of Floreana shows us a situation with all these tensions (Figure 12.2) between the different components of each AS as well as between both AS.

Within-Level Challenges

At the regional level, we see two fundamental problems. On the one hand, there is a tension between worldviews and intended goals. The apparent coherence of the process establishing governance tools, rules crafting, and outcomes contrasts with the divergent knowledge that divide the main actors participating in the AS into two groups. This is an important factor for understanding the internal dynamic of this AS, since it ultimately means a larger compromise for a group aiming primarily at environmental conservation. On the other hand, the formal exclusion of regional and national entrepreneurs from the AS (represented in Figure 12.2 with black boxes and a separation line) implies a weakening of the AS itself, motivating this group to form a lobby that we know has pressured and will continue to do so at the state level to block the process of rule-crafting and consequently undermine the intended outcomes (that undoubtedly go against their interests).

At the local level, the tensions and contradictions increase as the local entrepreneurs are included in the AS. It is also evident that there is a need for a plural integration of multiple stakeholders in the CBT model at the local level, despite the fact that it may increase complexity because of the heterogeneity of worldviews, proposed governance tools, and expected outcomes. The tensions are multiplied, but they can be solved only in their emergence and through an adaptive process. This ethnographic case has demonstrated that Floreanos analyze the costs and benefits of this process beyond their economic dimension and clearly shows that even such a small community is not a homogeneous entity. The results indicate that one of the central aspects of the development of CBT is located at the community level. Thus, integrating individual and collective interests must have the central role in the collective-action process required to change tourism from business-as-usual to CBT model of tourism.

Cross-Level Challenges

The two ASs do not reflect only two different levels of collective action and institutional interplay, they also exhibit different sociocultural contexts.

While differences in worldviews are common to both levels, it is also obvious that each level has different expectations of outcomes, that is, CBT as means to environmental conservation or to economic development. While there has been some coordination between levels toward the development of CBT, reconciling these differences will require more attention to the development of monitoring, sanctions, and conflict-resolution mechanisms. Regarding the development of CBT in Floreana, the central actors are sufficiently represented in both AS (GNP, NGOs, and local government). At the local level, participation and collective decision making is direct, occurring through assemblies. The problems of different worldviews are not as significant as those that habitually occur between scientific and indigenous knowledge (Natcher, Davis, and Hickey 2005). In this case, it is a question of differing perspectives within the same cultural context. Consequently, applying Young's (2006) terminology, the multilevel analysis in Floreana is similar to a "negotiated agreement," with the possibility that it will evolve into a comanagement system with strong governance mechanisms at the local level (Berkes 2002). There are inherent tensions that occur in all processes of changing resource management (Carlsson and Berkes 2005; Cash et al. 2006). As we see in the description of the AS, the regional actors are varied and do not share a unified perspective of "the regional." The community, for its part, is perhaps even more complex and heterogeneous. Nonetheless, as these two levels maintain a clear relationship of interdependence, it is worthwhile considering them as "adjacent action situations" (McGinnis 2011b); in other words, as "outcomes generated in one action situation help determine the rules under which interactions occur within the other action situation" (2011b, 52). Even if we consider other levels (such as the state or market), both form a coalition against national and regional entrepreneurs on one hand, and, on the other, both seek to pressure the state in the concessions necessary for the development of CBT on the island.

Nonetheless, once the process of transforming a multilevel management regime has begun, as in Floreana, it is likely to be subjected to nonlinear trends according to its inherent complexity. The development of the process will be determined by events, agency, and contingencies more than by a priori rules or arguments, which can lead to different trajectories from specific events that create uncertainty. An example is the importance that particular leaders have in the two action situations studied. The personalities and visions of the park director, the local government president, or NGOs representatives strongly influence together with structural aspects the dynamic of crafting a plan for CBT. Any change among these actors at particular stages of the process is also likely to influence the outcome.

The complex nature of multilevel governance of CPRs implies that diverse worldviews and different forms of interpersonal relationships (contexts and forms) are important components of collective-action processes. They influence the negotiation of trade-offs needed to balance differences in expected outcomes (e.g., reconciling environmental conservation and local development). CBT is intended to promote management that takes into account that different resources associated with tourism are held not only under different ownership systems but also under different perspectives of management and use.

Conclusions

This case study sheds light on a number of theoretical and practical premises. On the one hand, it demonstrates the utility of combining institutional analysis (the IAD framework) with an ethnographic methodology. This strategy allows us to study the transformation of a CPR governance system as a process involving different levels of analysis and, at the same time, the internal dynamics of each of them. Ethnography confronts the complexity of study settings and cautions against the danger of schematic and mechanic simplification that an analytical model could impose in the absence of a real-world application. Confronting formalism and abstraction, ethnography not only brings us closer to the multiple dimensions of the process analyzed here but also the internal heterogeneity of its components even in a very small community such as Floreana. The IAD, on the other hand, offers a flexible analytical tool and a rich terminology that helps the systematization and comparative aspects of a case study (Ostrom 2011; Poteete, Janssen, and Ostrom 2010). Departing from this position and taking into account the complexity and inherent multilevel nature of the processes of CBT development, the IAD framework helped us to organize ethnographic data to facilitate within- and between-level analysis. We hope that the case study presented here helps to shed light on the complexity of developing rules and institutional arrangements for tourism activities in protected areas.

Acknowledgments

This chapter is a partial result of the research projects "Anthropology of Conservation in the Galápagos" (Charles Darwin Foundation and the Pablo de Olavide

University); and "Retóricas de la naturaleza y Turismo de Base Local: Estrategias de sostenibilidad" (Ministry of Economy, CSO2012–33044). Pedro Cantero and Javier Andrada participated in the fieldwork in Floreana. The combined work of the authors of this chapter was carried out during Esteban Ruiz-Ballesteros' position as visiting scholar at the Anthropological Center for Training and Research on Global Environmental Change at Indiana University Bloomington, financed by the Spanish Ministry of Education in 2012. Brondizio also thanks the Institut d'Etudes Avances–Paris for its support during the revision and resubmission of this chapter. The authors thank Gustavo Garcia for his careful editing and constructive comments on the initial manuscript.

Note

This chapter was originally published in *Human Organization* 72(4) (2013): 323–35. Reprinted with the permission of the Society for Applied Anthropology.

References

Acheson, James M. 2006. "Institutional Failure in Resource Management." *Annual Review of Anthropology* 35: 117–34.

———. 2011. "Ostrom for Anthropologists." *International Journal of the Commons* 5(2): 319–39.

Andrada, Javier, Pedro Cantero, and Esteban Ruiz-Ballesteros. 2010. *Habitar Galápagos: Encrucijada de Naturaleza y Cultura*. Quito, Ecuador: Presidencia de la República del Ecuador, Universidad de Cuenca.

Berkes, Fikret. 2002. "Cross-Scale Institutional Linkages: Perspectives from the Bottom Up." In *The Drama of the Commons*, edited by Elinor Ostrom, Thomas Dietz, Nives Dolšak, Paul Stern, Susan Stonich, and Elke Weber, 293–321. Washington, DC: National Academies Press.

Briassoulis, Helen. 2002. "Sustainable Tourism and the Question of the Commons." *Annals of Tourism Research* 29(4): 1065–85.

Brondizio, Eduardo S., Elinor Ostrom, and Oran R. Young. 2009. "Connectivity and the Governance of Multilevel Social-Ecological Systems: The Role of Social Capital." *Annual Review of Environmental Resources* 34: 253–78.

Carlsson, Lars, and Fikret Berkes. 2005. "Comanagement: Concepts and Methodological Implications." *Journal of Environmental Management* 75(1): 65–76.

Cash, David W., W. Neil Adger, Fikret Berkes, Po Garden, Louis Lebel, Per Olsson, Lowell Pritchard, and Oran Young. 2006. "Scale and Cross-Scale Dynamics: Governance and Information in a Multilevel World." *Ecology and Society* 11(2): 8.

Consejo de Gobierno de Galápagos (INEC). 2009. *Encuesta de Condiciones de Vida*. Puerto Ayora, Ecuador: Consejo de Gobierno de Galápagos.

———. 2011. *Censo población Ecuador*. Quito, Ecuador: Consejo de Gobierno de Galápagos.

Cox, Michael, Gwen Arnold, and Sergio Villamayor Tomás. 2010. "A Review of Design Principles for Community-Based Natural Resource Management." *Ecology and Society* 15(4): 38.

Gardener, Mark, R. Rachel Atkinson, and Jorge Luis L. Rentería. 2010. "Eradications and People: Lessons from the Plant Eradication Program in Galápagos." *Restoration Ecology* 18(1): 20–29.

Gonzalez, José, Carlos Montes, José Rodriguez, and Washington Tapia. 2008. "Rethinking the Galápagos Islands as a Complex System: Implications for Conservation and Management." *Ecology and Society* 13(2): 13.

Grenier, Christophe. 2007. *Conservación contra natura: Las islas Galápagos*. Quito, Ecuador: Abya-Yala.

Healy, Robert G. 2006. "The Commons Problem and Canada's Niagara Falls." *Annals of Tourism Research* 33(2): 525–44.

Hiwasaki, Lisa. 2006. "Community-Based Tourism: A Pathway to Sustainability for Japan's Protected Areas." *Society and Natural Resources* 19(8): 675–92.

Holden, Andrew. 2005. "Achieving a Sustainable Relationship between Common Pool Resources and Tourism: The Role of Environmental Ethics." *Journal of Sustainable Tourism* 13(4): 339–52.

Kruger, Oliver. 2005. "The Role of Ecotourism in Conservation: Panacea or Pandora's Box?" *Biodiversity and Conservation* 14(3): 579–600.

Li, WenJun. 2006. "Community Decision Making, Participation in Development." *Annals of Tourism Research* 33(1): 132–43.

McGinnis, Michael D. 2011a. "An Introduction to IAD and the Language of the Ostrom Workshop: A Simple Guide to a Complex Framework." *Policy Studies Journal* 39(1): 169–83.

———. 2011b. "Networks of Adjacent Action Situations in Polycentric Governance." *Policy Studies Journal* 39(1): 51–78.

Moore, Susan A., and Kate Rodger. 2010. "Wildlife Tourism as a Common Pool Resource Issue: Enabling Conditions for Sustainability Governance." *Journal of Sustainable Tourism* 18(7): 831–44.

Natcher, David C., Susan Davis, and Clifford G. Hickey. 2005. "Co-Management: Managing Relationships, Not Resources." *Human Organization* 64(3): 240–50.

Neves-Graça, Katja. 2004. "Revisiting the Tragedy of the Commons: Ecological Dilemmas of Whale Watching in the Azores." *Human Organization* 63(3): 289–300.

Okazaki, Etsuko. 2008. "A Community-Based Tourism Model: Its Conception and Use." *Journal of Sustainable Tourism* 16(5): 511–29.

Ostrom, Elinor. 1990. *Governing the Commons: The Evolution of Institutions for Collective Action*. New York: Cambridge University Press.

———. 2005. *Understanding Institutional Diversity*. Princeton, NJ: Princeton University Press.

———. 2011. "Background on the Institutional Analysis and Development Framework." *Policy Studies Journal* 39(1): 7–27.

Ostrom, Elinor, Roy Gardner, and James Walker. 1994. *Rules, Games, and Common-Pool Resources*. Ann Arbor: University of Michigan Press.

Parque Nacional Galápagos (GNP). 2012. *Parque Nacional Galápagos*. http://www.galapagospark.org.

Poteete, Amy R., Marco Janssen, and Elinor Ostrom. 2010. *Working Together: Collective Action, the Commons, and Multiple Methods in Practice*. Princeton, NJ: Princeton University Press.

Roberts, Sherma, and John Tribe. 2008. "Sustainability Indicators for Small Tourism Enterprises An Exploratory Perspective." *Journal of Sustainable Tourism* 16(5): 575–94.

Ruiz-Ballesteros, Esteban. 2011. "Socio-Ecological Resilience and Community-Based Tourism: An Approach from Agua Blanca, Ecuador." *Tourism Management* 32(3): 655–66.

Ruiz-Ballesteros, Esteban, and Macarena Hernández-Ramírez. 2010. "Tourism That Empowers? Commodification and Appropriation in Ecuador's Turismo Comunitario." *Critique of Anthropology* 30(2): 201–29.

Sick, Deborah. 2008. "Social Contexts and Consequences of Institutional Change in Common-Pool Resource Management." *Society and Natural Resources* 21(2): 94–105.

Stem, Caroline, James P. Lassoie, David R. Lee, David D. Deshler, and John W. Schelhas. 2003. "Community Participation in Ecotourism Benefits: The Links to Conservation Practices." *Society and Natural Resources* 16(5): 387–413.

Stronza, Amanda. 2010. "Common Management and Ecotourism: Ethnographic Evidence from the Amazon." *International Journal of the Commons* 4(1): 56–77.

Tao, Teresa, and Geoffrey Wall. 2009. "Tourism as a Sustainable Livelihood Strategy." *Tourism Management* 30(1): 90–98.

Taylor, Peter Leigh, and Antony S. Cheng. 2012. "Environmental Governance as Embedded Process: Managing Change in Two Community-Based Forestry Organizations." *Human Organization* 71(1): 110–22.

Theodori, Gene. 2005. "Community and Community Development in Resource-Based Areas: Operational Definitions Rooted in an Interactional Perspective." *Society and Natural Resources* 18(7): 661–69.

Tosun, Carl, and Dallen J. Timothy. 2003. "Arguments for Community Participation in Tourism Development." *Journal of Tourism Studies* 14(2): 2–11.

Wagner, John, and Malia Talakai. 2007. "Customs, Commons, Property, and Ecology: Case Studies from Oceania." *Human Organization* 66(1): 1–10.

Watson, James, Mandy Trueman, Marta Tufet, Scott Henderson, and Rachel Atkinson. 2010. "Mapping Terrestrial Anthropogenic Change across the Galápagos Archipelago." *Oryx* 44(1): 79–82.

West, Paige, James Igoe, and Dan Brockington. 2006. "Parks and Peoples: The Social Impact of Protected Areas." *Annual Review of Anthropology* 35(1): 251–77.

World Tourism Organization (WTO). 2006. *Poverty Alleviation through Tourism: A Compilation of Good Practices*. Madrid, Spain: World Tourism Organization.

World Wide Fund for Nature. 2001. *Directrices para el desarrollo del turismo comunitario*. Gland, Switzerland: World Wide Fund for Nature.

Wunder, Sven. 2000. "Ecotourism and Economic Incentives: An Empirical Approach." *Ecological Economics* 32(3): 465–79.

Yin, Robert. 2009. *Case Study Research, Design, and Methods*. Thousand Oaks, CA: Sage.

Young, Oran. 2006. "Vertical Interplay among Scale-Dependent Environmental and Resource Regimes." *Ecology and Society* 11(1): 27.

PART V

Foundations for Future Extensions

13

Institutional Analysis, Policy Analysis, and Performance Evaluation

VINCENT OSTROM

At the Bloomington conference in 1981, a group of colleagues in both Europe and North America undertook to clarify for one another the theoretical concepts and methodological tools that they were using to conduct inquiries at the interorganizational and intergovernmental level of analysis in the public sector. The key concepts being utilized were networks, implementation structures, and public service industries. The concept of network supplies an important heuristic for mapping the configuration of relationships that is likely to be involved in patterns of interaction in the advanced industrial societies of Western Europe and North America. Much of the discussion, however, focused upon the conceptual orientation and methodologies being used to study implementation structures and public service industries.

As sometimes happens in the exploration of new concepts and methodologies, the conferees were not able to clarify how the two different approaches were related to one another. Much of the discussion proceeded as though the two approaches were competitive. Yet there were important disjunctions. The essential complementarity did not get clarified because of the failure to specify the essential relationships between policy studies and service delivery studies.

This failure has been a stimulus to further reflection on my part. I have sought to understand different modes of political inquiry and the importance of establishing appropriate linkages among these modes of analysis if we are to develop adequate programs of inquiry into the study of political phenomena generally. Basic distinctions are difficult to establish because so much of political experience depends upon making comparisons across a multitude of conceptual sets that people draw upon in relating themselves to one another and that scholars in turn use to study the action tendencies that are derived from the use of those conceptual sets.

Political phenomena rely minimally upon overtly observable phenomena. Types of buildings provide clues about the activities that are likely to occur in those locations. Uniforms or patterns of dress provide other clues about action tendencies that can be expected. But the conceptions that people have in relating themselves to one another are of more importance in understanding what is giving order to human activities and relationships. Organizations are artifacts that contain their own artisans and an understanding of the nature of these artifacts depends upon the conceptions and explanations of the artisans who use these artifacts to relate themselves to one another. What Bielefeld University, for example, is depends upon the conceptions and explanations offered by those who identify themselves as being a part of Bielefeld University. The scholars who seek to understand the cognitively pregnant phenomena of human organization must, in turn, fashion their own cognitive tools where the referent is often difficult to specify. There is little wonder that problems arise in specifying cognitions of cognitions when human beings cannot directly read one another's minds.

An explicit and self-conscious effort to study the phenomenon of interorganizational and intergovernmental relationships when viewed from the perspective of studying cognitively pregnant experiences is something of a heroic effort in itself. The overwhelming preoccupation in the study of political phenomenon has usually focused upon the study of relationships inherent in a particular organization or unit of government. It is relatively easy to put boundaries upon patterns of relationships, to reify the concept of an organization and to imagine it to be a discrete thing. Where the focus shifts to the structure of interorganizational relationships and how one defines and conceptualizes those particular structures is itself a difficult task in human cognition.

In this chapter, I shall focus upon some basic cognitive distinctions that scholars make when they engage in the study of political phenomena. The distinctions I want to make pertain to what I shall refer to as policy analysis, institutional analysis, and operational analysis. First, I wish to show how these different modes of analysis are related to one another and show some of the difficulties that are likely to occur when studies are conducted without an awareness of the essential complementarity of these different modes of analysis. I shall turn first to policy analysis, to operational analysis, and then to institutional analysis. Finally, I shall indicate how the focus upon implementation structures and upon public service industries to study patterns of interorganizational relationships are essentially complementary to one another. The task confronting us, then, is to develop a conscious awareness of the importance of making proper linkages in scholarship drawing upon these different ways of conceptualizing patterns of interorganizational relationships.

Public Policy Analysis

In the contemporary social sciences and in political science particularly, a mode of analysis characterized as public policy analysis has been a major preoccupation of many scholars and professional policy analysts. In a most general sense, policy analysis is as old as efforts of legislators or others to explain the implications that would follow from a proposed course of legislative action. While this ancient perspective still has considerable relevance, the contemporary modes of policy analysis have taken somewhat different stances in relation to place of legislation in policy analysis.

One mode of analysis takes the legislative specification of goal or purpose as given and proceeds to conceptualize a means-ends analysis as being the appropriate mode of inquiry for conceptualizing the nature of a program that would entail the appropriate operation to realize the specified goal. This is an effort to construe or explain the relationships of an administrative program to the execution of public policy.

Another mode of analysis again takes the specification of legislative goal as defining the task to be accomplished and focuses upon the implementation of public policy. Implementation is considered successful when the legislative goal is realized and relatively unsuccessful as implementation efforts depart from the realization of legislative goals. Taking the legislative goal as controlling is sometimes referred to as a "top-down" approach. A variation in implementation studies are those that focus upon the configuration of different organizations that are implicated by any policy decision and examine the pattern of interorganizational arrangements that are involved in working out the implementation of a legislative enactment. This latter variation is the context for specifying implementation structures in "analysing policy production."[1]

There are critical problems that arise in these modes of analysis. One is the place assumed by the specification of the "goal" or "goals" in the legislative enactment. This aspect of a legislative action includes the specification of basic considerations of value. The goal is the value to be sought. Further, the mode of analysis proceeds on a presumption that a legislature is the legitimate instrumentality to make such decisions and the legislative decision is not itself to be subject to critical assessment and examination. Little or no consideration is given to the circumstance that political discourse at a legislative level, especially as one has recourse to only one legislature for a large nation-state, has strong tendencies to rely upon simple formulations that have the import of slogans: "war on poverty," "social justice," "pure water," "clean air," "good health." There may, then, be reasons why goals formulated in legislation are not properly specified or are misspecified.

The emphasis placed upon a means-ends calculus as applying to policy analysis suggests that the transformations in the means-end process yield some specifiable state. Problems at this point abound in determining whether the resulting state is a physical state such as "pure water" or "good health" would clearly imply, or a state of social relationships as a term like "social justice" might imply.

A means-ends calculus would need to specify the causal conditions that would yield something that is properly specified as "pure water." Can such conditions be specified so that the production of "pure water" is yielded as an end-state? If such a process were technically feasible, what would it cost and what would be its effects? Presumably, distilled water comes reasonably close to providing a technical criterion for pure water. Is this the goal being specified? What would be the costs of yielding such an end-state? What would be its effects? Can such a process be organized so that it would apply to a nation as a whole? If not, what are the conditions of variability that would require variable production processes in the way that particular enterprises or combinations of enterprises might be organized to produce comparable end-states?

In the allusions to means-ends analysis, the traditional modes of public-policy analysis rarely proceed with rigor in specifying a technically feasible engineering solution, but instead use a means-ends language as a crude heuristic to presume that an administrative process can be organized to yield the desired effect. The specification of end-states is abandoned for a crude and unspecified criterion of choice that is assumed to function in a set of rule-ordered relationships. The problem is shifted from being an engineering problem to a regulatory problem, where the assumption is made that administrative authorities are competent to enforce whatever regulations are adopted.

The rationale for implementation studies arises primarily from the circumstance that the thrust of the policy problem is not primarily one of engineering but one of regulation. The instrumental quality of a means-ends calculation then shifts to one of administration. Bureaucracies as ideal-types are often assumed to be rational means for attaining the goals sought in policy decisions. Perfectly obedient public servants held accountable by a well-integrated hierarchy of command are viewed as the appropriate means for the translation of legislative specification of goals into effects. The discrepancy between goal specification and performance is the issue addressed in implementation studies.

This shift in the nature of the problem with an assumption about the appropriateness of a means-ends calculation usually ignores the fundamental differences that are involved in physically producing "pure water" from regulating patterns of human conduct by reference to rules and rule enforcement. This latter problem requires reference to human institutions as rule-ordered relationships and a range of difficulties that are entailed in those relationships that are of a radically different order of magnitude than those that have to do with the properties of H^2O.

One of numerous difficulties is the issue of enforcement and the costs that apply to enforcement procedures. Most societies have elaborate procedures with exacting standards of judgment that apply to the imposition of criminal penalties. The imposition of sanctions for the violation of rules of law normally involves criminal jurisprudence.

The procedures in criminal jurisprudence in the United States, for example, require that special criteria be met that are in the legal competence of only specialized authorities. These authorities exist apart from the normal administrative channels that have to do with the implementation of public policy. Before an indictment can be issued in criminal proceedings, it is necessary to engage in "preliminary" proceedings that are designed to determine whether "probable cause" exists for prosecution. These proceedings uniformly require recourse to a grand jury, a prosecuting attorney, or an attorney general as independent law officers to establish the appropriate grounds for an indictment. Conviction of a criminal offense requires evidence that must meet demanding conditions of proof including that of unanimous agreement by a trial jury. The condition of unanimous agreement is designed to establish proof "beyond reasonable doubt." Enforcement costs associated with criminal proceedings, thus, entail high costs both for the enforcers and for those subject to enforcement efforts. Given these costs, one would not expect to find high levels of enforcement for those policies that entail high costs for "target groups" and proportionately small or negligible benefits for anyone else.

Implementation studies that view the relevant structure of relationships as involving multiple organizational arrangements have abandoned the assumption that a theory of bureaucracy provides the appropriate instrumentality for translating authoritatively specified goals into effects. But the problem is still viewed as one of "policy production" without having specified the problems of entrepreneuring the desired effects. In beginning to understand some of the difficulties involved, we need to specify more precisely the nature of policy decisions and their relationships to other decisions that are brought into focus by reference to the operational and the institutional modes of analysis.

Clarity is added if we recognize that the legislation is confined to words. Resolutions and statutes are nothing but words. A policy decision, then, is a set of instructions. If well formulated, that set of instructions may specify the attainment of some objective or goal with accompanying instructions that assigns certain powers with commensurable obligations to some who are to exercise entrepreneurial responsibilities in the realization of those objectives in relation to correlative obligations and entitlement on the part of the community of people who will presumably benefit from efforts being undertaken. We should never forget that policies are no more than a set of instructions and that the legislative process entails no more than producing sets of instructions.

Operational Analysis: Service Delivery Systems

To see the effect of a set of instructions upon end-states as tangible events requires a shift in the focus of inquiry. One needs to be concerned with states of the world including states of human social relationships and human development if the intended effect, as in education, bears critically upon the development of individual potentials. The focus is upon the effects that are yielded and upon the conduct of those enterprises that bear most closely upon yielding those effects. A focus upon service delivery rather than policy implementation provides a closer approximation to the tangible effects that occur.

Problems also abound in the study of service delivery and what constitutes appropriate indicators of outputs when inquiry focuses upon performance in the public sector at an operational level. The defining characteristics of many public goods and services are such that those goods and services are not easy to unitize or package into equivalent units. Measurements are difficult to attain. While difficulties abound, those difficulties need not foreclose the use of human ingenuity to conceptualize proxy measures that can be used as indicators of performance. Issues then arise in critically evaluating the limits and usefulness of different types of indicators.

For example, the Federal Bureau of Investigation (FBI) in the United States has for a long time used an index of major crimes to report on law enforcement efforts. Ostensibly, such an index would appear to be a good indicator of performance in the delivery of police services. However, serious difficulties arise that make this measure into a highly unreliable indicator. First, the data are derived from crimes as classified and reported by thousands of different police agencies. Either lax reporting or lax law enforcement is likely to create low measure on the crime index. Efforts to improve law enforcement efforts are likely to yield an increased score on the crime index. The measure creates false impressions about relationships of effort expended to results attained. These problems lead professional law enforcement officers to have little or no confidence in the FBI crime index as a measure of performance.

The insufficiency of the FBI crime index need not foreclose efforts to devise more appropriate indicators of the presence of crime and of police performance. Measures of criminal victimization may be important indicators. The reliability of different methods for estimating criminal victimization by a sample survey or a census of relevant population is a proper subject of inquiry. So is the analysis of calls for service, speed of response, degree of follow-up and referral, and evaluation of the quality of the service rendered. A variety of different indicators of performance can be used; and the use of a multimode approach might be expected to compensate for the bias of any single indicator.

The close relationship of fire protection to the value of property protected by fire insurance introduces a close proximity between effort and measurable effect in assessing the performance of fire protection agencies. Similar circumstances apply to the collection and disposal of trash and a variety of similar services. Measuring the output of an educational system poses greater difficulties analogous to those involved in police protection services.

The need to extend the horizons of public policy studies to take account of the effects yielded by studies of service delivery systems should be apparent if there is to be an assessment of the effect of public policies upon states of affairs in human communities and the environmental circumstances in which human beings relate to one another and to their world. All of those different relationships may be difficult to take into account or impossible to contain within the confines of a single study. Yet, it is important to appreciate the limits inherent in any one study and to be sensitive to establishing proper linkages that enable scholars to draw properly qualified conclusions from the limits that apply to particular studies. One type of essential linkages are those that appropriately relate policy studies to studies of service delivery systems.

Institutional Analysis

Policy analysis by focusing upon the prescriptive messages adopted by legislative bodies is necessarily related to other realms of inquiry that might be characterized as institutional analysis. Here, various types of rule-ordered relationships, as such, are subject to inquiry. Particular structures of rule-ordered relationships in legislative bodies, administrative agencies, judicial instrumentalities, and the relationships among different decision-making units in a system of government can all be subject to inquiry.

For example, reference to a hierarchy of superior-subordinate command structure to coordinate relationships both within and among governmental agencies can be subject to inquiry where inferences can be drawn about the implications that follow from such structures of relationships. On the one hand, the coordination of relationships through an integrated chain of command has been used to imagine a rational legal order that maintains a uniform rule of law throughout a public domain including that of a large nation-state. The same structure of relationships has been used to imagine radically different implications. When individuals are assumed to act strategically to advance their career potentials rather than being perfectly obedient public servants, the inference is that information will be systematically distorted to discount failures and to emphasize successes. Such filtering of information can reach a point where expectations depart radically from performance. This propensity can be expected to assume more extreme magnitudes in the public sector where outputs or outcomes are not easily observable and measurable. If the desired result does not apply uniformly over the domain of a nation-state, then the attainment of the desired variability might better be realized by multiple organizations.

Many similar questions can be raised about the effect of legislative structures upon the policy decisions that are reached. For example, the legislative process, including legislative debate, may be so organized that only those arguments considered to have a significant bearing upon the future prospects of the major political parties will have an opportunity to be heard. Legislative bodies such as the British House of Commons do not even permit all members to be present at any one time. Recognition to speak may not be available to individual members of the House of Commons. What any speaker has to say may be well delimited by party leadership in advance of presentation. Members of Parliament normally vote as instructed by party whips. The probability that legislative deliberation will serve to clarify the different implications that are likely to follow from legislative decisions is reduced when the legislative process is so organized to foreclose more open inquiry. The probability of "unanticipated consequences" is increased. Variable conditions of legislative organization can be expected to affect the way that policies and policy objectives are specified.

The conditions of legislative organization need to be viewed as reflecting variable institutional arrangements. To understand how these conditions are taken into account requires one to take a constitutional perspective where one might consider the effects that variable conditions would have in specifying the terms and conditions of legislative organization and of the relationship of legislatures to other decision structures within a system of government. A constitutional perspective would in addition require one to consider whether other principles of organization and criteria of choice need to be taken into account in considering legislative exercise of authority.

One of the more important design criteria that might apply to a system of government, including the exercise of legislative authority, is whether the terms and conditions specified in a constitution are enforceable as positive law. Jurisprudence would then be informed by constitutional law and the precepts of justice that give meaning to the language of law. In such circumstances, the exercise of governmental prerogatives would themselves be subject to general rules of law. That would limit the range of discretion.

The conditions that apply the maintenance of an enforceable system of constitutional law have radical implications. All exercises of authority would be subject to limits and no exercise of authority would be unlimited. This condition stands in antithesis to the doctrine of unlimited sovereignty on the part of those who exercise leadership positions in a government. A legislative specification of goal would in such conditions be an insufficient basis for determining its legitimacy and for making the inference that such a specification of goal is deserving of unqualified implementation.

The same issue can be addressed from a slightly different perspective. Do we have reason to believe that specification of a winning coalition in a legislature meets the necessary and sufficient condition for establishing a just policy that takes proper account of the larger community of interest or only serves the interests of those comprising the winning coalition? Where the latter possibility exists, the specification of rules of constitutional law that constrain the legislative exercise of discretion so as to reduce improper exercises of discretion would be justified.

From a constitutional perspective, one might then contemplate the conditions that might properly apply to legislative specifications of goals. Grounds might then exist for determining when a legislative specification of goal had not been properly specified. An issue might then exist in constitutional law about the criteria that apply to a proper specification of legislative standards. Such criteria would have substantial implications for conceptualizing standards that are relevant to the analysis of implementation efforts.

The problem can be illustrated by reference to an essay by Mazmanian and Sabatier (1981) that makes a general assessment of implementation studies. Mazmanian and Sabatier advance the thesis that "many of the case studies that form the bulk of the implementation literature become so immersed in the details of program implementation that they lose sight of the macro-level legal and political variables that structure the entire process" (1981, 3). These "macro-level legal and political variables" that structure the entire legislative and implementation process derive their meaning from their constitutional context.

In the course of their assessment of the implementation literature, Mazmanian and Sabatier formulate a list of items that is offered as a checklist for legislative staffs and other framers of legislation to take into account in drafting legislation so as to facilitate implementation. This list is reproduced as Table 13.1. This table can be construed as advice pertaining to the standards that are relevant to the exercise of legislature authority as derived from implementation studies.

Item 4 advises that "the number of veto points within and among implementing institutions" be minimized and that "sufficient sanctions and inducements" be provided "to enable supportive officials to overcome resistance among their colleagues and among target groups" (1981, 25). "Supportive officials" are those who support and advocate the legislation. "Target groups" are those who are subject to enforcement efforts. Efforts to invoke procedures giving opportunities to advance arguments about the probable effect of legislation and rules adopted under legislation would presumably be reduced or eliminated. Item 5 calls for supporting provisions including that of placing the burden of proof upon those subject to enforcement efforts. Items 7, 10, and 11 urge that legislation be drafted to strengthen the capability of supporters to act on behalf of the program, engage in legislative oversight, and participate in implementation processes. Special standing is to be given to supporters of the legislation, presumably at the cost of equivalent opportunities for those who have reason to oppose the legislation.

The purport of these recommendations has substantial significance for issues of a constitutional nature. Placing the burden of proof upon those subject to enforcement efforts stands at variance with long-established constitutional principles of due process of law. Extending special standing and resources to supporters of legislation would have a strong biasing effect upon the consideration of arguments and evidence in assessing the impact of implementation efforts. Winning coalitions are encouraged to formulate legislation in a way that mobilizes constituency support to facilitate both the short- and long-term dominance of those interests. Presumptions of equal justice in a procedural due process of law is abandoned to a presumption that winning legislative coalitions meet the necessary and sufficient conditions for properly specifying legitimate goals for mobilizing sanctions and taking collective actions in a society.

Whether such a presumption is correct or not can only be resolved by inquiries directed at institutional variables that are potentially relevant to constitutional choice. An extended tradition of inquiry about the effect of alternative voting arrangements both in selecting legislators and in making legislative decisions has developed over the last two decades. The overwhelming conclusion of this research is that no single voting rule whether applied to general elections or legislative decisions provides, by itself, an adequate mechanism for translating individual preferences into social decisions in a fair, reliable, and stable manner. This tradition of inquiry also demonstrates that skillful manipulation of the agenda within a set of rules can lead to a majority decision for a policy that is less preferred by a majority than other available alternatives. It is possible for minorities strategically to manipulate agendas so that minority preferences prevail over majority preferences. William Riker's book on *Liberalism against Populism* (1982) reviews the conclusions drawn from these inquiries. From these inquiries, there appears to be little justification for presuming that winning coalitions in legislatures will establish just policies that take proper account of the larger community of interest. Other structural and procedural constraints pertaining to due deliberation and due process of law are necessary conditions to facilitate the just exercise of authority in a society.

Table 13.1. The Mazmanian and Sabatier checklist: Will a proposed statute achieve its legislative objectives?

Toward this end, we propose the following checklist that legislative staff and other statutory framers can use in estimating the probability that a statute will achieve its mandated objectives. In so doing, we simplify the situation somewhat by making the following assumptions concerning the tractability of the problem—the most important being (1) that the statute seeks a rather substantial change in target group behavior and (2) that there is a reasonably valid theory relating changes in such behavior to the "solution" of the problem being addressed; in other words, the principal difficulty facing statutory framers is obtaining compliance from target groups.

1. Are the statutory objectives precise and, if multiple, clearly ranked in importance? Moreover, if the statute is assigned to an existing agency, does it indicate the relative priority of these new objectives in the totality of the agency's programs?
2. Does the statute actually incorporate a valid causal theory?
3. Does the statute provide sufficient financial resources to the implementing institutions to enable them to conduct the necessary technical analyses, to apply the general objectives to thousands of specific cases, and to monitor target group compliance?
4. Does the statute minimize the number of veto points within and among implementing institutions and does it provide sufficient sanctions and inducements to enable supportive officials to overcome resistance among their colleagues and among target groups? If dealing with a regulatory function, does it provide for tax breaks or other forms of compensation to members of target groups who are particularly hard-hit by adjudicatory decisions?
5. Are the decision rules contained in the statute consistent with statutory objectives? For example, do they place the burden of proof on target groups? Do they give as much authority as possible within implementing institutions to those officials most likely to support statutory objectives? Do they make the granting of permits or licenses contingent on specific findings consistent with statutory objectives?
6. Does the statute assign the responsibility for implementation to institutions (agencies) that are strongly supportive of its objectives and likely to grant the program high priority? Specifically, is it possible to create a new agency to administer the program or else to assign it to a prestigious existing agency that supports the objectives and is looking for a new program?

7. Does the statute maximize the opportunities for supporters external to the implementing agencies to participate actively in the implementation process? Specifically, does it provide standing for supporters to actively intervene in agency proceedings and to appeal agency decisions to the courts? Does the statute provide for evaluation studies by prestigious independent organizations to monitor the extent to which agency decisions and the impacts of those decisions are consistent with statutory objectives? Finally, is it possible to somehow centralize legislative oversight in the hands of supportive legislators?
8. What is the probability that changes in socioeconomic conditions or in technology during the foreseeable future are likely to undermine political support for statutory objectives? If the achievement of those objectives is contingent on technological innovation, what steps does the statute take to foster such progress?
9. What can be done to counter the short issue-attention span of the mass media and the general public? In particular, is it possible to convince some of the more important media to hire specialist reporters to cover the general issue addressed by the statute?
10. What steps can be taken to activate any latent supportive constituencies and to assure that supportive groups have the necessary staff and other resources to monitor and to actively participate in the implementation process?
11. What can be done to assure that legislative and executive sovereigns who support the statute will actively monitor and intervene in the implementation process? In particular, is anyone available to serve as a "fixer" and does he have the staff and other resources to do so effectively? Moreover, what can be done to assure that subsequent legislation in policy areas relevant to the statute does not undermine statutory objectives and that attempts to revise the statute do not emasculate it?
12. Can anything be done to appoint implementing officials who are not only committed to the achievement of statutory objectives but also have above-average managerial and political skills?

The answers to these questions should provide a reasonable estimate of the probability that the policy decisions of implementing agencies will be consistent with statutory objectives and that target groups will actually comply with those decisions until the objectives are attained.

Source: Mazmanian and Sabatier (1981, 25–27).

Linkages among Modes of Analysis

Public policy analysis, thus, needs to be conducted with a recognition that policy considerations need to take account of studies done in the mode of institutional analysis where the effort is made to ascertain the effect of variable institutional arrangements upon processes of policy making. These analyses need to take account of design criteria relevant to an assessment of the implementation process itself.

Since all human beings are prone to error and are subject to limited and biased perception, it would be an error not to subject legislative deliberation and implementation processes to the error-correcting procedures of critical inquiry in the exercise of human judgment. An awareness of the problems that arise in the organization of political processes and the way that different institutional arrangements may have differential effects in coping with such problems is of importance in understanding the policy process and the problems that are likely to arise in policy implementation.

While policies can be reviewed as a set of instructions that apply to the assignment of responsibilities for transforming states of affairs in the world of events, we also need to recognize that processes of legislation, implementation, and adjudication may also occur within sets of constitutional instructions that establish the relevant conditions and criteria of choice that apply to political processes more generally. It is an error to assume that implementation somehow acquires an imperative quality that dominates all other considerations in human societies.

The effects of these different sets of instructions must in turn be established by the way that they affect patterns of human interaction to yield tangible effects in reordering the world of events, relationships in human societies, and the development of individual human potentials. The effects of both institutional arrangements and policy decisions can be assessed only as attention can appropriately be focused upon outputs and outcomes. Thus, policy studies must be conceived as having a basic relationship to the study of service delivery systems and their effect upon events in the world.

The great difficulty that is presented is that any one study must be confined in a way that can address only a few questions at a time. It is not feasible for any one study to take account of all variables relevant to institutional, policy, and operational modes of analysis at any one time. Instead, it is necessary that scholars design particular studies so that they are cognizant of relevant conditions addressed in different modes of inquiry that are essential in specifying the logic of the relevant decision situation. To do this, we need to give much more serious attention to the linkages between institutional, policy, and operational modes of analysis and how they can be constructively related to one another.

It is possible to design inquiries about service delivery systems where pertinent institutional variables can be treated as independent variables to determine the differences, if any, in the effects that are yielded by variable institutional arrangements. Policy formulations that include reference to implementation structures that embody particular types of institutional arrangements can be treated as elements in a hypothetical set. Evidence derived from implementation studies could be tested for its consistency or inconsistency with findings derived from an examination of the relevant institutional variables for their effect upon service delivery.

Legislative specification of policy objectives and the terms and conditions pertaining to the attainment of those objectives can be construed at a theoretical level so that criteria pertinent to legislative decisions and the implications that follow from particular structures of electoral and legislative arrangements can be assessed for potential relevance. The empirical relevance of constitutional specifications regarding institutions of government, thus, depends upon establishing proper linkages between those considerations and the outputs and outcomes yielded by service delivery systems. Tangible evidence at the level of outputs and outcomes must be traced back through the conduct of enterprises in service delivery systems, through policy instructions to the terms and conditions that apply to the setting of those policy instructions, and their application, enforcement, and revision. In this way, we might hope to determine how structures affect performance.

An improvement in the quality of knowledge about the instrumental effect that different types of institutional arrangements have upon the outputs and outcomes yielded by service delivery systems should provide better grounds for exercising constitutional decisions relevant to the guidance and control of governing institutions. When the governed can establish and enforce appropriate constraints and criteria upon the conduct of those who govern, human societies would have the appropriate basis for maintaining patterns of reciprocity where all would be held accountable to the same basic standards of conduct. Where such arrangements are subject to critical inquiry, human societies might gradually acquire increasing capabilities for self-government.

Implications for the Study of Interorganizational Arrangements

The difficulties experienced at the Bloomington conference in identifying the relationship of implementation structures as formulated by Hjern, Hull, and Porter at the International Institute of Management (IIM) to public service industries as formulated by the community of scholars associated with the Workshop in Political Theory and Policy Analysis should now be apparent. The focus upon multiorganizational implementation structures is centrally directed to issues of policy analysis and "to analyzing policy production in a systematic manner in this corporatist world of fuzzy political responsibilities," as Hjern has put it.[2] The public service industry studies were conceived and conducted as inquiries concerned with service delivery systems. The two approaches are complements to one another. Both types of studies need to be placed in the context of a more general system of inquiry that has reference to institutional, policy, and operational modes of analysis.

The IIM studies are concerned with manpower training programs in Sweden and Germany. A multiplicity of agencies with different structures are involved in the complementation of policies pertaining to the development of manpower training programs. If the confines of the policy study were to be extended to service delivery arrangements, the focus of inquiry would then shift to an effort to assess the structure and performance of labor markets in an effort to determine what effect differently structured manpower training programs have upon the performance of labor markets. Presumably, such market arrangements would include both private and public employment and the operation of black markets in labor services as well as fully legitimate markets. The conceptualization of the relevant industry structure would presumably have reference to both private and public instrumentalities and voluntary associations contributing to the supply of labor services in relation to potential users of such services.

Studies in the delivery of police services might also be complemented by studies of policy implementation where an effort would be made to determine how a general policy to be applied to all police agencies would be considered within the context of fora organized on an interorganizational basis to determine how relationships should be reconstituted to facilitate the attainment of the policy objective. It is imaginable that unanticipated problems might arise at this level of inquiry requiring a reconsideration of policies. The assessment of these calculations would have a critical relevance for determining the effect of a policy decision upon service delivery and the effects yielded for communities of people. It is imaginable that a policy decision might adversely affect performance when measured by one criterion and improve performance when measured by another criterion. Those involved in a public service industry may well form themselves into an implementation structure in considering the effects of a polity upon their joint operations. But this does not imply that an industry structure is the same as an implementation structure. If patterns of entitlement are established in law where citizens can make enforceable demands upon service delivery agencies, we might expect quite different patterns of compliance than where enforcement prerogatives are confined to a central regulatory agency and the Department of Justice. Again, institutional variables enter into the calculation of probable effects.

Different modes of analysis and different conceptual terms are appropriately used to complement one another in undertaking parallel modes of inquiry. Clarifying the different modes of analysis, their patterns of complementarity to one another, and their ties to a more general framework of analysis are important steps in the development of interorganizational studies that draw concurrently upon institutional, policy, and operational modes of analysis.

It is also important to recognize that different intellectual disciplines have diverse resources that can be mobilized for these different modes of analysis. Students of philosophy and jurisprudence have strong interests that bear upon critical issues in institutional analysis. Political scientists and sociologists have been centrally concerned with policy analysis. Economists have had more strongly focused interests in operational analysis. Yet, inquiry is not narrowly compartmentalized. Studies broadly concerned with guidance, control, and performance evaluation in the public sector need to draw upon diverse capabilities across a variety of different scholarly disciplines. Effective collaboration depends upon a clarification of the essential complementarity of different approaches and the mobilization of critical capabilities to be derived from different points of view.

Notes

This chapter was originally prepared for a Workshop on Interorganizational Arrangements in the Public Sector held at the International Institute of Management (IIM) in Berlin, Germany, on July 26–28, 1982, and was originally published in *The Quest to Understand Human Affairs: Natural Resources Policy and*

Essays on Community and Collective Choice, vol. 1, edited by Barbara Allen (Lanham, MD: Lexington Books, 2011), pp. 319–37. Table 13.1 reprinted with the permission of the authors.

1. Benny Hjern to Vincent and Elinor Ostrom, December 3, 1983.
2. Letter to Vincent and Elinor Ostrom, December 3, 1982.

References

Kiser, Larry, and Elinor Ostrom. 1982. "The Three Worlds of Action: A Metatheoretical Synthesis of Institutional Approaches." In *Strategies of Political Inquiry*, edited by Elinor Ostrom, 179–222. Beverly Hills, CA: Sage. Reprinted in Michael McGinnis, *Polycentric Games and Institutions: Readings from the Workshop in Political Theory and Policy Analysis* (Ann Arbor: University of Michigan Press, 2000), 56–88.

Mazmanian, Daniel, and Paul Sabatier, eds. 1981. *Effective Policy Implementation*. Lexington, MA: Lexington Books.

Ostrom, Vincent. 1982. "A Forgotten Tradition: The Constitutional Level of Analysis." In *Missing Elements in Political Inquiry: Logic and Levels of Analysis*, edited by Judith Gillespie and Dina Zinnes, 237–52. Beverly Hills, CA: Sage.

———. 2008. "The Normative and Limiting Conditions in a Polycentric Political Order." In *The Struggle to Constitute and Sustain Productive Orders*, edited by Mark Sproule-Jones, Barbara Allen, and Filippo Sabetti, 29–43. Lanham, MD: Lexington Books.

Parks, Roger B., and Elinor Ostrom. 1981. "Local Service Delivery Structures: Modelling Interorganizational Effects on Intraorganizational Decision Making." Presented at the International Conference on the Analysis of Intergovernmental and Interorganizational Arrangements in Public Administration, Indiana University, Bloomington, May 11–14, 1981.

Riker, William H. 1982. *Liberalism against Populism*. San Francisco, CA: Freeman.

14

Learning from the Field

ELINOR OSTROM

Let me first extend my thanks to Michael Szenberg and his colleagues for inviting me to contribute a chapter to this distinguished volume. It has given me an opportunity to rethink some of the foundations of my own work.

While many of the economists who have contributed to this volume began their academic journeys in high school or college, mine did not begin until I was a graduate student at UCLA in the early 1960s. As a poor kid born in the Depression (1933), my early years were focused primarily on survival. We were fortunate to have a relatively large backyard in our home in Los Angeles, where we had a variety of fruit trees and room to plant a vegetable garden. As a kid, I learned how to garden and also how to preserve fruits by standing over a hot stove to can them. Now I must confess that the long, hot August days that I spent canning peaches and apricots are not my favorite memories of my childhood, but I certainly learned a lot about the household economics of a poor family—long before I studied these problems in developing countries.

Since neither of my parents had more than a high school education, I received no encouragement to obtain a college degree. My mother, in fact, strongly discouraged any thought of college. Fortunately, she had transferred me to Beverly Hills High School from the Los Angeles school system, and 90 percent of my high school classmates planned to go to college. Consequently, I wanted to go to college just to "keep up" with my friends. I entered UCLA in 1951. When asked by a counselor what major I wanted to adopt, I responded "debate," as I had really enjoyed and learned a lot from debating in high school. The counselor somewhat indignantly told me there was no such major in college. The counselor then noted my major as education, as this was the only major that the counselor thought was appropriate for a girl at that time. Girls who received good grades in college (as I had done in high school) could find a job teaching grammar school or high school, but the counselor did not know of any other opportunities for girls with a BA degree in the early 1950s.

My most pressing need was to find part-time work to support myself in college. Fortunately, I was able to combine teaching swimming during the summers (I had been on a swim team in high school) with a variety of part-time jobs in the library and in local stores. Given UCLA's low tuition fees in that era, I was able to graduate from college without any debt by working twenty-five to thirty hours a week. After taking an interesting political science course in my first semester, I became a political science major, not because of job opportunities but because of enjoyment of the class. I also took a variety of economics classes for enjoyment, and I received good grades in both. I was asked to become a grader for freshman economics courses during the last year and a half of my undergrad program.

After graduation in 1954, I married my high school steady date and moved to the Boston area to help finance his training at Harvard Law School. After an extensive job search, I spent my first year in a clerical job, since very few positions were available in those days to a young woman with a college degree. Then, I stubbornly talked my way into a position as the assistant personnel manager for the home office of Godfrey Lowell Cabot located in downtown Boston. As the first woman in a professional position for the firm, I worked hard and was quite pleased that I was successful in opening up the staff to the possibility of a greater variety of religious, gender, and racial characteristics among employees than when I joined, while also receiving strong recommendation letters for the future. After returning to Los Angeles, I was surprised when my husband took a position with a private business corporation rather than a law firm. Over the next few years, our paths continued to go in different directions, and we decided on a divorce before having children.

My experience in personnel administration in Boston enabled me to obtain a good professional position as a personnel analyst at UCLA, and I began taking courses leading to an MPA degree in personnel management. I really enjoyed the content of my initial graduate courses in political science and economics, and I did well. I began to dream about entering a PhD program in economics or political science. Because of the lack of mathematics in my undergraduate program (due to the counseling I had received as an undergraduate), the UCLA Economics Department rapidly turned down my application but encouraged me to take an outside minor in economics if I was accepted by the Political Science Department. Some political science faculty members strongly objected to the admission of women to their doctoral program, but I was admitted in the fall of 1960 and began to dig into an exciting interdisciplinary program. I was very fortunate that several faculty members in economics and political science, including Jack Hirshleifer, Vincent Ostrom, and Charles Tiebout, were engaged in active research programs on the organization of governance in metropolitan areas and the governance of the water industry in California (Hirshleifer, DeHaven, and Milliman 1960; V. Ostrom, Tiebout, and Warren 1961; see also Bain 1959).

Their early work challenged the notion that order in the public sector stemmed only from central direction. Instead of prejudging the performance of complex organizations in metropolitan areas, Ostrom, Tiebout, and Warren proposed, for example, that the multiplicity of local jurisdictions in a metropolitan area be conceived as a "polycentric political system."

> "Polycentric" connotes many centers of decision-making which are formally independent of each other. . . . To the extent that they take each other into account in competitive relationships, enter into various contractual and cooperative undertakings or have recourse to central mechanisms to resolve conflicts, the various political jurisdictions in a metropolitan area may function in a coherent manner with consistent and predictable patterns of interacting behavior. To the extent that this is so, they may be said to function as a system. (V. Ostrom, Tiebout, and Warren 1961, 831)

This brought a different perspective to the study of governance. Instead of presuming the existence of only two kinds of order—the market and the government—they concluded that order could be achieved in *public industries* where large, medium, and small governmental and nongovernmental enterprises engage in both competitive and cooperative relationships.

Public Entrepreneurship

In a research seminar organized by Vincent Ostrom on the water industry in Southern California, each graduate student was assigned one groundwater basin underlying Los Angeles County or the adjacent Orange County and asked to gather and analyze data regarding how water producers were coping with or ignoring growing overdrafts. I was assigned West Coast Basin, which underlay the coast from approximately the Los Angeles International Airport south to the Palos Verdes peninsula. Water production had expanded during the war years of the early 1940s. By 1945 there were approximately 350 groundwater producers composed of public water utilities and private water companies, oil companies, industrial producers, and 250 nonindustrial groundwater pumpers, many of which produced vegetables and fruit for the Los Angeles market.

In 1945 the West Basin Water Association was formed to provide an arena where the multiple issues of groundwater overdraft and saltwater intrusion could be discussed on a regular basis. In 1961, when I started my study—not knowing at that time that I would continue to study West Basin for my doctoral dissertation—the leaders of the West Basin Water Association invited me to attend their regular meetings and to examine their extensive archives. The problems faced in West Basin were substantial and complicated, involving the major overdraft of the basin and substantial disagreements regarding how to arrive at agreed-upon water rights, how to gain sufficient and accurate information about the underground structure and flow of water into the basin, and how to create and sustain new enterprises.

After my first-semester report on the developments I observed in West Basin, I realized that the resource problems of West Basin represented a variety of classic problems that I was reading about in the literature. I was studying the work on entrepreneurship by Joseph Schumpeter (1936) and Frank Knight (1921), as well as Ciriacy-Wantrup's (1952) work on the economics of resource conservation, Musgrave's (1959) work on public finance, and Buchanan and Tullock's (1962) analysis of constitutional choice at multiple levels. I was witnessing forms of public entrepreneurship that would be hard to match if one were studying elected public officials representing state or federal agencies with limited access to relevant records or the officials themselves.

Fortunately, I began my study sixteen years after the initial formation of the West Basin Water Association, and I had full access to all of its correspondence and records. Therefore, I was able to obtain detailed records of many of the concrete actions that the local leaders had already adopted to overcome the threat of losing a valuable natural resource—a groundwater basin—through overuse and saltwater intrusion. I could hear and read about years of head-on conflict that was slowly resolved in the shadow of an equity court jurisdiction by an agreement negotiated by a committee of attorneys and engineers that was finally agreed to by more than 80 percent of those pumping water from the basin. Further, these public entrepreneurs invented several physical structures to create a barrier against further saltwater intrusion and means of using reclaimed fresh water to replenish the supply of water in the basin. I do not want to go into further detail here, but interested readers can find more in Ostrom (1990, chap. 4), Blomquist (1992), and Blomquist and Ostrom (2008).

What were the major lessons I learned from my dissertation research that have influenced my academic career in the more than fifty years since I defended?

First, I recognized how difficult it is to find economically efficient allocations for what I now know are common-pool resources.

Second, I witnessed the incredible amount of time and energy that some participants facing a tough public problem are willing to devote to achieving solutions that reflect long-term gains to their own entity and are relatively fair to the interests of others.

Third, I learned about large-scale government facilities—such as equity jurisprudence in a state court system, the creation of special districts, and national agencies (such as the US Geological Survey) that can provide rigorous scientific information about local unknowns (such as the hidden underground boundaries of a groundwater basin) that increase the capabilities of locals to solve tough problems.

Fourth, I learned about the operational advantages of polycentric systems (V. Ostrom, Tiebout, and Warren 1961), which were under considerable development and discussion at UCLA, for helping solve public problems that did not conform to any of the boundaries of core public and private actors involved. I also learned that involving multiple agencies in coping with a complex problem was not automatically chaotic in nature. Rather, some combination of agencies potentially enabled citizens, private industry, and local, regional, state, and national public agencies to work together to bring diverse knowledge and capabilities to bear on difficult problems.

Fifth, I learned the advantage of drawing on multiple disciplines for the study of complex public problems.

Sixth, I learned the importance of patience and persistence. The public entrepreneurs of West Basin spent the better part of two decades working out the system of public and private industry that was basically in place by 1965. Further studies backed up my initial findings. Blomquist (1992) studied eight groundwater basins in Southern California that documented further progress in West Basin (but not uniformly across all eight basins he studied). Brian Steed (2010) has examined the achievements fifty years later and found that the groundwater conditions of West Basin have continued to improve significantly over time.

After completing my dissertation (1965), I learned that the basic theory of "collective *in*action" propounded by Mancur Olson (1965) and the "tragedy of the commons" articulated by Garrett Hardin (1968) were both correct in pointing to the difficulty of solving collective-action problems. I had, however, substantial evidence that it was *not impossible* for those involved to solve these challenging problems if allowed to engage in public entrepreneurship.

Studying Scale of Public Organization to Provide Public Goods

For the next phase of my work, the work of Vincent Ostrom (1999) on polycentricity and that of Herbert Simon (1957a, 1957b, 1978) on public administration and ways of thinking about human choice were both foundational. Both Ostrom and Simon stressed the lack of well-developed and tested theory related to the provision of public goods and services by governmental agencies in urban areas. Both stressed the essential complexity of governmental relationships in urban areas and criticized the many public administration scholars (e.g., Gulick 1957; Friesema 1966; Hawley and Zimmer 1970; Wood 1961) who propounded the untested theory that concentrating governance in a single hierarchical unit in a metropolitan area was the most efficient way to organize the provision of public services.

On the basis of this untested theory, public administration scholars strongly recommended massive consolidation of urban government units. The basic textbook on urban governance during the second half of the nineteenth century recommended that "as far as possible in each major urban area *there should be only one local government*. . . . Furthermore, the *administration should be organized as a single integrated system* upon the hierarchical principle, tapering upward and culminating a single chief executive officer" (Anderson and Weidner 1950, 609–10; original emphasis; see also Committee for Economic Development 1970).

Simon strongly criticized the repeated calls for reform without a sound theory or careful field research to test that theory. In his treatise *Administrative Behavior*, he asked what steps research should take to improve our understanding of diverse governance arrangements:

> First, it must develop adequate case studies of existing administrative situations. It will do well to initiate these on a small scale—dealing in

> minute detail with organizational units of moderate size. Only in this way can superficiality be avoided.
>
> Second, techniques must be developed and improved for measuring the success of particular administrative arrangements. . . . The only procedure of evaluation that can possibly be valid is the comparison of alternative administrative schemes in terms of their objective results. (Simon 1957a, 247)

In the early 1970s, I had an opportunity to take Simon's advice seriously. After a period of administrative responsibility as the graduate advisor for the Department of Political Science during the Vietnam era, where the administrative load was very large, I had my first opportunity to teach a yearlong graduate seminar. I chose to focus on the challenge of developing better theory and empirical methods for understanding the incentives generated by diverse ways of organizing the production of diverse urban goods and how this affected outcomes. Fortunately, Roger Parks, Gordon Whitaker, Dennis Smith, and several other advanced graduate students joined in an initial effort to understand how police were organized and performed. Without a research grant, it was challenging to think about how structure and performance could be studied effectively, but Roger Parks came up with an excellent idea, and my spring undergraduate seminar involved students who wanted to participate in a real research project.

In the nearby Indianapolis metropolitan area, there were three small, independent police departments located immediately adjacent to the city of Indianapolis. The neighborhoods inside Indianapolis were quite similar to the neighborhoods served by these small departments. From reading extensively on the causes of crime, we had come to a basic understanding that the level of crime in an area was a function of both the socioeconomic status of the neighborhood and how local government and police services were organized and provided. The location of these neighborhoods side-by-side provided an opportunity to take Simon's advice to compare "alternative administrative schemes in terms of their objective results" by designing a small, "most-similar systems" comparative case study of how the size of a police department affected crime rates, citizen evaluations and willingness to call on the police, police response times, internal work patterns in the different departments, and other measures of performance.

When we drew our initial frame for doing a random sample of households to be interviewed, we were very concerned that we draw boundaries in such a way that we selected neighborhoods inside the city of Indianapolis that were very similar to those being serviced by the three independent departments. Consequently, after working with census block data, we took students, who were not at all familiar with Indianapolis, there for a day. We drove them through the independent communities and crossed into Indianapolis without mentioning that we had crossed boundaries. After we had gone back and forth several times, we asked the students if they had noticed any obvious change in the basic structure of the neighborhoods they were observing, and they had not. We also conducted statistics analyses, after we had finished our interviews, to ascertain whether the social and economic structure of the respondents sampled in the independent communities was similar to that of the three Indianapolis neighborhoods. We were relieved to find that very few differences existed in the socioeconomic characteristics of the respondents in the survey data (see E. Ostrom et al. 1973).

On the other hand, there were major statistical differences in regard to basic data related to police performance. We found that the citizens living in the small, independent communities had a statistically significant lower victimization rate, a greater willingness to report victimization when it occurred, faster and more extensive police follow-up, and higher evaluations of promptness, police-citizen relations, and general evaluations of the job being done by their police department (E. Ostrom et al. 1973). Research conducted two decades later demonstrates that the relationships found in Indianapolis in the 1970s were still valid twenty-five years later (Parks 1999).

This first study of the impact of police organization was replicated in relatively similar neighborhoods in Grand Rapids, Michigan, by Samir IsHak (1972) and in the Nashville–Davidson County metropolitan areas by Bruce Rogers and C. McCurdy Lipsey (1974). Then we conducted a closely related study of two poor black communities with their own police departments and three similar black communities located within the city of Chicago and served by that city's large police department (E. Ostrom and Whitaker 1974). We found that the allocations of resources to the two types of neighborhoods were extremely different in that more than fourteen times as many resources were devoted to police services in the city of Chicago neighborhoods than in either of the two small, independent communities. The major difference in allocated resources, however, did *not* increase the service levels received by black citizens in the city of Chicago.

With our increased confidence in our findings and ability now to obtain research grants to conduct broader studies, we decided to do a major study of policing in the St. Louis metropolitan area. The residents of the city of

St. Louis were served by a very large department with more than 2,000 officers. Two-thirds of the ninety-three independently incorporated cities had their own police departments, ranging from one with only part-time officials to one with seventy-six full-time officers (E. Ostrom 1976). We again utilized a most-similar systems research design to generate a design matrix that included three strata of neighborhood wealth and racial characteristics served by police departments that ranged from very small to the St. Louis Department with more than 2,000 officers. We conducted citizen surveys, interviewed officers serving these neighborhoods, rode with officers as observers, and recorded data obtained from official police records and reports to their citizens.

We found that the size of a police department was positively and significantly related to the victimization rate within a neighborhood and citizen's sense that crime was increasing. Size was negatively related to (1) the percentage of citizens assisted, (2) the percentage of citizens indicating that police responded "very rapidly" in their neighborhood, (3) the percentage of citizens rating the job being done by their police as "outstanding," (4) the percentage of citizens strongly agreeing with the statement that "police are honest," and (5) the percentage of citizens strongly agreeing that "police treat all citizens equally" (E. Ostrom and Parks 1973).

Our findings strongly negated the presumption that the size of police departments was positively related to performance across this series of studies. However, we received considerable criticism when we presented papers at professional meetings about our reliance on survey data, rather than official crime data, as measures of performance. There was substantial skepticism that citizens would be able to provide accurate data about police department performance. Some scholars urged us to use official crime statistics rather than survey data, even though multiple scholars who had examined police service delivery and quality of service had challenged the notion that police were measured well by crime data. Obviously, one problem that many scholars pointed out is that aspects of the neighborhood itself affected crime rates, but this is why we very carefully matched neighborhoods before examining the impact of differently organized police departments.

This skepticism about citizen capacity to measure performance led us to conduct a very careful "measurement study" (E. Ostrom et al. 1975). We studied a variety of ways of measuring street lighting and developed a method for taking measurements of street brightness using a light meter. We then developed two methods for measuring road roughness. One was a "roughometer" that we dragged behind a car in order to produce a graph of the smoothness to roughness of a neighborhood street. The second was a way of sampling urban streets and observing how smooth they were and whether there were potholes and, if there were, measuring their depth. Then, we did a random sample of citizens on each street sampled and asked questions regarding their estimates of road roughness and brightness of street lighting. Findings from this study showed us that citizens accurately reported the road roughness in front of their homes. Their evaluation of street lighting turned out to be less accurate, but lighting experts later explained that the color of the street lighting affects what citizens see as contrasted with our physical measurements. The experts concluded that the citizen evaluations were relatively accurate, given the diversity of colors of street lighting in the neighborhoods we studied.

Our growing sense that citizens could give us reasonable evaluations of public services was also reinforced by our efforts to obtain good data about how police were organized internally. In most of the departments studied, we drew a random sample of officers' beats and rode with the officers for an eight-hour shift. This gave us an excellent opportunity to see if there were differences in the knowledge of the police officers and the way that police related to neighborhoods served. We did observe differences. When we rode in police cars assigned to small- to medium-sized departments, officers would spend time on our first observation, telling us about the background of the neighborhood and showing us where particularly safe neighborhoods were located and where there were problematic areas in which they kept a careful watch. On our first observation in a large police department, on the other hand, officers would frequently apologize for not knowing the neighborhood they were patrolling very well since they had to rotate every twenty-eight days. These rotation shifts represented an attempt by large departments to deal with threats of corruption, but our citizen surveys revealed that there was a higher level of police corruption in the large jurisdictions than in the small (Parks 1984).

Studying Police Industry Structure and Performance

In our studies of the effect of the size of a police department on performance, we shared the skepticism of Vincent Ostrom, Charles Tiebout, and Herbert Simon regarding the naive theory advanced in public administration regarding the advantages of hierarchical organization for the production of public goods. We also followed Simon's (1957a) advice to conduct careful case studies of existing administrative structure, as well as his skepticism about the performance of public hierarchies. As previously discussed, we started with a carefully designed but small study of police organization and performance for six very similar neighborhoods served by one large and three small police departments. We found that the presumptions made by the Committee for Economic Development (1970, 1972) and many scholars that larger departments would produce better services were not supported in Indianapolis. Nor were they supported in Grand Rapids, Nashville, or Chicago, with similar designs but different types of neighborhoods, or in our large study of diversely organized departments and neighborhoods in St. Louis.

While we were able to publish our results in reputable journals, not much attention was paid to our surprising findings by national commissions or public administration scholars. Major reports were still recommending the consolidation of most police agencies serving urban areas into metropolitan-wide departments (National Advisory Commission on Criminal Justice Standards and Goals 1973). Two observations tended to dominate the thinking of scholars who assumed that hierarchy was the best way to organize public-service delivery. First, it was noted that small- to medium-sized police departments rarely had their own crime laboratories. Because few studies were made of the day-to-day administrative life of police departments, the presumption was made that police serving smaller communities did not have access to *any* criminal laboratories to conduct blood tests and analyze other crime investigation data. Second, it was observed that many different agencies engaged in traffic patrol in a single metropolitan area. The presumption drawn from this observation was that the distribution of this service was chaotic and thus of low quality.

Given the theoretical tradition that focused on public-service industries among those active in the early development of the Workshop in Political Theory and Policy Analysis at Indiana University, we thought it would be important to do a careful, large-scale study of the structure and performance of the police service industry in metropolitan areas. This would require the development of a new approach to the study of police *industry* rather than the study of individual police *organizations*. Further, we needed to develop completely new research instruments to measure the structure of the police industry accurately in multiple metropolitan areas so that we could assess how structure affected performance. We spent time studying the research strategies and methods of those studying private-service firms and industries (Caves 1964; Williamson 1964, 1967; Robinson 1958; Bain 1959; McKean 1964; Margolis 1964) but realized we could not use exactly the same methods developed to assess the structure and flow of private-good industries.

We had to invest heavily in a new analytical approach to characterize direct and intermediate police services. *Direct services*, such as general area patrol, traffic regulation and patrol, and various types of investigatory services, are produced directly by police for citizens. *Intermediate services* are required in the production of direct services and include radio communications, detention, training, and crime laboratory analyses. We identified six characteristics of local collective goods as they combine with institutional arrangements to affect performance in providing or producing direct and intermediate police services. On the production side, these were (1) economies of scale in production, (2) coproduction, and (3) measurability. On the provision side, these were (1) the size and location of the group of individuals who jointly consume a service, (2) the diversity of preferences about service styles and levels, and (3) the degree of choice that citizens have concerning their consumption of a service.

Economies and Diseconomies of Scale

Economies of scale occur when the average costs of production decrease with increases in the amount of the good being produced. Many intermediate police services are capital intensive, and economies of scale are reached in large production units. Average costs of crime laboratory analysis, for example, tend to fall over an extended range of output. Initial capital expenditures involved in purchasing equipment are large. Highly trained personnel are needed to run analyses. Training of new police officers can also involve substantial economies of scale. When training is conducted in an "academy," substantial investments must be made in a building and a staff so that training a large number of recruits will be less expensive (per recruit) than training only a small number. Radio communications also involve the purchase of relatively expensive equipment and the likelihood of economies of scale.

In contrast, direct services are highly labor intensive. Between 85 and 90 percent of the costs of direct services relate to personnel or variable expenses, such as gasoline. Serving a larger jurisdiction may increase average costs rather than reducing them for most direct services. In regard to the investigation of infrequent events, such as homicides, one might expect that specialized units serving a large area might process a sufficient number of cases to enhance skills at production.

Coproduction of Police Services by Citizens

Physical goods can be produced independently of the inputs of those who eventually may consume them. However, the production of all services involves some input by the consumers being served (Parks et al. 1981). If students, for example, do not participate actively in their own education, input resources devoted to education have little effect on results achieved. Students are essential coproducers of education. In regard to safety in a community, citizens are important coproducers. They provide the "public eyes" that may prevent criminal activities or alert the police to problems. Without the active help of citizens giving information and being willing to serve as witnesses in court, police are less effective in solving crimes or in building cases that can be prosecuted in court. Citizens can prevent many types of criminal activities by taking precautionary efforts of many kinds.

Coproduction of direct police services by citizens is likely to be more intensive in small collective consumption units where citizens perceive themselves to have a stake in preserving the peace and safety of their neighborhoods and view the police as providing valuable services to assist in those efforts. Officers serving in small police departments should also be more oriented to encouraging citizens to help in the coproduction of direct services. In regard to intermediate services, citizens are not normally involved as coproducers, but the direct and indirect-service producers themselves may be involved in coproduction activities.

Measurability

Satisfactory measures of direct police services are difficult to obtain. Conceptually, the outputs of direct services are "states of affairs" improved to some degree by the efforts of police. Thus, the output of general area patrol is the extent to which it is safer to walk on the streets or keep valuable possessions because of the efforts of police.

One can never directly measure the output of direct services, as it requires reference to a counterfactual situation: the state of affairs that would have existed in the absence of police services. Measurement must rely on either statistical inference or proxy measures. Reliable statistical inference would require that we *know* the set of factors that cause crime and could accurately predict the level of crime that would occur without any police services. Such knowledge is not available. Police and citizens alike tend to rely on three types of proxy measures: (1) resource inputs, (2) activity levels, and (3) crime rates.

Indicators of *resource inputs* include the total budget or expenditures and the number of employees. These provide information only about the resources available to produce services and give no information on the level or quality of output. While many social scientists have presumed that output is linearly associated with resource inputs, our own studies made us skeptical about this assumption. Indicators of *activity levels* include number of miles driven, number of tickets issued, number of calls answered, number of arrests, and number of crimes solved. These are "closer" to what we mean by the output of police, but are still proxy measures and are largely under the control of the producer. A police department can increase its "output" by increasing the number of people arrested or the number of traffic tickets issued. In other words, police can arrest more drunks on Saturday night and increase their "productivity." Whether that reflects an increase in "output" is highly questionable.

Crime rates, the third type of proxy measures, are trace data that survive a long series of transformations under the control of many different actors. Some information is lost at each transformation, and systematic distortion can occur at each step. For example, police can record information so that a lesser crime is coded when they want to reduce serious crime, while increasing the "seriousness" of the offense when they want to produce a local "crime wave." Since budgetary allocations are frequently increased after a local crime wave has occurred, internal incentives exist within departments to bias data recordation so as to produce the given results.

The difficulties of developing reliable and valid quantitative measures of direct services output make it advantageous to organize both the production and the provision of direct police services in relatively small units. The police chief of a very large department is a captive of the statistical reports on activities and crime rates that he receives. He cannot have a good "feel" for what is happening on the street, as he is too far removed by status and physical barriers. On the other hand, the police chief of a small department, who actively patrols and observes his officers on a day-to-day basis, is better able to monitor performance. Police chiefs of small departments are *not* entirely dependent upon statistics to estimate the quality of police work. In medium-sized departments, the chain of command is quite shallow, and police chiefs still have a relatively accurate picture of what is happening on the street. Thus, police chiefs in small- to medium-sized departments can monitor internal performance on the basis of more detailed and accurate information than police chiefs of larger departments.

On the provision side, local public officials representing a large community cannot know first-hand what is happening in many different locations. They are also captives of the statistical information they receive. Thus, they have difficulty articulating demands related to the real performance of officers on the street. In a small community, mayors and local councils have a chance to observe the activities of their local police on a day-to-day basis and are able to specify far more precisely what they want and what they do not want in their community.

While measurement problems are severe in regard to direct services, intermediate services are easier to measure. Many private-sector "for-profit" firms sell equivalent types of services, such as telephone answering services, laboratory services, and training services. Since meaningful records of such services can be kept, a direct-service producer may easily arrange for intermediate services with alternative producers of those services.

Size and Location of the Group of Individuals Jointly Consuming a Service

Only a relatively small group of citizens simultaneously consumes the benefits of most direct services. Those who receive the protection of a police car on patrol, for example, live in small and concentrated areas. Traffic patrol and accident investigation on major freeway systems, however, serve a larger community of individuals, some of whom live and work in a particular metropolitan area and some of whom are traveling between more distant locations. Most intermediate services may jointly affect a relatively large group.

Diversity of Preferences

Citizens' preferences vary substantially in regard to the level and type of police services. In poor neighborhoods where the streets are extensively used for recreational purposes, citizens strongly prefer a sense of public order that involves an extensive use of sidewalks and streets for outdoor activities. The same level of noise and commotion would be viewed negatively in a wealthy neighborhood where citizens have a strong preference that police maintain quiet and peaceful streets.

When exclusion is of low-cost to the supplier, as with private goods, preferences for the amount and quantity of a good are revealed as a result of many quid pro quo transactions. Producers learn about preferences through consumers' willingness to pay for various goods offered for sale. Where exclusion is difficult, designing mechanisms that honestly reflect beneficiaries' preferences and their willingness to pay is difficult and complex, regardless of whether the providing unit is organized in the public or the private sphere. In very small groups, those affected are usually able to discuss their preferences and constraints on a face-to-face basis and to reach a rough consensus. In larger groups, decisions about provision are apt to be made through mechanisms such as voting or the delegation of authority to public officials. The extensive literature on voting systems demonstrates how difficult it is to translate individual preferences into collective choices that adequately reflect individual views (Arrow 1951; Shepsle 1979; Buchanan and Tullock 1962). The problem of preference aggregation is intensified when individuals with radically differing preferences are combined into one collective consumption unit. Consequently, smaller provision units with a greater homogeneity of preferences reduce some of the difficulties of arriving at collective decisions (Bish 1971).

Degree of Choice That Citizens Have Concerning Consumption of a Service

Citizens have extremely little choice about whether to consume most direct police services. The existence of a particular style of patrolling in a neighborhood, for example, makes it difficult for those living in the neighborhood to avoid being affected unless they physically move from the neighborhood. When aggressive patrol techniques are utilized and individuals are frequently stopped and frisked, all families living in the neighborhood are forced to consume this type of order. Any in-person protest to the officers on patrol may result in physical harm. From the consumers' point of view, living in a small jurisdiction where the voices of individual citizens may carry greater weight is an important institutional factor offsetting to some extent the degree of coercion imposed upon local residents. Citizens can articulate more effectively preferences about how their neighborhoods should be served. More effective voice is particularly important for poorer families who cannot easily move and who are thus more exposed to threats of coercion either from those who offend against the law or from those who serve as police officers.

In regard to intermediate services, citizens are not the actors who can exercise direct choice in any case. It is producers of direct services who may be able to exercise some degree of choice. Choice depends upon the availability of alternative suppliers. If a police department has its own radio transmitter and is tied into other networks, it can exercise some degree of choice concerning its use of alternative facilities.

Measuring Industry Structure

Drawing on work related to the structure of private industry, we developed a method for recording how police were organized in a metropolitan area by using police service matrices. For each of the direct and intermediate services observed in a metropolitan area, we recorded the producers as columns in the matrix. Then we recorded the consumption units, such as local city governments, as rows in the matrix. For each direct or intermediate service, we could then assess whether there was any duplication of services whereby one producing agency (columns) served more than one provision agency (rows). This enabled us to array metropolitan areas into those that were more consolidated, where there were fewer producers for the population served, as compared with those that were more "fragmented," meaning there were a larger number of distinct organized consuming units for any particular service in question. We developed a relative *fragmentation* measure by dividing the absolute fragmentation by the population of the metropolitan area.

We also developed a measure for *multiplicity*. The absolute measure was the number of producers for a particular service, while two relative measures were obtained by dividing the absolute number by the number of consuming units for that service as well as dividing it by population size. We measured *duplication* by examining the matrix to determine when two or more consuming units regularly received a service from more than one producer.

We carried out our study of police industry structure in a random sample of eighty metropolitan areas (E. Ostrom, Parks, and Whitaker 1978). We identified a total of 1,159 direct-service producers. Most of these agencies produced general area patrol, traffic patrol, accident investigation, and burglary investigation services. In regard to intermediate services, we found that 70 percent of the direct-service producers also produced their own radio communications, but only a small proportion of any of the direct-service producers produced the other intermediate services such as crime labs or entry-level training. However, in *all* eighty metropolitan areas, indirect services were made available to *all* direct-service producers, contrary to the assertions of those proposing major consolidation of police departments. Our findings regarding the structure and performance of police industry in these eighty metropolitan areas substantially challenged the presumptions made by many scholars.

Our measures of performance included the allocation of police personnel to on-the-street assignments and the relative efficiency of agencies in producing response capacity and solving crime. For each of the eighty metropolitan areas, we calculated the number of producers of each type of service (multiplicity) and the proportion of the population being served by the largest producer of each type of service (dominance). Metropolitan areas with low scores in regard to multiplicity and high scores in regard to dominance come closest to approximating the "consolidated" model so frequently recommended by consolidation proponents. Metropolitan areas with high scores in regard to multiplicity and low scores in regard to dominance came closest to approximating the "fragmented" metropolitan areas criticized by these same proponents.

We found a distinct difference in the availability of sworn officers to engage in patrol activities in the metropolitan areas depending upon the industry structure. While more officers per capita were employed in the most consolidated areas, a lower percentage of these officers were actually assigned to patrol divisions in these metropolitan areas. One-third more officers were required in the most consolidated metropolitan areas to place the *same* number of officers on patrol as compared with the least consolidated metropolitan areas. Citizens living in the most fragmented metropolitan areas received more police presence on the streets for their tax expenditures than did citizens living in the most consolidated areas (Parks 1985).

The Underlying Philosophy of My Work

In this essay, I have focused on my early career rather than the research carried on over the past forty years. The philosophical foundation of my research program was well established by the early 1980s, even though I have ventured forth on a rich program of research focusing on how institutions affect incentives related to common-pool resources (E. Ostrom 1990; E. Ostrom, Gardner, and Walker 1994; Poteete, Janssen, and Ostrom 2010). The most important theoretical foundation has continued to be the theory of polycentricity initially developed by V. Ostrom, Tiebout, and Warren (1961) and V. Ostrom (1999), as well as Herbert Simon's (1957b,

1978) theory of bounded rationality and his stress on the importance of field research. I have also been deeply enriched by important studies in public choice (Brennan and Buchanan 1985; Buchanan 1968; Buchanan and Tullock 1962) and the new institutional economics tradition (North 1978, 1990, 2005). The extensive field research conducted early in my career generated findings contrary to the presumption that when the market is not an efficient solution to a problem, hierarchy is the only other viable solution.

Basically, I believe that solving problems related to the long-term sustainability of common-pool resources and the efficient provision of public goods is difficult but not impossible. Further, the theoretical presumption that public officials in hierarchical governments are most likely to find efficient and fair solutions does not have an empirical foundation. Imposing policies based on a faulty theory can generate substantial problems.

Instead of using different models for citizens and public officials, I prefer to think of all individuals in most situations as facing incomplete information but having the capacity to learn over time if they continue their interactions. Further, individuals can learn norms regarding what they should, should not, or may do in particular situations given the actions of others in that situation. Individuals also acquire diverse preferences for outcomes (both positive and negative) to be achieved by others. Thus, instead of expecting to find narrow utility-maximizing individuals in most settings, I expect to find a mixture of types of individuals. In repeated social dilemmas that generate relatively accurate information about the actions that other individuals have taken in the past and that facilitate communication, I expect to find that many individuals adopt strategies that improve their own and other persons' outcomes, but not necessarily the outcomes of all participants. An important factor affecting individual orientations to benefits for self and others is whether those involved are able to change the structure of frequent encounters so as to increase the likelihood of jointly positive outcomes. Thus, the possibilities of public entrepreneurship have continued to fascinate me throughout my career.

It is indeed important to build a stronger theoretical foundation for understanding public economies at local community, metropolitan, national, and international levels. But to do so requires a behavioral theory of human behavior and a rigorous, but more complex analysis of the diverse contexts that affect the initial incentives of participants, information that participants obtain about a situation over time, and their capacity to adapt to changes in that environment (these ideas are developed in greater depth in E. Ostrom 2010; Poteete, Janssen, and Ostrom 2010).

Note

This chapter was originally published in *Eminent Economists II: Their Life and Work Philosophies*, edited by Michael Szenberg and Lall B. Ramrattan (New York: Cambridge University Press, 2014), pp. 316–37. Reprinted with the permission of Cambridge University Press.

References

Anderson, William, and Edward Weidner. 1950. *American City Government*. New York: Henry Holt.

Arrow, Kenneth J. 1951. *Social Choice and Individual Values*. New York: Wiley.

Bain, Joe S. 1959. *Industrial Organization*. New York: Wiley.

Bish, Robert. 1971. *The Public Economy of Metropolitan Areas*. Chicago, IL: Markham.

Blomquist, William. 1992. *Dividing the Waters: Governing Groundwater in Southern California*. San Francisco, CA: ICS Press.

Blomquist, William, and Elinor Ostrom. 2008. "Deliberation, Learning, and Institutional Change: The Evolution of Institutions in Judicial Settings." *Constitutional Political Economy* 19(3): 180–202.

Brennan, Geoffrey, and James Buchanan. 1985. *The Reason of Rules: Constitutional Political Economy*. New York: Cambridge University Press.

Buchanan, James M. 1968. *The Demand and Supply of Public Goods*. Chicago, IL: Rand McNally.

Buchanan, James M., and Gordon Tullock. 1962. *The Calculus of Consent*. Ann Arbor: University of Michigan Press.

Caves, Richard. 1964. *American Industry: Structure, Conduct, Performance*. Englewood Cliffs, NJ: Prentice-Hall.

Ciriacy-Wantrup, Siegfried V. 1952. *Resource Conservation, Economics, and Policies*. Berkeley: University of California Press.

Committee for Economic Development. 1970. *Reshaping Government in Metropolitan Areas*. New York: Committee for Economic Development.

———. 1972. *Reducing Crime and Assuring Justice*. New York: Committee for Economic Development.

Friesema, H. Paul. 1966. "The Metropolis and the Maze of Local Government." *Urban Affairs Quarterly* 2: 68–90.

Gulick, Luther. 1957. "Metropolitan Organization." *Annals of the American Academy of Political and Social Sciences* 314: 57–65.

Hardin, Garrett. 1968. "The Tragedy of the Commons." *Science* 162(3859): 1243–48.

Hawley, Amos H., and Basil G. Zimmer. 1970. *The Metropolitan Community: Its People and Government*. Beverly Hills, CA: Sage.

Hirshleifer, Jack, James C. DeHaven, and Jerome Milliman. 1960. *Water Supply: Economics, Technology and Policy*. Chicago, IL: University of Chicago Press.
IsHak, Samir. 1972. "Consumers' Perception of Police Performance: Consolidation vs. Deconcentration—The Case of Grand Rapids, Michigan Metropolitan Area." PhD diss., Indiana University.
Knight, Frank H. 1921. *Risk, Uncertainty, and Profit*. Boston, MA: Houghton Mifflin.
Margolis, Julius. 1964. "The Structure of Government and Public Investment." *American Economic Review* 54 (May): 236–42.
McKean, Roland N. 1964. "Divergences between Institution and Total Costs within Government." *American Economic Review* 54 (May): 243–49.
Musgrave, Richard. 1959. *The Theory of Public Finance: A Study in Public Economy*. New York: McGraw Hill.
National Advisory Commission on Criminal Justice Standards and Goals. 1973. *Report on Police*. Washington, DC: US Government Printing Office.
North, Douglass C. 1978. "Structure and Performance: The Task of Economic History." *Journal of Economic Literature* 16: 963–78.
———. 1990. *Institutions, Institutional Change and Economic Performance*. New York: Cambridge University Press.
———. 2005. *Understanding the Process of Institutional Change*. Princeton, NJ: Princeton University Press.
Olson, Mancur. 1965. *The Logic of Collective Action: Public Goods and the Theory of Groups*. Cambridge, MA: Harvard University Press.
Ostrom, Elinor. 1965. "Public Entrepreneurship: A Case Study in Ground Water Basin Management." PhD diss., University of California, Los Angeles.
———. 1976. "Size and Performance in a Federal System." *Publius* 6(2): 33–73.
———. 1990. *Governing the Commons: The Evolution of Institutions for Collective Action*. New York: Cambridge University Press.
———. 2010. "Beyond Markets and States: Polycentric Governance of Complex Economic Systems." *American Economic Review* 100(3): 641–72.
Ostrom, Elinor, William H. Baugh, Richard Guarasci, Roger B. Parks, and Gordon P. Whitaker. 1973. *Community Organization and the Provision of Police Services*. Beverly Hills, CA: Sage.
Ostrom, Elinor, Roy Gardner, and James Walker. 1994. *Rules, Games, and Common-Pool Resources*. Ann Arbor: University of Michigan Press.
Ostrom, Elinor, and Roger B. Parks. 1973. "Suburban Police Departments: Too Many and Too Small?" In *The Urbanization of the Suburbs*, edited by Louis H. Masotti and Jeffrey K. Hadden, 367–402. Beverly Hills, CA: Sage.
Ostrom, Elinor, Roger B. Parks, et al. 1975. "Measuring Urban Street Conditions." In *Measuring Urban Services: A Multi-Mode Approach*, pamphlet 2, Portfolio of Professional Papers on Measuring Urban Services (The Measures Project). Bloomington: Indiana University, Workshop in Political Theory and Policy Analysis.

Ostrom, Elinor, Roger B. Parks, and Gordon Whitaker. 1978. *Patterns of Metropolitan Policing*. Cambridge, MA: Ballinger.

Ostrom, Elinor, and Gordon P. Whitaker. 1974. "Community Control and Governmental Responsiveness: The Case of Police in Black Neighborhoods." In *Improving the Quality of Urban Management*, edited by Willis Hawley and David Rogers, 303–34. Beverly Hills, CA: Sage.

Ostrom, Vincent. 1999. "Polycentricity" (Part 1 and Part 2). In *Polycentricity and Local Public Economies: Readings from the Workshop in Political Theory and Policy Analysis*, edited by Michael McGinnis, 52–74; 119–38. Ann Arbor: University of Michigan Press.

Ostrom, Vincent, Charles M. Tiebout, and Robert Warren. 1961. "The Organization of Government in Metropolitan Areas: A Theoretical Inquiry." *American Political Science Review* 55(4): 831–42.

Parks, Roger B. 1984. "Linking Subjective and Objective Measures of Performance." In *Understanding Police Agency Performance*, edited by Gordon P. Whitaker, 148–59. Washington, DC: US Department of Justice, National Institute of Justice.

———. 1985. "Metropolitan Structure and Systemic Performance: The Case of Police Service Delivery." In *Policy Implementation in Federal and Unitary Systems*, edited by Kenneth Hanf and Theo A. J. Toonen, 161–91. Dordrecht, the Netherlands: Martinus Nijhoff.

———. 1999. "Do We Really Want to Consolidate Urban Areas? [It's Like Déjà Vu All Over Again]." In *Polycentricity and Local Public Economies: Readings from the Workshop in Political Theory and Policy Analysis*, edited by Michael McGinnis, 349–351. Ann Arbor: University of Michigan Press.

Parks, Roger B., Paula Baker, Larry Kiser, Ronald J. Oakerson, Elinor Ostrom, Vincent Ostrom, Stephen L. Percy, Martha Vandivort, Gordon P. Whitaker, and Rick Wilson. 1981. "Consumers as Coproducers of Public Services: Some Economic and Institutional Considerations." *Policy Studies Journal* 9(7): 1001–11.

Poteete, Amy, Marco Janssen, and Elinor Ostrom. 2010. *Working Together: Collective Action, the Commons, and Multiple Methods in Practice*. Princeton, NJ: Princeton University Press.

Robinson, E. A. G. 1958. *The Structure of Competitive Industry*. Chicago, IL: University of Chicago Press.

Rogers, Bruce D., and C. McCurdy Lipsey. 1974. "Metropolitan Report: Citizen Evaluations of Performance in Nashville–Davidson County, Tennessee." *Publius* 4(4): 19–34.

Schumpeter, Joseph A. 1936. *The Theory of Economic Development*. Trans. Redvers Opie. Cambridge, MA: Harvard University Press.

Shepsle, Kenneth A. 1979. "Institutional Arrangements and Equilibrium in Multidimensional Voting Models." *American Journal of Political Science* 23(1): 27–59.

Simon, Herbert A. 1957a. *Administrative Behavior: A Study of Decision-Making Processes in Administrative Organization*. New York: Free Press.
———. 1957b. *Models of Man: Social and Rational*. New York: Wiley.
———. 1978. "Rationality as Process and as Product of Thought." *American Economic Review* 68(2): 1–17.
Steed, Brian C. 2010. "Natural Forces, Human Choices: An Over Time Study of Responses to Biophysical and Human Induced Disturbance in Los Angeles, California Groundwater Governance." PhD diss., Indiana University.
Williamson, Oliver E. 1964. *The Economics of Discretionary Behavior: Managerial Objectives in a Theory of the Firm*. Englewood Cliffs, NJ: Prentice Hall.
———. 1967. "Hierarchical Control and Optimum Firm Size." *Journal of Political Economy* 75(2): 123–38.
Wood, Robert C. 1961. *1400 Governments*. Garden City, NJ: Doubleday, Anchor Books.

Index

5MHRP. *See* Five Million Hectare Reforestation Programme

accountability, 65, 218n5
action arena, analysis of, 79–80; definition of, 28–29, 52; linking, 78–80; types of, 63
action-outcome evaluation, 253–56
action situation, xiv–xx, xxiii, xxv, 29, 241; adjacent, 95–97, 100–101, 190, 363; changing contextual factors in, 100–104; collective-choice, 189; comparing, 97–100; consequential, xvi; definition of, xiv, 54, 59, 184, 228; within IAD framework, 184; identifying, 92–93; information flow in, 94–95; knowledge in, 96; linked to potential outcome, 250–53; operational, 188; physical and material conditions of, 72–77; related to rules, *309*; selecting, 97; structure of, 52–53, 59–60. *See also* Floreana in Galápagos National Park, as a local-level action situation; Galápagos National Park, as an action situation; policy action situation
actor, assumptions about, 55; broad conception of, 55–56; characterization of, 53–54; decision-making capabilities of, 30–31; definition of, 54–55; identification of, 212
adaptability, 66
analysis, linkages among modes of, 384–85, 387; multidisciplinary, 50; multilevel, 50, 79–80; multilevel or multiscale, 214–15; shifting from institutions to linkages, 212–13; social network, 163. *See also* institutional analysis; operational analysis; policy analysis; public policy analysis
analytical framework, changing, 211–15; choice of, 203–204
Angelsen, Arild, on hybrid nested approach to REDD+, 278
asset specificity, 159

"Balkanization," 135
banking as example for policy analysis, 26–28
blueprint approach, 15
bounded rationality, 56, 174
Brautigam, Deborah, on incentives in development aid, 226

CBT. *See* community-based tourism
Clark, James, on sustainability in urban forests, 191
Coase Theorem, 155
collaborative group, 155–56

collective action, 234; context of regional, 157–58; individual exchange and, 150–51; institutional, xxii, 147–57; situation, 234
collective-action problem, 235; functional, 149; horizontal, 148–49; vertical, 149
common-pool resource, centrally managed, 98; flow of, 76–77; governance of, 91–92; within IAD framework, 93–94; open-access, 97–98; privatized, 98; study of, 37–39; in tourism, 344–45. *See also* Floreana in Galápagos National Park; governance, multilevel
community attributes, 22–23, 77–78, 160, 346
community-based tourism, challenges, 360–64; in protected area, 343. *See also* Floreana in Galápagos National Park, tourism development in
Community Resource Management Areas in Ghana, 290
conditions, physical and material, 19, 72–77
conflict, 120; and resolution, 135–36, 140
constitutional decisions, 120
constitutive process, 95–96
consumption, 113–14; collective, 118–20, 127; diverse scales of, 125–26, 137–38; patterns of, 134–35; production unit and, 121, 128–36
context, setting, 52
coproduction, 116–17, 139–40. *See also* public service, citizen coproduction of
coupled human-environment system, 171
CPR. *See* common-pool resource
CREMAs. *See* Community Resource Management Areas in Ghana
criminal jurisprudence in enforcing rules, 375
critical realism and institutional analysis, 318
cultural change, 97

decisions, contextualizing, 312–13; multilevel, 352
design principles for resource management, 89, 98–99, 186; in dependent communities vs. technical systems, 102–3
Detroit, government of, 111; questions for policy makers in, 136–41
development, cooperation, 242; definition of, 230; democratic, 233–35; progress toward, 232–33. *See also* development aid
development aid, cautions about, 59; centered on beneficiaries, 265–67; chain of delivery, 243–44; donor-recipient strategies in, 249–56; impact on recipient's budget, 268n10; major actors in, 244, 246; ownership in, 224, 236–41, 261–65; sustainability of, 223, 224, 244, 261–65, 268n11. *See also* donor-recipient relationship; REDD+, international aid for; Swedish International Development Cooperation Agency
development assistance. *See* development aid
development cooperation octangle. *See* international development cooperation octangle
development policy, xxv–xxvi
discourse, policy and, 314–16
dispute resolution, 96
donor-recipient relationship, negotiation in, 258–60; understanding, 248–58

economic efficiency, 64
The Economist, on donor-recipient "dance," 254–55

ecosystem service, sustaining, 173–75
equity, assessing, 64–65
excludability, 19–21, 74–76, 112–15
exclusion. *See* excludability

fallible learner, 56–57
FECOFUN. *See* Federation of Community Forestry Users of Nepal
Federation of Community Forestry Users of Nepal, 289
Five Million Hectare Reforestation Programme, 319, 322; lack of livelihood improvement and, 324; as a panacea, 327–28; prominent drivers for decisions regarding, *325*. *See also* Vietnam
Floreana in Galápagos National Park, *348–49*; economy in, 350; governance of, *351–54*; as a local-level action situation, 357–60; tourism development in, 350–54
Folk Development Colleges, 236
forest ownership by national governments, 283
forest rights movements in REDD+, 290–92
forest users, associations, 284, 289–90, 291; in REDD+, *282–84*
forestry agencies in REDD+, 284–85
Foucault, Michel, on power, 310
fragmentation of policy making, 147
framework, definition of, 51
framing of observation, 216–18
free-riding, 49, 75

Galápagos National Park, 343, 347; as an action situation, *354–57*
game theory, 11
GNP. *See* Galápagos National Park
goods, nature of, 112–18; taxation for, 129–30; transaction characteristics of, 159; types of, 115
governance, autonomous units of, 123; effective, 184–85; multilevel, 345–46, 364; questions for reform of, 136–41; regional, 150–52, 161
Governing the Commons, 89, 99–100

Hajek, Frank, on REDD+ planning, 293
Hardin, Garrett, on commons, 60, 90–92
holon, 193
homeowners' association, 118–19
homo economicus, 55
human and environmental agency in IAD framework, 318–19

IAD. *See* institutional analysis and development framework
ICA. *See* institutional collective action framework
IFRI. *See* International Forestry Resources and Institutions
incentive, definition of, 224, 229
incentive analysis, 80–81
incentive in development aid, perverse, 223, 224–27; problem of, 237, 245–46
individual, behavior, 55–56; boundedly rational, 56; in rule-making, 5–7
inquiry, 4, 175, 371–73, 376, 378–79, 381, 385–87
institutional analysis, 8–12, 14, 52, *378–83*; alternative frames for, 203–204; applied to development aid, 226, 246–47; applied to urban forest ecosystems, 187–91; elements of, 53; rules-in-use and, 71–72, 312; steps in, 87–89, 90–105; steps exemplified, 90–105; in sustaining natural resources, 183; in urban systems, 172
institutional analysis and development framework, xiii–xvii, xix–xxv, xxvii, 16–17, 49–54, 87, 294,

306–9, 315–17, 319; adaptability of, 317–18; application of, 36–40, 60–62, 89–105, 183–87, 246–58, 308, *319–28*, 345–46, 352, 364; components of, *316–17*; as an inexhaustible source of questions, 105–7; three choice levels of, *309*; in urban ecosystem studies, 180–81, 191–92; using, 17–26, 80–81
institutional arrangement that encourages coproduction, 139–40. *See also* coproduction
institutional change, 79
institutional collective action framework, 148, 163. *See also* collective action, institutional
institutional failure, 191
institutions, 4, 14, 218n1, 224, 227–29; accountability in, 207–208; within context of IAD framework, 183–84; coordination problems in, 207; defining, 176–78, 310; as equilibria, 176, 177; influencing urban forest ecosystems, 181–83; lacking inquiry, 378–79; multilevel, 203–208; nested, 181; as norms/rules, 176–77; power and, 308–12; in urban ecosystem research, 177–81. *See also* institutional analysis
international development cooperation octangle, 241–46
International Forestry Resources and Institutions, 38, 180
interorganizational arrangements, study of, 386–87

JNR. *See* Jurisdictional and Nested REDD+ Initiative of Verified Carbon Standards
joint decision trap, 207
Jurisdictional and Nested REDD+ Initiative of Verified Carbon Standards, 278–79

knowledge, in action situation, 96; incomplete, 56; localized, 241

legislation, by elected officials for self-governance, 7; to facilitate implementation, 380–83; federal vs. state, 28; goals in, 374–75, 380, *382–83*; variables affecting, 73, 140, 187, *189*, 378–79, 381. *See also* policy, is only words
level vs. scale, 209, 214–15
linkages, analysis of, 213; cross-scale, 276; efficiency of, 241–42; multidimensional, 215–18; multiscale, 203–204, 208–11. *See also* REDD+, institutional linkages in
Long Term Ecological Research, 179
LTER. *See* Long Term Ecological Research
Lukes, Steven, on power, 310

market conditions, 96
Mazmanian, Daniel. *See* legislation to facilitate implementation
measurement of goods, difficulty in, 159–60
Millennium African Renaissance Programme, 268n5
model as part of analysis, 51
monitoring, commons, 97–98; forests, 186, 286–87; goods, 159–60; in the IAD, 94; policy reform, 100–101
monitoring, reporting, and verification, 275–76
monopolies, natural, 74
MRV. *See* monitoring, reporting, and verification

National Estuary Program, 163
natural resource management, decentralization of, 305; political ecology and, 312–13

Neenan, William, on fiscal relations in Michigan, 141
nesting, complex, 6
network, contract, 154–55, 158; managed, 152–53; policy, 156, 158
new institutional economics scholar, 176–77
New Regionalist, 150–51
NIE scholar. *See* new institutional economics scholar
norm, general, 66; internal, 57–58, 228–29
North, Douglass, on separating concepts of organization and institution, 228; theory of institutions, 318
NRM. *See* natural resource management

octangle. *See* international development cooperation octangle
operational analysis, 376–78
opportunism, 56
organization, 14–15; functionally defined, 205–206; questions for reform of, 136–41; regional, 153–54; territorially defined, 205
Ostrom, Elinor, 89, 389–91; on action situations, xv–xvi, xvii–xviii; on analytical complexity, xix–xx; on design principles, 89, 105–6; on nested framework, 281; underlying philosophy of, 406–7; on working with rules, xxvix
Ostrom, Vincent, on evaluating policy implementation, xxviii; on local jurisdictions in a metropolitan area, 391. *See also* legislation to facilitate implementation; public policy analysis
outcome, analysis of, 18; changing, 78; evaluating, 64–67, 253–56; gap between intention and, 324, 326; linked to action situation, 250–53; predicting, 62–63
ownership, collective action and, 238–39; four dimensions of, 239–40

payment for environmental services, 277
PES. *See* payment for environmental services
police services, analysis of, 36–37; citizen preferences and choices for, 403–5; direct and intermediate, 400; measurability, 401–3; performance measures of, 377, 405–6; promoting hierarchy of, 398–99; survey data vs. crime data, 397. *See also* public good; public service
policy, design, 15; evaluating equity of, 33; is only words, 100, 376
policy action situation, 22–23, 27–28; constrained, 31
policy analysis, xxi–xxii, 14–15; community attributes' influence in, 22–23; defining objective and approach of, 17–19; integrating, 28–31; outcomes in, 32–34; patterns of interaction in, 31–32; physical and material conditions' influence in, 17–22; rules-in-use aspects of, 23–28. *See also* public policy analysis
policy arena, 149
policy decision, 376; goal of 373–75, 380
policy issue, defining, 17–18
policy system, 26–27; fragmentation of, 147
political ecology, 305
political structure, 160–61
polycentric system, 6, 391
private goods, 73–74; measurement of, 115–16
private vendor, 121–22

process, configural, 50–51
production activity, 21–22; advantage of diverse scales for, 125–26; bargaining for, 127
production unit, 120–23; mix of public and private firms in, 138; problems with collective-consumption unit and, 128–36
property rights, of forest users, 277; privatization of, 174
provision activity, 21–22
PROW. *See* public right-of-way
public economy, complex structure of, 125–27; in metropolitan areas, 118–25
public entrepreneurship, 391–94
public good, 74–76, 117–18; case study of, 99–100; contracting, 122–23; equitable delivery of, 130–33; measurement of, 115–16; options for obtaining, 124; scale of organization to provide, 394–98
public policy analysis, 373–76; focus on multiorganizational implementation, 386–87; studying effects of, 377
public right-of-way, 187; confusion in management of, 190
public service, citizen coproduction of, 401; finance and, 138–39; industry, 123–25; questions for policy makers in, 136–41; studying delivery of, 395–400

rationality, strict, 41n10
REDD+, 275–76; carbon auditing and accounting in, 287–88; evolution of, 277; existing proposals for, 278–79; goal of, 292; institutional linkages in, 276, 283–84, 288–92; international involvement in, 280, 285–86; monitoring, 286–88; national and subnational governments' roles in, 277, 279–80, *283*, 285–86, 289–90, 292–93; nested, 276, 278–79; new proposal for nested, *281–86*, 294; NGOs in, 288–89; transaction costs of, 293. *See also* forest rights movements in REDD+
redistribution policy, 131–33, 141
Reducing Emissions from Deforestation and Forest Degradation, and Enhancement of Forest Carbon Stocks in Developing Countries. *See* REDD+
regime change, 96–97
research design, as a foundation, 91; selecting cases based on, 103–5
resolution, courts' role in, 135–36; of observation, 216–18
right to alienate, 240–41
Robbins, Paul, definition of political ecology, 305
rules, definition of, 68, 178; -in-form, 69–70; nested, 27–28, 79, 185–86; operational, 187; origins of, 68–70; state-level, 159; transformation of, *353*; types of, 185, 187–90. *See also* policy, is only words
rules-in-use, 228, 307; configurations of, 70–72; types of, 24–26, 71–72

Sabatier, Paul. *See* legislation to facilitate implementation
sanctions, cost of developing, 78; necessity of, 6, 33, 118, 287; vs. norms, 177. *See also* criminal jurisprudence in enforcing rules
scale, concept of, 209–10; economies and diseconomies of, 400
Searle, John, on institutions and power, 310
self-governance, designing, 5–8; four "I's" of, 4; rules in, 4–5; setting for possibility of, 6–7

self-governing groups, size of, 6
self-organization, benefits of, 151; limitations of, 156–57; in metropolitan areas, 161–65
SEM. *See* Southeastern Michigan
SES. *See* social-ecological system
Sida. *See* Swedish International Development Cooperation Agency
Simon, Herbert, xxviii; on complexity of design, 105; on improving governance arrangements, 394–95
social-ecological system, 172–73; multiples in, 203–204
Southeastern Michigan, special public service districts in, 119
strategy, 229; based on information and learning, 56–57; in game theory, 51; as a result of interaction, 31–32, 148, 210. *See also* action situation; development aid, donor-recipient strategies in; *homo economicus*
street tree, 187
subtractability, 19–21, 76–77, 113–15, 134
sustainability, 231–32; evaluative criteria linked to, 64–67, 77; thinking about improving, 105–106; threats to, 104
Swedish International Development Cooperation Agency, concepts of sustainability, 231–32; on incentives, 224–25; six goals of, 230

tenure rights, 282; exclusionary, 280
theories as part of analysis, 51
Tiebout, Charles, on local jurisdictions in a metropolitan area, 391
toll goods, 20
tourism, 343; in the Galápagos Islands, 345, 348. *See also* community-based tourism
tragedy of the commons, 91, 97–98
transaction cost, regional, 157–61, 163

UNFCCC. *See* United Nations Framework Convention on Climate Change
United Nations Framework Convention on Climate Change, role in REDD+, 285–86
urban ecological research, 178–79
urban forest, 171, 180; vs. community forest, 193; management of, 181–83; as matrix of property rights and management, 181; municipal codes for, 181
UTV. *See* Swedish International Development Cooperation Agency

van Ufford, Philip, on studying interorganizational linkages, 245
Vietnam, afforestation program in, 322–23; deforestation and remedies, 320–21; land classification in, 321; land-use rights in, 321–22
voucher system, 122

Warren, Robert, on local jurisdictions in a metropolitan area, 391
West Basin Water Association in Los Angeles, 392
working rules. *See* rules-in-use
Workshop in Political Theory and Policy Analysis, 13, 91

Contributors

Krister P. Andersson is professor of political science and the director of the Center for the Governance of Natural Resources at the University of Colorado at Boulder. His main area of research deals with the politics of environmental governance, and focuses on the role local institutional arrangements play in explaining variation in environmental policy outcomes in Latin America. His research has been published in five books, some sixty peer-reviewed journal articles and book chapters.

Eduardo S. Brondizio is professor of anthropology at Indiana University Bloomington, where he serves as the codirector of the Center for the Analysis of Social-Ecological Landscapes (CASEL); he is an affiliated faculty member of the Vincent and Elinor Ostrom Workshop. An environmental anthropologist, Brondizio's research combines long-term studies of the transformation of rural and urban areas and populations in the Amazon with research on the human dimensions of global environmental change. He is a member of the Science Committee of Future Earth and the International Geosphere-Biosphere Programme (IGBP) and coeditor-in-chief of Elsevier's *Current Opinion in Environmental Sustainability*.

Floriane Clement is a researcher and Sub-Theme Leader Gender and Poverty at the International Water Management Institute (IWMI). She has a strong interest in the study of human-environment interactions in the context of development and has drawn from multiple bodies of literature for her research, including institutional analysis of common-pool resources, political ecology, discourse analysis, gender studies, and development studies. Two of Floriane's publications were assigned by Elinor Ostrom as essential readings at the fall seminars of the Workshop in Political Theory and Policy Analysis, Indiana University, in 2006 and 2010.

Daniel H. Cole is professor of law and professor of public and environmental affairs at Indiana University Bloomington, where he also serves on the Affiliated Faculty of the Vincent and Elinor Ostrom Workshop. Professor Cole is author or editor of eight books, including *Property in Land and Other Resources* (Lincoln Institute, 2012), which he coedited with Elinor Ostrom, and more than fifty articles, book chapters, and essays, most of which cross the boundaries of law, economics, and political science. He is a member of the Advisory Board of the Institute for Policy Integrity at the NYU Law School, and a Life Member of Clare Hall (College for Advanced Study), University of Cambridge.

Tom Evans is a professor in the Department of Geography and senior research fellow with the Vincent and Elinor Ostrom Workshop at Indiana University. His work addresses the intersection of social and environmental systems with an emphasis on household-level decision making in the context of diverse governance arrangements. Previous work focused on dynamics of deforestation/reforestation while more recently his work has investigated the impact of climate change on smallholder farming systems in Kenya/Zambia and the ability of multilevel governance regimes and farmer adaptive capacity to mitigate effects of drought.

Richard Feiock holds the Jerry Collins Eminent Scholar Endowed Chair and is the Augustus B. Turnbull Professor of Public Administration and Policy in the Askew School at Florida State University where he directs the FSU Local Governance Research Laboratory. He is an elected fellow of the National Academy of Public Administration, serves on the US Environmental Protection Agency, Board of Scientific Counselors, and is editor of *Public Administration Review*. He has published four books and more than 220 refereed articles. He has received numerous research and career awards and has been principal investigator on six National Science Foundation research grants.

Burnell "Burney" C. Fischer, PhD, CF, is clinical professor emeritus, School of Public and Environmental Affairs, and former director of the Vincent and Elinor Ostrom Workshop at Indiana University. He leads the Bloomington Urban Forestry Research Group (BUFRG) at the Center for the Study of Institutions, Population, and Environmental Change (https://www.indiana.edu/~cipec/research/bufrg_about.php), and teaches Urban Forest Management and Urban Ecology. He is the former state forester and director, Indiana Division of Forestry. Professor Fischer received the

Arbor Day Foundation's Frederick Law Olmsted Award (2013), which recognizes an outstanding individual who has had a positive impact on the environment due to their lifelong commitment to tree planting and conservation at a state or regional level.

Clark Gibson is professor of political science and director of the International Studies Program at the University of California San Diego (UCSD). He studies the politics of development, democracy, and the environment. He has explored issues related to these topics in Africa, Central and South America, and the United States. His current research focuses on the accountability between governments and citizens in Africa, especially during the electoral process and in the provision of public services.

Robert Holahan is assistant professor of environmental policy and political science at Binghamton University (SUNY). He received his PhD in Political Science from Indiana University in 2011 and his MA in Political Economy and Public Policy from Washington University in St. Louis in 2005. His research focuses on the emergence and evolution of institutions that govern the human use of natural resource systems. Current projects include investigating the institutions used to regulate the production of oil and gas in the United States and an investigation of the public goods nature of urban sustainability initiatives.

Miranda Hutten is a graduate of the School of Public and Environmental Affairs at Indiana University with a Masters in both Natural Resources Management and Applied Ecology. As a Presidential Management Fellow for the US Forest Service, she provided technical and financial assistance on Forest Service landowner assistance programs. Currently, Miranda is the US Forest Service Urban and Community Forestry Program Manager for the Pacific Southwest Region. Her goal is to further partnerships with states, cities, communities, and nonprofit organizations to increase community awareness on the importance of trees in sustaining healthy and viable cities; to improve the social, natural, and economic environment of urban and community areas; and to enable the development of self-sufficient local urban and community forestry programs.

Prakash Kashwan is assistant professor of political science at the University of Connecticut. He received his PhD in Public Policy (2011) from Indiana University Bloomington, and a MS from the Indian Institute of Forest Management, Bhopal. His research focuses on political economy of institutions in the areas of comparative and international environmental policies and international development. His current research project includes a book-length project to examine institutional change over time in forest property regimes in India, Tanzania, and Mexico. Prakash is especially interested in how power endowments and power asymmetries shape institutional development and institutional change.

Michael D. McGinnis is associate dean for social & historical sciences and graduate education in the College of Arts and Sciences, and professor of political science, at Indiana University Bloomington. He is a senior research fellow (and former director) of the Vincent and Elinor Ostrom Workshop. He has a PhD in political science from the University of Minnesota and a BS in mathematics from The Ohio State University. He has published articles and book chapters on topics in public policy, institutional analysis, humanitarian aid, arms control, game theory, faith-based organizations, and US health policy.

Sarah Mincey is a social-ecological systems scientist who studies community-based natural resource management and environmental governance, with particular emphasis on urban forest management. In her current role as faculty at the School of Public and Environmental Affairs at Indiana University, she serves as the associate director for the Integrated Program in the Environment and administrative director for the IU Research and Teaching Preserve. She maintains much of her research activity through her faculty affiliation with the Vincent and Elinor Ostrom Workshop.

Elinor Ostrom was founding director and senior research director of the Vincent and Elinor Ostrom Workshop in Political Theory and Policy Analysis, Distinguished Professor and Arthur F. Bentley Professor of political science, and professor in the School of Public and Environmental Affairs at Indiana University Bloomington. She was the cowinner of the 2009 Sveriges Riksbank Prize in Economic Sciences in Memory of Alfred Nobel.

Vincent Ostrom was founding director of the Vincent and Elinor Ostrom Workshop in Political Theory and Policy Analysis and Arthur F. Bentley Professor Emeritus of political science at Indiana University Bloomington.

Margaret M. Polski is a researcher in the field of national security policymaking, strategic planning, and operational design. She serves as a research analyst with the Center for Naval Analyses (CNA); an affiliate research fellow in the Krasnow Institute for Advanced Study; a consultant to the National Academy of Sciences; a panel member for the National Science Foundation; and supports the US Department of State in public diplomacy. Dr. Polski has a PhD from Indiana University in Political Science; an MPA from Harvard University in Business Economics and Policy; and a Bachelor's in Elected Studies from the University of Minnesota.

Amy R. Poteete is an associate professor of political science at Concordia University in Montreal. Her research focuses on natural resource policies and electoral politics in Africa, particularly in Botswana and Senegal. Another strand of writing concerns methodological issues. She is the coauthor, with Marco A. Janssen and Elinor Ostrom, of *Working Together: Collective Action, the Commons, and Multiple Methods in Practice* (Princeton University Press). Other publications include chapters in edited volumes and articles in a variety of journals, including *Development and Change*, *Journal of Development Studies*, *Journal of Modern African Studies*, and *World Development*.

Esteban Ruiz-Ballesteros is professor of social anthropology at Pablo de Olavide University in Seville, where he is director of the Department of Social Anthropology, Psychology and Public Health. He is a member of the Social Research and Participatory Action Group (GISAP). His current research fields are community-based tourism, commons, and environment-human relationships, carrying out fieldwork in Andalusia, Ecuador, and the Galapagos. His recent work has been published in *Human Ecology*, *Land Use Policy*, *Human Organization*, *Tourism Management*, *Journal of Material Culture*, *AIBR*, and *Revista de Dialectología y Tradiciones Populares*.

Sujai Shivakumar is a senior policy advisor with the Board on Science, Technology, and Economic Policy at the National Academies of Sciences, Engineering, and Medicine, where he directs a portfolio of studies on innovation, entrepreneurship, manufacturing, and workforce issues. Dr. Shivakumar holds a doctorate in economics from George Mason University and was a visiting scholar from 1997 to 2001 at the Workshop in Political Theory and Policy Analysis at Indiana University Bloomington. He is the author of *The Constitution of Development* (Macmillan, 2005) and coauthor of *The Samaritan's Dilemma: The Political Economy of Development Aid* (Oxford University Press, 2005).

Susan I. Stewart earned her PhD in Recreation with a specialization in Resource Economics from Michigan State University in 1994. After almost twenty years in Forest Service Research, she returned to her northern Michigan roots in July 2012, relocating from the Chicago suburbs to Harbor Springs. She is currently a staff scientist at the University of Wisconsin-Madison, where she works with an interdisciplinary group of researchers to study housing growth and its ecological impacts (http://silvis.forest.wisc.edu/).

Jess Vogt conducts social-ecological research on urban forests in the context of sustainability science. Vogt is an assistant professor in the Department of Environmental Science and Studies at DePaul University in Chicago, Illinois. She received her PhD, MPA, and MSES from the School of Public and Environmental Affairs at Indiana University Bloomington. Vogt is also a researcher with the Bloomington Urban Forestry Research Group, an active member of the International Society of Arboriculture, and an assistant editor at the journals *Forests*, and *Urban Forestry & Urban Greening*.